Aristocratic Power in the
Spanish Monarchy

Aristocratic Power in the Spanish Monarchy

The Borromeo Brothers of Milan, 1620–1680

SAMUEL WEBER

OXFORD
UNIVERSITY PRESS

Great Clarendon Street, Oxford, OX2 6DP,
United Kingdom

Oxford University Press is a department of the University of Oxford.
It furthers the University's objective of excellence in research, scholarship,
and education by publishing worldwide. Oxford is a registered trade mark of
Oxford University Press in the UK and in certain other countries

© Samuel Weber 2023

The moral rights of the author have been asserted

All rights reserved. No part of this publication may be reproduced, stored in
a retrieval system, or transmitted, in any form or by any means, without the
prior permission in writing of Oxford University Press, or as expressly permitted
by law, by licence or under terms agreed with the appropriate reprographics
rights organization. Enquiries concerning reproduction outside the scope of the
above should be sent to the Rights Department, Oxford University Press, at the
address above

You must not circulate this work in any other form
and you must impose this same condition on any acquirer

Published in the United States of America by Oxford University Press
198 Madison Avenue, New York, NY 10016, United States of America

British Library Cataloguing in Publication Data
Data available

Library of Congress Control Number: 2022951995

ISBN 978–0–19–887259–7

DOI: 10.1093/oso/9780198872597.001.0001

Printed and bound in the UK by
TJ Books Limited

Links to third party websites are provided by Oxford in good faith and
for information only. Oxford disclaims any responsibility for the materials
contained in any third party website referenced in this work.

To my nonni

Acknowledgments

This book started life as a Ph.D. thesis I wrote as part of a joint doctorate at the Universities of Bern and Durham. As I send it off to print, it is a pleasure to acknowledge the many people who helped me with this project over the years of its gestation.

My most heartfelt thanks go to the four people who supervised the Ph.D. and its subsequent metamorphosis into a monograph. My greatest debt is to my two doctoral advisers, Christian Windler and Toby Osborne. Christian not only made me aware of the correspondence of Federico IV Borromeo that became the main source of this book; he has also shaped me as a scholar. Indeed, anyone familiar with his work on the early modern Maghreb and Persia will immediately recognize the profound impact that his subtle analyses of structural power and the agency of subalterns have had on me. Toby's knowledge of Italian elites is as impressive as his willingness to go far beyond the call of duty for his students. No one has read more half-baked drafts of this work than he has over the years. I also want to acknowledge the constant encouragement and unstinting support of the internal and external examiners of the Ph.D., Nicole Reinhardt and Birgit Emich. Without their landmark studies on patronage in seventeenth-century Italy, I could not have conceived the original Ph.D. project, let alone written this book. I can only aspire to become the scholar and mentor that Christian, Toby, Nicole, and Birgit have been to me.

During the research for the Ph.D. and the book, countless people have been generous with their time and expertise. I want to thank former and current colleagues in Bern, whose work I admire greatly and whose friendship has sustained me over the years. I also want to acknowledge the audiences of research seminars and conferences in numerous countries for engaging with papers that later became chapters of the book. Many more colleagues were forthcoming with advice big and small throughout the research for and the writing of this book. While I cannot mention them individually, I do want them to know that each interaction meant the world to me.

Thanks are due to the institutions whose material assistance made the research for this book possible in the first place. Research toward the Ph.D. was funded by the Department of History and the Faculty of Humanities of the University of Bern, Swissuniversities, and the Swiss National Science Foundation. In Rome, I was lucky to be hosted by the Istituto Svizzero and the German Historical Institute on several occasions, and I want to thank the directors of these institutions and my fellow *borsisti* for a wonderful time in the Eternal City.

viii ACKNOWLEDGMENTS

I am equally grateful to the institutions where the archival research for this book was carried out. A heartfelt *grazie* goes to the former and current archivists of the Archivio Borromeo dell'Isola Bella, the late Carlo Alessandro Pisoni and Lorena Barale, who were excessively generous in allowing me to pore over the previously untapped Borromeo private papers on which this book is based. I also want to thank the many collaborators of the archives I visited across Italy and Spain. Over the last two decades, they have borne the brunt of the philistine attacks on the humanities that have sadly become *de rigueur* in governing circles. I salute the services they continue to provide to researchers in spite of their own unsustainable working conditions that should worry anyone who cares about an impartial engagement with the past.

Numerous people have read this text in one of its many iterations from draft chapters of a doctoral thesis to monograph. I must acknowledge the thoughtful and reassuring feedback of Nadine Amsler, Giuanna Beeli, Enrique Corredera Nilsson, Birgit Emich, Toby Osborne, Nicole Reinhardt, Nicolas Rogger, Nadir Weber, and Christian Windler. Last but not least, I thank the two anonymous reviewers for Oxford University Press for their probing questions and insightful comments, which have improved this book substantially. It goes without saying that any shortcomings that remain are my fault alone.

I am grateful to the people who helped me navigate the publication process. Tom Hamilton, Regine Maritz, Toby Osborne, and Nicole Reinhardt offered invaluable advice on earlier versions of the book proposal I ended up sending to Oxford University Press. At Oxford University Press, I thank Karen Raith for believing in the manuscript I submitted, and Luciana O'Flaherty and Cathryn Steele for shepherding the project across the finish line. Thanks are due to Vasuki Ravichandran for overseeing the production process and Louise Larchbourne for her eagle-eyed copyediting of the manuscript. Marina Stone provided much-appreciated last-minute help with footnoting before submission.

I could not have written this book in the midst of a devastating pandemic without the practical help and emotional support of friends and family in places near and far. They are far too numerous to mention all of them by name, and the tiredness that comes with wrapping up a project of this scope would inevitably entail regrettable oversights and omissions. I am sure they know who they are. I would, however, be remiss if I did not acknowledge my sisters and my parents. Their unwavering commitment to social justice inspires me every day, and I can only hope that they will accept this monograph as my way of honoring the values they live by. I dedicate this book to my grandmother and to the memory of my late *nonni*, whose bold dream of a world without privilege gave me hope when the sources I was studying threatened to quash it.

Contents

List of Figures	xi
List of Abbreviations	xiii
Maps	xv
Family Tree	xvii
Introduction: The Borromeos' Hidden Spanish Connection	1
Historiography: Spanish Italy, *c.*1550–1700	3
Methodology and Sources	9
Outline of the Argument	15
Prologue: The Unraveling of an Ecclesiastical Dynasty	18

I. BUCCANEERING

1. *Olivaristas* on the Make: The Borromeos and the Government of the Count-Duke of Olivares	25
The Rise of the Minister-Favorite	26
Court Patronage under Olivares	30
The "Misrecognition" of Favoritism	36
Conclusion	41
2. Becoming Military Leaders: The Borromeos, the Union of Arms, and the Franco-Spanish War in Italy	43
The Union of Arms	44
The Milanese Warrior Nobility under Olivares	48
The Borromeos and Popular Opposition to the War	53
Conclusion	59
3. The Pitfalls of Patronage: Giovanni Borromeo as Commissioner-General of the Army in Lombardy	61
Milan under Military Occupation	63
Giovanni Borromeo and Troop Allocation	66
The End of Giovanni Borromeo's Billeting Scheme	72
Conclusion	79
4. The Decline and Fall of an *Olivarista*: Giovanni Borromeo's Failed Quest for Admission to the Spanish Governing Elite	81
Spanish Honors and Rewards	83
The Campaign against Giovanni Borromeo	86
The Fall of Giovanni Borromeo	91
Conclusion	97

X CONTENTS

II. BLEARING

5. "A Faithful Vassal of His Majesty": Federico Borromeo as
   Papal Nuncio and the Ideology of Disinterested Service — 101
   The Education of Federico Borromeo — 103
   The Crisis of Nepotism in the Papal Court — 105
   Federico Borromeo's Career in the Court of Alexander VII — 109
   Conclusion — 118

6. Moral Panics and the Restoration of Consensus: Federico
   Borromeo and the Jurisdictional Controversies in Spanish Italy — 120
   Jurisdictional Conflicts in Spanish Italy — 122
   Federico Borromeo and the Congregation of Ecclesiastical Immunity — 126
   The Settlement of the Jurisdictional Conflicts — 131
   Conclusion — 136

7. Dissimulation and Subterfuge: Federico Borromeo as Nuncio
   in Spain and Papal Secretary of State — 137
   The Court of Madrid after Philip IV — 138
   Federico Borromeo and the Nithard Crisis — 141
   The Making of the Baroque State — 149
   Conclusion — 152

8. Pining for Stability: Antonio Renato Borromeo and the
   Uses of Symbolic Power — 154
   The Borromeos as Patrons of the Arts — 155
   The Rise of Antonio Renato Borromeo — 161
   The Aristocratic Government of Juan José of Austria — 169
   Conclusion — 173

   Epilogue: The Crisis of Favoritism and the Courtization
   of the Nobility — 175

Bibliography — 181
Index — 205

List of Figures

0.1 Map of the State of Milan — xv

0.2 Map of Lake Maggiore — xvi

0.3 Borromeo Family Tree — xvii

4.1 Melchiorre Gherardini, *Giovanni Borromeo Drives the Goths out of Rome,* *c.*1650 (Angera, Rocca di Angera) — 82

8.1 Cesare Fiori (attr.), *Portrait of Federico Borromeo Jr.*, 1670 (Milan, Pinacoteca Ambrosiana) — 157

8.2 Anon., *Portrait of Federico Borromeo Sr.*, *c.*1650 (Milan, Pinacoteca Ambrosiana) — 158

8.3 Filippo Abbiati, *Solemn Banquet Offered by Vitaliano I Borromeo to the King of Naples, Alfonso of Aragon, and the Duke of Milan, Filippo Maria Visconti*, 1683–1685 (Angera, Rocca di Angera) — 165

8.4 Filippo Abbiati, *Solemn Entry of Isabella d'Aragona, Bride of Gian Galeazzo Sforza, Taken to Milan by Giovanni Borromeo*, 1683–1685 (Angera, Rocca di Angera) — 166

List of Abbreviations

AAV	*Archivio Apostolico Vaticano, Vatican City*
ABIB	*Archivio Borromeo dell'Isola Bella, Stresa*
ASCM	*Archivio Storico Civico, Milan*
ASDM	*Archivio Storico Diocesano, Milan*
ASM	*Archivio di Stato, Milan*
ASR	*Archivio di Stato, Rome*
AGS	*Archivo General, Simancas*
BAM	*Biblioteca Ambrosiana, Milan*
BAV	*Biblioteca Apostolica Vaticana, Vatican City*
BNB	*Biblioteca Nazionale Braidense, Milan*
BNE	*Biblioteca Nacional de España, Madrid*
EST	Estado collection, *AGS*
FB	Famiglia Borromeo collection, *ABIB*
FCS	Fondo Crivelli Serbelloni, *SSL*
SSP	Secretarías Provinciales collection, *AGS*
SSL	*Società Storica Lombarda, Milan*
b.	*busta*
cart.	*cartella*
fasc.	*fascicolo*
leg.	*legajo*
lib.	*libro*
p.a.	*parte antica*

Maps

Fig. 0.1 Map of the State of Milan
(Lucas Pfister, Bern)

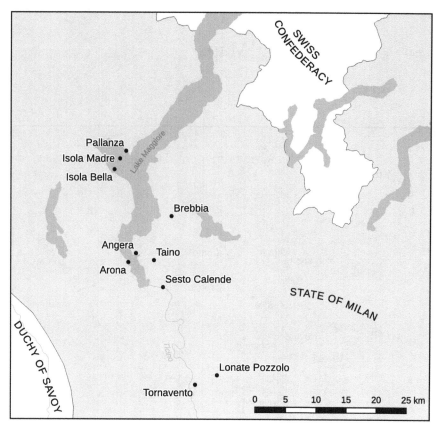

Fig. 0.2 Map of Lake Maggiore
(Lucas Pfister, Bern)

Family Tree

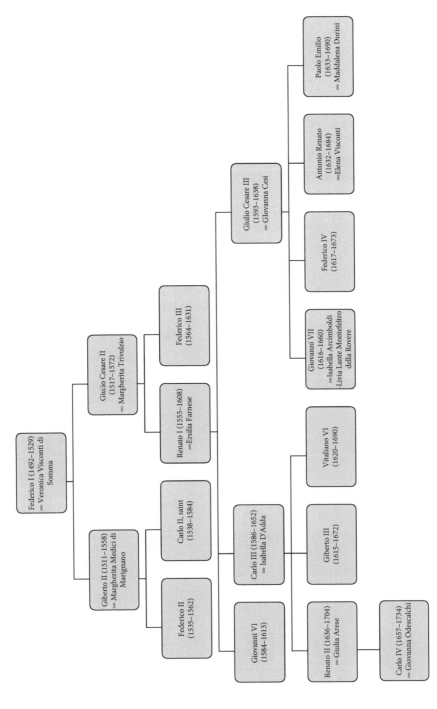

Fig. 0.3 Borromeo Family Tree

Introduction

The Borromeos' Hidden Spanish Connection

Alessandro Manzoni's 1840 novel *The Betrothed* is a canonical work of Italian literature. At its heart, the book is a love story about a young couple, Renzo and Lucia. Critics, however, have been most interested in the novel's backstory: its portrait of Milanese society in the 1620s. In Manzoni's rendition, Milan at the time was in the grips of a major crisis. In the Renaissance, the territory in northern Italy had been a flourishing center of protoindustrial production and a major hub for agricultural produce from the Po Valley. By the time Manzoni's story sets in, however, Lombardy's advanced agriculture was no longer able to feed the population of what was, by many accounts, Europe's fourth largest metropolis.[1] In fact, as Manzoni recounts in moving prose, the poor were roaming the city streets, asking for charity from the equally impoverished nobility and middle classes. When the military skirmishes on Milan's borders exacerbated the famine, the lower orders revolted against the Spanish high nobility who had been administering the State of Milan since 1535 when it had become the northern Italian outpost of the Spanish Habsburgs' global empire. In one of the more memorable scenes of the book, the destitute masses targeted the man who had been sent in from Madrid to command the sizeable Spanish army stationed there, Governor Gonzalo Fernández de Córdoba (r. 1625–1629). As the rioting masses escorted his carriage out of the city gate, they started to "pelt it with rocks, bricks, and garbage of all kinds," shouting: "Down with the famine, down with bleeding the poor."[2]

Even though Manzoni centered the hardship of ordinary Milanese, his interest was less in the abolition of elite rule than in the substitution of one ruling class by another. In *The Betrothed*, the voracity of the Spanish governing class is contrasted with the benevolent paternalism of Milan's local elite. The man who best embodies these values is Don Gonzalo's antagonist, the archbishop of the city, Cardinal Federico Borromeo (1564–1631). Where the Spanish governor was too callous to deal adequately with the famine, Borromeo, the offspring of one of the city's leading families, was "supremely charitable and generous."[3] When faced with a hunger-stricken flock, this clergyman tapped his family trust fund to set up a

---

[1] D'Amico, *Spanish Milan*.   [2] Manzoni, *The Betrothed*, p. 476.   [3] Ibid., p. 363.

Aristocratic Power in the Spanish Monarchy: The Borromeo Brothers of Milan, 1620–1680. Samuel Weber,
Oxford University Press. © Samuel Weber 2023. DOI: 10.1093/oso/9780198872597.003.0001

charity organization. Along with the parish priests under his aegis, the indefatigable archbishop walked the city streets, handing out 2,000 bowls of rice soup a day to the hungry and offering shelter to the homeless in the palaces of those who could afford to put them up. In Manzoni's reading, Borromeo's response to the hunger crisis of the 1620s emanated from a long family tradition of voluntary poverty and paternalist largesse. Cardinal Borromeo, Manzoni assures his readers, "was one of those rare men of any era who dedicated great intellect, the resources of his vast wealth, all the advantages of a privileged status, and an unwavering sense of purpose in seeking out and practicing good."[4] Born with a silver spoon, Federico Borromeo chose a lifestyle of abnegation: "he did not seek or even studiously avoided any of the advantages his status could have granted him."[5] In a deeply corrupt and corrupting society, Manzoni avers, Cardinal Borromeo hovered above the fray, ostentatiously disinterested in the self-enrichment that animated other nobles in this "dirty and gaudy era."[6]

Given the novel's prominence in Italian culture, Manzoni's flattering portrait of Federico Borromeo has exerted a tenacious hold on the collective imaginary.[7] To Manzoni's contemporaries embroiled in the struggle to shake off the yoke of Austrian rule and unite Italy as a nation-state, Cardinal Borromeo was the prototypical representative of a coming national elite. Men like him could chaperone the masses out of the foreign rule of the Spanish Habsburgs' Austrian cousins who still governed Milan and much of northeastern Italy in the 1840s. Interestingly, this optimistic view of big-hearted elites far outlived the *Risorgimento*. After World War II, the nationalist reading fused with a Catholic interpretation of *The Betrothed*: the values of paternalism Federico embodied became the creed of the ruling Christian Democrats who made sure to turn the novel into a staple of every Italian high-school education.[8] Read by generations of Italians, the novel and its untold numbers of screen adaptations have inculcated the image of the benevolent cardinal to such an extent that even professional historians have rarely interrogated it. In fact, in the limited historiography on the subject, Federico is unfailingly portrayed as a man of the Church, an exemplar of compassion, aloof from the wrangling other nobles routinely engaged in.

This book challenges this comforting narrative of the Borromeo family. Tapping previously unknown sources from the Borromeo private papers, it reconstructs the fag end of Cardinal Federico's life and the tortuous trajectory of his heirs from a cadet branch of the house, known as the Borromeos of Angera. It covers a period stretching from roughly 1620 through 1680 to make two related claims. First, it reveals that, contrary to the received wisdom, the Borromeos became increasingly involved with the Spanish high nobility with whom Manzoni

---

[4] Ibid., p. 357.   [5] Ibid., p. 358.   [6] Ibid., p. 360.
[7] On the novel's reception in Italy, see Martin, "Introduction," pp. 5–8.
[8] Mozzarelli, "Il nero tunnel," p. 17.

contrasted them. Far from being harmless spectators or even silent saboteurs of the acquisitiveness of fellow nobles, the Borromeos partook fully in the "dirty and gaudy era" in which they lived. Second, the book argues that this Spanish connection has largely gone unnoticed because the Borromeos themselves expended considerable effort to transmute their rapacity into apparent charity. *Aristocratic Power in the Spanish Monarchy* is at once a reconstruction of the Borromeos' growing entanglement with the Spanish rulers of Lombardy and an exposé of their incessant labor to erase the traces of their cronyism. It constitutes both a study of the nobilities of Spanish Italy and an analysis of a form of negation of privilege so efficacious that even such a conscientious scholar of the past as Alessandro Manzoni ended up falling for it.

Historiography: Spanish Italy, *c.*1550–1700

Around the same time that Spain expanded its dominion to the New World, its ruling family also set eyes on the Italian peninsula. With its fragmented political landscape, Italy around 1500 was particularly vulnerable to the appetites of this emerging world power, and when the Italian Wars (1494–1559) broke out, the Spanish kings quickly gobbled up a sizeable chunk of the peninsula. By the end of the great power rivalry between Spain and France in Italy in 1559, three territories found themselves under direct Spanish rule: the State of Milan in the north, the Kingdom of Naples in the south, and the island of Sicily. Others, such as the Papal States in central Italy and the Republic of Genoa in the northwest, remained formally sovereign, but there, too, the Spanish Habsburgs' influence among sections of the local oligarchies ran deep. Granted, once the French Wars of Religion (1562–1598) had fizzled out and France began to reassert itself in the Italian peninsula in the early decades of the seventeenth century, Spain's predominance received a dent. But, on the whole, the Catholic monarchy remained the hegemonic superpower throughout the seventeenth century, right up until the War of the Spanish Succession (1701–1714), which ended formal Spanish rule in Italy.[9]

The reckoning with the period of "Spanish preponderance" in Italy's history set in almost as soon as the rule of the Spanish Habsburgs collapsed in the early eighteenth century. Most assessments of the period have been entirely negative. Enlightenment thinkers set the tone for what was to obtain for the next 200 years: Ludovico Antonio Muratori (1672–1750) and Pietro Verri (1728–1797) were the first to argue that the incorporation of much of Italy into the Habsburgs' sphere of influence put an abrupt end to the splendors of the Renaissance and brought

---

[9] For Milan, the most comprehensive account in English is D'Amico, *Spanish Milan*. For an overview of other territories, including detailed bibliographies, see the contributions to Dandelet and Marino, eds., *Spain*.

4 ARISTOCRATIC POWER IN THE SPANISH MONARCHY

about an age of economic and social decay.[10] In the nineteenth century, nationalists, hard-pressed to explain Italy's supposed backwardness, padded the Enlightenment trope of Spanish decadence with a lachrymose story of foreign rule. Spanish "misgovernment" (*malgoverno*), along with that of venal popes, had supposedly delayed the forward-march to national self-determination by several centuries. Thanks to Pietro Verri in the eighteenth and Alessandro Manzoni in the nineteenth century, Milan held pride of place in the nationalist mythmaking about Spanish coercion and valiant Italian resistance to the quasi-colonial exploitation of what had once been a prosperous and highly advanced economy.[11] Honed in the struggles of the Enlightenment and the *Risorgimento,* the dark legend proved remarkably long-lived. Over the course of the late nineteenth and well into the twentieth century, the narrative of foreign rule survived, virtually unscathed, several changes in political regime and shifts in historiographical sensibilities.

Indeed, historians of Spanish Italy started to question these well-worn explanatory categories only when nationalism subsided as a trans-epochal mode of historical explication in the 1980s.[12] As part of the migration to post-nationalist interpretations of the early modern period writ large, specialists of Spanish Italy buried the old paradigm of foreign rule in favor of a narrative of cooperation and compromise.[13] Where the nationalist historiography had painted a picture of widespread local resistance to Spanish rule, a new generation of Italian and Spanish historians now insisted on the Habsburgs' ability to buy off portions of the Italian nobility and enlist them for their empire building.[14] Operating in a world where national origin did not dictate political affiliation, the Iberian ruling class was able to appeal to a shared dynastic and aristocratic culture that allowed it to overcome what nationalist historians would later identify as an insurmountable obstacle: the lack of ethnic, linguistic, and legal commonalities between Italy and Iberia.[15] Recognizing Italian nobles' usefulness to the imperial project, the Habsburgs tantalized local elites with the riches and symbolic signs of preeminence that cooperation with Spain could afford them.[16] Italian nobles were actively encouraged to view the centralized court in Madrid,[17] which emerged in the latter half of the sixteenth century, as a marketplace where honor, that distinguishing characteristic of nobility, could be enacted in exciting new ways.[18] In so doing, the Spanish monarchs lured Italian nobles into an elite conglomerate in

---

[10] Mozzarelli, "Il nero tunnel," p. 17; Verga, "La Spagna."

[11] See the overview in Signorotto, "Dalla decadenza."   [12] Mozzarelli, "Dall'antispagnolismo."

[13] The first formulations can be traced back to two conferences that took place in the early 1990s and whose proceedings were published in Pissavino and Signorotto, eds., *Lombardia borromaica,* and Brambilla and Muto, eds., *La Lombardia.*

[14] Ribot García, *La Monarquía,* pp. 530–1, 636–8.   [15] Galasso, *Alla periferia,* p. 20.

[16] For a similar perspective on the Viennese court, see Pečar, "Status-Ökonomie."

[17] On the court of Philip III, see the monumental Martínez Millán and Visceglia, eds., *La Monarquía.* For an innovative approach to courts as centers of elite networks, see Duindam, *Vienna.*

[18] Mozzarelli, "Onore"; Visceglia, "'Non si ha da equiparare.'"

INTRODUCTION: THE BORROMEOS' HIDDEN SPANISH CONNECTION   5

which the king of Spain functioned as the sole protector of a fledgling pan-Hispanic society of gentlemen.[19] Rather than acting as subjugators, this new school of thought has claimed, the Spanish rulers presented themselves as patrons of local elites who in turn readily inserted themselves into trans-local networks of families, glued together by a shared allegiance to the king of Spain.[20]

What was a historiographical paradigm shift in the early 1990s has since produced more nuanced results. An increasingly mature historiography has revealed that the client networks the Habsburgs forged in Italy underwent significant changes as the kings responded to the demands of the crown's Italian subjects.[21] Over time, Habsburg administrators extended the circle of potential beneficiaries of the crown's material and symbolic riches. After the peace of Cateau-Cambrésis had sealed the *pax hispanica* in the Italian peninsula in 1559, Philip II (r. 1555–1598) spent the remainder of the century wooing the nominally sovereign heads of Italy's principalities in the north and the center of the peninsula, as well as the leading families of territories with aristocratic governments, such as the papacy (an elective monarchy) and the Republic of Genoa. As the sixteenth turned into the seventeenth century, the existing networks were beefed up. With France rebounding from its Wars of Religion, the Habsburgs sought to pander to heads of households from the three territories under direct Spanish rule. During the reigns of Philip III (r. 1598–1621) and Philip IV (r. 1621–1665),[22] both established noble houses and social strivers were animated to take advantage of the guerdons that the Spanish monarchs dangled before them.[23] Thanks to their solicitude, the crown succeeded in building a resilient Italian "subsystem" within the world-spanning "Spanish system."[24]

The opening up of the spoils system to lower-ranking nobles and the consequent massification of honorifics in the seventeenth century sparked a reorganization of the administration of royal patronage. Starting in 1598, the management of the crown's network was placed in the hands of a new figure, the minister-favorite (*valido* in Spanish).[25] After a relatively shy start and tentative attempts to rope in nobles from Milan, Naples, and Sicily under Philip III's favorite, the Duke of Lerma (r. 1598–1618),[26] the novel form of governance peaked under Lerma's successor, the Count-Duke of Olivares (r. 1623–1643). By appealing to the warrior instincts of Spanish Italy's hereditary nobility, Philip IV's favorite constructed a support base of Italian clients. As the Thirty Years' War (1618–1648) reached Italy in the 1630s, these *olivarista* nobles actively contributed to the construction

---

[19] Visceglia, "La nobiltà napoletana," p. 44. More generally, see Yun Casalilla, ed., *Las redes.*
[20] Elliott, "A Europe."   [21] The following paragraph is based on Spagnoletti, *Principi.*
[22] Martínez Millán, ed., *La corte.*
[23] Case studies from Milan include Visconti, *Il commercio*; Cremonini, *Le vie.*
[24] The terminology is borrowed from Musi, "L'Italia," and Musi, *L'impero*, ch. 3.
[25] The literature on the topic is vast. See Feros, *Kingship*; Elliott, *The Count-Duke.*
[26] For Lerma's Italian network, see Enciso Alonso-Muñumer, *Nobleza.*

6 ARISTOCRATIC POWER IN THE SPANISH MONARCHY

of a war government with massively expanded emergency powers.[27] As this book uncovers, during Olivares's ascendancy, his Italian sub-patrons created a shareholder culture that went far beyond the rarefied circles of the high nobility. With their help, resources were funneled down to a growing roster of clients amongst the "middling sorts" in towns across Lombardy, creating new dependencies, as well as enmity toward Spain in a territory that prided itself on its loyalty to the crown.

As Spanish Italy's elites and their punters basked in the bounty of the Catholic king, storm clouds were gathering. By the 1640s, the Spanish empire was the worst hit by the apogee of the general crisis of the seventeenth century.[28] Of the "six contemporaneous revolutions" that rocked Western Europe in the 1640s, four took place within the composite Spanish monarchy.[29] In 1640, Catalonia and Portugal rose against the Habsburgs, only to be followed by two of the crown's Italian possessions, Sicily and Naples, in 1647.[30] To what extent the networking of successive minister-favorites had contributed to the crisis of Spanish rule in the Italian peninsula remains a moot point. Specialists in the history of southern Italy have linked the revolts in Sicily and Naples to the local nobilities' connivance with Spanish power and the large-scale redistribution of resources it entailed.[31] The widespread protests, according to this view, emanated from discontent with a nobility hooked on crown patronage and culminated in a social movement calling for the establishment of a constitutional monarchy capable of reining in an elite running amuck.[32]

In Milan, which was spared the upheavals that tore asunder southern Italy, the dynamics were perhaps more similar to those in the south than historians have allowed. Early interventions highlighted the differences between Naples and Milan. Cesare Mozzarelli famously argued that, in the absence of a feudal system conferring any real power on feudatories, Milanese nobles were so wedded to the institutions of the state that they had no interest in rebelling against the Spanish monarch.[33] Gianvittorio Signorotto later added nuance to that argument. Teasing out the networks into which the Milanese nobility enrolled massively in the central decades of the seventeenth century, Signorotto suggested that the crown's largesse procured Milan stability at a time of widespread unrest.[34] More recently, however, historians have poked holes in the narrative of Milan's loyalty. Alessandro Buono, in his work on opposition to the war economy, has argued

---

[27] Benigno, *L'ombra*. On the military as a transmission belt in Lombardy, see Rizzo, "Centro"; Maffi, *Il baluardo*, and Maffi, *La cittadella*.

[28] The two foundational texts, representing the polar opposites in the debate, are Hobsbawm, "The General Crisis," and Trevor-Roper, "The General Crisis." The latest overview is Parker, *Global Crisis*.

[29] Merriman, *Six Contemporaneous Revolutions*.

[30] Elliott, Villari, and Hespanha, eds., *1640*.   [31] Benigno, *Specchi*; Benigno, *Favoriti*.

[32] Villari, *Un sogno*.   [33] Mozzarelli, "Strutture," pp. 435–6, 441–3.

[34] Signorotto, *Milano*.

INTRODUCTION: THE BORROMEOS' HIDDEN SPANISH CONNECTION   7

that the induction of Milanese nobles was a source of disquiet rather than stability.[35] This book builds on Buono's insights and reveals that Milan faced opposition to elite profiteering in similar forms to those manifest in southern Italy and may have averted an open revolt by chance rather than through careful design.

The brush with catastrophe in the 1640s heralded a "struggle for stability" throughout the Spanish empire.[36] Recent work on the court of Madrid has unveiled some of the consequences of the intense soul-searching that obtained in the aftermath of the breakdown of order. By far the most important of the changes that materialized was the occlusion of the minister-favorite. In the wake of the first revolts in the Iberian peninsula, Olivares was dismissed in 1643, and even though his cousin, Luis Méndez de Haro (r. c.1647–1661), tried to impose himself as the next *valido*, that model of governance had by then clearly run its course. Haro was duly kept in check by fellow grandees, who were determined to ensure that no one attained the same level of unchallenged authority over the king's patronage as that which had led to such disastrous outcomes for the empire.[37] As the monarchy rebounded from its deepest crisis in the 1650s, the high nobility took collective responsibility as an oligarchy dependent on the king.[38] Having stared into the abyss, the Spanish aristocracies of the seventeenth century reinvented themselves as the king's loyal servants in what I. A. A. Thompson aptly called a "monarcho-señorial regime."[39]

Much less is known about the fallout of this redefinition of monarchical government in Spanish Italy. Recent studies on Naples yield the sense that local elites responded to the uprisings of the 1640s by implementing new forms of administration that relied heavily on symbolic power and a commitment to "good government."[40] In northern Italy, the absence of a revolt and the resulting lack of a clear rupture has meant that the latter half of the seventeenth century has never received sustained attention from scholars.[41] Yet, if research on Castile, the other non-revolutionary territory of the empire, is anything to go by, the crisis wrought important changes in the management of the commonwealth even in regions that emerged relatively unscathed from the calamity of the 1640s.[42] This was certainly true of Milan, where local elite families consciously relegated profiteering to a "backstage" that was shielded from view by an elaborate "front stage" of royal munificence.[43] As we will see, such performative royalty was not foisted upon the nobility, as was once argued, but actively constructed with its help. In a bid to

---

[35] Buono, *Esercito.*   [36] The term is borrowed from Rabb, *The Struggle.*
[37] Valladares, ed., *El mundo.*   [38] Malcolm, *Royal Favouritism.*
[39] Thompson, "The Nobility," p. 204.
[40] Minguito Palomares, *Nápoles;* Carrió-Invernizzi, *El gobierno.*
[41] The only notable exception, though it does not cover the period immediately following the 1640s, is Álvarez-Ossorio Alvariño, "La república."
[42] MacKay, *The Limits.*
[43] The terminology is borrowed from Stollberg-Rilinger, "The Baroque State," p. 828. I refer to the "Methodology and Sources" section for more on this.

8 ARISTOCRATIC POWER IN THE SPANISH MONARCHY

recuperate the legitimacy they had lost through their self-seeking behavior, Milanese aristocrats actively contributed to the "resilience" of the Spanish monarchy in the latter half of the seventeenth century.[44]

Even though the nobility was at the heart of the transformations in Spanish Italy and the imperial center, we know surprisingly little about the evolution of that social group during the seventeenth century. For the Iberian peninsula, this period has been shown to have wrought profound changes within that group, which proved surprisingly adaptable to the ever-changing world of the court, with its constant pressure for reinvention as new elements acceded to the ranks of the nobility.[45] What happened in Italy is less clear. Granted, in the 1980s and 1990s, Neapolitan historians in particular published detailed studies of single aristocratic clans based on extensive research in family archives.[46] However, many of these analyses remained indebted to the classic methodologies of social and economic history and, as a result, were more focused on the long-term evolution of landed estates and on marital alliances than the more volatile *histoire événementielle* of court politics. In an essay taking stock of this historiography in 1996, Maria Antonietta Visceglia lamented the dearth of studies on the trans-local ties of Italian families in the context of Spain's imperial politics, which, she argued, heavily inflected the social reproduction of dynasties from Spanish Italy.[47]

In the meantime, Visceglia's call has clearly been heeded. Several scholars working on Naples have investigated local families through the prism of their ties to the Habsburgs.[48] While these pioneering studies have offered a bird's-eye view, often covering the entire early modern period, Giuseppe Mrozek Eliszezynski has recently shown the usefulness of a microhistory of the networks of a Neapolitan family during the relatively short, though also extraordinarily tumultuous, central decades of the seventeenth century.[49] Despite its crucial importance in the geo-strategy of the Spanish monarchy, Milan has been neglected in these new social and cultural histories of Italian families' trans-local networks. This book endeavors to fill this gap. It probes the vagaries of social collaboration between a noble family and the king of Spain by focusing on a particularly tense period—the middle decades of the seventeenth century—and revealing how that watershed moment affected the ties of one pre-eminent clan—the Borromeos—with the crown. Homing in on the family's growing dependence on the Madrid court, the book scrutinizes that process itself, as well as the contradictions and unintended consequences this complicity spawned.

---

[44] Storrs, *The Resilience.*   [45] Soria Mesa, *La nobleza.*

[46] See Astarita, *The Continuity*, which contains bibliographical references to comparable studies in Italian.

[47] Visceglia, "La nobiltà napoletana," pp. 54, 51.

[48] Sodano, *Da baroni*; Papagna, *Sogni*; Noto, *Élites.*

[49] Mrozek Eliszezynski, *Ascanio Filomarino.*

Methodology and Sources

Families have come to hold a central place in the historiography of early modern Europe. Following pathbreaking research into village communities,[50] scholars studying the nobility have also developed an interest in the behavior of individual aristocratic clans. Underlying this research is the idea that early modern societies were familist entities. Early modern nobles inhabited a world in which the elite household was the default unit of society. This led to much of politics being dominated by the pursuit of family interests and the resulting competition between houses.[51] Increasingly, these interests were battled out in princely courts.[52] The reason for this centralization was simple. The defense of clan interests necessitated alliances: noble heads of household needed to cooperate with other families both to advance their own cause and to oust potential antagonists. As a result, the early modern period saw an intensifying of networks between noble families, which converged on princely courts.

As historians have shown, the lifeblood of these networks was patronage, the preferment of friends and relatives.[53] Historians' appreciation of patronage has shifted considerably since the term first entered their vocabulary via anthropology in the 1970s. Pioneers in the field took a functionalist approach to patronage.[54] Wolfgang Reinhard, in his work on the papacy, and Sharon Kettering, in her writings on the French monarchy, both contended that the networks elite families built for dynastic reasons wound up serving as handmaidens to the modern state infrastructure of the nineteenth century: in their master narrative, power-hungry elites lent their jockeying bureaucratic forms through increasingly complex bodies set up to adjudicate the scramble for resources, which ended up taking on a life of their own.[55] As Reinhard once quipped, the networks of noble oligarchies in the seventeenth century were not a "cesspool of corruption" but, rather, "a necessary and altogether functional and appropriate stage in the development of the modern state."[56]

More recently, scholars of clientelism have moved away from these teleological accounts and have transitioned toward studying patronage as an emic concept. A number of historians have shown that while modern, bureaucratic institutions may have been the ultimate result of the institutionalization of clientelism, that outcome was far from intended by the nobilities who partook in that process.[57] As a consequence, scholars have tried to understand patronage as an emanation of the political culture of the Old Regime rather than as a category of sociological

---

[50] Sabean, Teuscher, and Mathieu, eds., *Kinship*.
[51] Osborne, *Dynasty*. A sociological interpretation is Adams, *The Familial State*.
[52] Spagnoletti, *Le dinastie*, pp. 190–3.   [53] Reinhard, "Amici," pp. 312–3.
[54] Reinhard, *Freunde*; Kettering, *Patrons*; Kettering, *Patronage*.
[55] Reinhard, ed., *Power Elites*.   [56] Reinhard, "Amici," p. 333.
[57] Rowlands, *The Dynastic State*; Parker, *Class*.

10 ARISTOCRATIC POWER IN THE SPANISH MONARCHY

analysis that was posthumously grafted upon early modern societies.[58] Adopting an ethnographer's perspective, early modernists have shown that notions of patronage were ubiquitous in the sources, denoting ties of mutual dependence that were couched in the disinterested language of the gift register.[59] By focusing on how early modern elites used patronage as a linguistic device, historians have shown the deliberate ambiguity of the term in contemporary parlance. Depending on one's specific interests at any given moment, patron-client ties could be perceived as "useful networks" (usually for oneself) or "corrupt coteries" (when others did it).[60]

What fed the ambiguity of patronage, specialists have argued, was the coexistence of competing and sometimes conflicting norms in early modern societies.[61] Patronage was the key component of the widely accepted social norm of *pietas*, the powerful's responsibility to kith and kin.[62] Yet, that social commandment sat in opposition to the equally binding norm of the preservation of the common good in whose name many members of the elite claimed to be acting.[63] Making matters worse, this intrinsic ambiguity could easily be leveraged against rivals in the competition over resources. As Hillard von Thiessen has argued, the commitment to the common good could be invoked to delegitimize the patronage of competitors who were regularly accused of corruption by people who often engaged in the very same practices as soon as the opportunity to do so presented itself.[64]

As von Thiessen's work indicates, the study of patronage has come to overlap with research into corruption. Like patronage, the definition of corruption was historically contingent and served a similar function as a rhetorical sleight of hand in the rush for resources.[65] Arising out of the conflict between social obligations and norms centered on the commonwealth, early modern corruption was defined as the pursuit of self-interest in violation of the collective good.[66] Given the early modern elite's structural dependence on patronage, anti-corruption existed almost exclusively as discourse and rarely as practice. According to the most authoritative scholars in the field, early modern anti-corruption remained a weapon that was cynically brandished to moralize the scramble for resources in princely courts but was rarely, if ever, conducive to interventions for the strengthening of the collective good.[67] In a society steeped in patronage, charges of

---

[58] Herman, "The Language."   [59] Neuschel, *Word*.

[60] The quotes are from the title of a collection of essays. See Karsten and von Thiessen, eds., *Nützliche Netzwerke*.

[61] Von Thiessen, *Das Zeitalter*, pp. 18, 35–117, 246–70.   [62] Reinhard, "Papa Pius."

[63] Asch, Emich, and Engels, "Einleitung," p. 10; von Thiessen, "Korruption," pp. 94–5; Andújar Castillo, Feros, and Ponce Leiva, "Corrupción," p. 291.

[64] Von Thiessen, "Korruption."   [65] Kroeze, Vitoria, and Geltner, "Introduction."

[66] Emich, Reinhardt, von Thiessen, and Wieland, "Stand," p. 236; von Thiessen, "Korruption," p. 92.

[67] Asch, Emich, and Engels, "Einleitung," pp. 7, 22; Andújar Castillo, Feros, and Ponce Leiva, "Corrupción," p. 293.

INTRODUCTION: THE BORROMEOS' HIDDEN SPANISH CONNECTION   11

corruption were meant to restore a semblance of balance between the competing demands of social and common good norms rather than tip the scale in favor of the latter.[68] That shift, the current consensus holds, materialized only in the eighteenth century, when the Enlightenment injected new ideas of the commonwealth into the debate.[69] The seventeenth century, according to this view, was a period when elites remained locked in an unproductive stalemate in which accusations of corruption were hurled without resulting in meaningful change, certainly not in the triumph of the commonwealth.

This book challenges the assumption that seventeenth-century elites failed to address the contradiction between social norms and the commonwealth.[70] While they did not end the preferment of kith and kin, they did grow increasingly uncomfortable with the open disavowal of the common good norms the jockeying of the age entailed. As the century progressed, families like the Borromeos sought to grapple with this uneasiness. As I argue in this book, the response they came up with was the symbolic politics that came to dominate the elite's public actions in the latter half of the seventeenth century. The initial impulse for the study of symbolic politics came from Peter Burke's now-classic treatment of the representations of Louis XIV of France (r. 1643–1715).[71] The idea undergirding the work of Burke and his many epigones has been that symbolic politics was an attempt by seventeenth-century monarchies to manufacture consent by grafting their vision of themselves on an impressionable public.[72] Challenges to this approach have come mostly from historians of the Holy Roman Empire. A group of scholars working around Barbara Stollberg-Rilinger has suggested that the investment in symbolism was a joint venture of the nobility and the monarch, who reinforced their hold on power in this way.[73] In the process, Stollberg-Rilinger has argued in her most recent intervention, princes and the high nobility built a "baroque state," whose defining feature was a "front stage" of pomp and pageantry that concealed the backroom deals of politics, which was still predominantly "dynastic action."[74] This skullduggery, Stollberg-Rilinger suggests, was an attempt to address the "fundamental tension between ideal order and factual disorder" that had emerged from the "extraordinary shocks" of the early modern age, leaving the elite hankering after "clarity, stability, and security" from the seventeenth century forward.[75] This book is the first to explore this idea further. It argues that patronage and symbolic politics—two phenomena at the heart of

---

[68] Von Thiessen, "Korruption," pp. 99, 120; Windler, "Redes," p. 127.

[69] Engels, "Corruption," p. 175; Bernsee, "For the Good," pp. 259, 263.

[70] In this sense, my book adds to the coping mechanisms Hillard von Thiessen has recently highlighted in his *Das Zeitalter*, pp. 271–320.

[71] Burke, *The Fabrication*.

[72] For examples from Spanish Naples, see Minguito Palomares, *Nápoles*; Guarino, *Representing*.

[73] Stollberg-Rilinger, *The Emperor's Old Clothes*, and Stollberg-Rilinger, *The Holy Roman Empire*. For an overview, see Krischer, "New Directions."

[74] Stollberg-Rilinger, "The Baroque State," p. 828.   [75] Ibid. pp. 826–7.

12   ARISTOCRATIC POWER IN THE SPANISH MONARCHY

recent historiography on early modern elites—were umbilically linked: in the eyes of its protagonists, symbolic predominance became necessary to deal with the inevitable corruption of a social order based on clientelism.

My approach relies heavily on the work of sociologist Pierre Bourdieu. Bourdieu posits that we need to conceive of societies as hierarchically stratified systems regulated by structures and processes that tend to reproduce extant inequalities.[76] Unlike many other scholars of elites, Bourdieu eschews economic reductionism: in his theoretical framework, inequalities are rooted in unequal access to education and influential contacts as much as in the dearth of economic capital.[77] Inequality, therefore, rests on more than one factor. What unifies these disparate sources and turns them into unequal power is a process Bourdieu calls "transubstantiation." Transubstantiation denotes the magicking of a vast array of valued resources ("capital" in Bourdieu's nomenclature) into symbolic power, or prestige, which is recognized as such by peers and social inferiors alike.[78] In Bourdieu's theory, then, symbolism is not a fanciful flight that is disconnected from more tangible forms of power. Far from being an exercise in futility, the transubstantiation of raw power into symbolic predominance is constitutive of, and crucial to the maintenance of, social difference, especially in premodern societies with less effective institutions of the state, which serve as the main delivery mechanisms of inequality in modern society.[79] What is more, symbolism is what makes power differentials palatable. As Bourdieu scholar David Swartz phrases it, "symbolic practices...deflect attention from the interested character of practices and thereby contribute to their enactment as disinterested pursuits."[80] By lending power an aura of disinterestedness, the transubstantiation into symbolic power guarantees stability to an extent that the exercise of brute force would not.[81]

Intimately tied up with Bourdieu's idea of transubstantiation is that of "misrecognition." Misrecognition signifies the strategies the powerful adopt to rationalize and, in the process, conceal the rapacious nature of their exercise of power. An integral part of the "labor of domination," misrecognition is a collective endeavor: the illusion needs to be upheld through the constant affirmation of people inside the same social group intent on embellishing the unsavory reality of their rule. What makes Bourdieu's concept so useful is that it factors out the ultimately unanswerable question of intentionality and redirects attention toward an analysis of the processes that perpetuate structures of inequality. As a semiconscious form of rationalization, misrecognition is as much self-deception within the elite as it is an attempt to pull the wool over the eyes of the ruled.[82]

---

[76] Swartz, "Metaprinciples," p. 21.   [77] Bourdieu, "The Forms."
[78] Bourdieu, "Rethinking," p. 8; Swartz, *Culture*, p. 93.
[79] Loyal, *Bourdieu's Theory*, p. 30. See Bourdieu, *The State Nobility*, on twentieth-century France.
[80] Swartz, *Symbolic Power*, p. 102.
[81] Ibid., p. 4; also see Stollberg-Rilinger, *The Emperor's Old Clothes*, pp. 3–4.
[82] Bourdieu, *Outline*, p. 6; Swartz, *Symbolic Power*, p. 38.

INTRODUCTION: THE BORROMEOS' HIDDEN SPANISH CONNECTION   13

Misrecognition operates wherever elites need to overcome a conflict between their material interests and the commitment to abstract ideas of the common-wealth. In her study of cadres of the Communist Party of the Soviet Union under Stalin, Sheila Fitzpatrick has shown that misrecognition allowed committed com-munists to make sense of the privileges they enjoyed in spite of their avowed commitment to equality.[83] This book argues that a similar process can be observed among seventeenth-century elites: as they sought to balance their entanglement in networks with a commitment to the commonwealth, they invested heavily in the transubstantiation of their self-seeking behavior into a symbolically exalted monarchy, misrecognizing their corruption as public service. In adopting Bourdieu's concept of misrecognition, not only does this monograph offer a new explanation of the stability of elite rule despite the rampant corruption of the sev-enteenth century; it also contributes to the rapidly growing field of elite studies in sociology, which has been particularly concerned with the ways power and privi-lege are camouflaged and masked.[84]

Aristocratic Power in the Spanish Monarchy offers an analysis of what sociolo-gist Loïc Wacquant has called the "division of the labor of domination" within a family.[85] As a generation of scholars has taught us, such divisions were usually moored in gender differences. By far the most prominent manifestation of this was the "working couple" of husband and wife.[86] Laboring in lockstep on a shared strategy, spouses in noble families advanced the interests of their households by performing distinct, yet complementary gender roles.[87] The Borromeos were no exception. Women were eminently important to their rise in the seventeenth cen-tury, and I have treated the significance of female power and maternity in a sepa-rate publication.[88] In this book, I want to focus on an oft-overlooked alternative gendered division of labor. As Renata Ago has shown, families in Catholic societ-ies often subsisted on the "teamwork" (*gioco di squadra*) of married laymen and celibate members of the clergy.[89] This book builds on Ago's pathbreaking research on the Roman nobility to look at the complementary masculinities of laymen and clerics, and to flesh out the cooperation between brothers of an elite household.[90] Specifically, it elucidates the adaptability of gendered male actors to parse the transition from a warrior to a courtier elite. While recent years have seen publica-tions on masculinities in the early modern period, this is the first monograph to

---

[83] Fitzpatrick, *Everyday Stalinism*, pp. 104–5; Swartz, *Symbolic Power*, pp. 37–8, 81–2.
[84] Savage, *The Return*. Laura Clancy has recently pointed out the continued importance of aristo-cratic power to the perpetuation of inequality. See her *Running*.
[85] Wacquant, "Foreword," p. x.   [86] The foundational text is Wunder, *He Is the Sun*.
[87] Most work has focused on princely families. See James, *A Renaissance Marriage*, and Aikin, *A Ruler's Consort*. For noble families lower down the social hierarchy, see Ferrier-Viaud, *Épouses*.
[88] Weber, "Una *mater*."   [89] Ago, "Giochi."   [90] Ago, "Ecclesiastical Careers."

14   ARISTOCRATIC POWER IN THE SPANISH MONARCHY

systematically probe their function in the social reproduction of a Catholic aristocratic family.[91]

This book addresses these large historiographical and methodological questions through a case study of the Borromeos in the seventeenth century. Most treatments of the family have focused on the sixteenth and the early decades of the seventeenth centuries when the Borromeos became one of the most important clans in Milan thanks to the prominent positions they held within the Milanese Church and their excellent ties to the papal court in Rome.[92] The only notable publication on the central decades of the seventeenth century is Cinzia Cremonini's work on the main branch of the family.[93] This book centers the cadet branch known as the Borromeos of Angera. Though studies on their role as patrons of the arts in seventeenth-century Milan exist, little is known about the wider context in which these paintings were commissioned.[94] This book reconstructs this broader picture by looking at Giulio Cesare III Borromeo and his three sons, Giovanni VII (1616–1660), Federico IV (1617–1673), and Antonio Renato (1632–1686). It shows how the Borromeos reinterpreted their ties to the papal court, turning them into an appendix to the family's overarching strategy of repositioning themselves as a Hispanic clan. Through tireless teamwork between laymen and clerics, the three Borromeo brothers at the center of this story turned a newly formed cadet branch into an imperial dynasty in what were crucial decades for Spanish rule in Italy and the Borromeo family.

The main source for this book is the previously untapped correspondence of Federico Jr., which consists mostly of his epistolary exchanges with his brothers and his mother. Additional, less complete collections of the epistles and personal documents that his two brothers left behind are also used. Together, the letters, housed today at the family archive on Isola Bella in Lake Maggiore, offer a rare glimpse into the strategic thinking that went into the preservation of social privilege and the individual parts played by family members as they mobilized their diverging male identities to advance what they understood as a shared cause: to place the Borromeos at the top of a burgeoning pan-Hispanic elite. Another important source is the patronage of the arts of the Borromeos, which in many instances gives more eloquent expression to what is often only hinted at in written sources: the twists and turns of the clan's deepening ties to the house of Habsburg. While the family papers are frequently candid, the deliberate omissions are often as palpable. I have tried to control the inherent bias of the main source by reading broadly in other archives. I have consulted additional material

---

[91] On early modern masculinities in a Protestant society, see Shepard, *Meanings*. On sibling rivalry in the Protestant nobility, see Pollock, "Younger Sons."

[92] See the Prologue of this book.   [93] Cremonini, "Storia."

[94] See Galli and Monferrini, *I Borromeo*, for a reconstruction of the careers and artistic commissions of the Borromeos of Angera. The authors had only very limited access to the Borromeo papers that are the main source of this book.

in state and church archives, including the repositories of the ducal tribunals in Milan, the archives of the Spanish monarchy, and the archives of the Church, in both Milan and the Vatican. Counterintuitively perhaps, the latter warrant particular attention with regard to the Borromeos' Spanish connection in the context of the shifting power dynamic between the Apostolic See and the court of Madrid in the latter half of the seventeenth century. The Vatican archives, as well as the other public repositories, contain the fragments left behind by the clan's elite opponents. These sources cast an altogether different light on the Borromeos' complacent depictions of themselves. As such, they work as an important corrective to the image the Borromeos projected to the court society they were trying to enter. It is through these documents that we are today able to grasp the complex misrecognition the Borromeos conjured in order to stay atop the social pyramid.

Outline of the Argument

This book is divided into two parts. Part I, titled "Buccaneering," explores how the Borromeos of Angera became clients of the Spanish monarchy and the legitimacy crisis this provoked. Part II, "Blearing," shows how they rationalized the self-interested nature of their clientelism and eventually succeeded in concealing their cronyism. The story commences in the early decades of the seventeenth century when Cardinal-Archbishop Federico Borromeo Sr. first sought *rapprochement* with the Catholic monarchy in what constituted a major shift in a family strategy that had hitherto been centered on the papal court in Rome (Prologue). The *détente* between the once rebellious archbishop and the crown allowed his nephews and great-nephews to benefit from the new opportunities the rise of the government of the minister-favorite in Madrid ushered in. Like other leading families from the monarchy's Italian territories, the Borromeos became imbricated in the crown's expanding patronage networks (chapter 1). In response to the ascendancy of the Count-Duke of Olivares and his appeals to the nobility's warrior instincts in the 1620s, the Borromeos presented themselves as military entrepreneurs in the service of the monarchy. This self-fashioning posed new problems, however. When the Borromeos geared up for a war against France, they claimed to do so to protect the populace in their sprawling fiefdom around Lake Maggiore. Yet, as the war got underway, their vassals exposed the alleged duty of care as a self-serving fiction that conveniently concealed the hopes of social advancement the Borromeos had pinned on Olivares's war government (chapter 2). As a result, when the Borromeos helped drag Lombardy into a devastating war against the French crown in the late 1630s, they had to deal with festering discontent among their subjects. Initially, they tried to stifle the growing protest movement by directing patronage resources of the war economy to local provisioners of military wherewithal. But this strategy, too, backfired. The vast majority of the population, who were made to pony up for the war profiteers, accused the Borromeos of undermining the principles of good government to which they had pledged allegiance (chapter 3). By the late 1650s, the chasm between lofty rhetoric and an unpleasant reality of mass destruction supplied arguments robust enough for the Borromeos' competitors to unmask them. Their rivals portrayed them as opportunists who claimed to be acting in the common good when all they were interested in was their advancement as an imperial family in the making. These charges proved almost fatal. As they were on the cusp of realizing their long-held dream of joining the in-crowd in the Madrid court, the Borromeos were unceremoniously ejected from these august ranks (chapter 4).

Having overplayed its hand, the family spent the better part of the 1660s overcoming the contradiction between its growing dependence on Spanish patronage and its claim that, in collecting its dues in Madrid, it was defending the commonwealth. To escape the whiff of self-interest hanging over them, the Borromeos pivoted to an old resource of theirs—the Catholic Church—which they now mobilized in novel ways. In an attempt to rebuild the burned bridge to Madrid, the family cardinal, an exemplar of public service to the papacy and the Catholic king, took over from the military entrepreneur (chapter 5). Using his symbolic capital as a member of the clergy, he assisted the king in resolving the jurisdictional controversies between the monarchy and the Church in Milan, carefully selling the initiative as a bid to restore the good government that the military entrepreneurs had, in the eyes of many, undermined (chapter 6). As a papal diplomat serving in Madrid and later in Rome, he took an active role in the court intrigues in Spain, presenting himself as a conscientious administrator who did the Spanish grandees' bidding in the hope that this would set the stage for the Borromeos' admission to the privileged circles from which they had been excluded in the 1650s (chapter 7). Thus, by the 1670s, the Borromeos had completed the great shift from warriors to courtiers, from self-seeking chancers to responsible administrators of the collective good. They had morphed into votaries of the monarchy who had learned to hide their pay-to-play behind the pomp and pageantry that now symbolized the benevolence of the king toward his subjects. Fashioning themselves as purveyors of good governance finally earned the family recognition as the pillar of Spanish power in Italy as which it had long seen itself (chapter 8).

Given the Borromeos' reputation as paternalists, they seem a particularly worthwhile object of study in coming to understand the workings of the "misrecognition" of privilege. The Borromeos are today best remembered as representatives of a socially minded elite who looked out for the indigent and downtrodden. This book shows that this image is itself the product of a long-term operation aimed at deflecting from the family's complicity in worldly affairs and its commitment to dynastic self-aggrandizement. That said, this monograph is as much a case study as a tell-all. For the transformation that particular family underwent to safeguard its privileged position speaks to a broader change in elite rule in the seventeenth century. As this book will show, the conflict between dynastic aspirations and the preservation of the common good developed a dynamic of its own that profoundly transformed monarchical rule and the nobility itself. The Borromeos may provide a particularly vivid example of the disturbing relationship between rapacity and philanthropy, but theirs is ultimately the story shared by many houses of their time and station: that of how the turbulence of the seventeenth century birthed the self-positioning of former warriors as courtiers who hid their self-interest behind an ideology of princely service.

Prologue

The Unraveling of an Ecclesiastical Dynasty

In July 1617, Federico Borromeo Sr. (1564–1631), the aging cardinal-archbishop of Milan, signed a treaty with Philip III (r. 1598–1621), king of Spain and duke of Milan.[1] The *concordia jurisdictionalis,* as the document was known, placed far-reaching restrictions on the holder of the highest ecclesiastical office in the Spanish-ruled statelet in northern Italy, hemming in the archbishop's police force and judicial powers.[2] As such, the *concordia* altered the relations between the Roman Catholic Church and the Spanish monarchy in the State of Milan. It put to bed what a papal diplomat involved in the negotiations had called a problem with "an infinite number of heads," not unlike "the Hydra, where the more heads one chops off, the more regrow."[3] Laying down unequivocal jurisdictional parameters and protocols, the treaty held the promise of a permanent settlement of the institutional rivalry between ecclesiastical and monarchical powerholders that had been eating away at the political stability of Milan. After six decades of wrangling over jurisdictional precedence, Borromeo had agreed to submit to, and recognize, the sovereignty of the king of Spain over certain aspects of the Milanese church.

To the uninitiated, the signing of the *concordia* came as a surprise. To them, it marked the sudden surrender of one of Milan's most prominent families to the king of Spain. The Borromeos had risen to the top of Milanese society as merchant bankers who acted as financiers to the dukes of Milan in the fifteenth century.[4] When the last Sforza died and the Habsburgs of Madrid integrated Milan into their global empire, the Borromeos briefly stared down the barrel of redundancy, only to reinvent themselves as an "ecclesiastical dynasty."[5] To counter what they deemed a Spanish power-grab against established local families such as themselves, they started to leverage the material and symbolic resources of the Church. The mastermind behind this survival strategy was Carlo Borromeo

---

[1] Gerolamo Caimi to Federico III Borromeo, Madrid July 9, 1617: *Biblioteca Ambrosiana, Milan,* mss. G 224 inf 24.

[2] Rimoldi, "L'età," p. 397. Also see "Concordia," p. 144.

[3] Quoted in Visceglia, *Roma,* p. 69. For a detailed description of the negotiations, see Rivola, *Vita,* pp. 445–51.

[4] Annoni, "Lo Stato."

[5] The term "ecclesiastical dynasty" was coined by J. A. Bergin to describe members of the French nobility who employed the wealth they drew from benefices of the Church to condition the actions of the Most Christian monarchy. See Bergin, "The Decline."

Aristocratic Power in the Spanish Monarchy: The Borromeo Brothers of Milan, 1620–1680. Samuel Weber, Oxford University Press. © Samuel Weber 2023. DOI: 10.1093/oso/9780198872597.003.0002

PROLOGUE: THE UNRAVELING OF AN ECCLESIASTICAL DYNASTY   19

(1538–1584). A highflyer, Carlo began serving as the right-hand man of his uncle, Pope Pius IV Medici (r. 1559–1565), aged just 20, overseeing the final and decisive phase of the Council of Trent, where the tenets of a renewed Roman Catholic Church were defined in response to the Protestant Reformation. Following his uncle's passing, Carlo, inspired by the reforms of the secular clergy decreed at Trent, took over the archbishopric of his hometown of Milan.[6] In the two decades from 1565 until his untimely death in 1584, he mobilized the reforming zeal of Trent to wage relentless lawfare against the Spanish crown and its institutions. Making the most of the hazy delimitations between overlapping legal spheres, Carlo revived the medieval doctrine of *plenitudo potestatis Ecclesiae* (full power of the Church), according to which monarchical institutions should at all times be subservient to the Church.[7] In Carlo's hands, that tenet became a battering ram. Citing Tridentine doctrine, he helped himself to powers to levy taxes and try all members of the clergy in his own law courts, privileges that remained unrivaled in the rest of the Catholic world.[8] In the eyes of many, the caviling over precedence was the beginning of something larger. The Spanish authorities feared that the popular archbishop might rouse the rabble and place himself at the helm of the strategically important state in northern Italy.[9] In the words of a panicking official, Carlo was "the most dangerous rebel that Your Majesty has ever had."[10] With this backstory in mind, the signing of the *concordia* might indeed have looked like a sudden about-face.

However, those who had cared to look closer over the years were possibly less astonished. Unbeknownst to most, the family had begun to turn its back on the self-fashioning as an exclusively ecclesiastical dynasty as early as the 1580s. As he became more experienced as archbishop, Carlo increasingly moved away from the hostility he had shown during the first fifteen years of his tenure. Toward the end of his life, he toiled for a settlement of the jurisdictional conflicts he had once thrived on. In 1580, he dispatched Carlo Bascapè (1550–1615), a confidant and the would-be bishop of Novara, to the court of Madrid. Bascapè lobbied Philip II (r. 1540–1598 as duke of Milan) for a formalized cooperation between the monarchy and the archbishop, which, he vowed, would save the Milanese's souls and result in political stability for the secular arm of government.[11] Carlo died a few years later, in 1584, without having made peace with the Spanish monarch. It would fall on his cousin Federico to seal the deal.[12] Like Carlo, Federico proceeded in fits and starts. Upon his appointment as archbishop of Milan in 1595, he

---

[6] The literature is vast. For an overview in English, see Headley and Tomaro, eds., *San Carlo*.

[7] Annoni, "Giurisdizionalismo," pp. 141, 151–2. Also see Prosdocimi, *Il diritto*, p. 15.

[8] Castiglione, *Il cardinale*, p. 92; Prosdocimi, *Il diritto*, p. 312; Wright, "Relations," p. 388.

[9] Borromeo, "Archbishop," p. 95.   [10] Quoted ibid.

[11] Bascapè, *I Sette Libri*, p. 482; Prodi, "San Carlo," pp. 222, 226, 234; Mellano and Molinari, "La 'Vita'," pp. 129, 137.

[12] On Federico Sr., see Jones, *Federico*; Zunckel, "Handlungsspielräume."

20 ARISTOCRATIC POWER IN THE SPANISH MONARCHY

adopted a rebellious pose, which promptly provoked a major crisis with the monarchy and sent him into a humiliating exile in Rome. As he nursed his wounds, the second archbishop of the Borromeo house came to understand that overt opposition would no longer pay off. By the turn of the seventeenth century, he had resurrected the memory of Carlo's more lenient stance in the final years of his life and tried hard to turn Carlo's idea of a peace treaty into reality.[13]

Aiding this *rapprochement* was a set of momentous changes to the governance of the Spanish monarchy. After the death of Philip II, the heir to the throne, Philip III, launched a major charm offensive to win over eminent members of the Italian high nobility. In the Spanish court, a new figure, variously known as *valido* or minister-favorite, held sway. Francisco Gómez de Sandoval, Duke of Lerma (r. 1598–1618), was tasked with the construction of a new network: using royal patronage, he was to convince Spanish grandees to enlist eminent local nobles in the Spanish monarchy's far-flung territories as surrogates of the crown. The man he dispatched to Milan to this effect was Pedro Enríquez de Acevedo, Count of Fuentes (r. 1600–1610).[14] In a sign of the *détente* underway, Fuentes visited Carlo's sepulcher in Milan's cathedral, embracing the crown's "most dangerous rebel" as an up-and-coming saint.[15] (Carlo would be canonized in 1610 as one of the first of many Spanish saints.[16]) Federico promptly returned the favor, writing a groveling letter to the Duke of Lerma, in which he explained away his past obstructionism as part of his duties as archbishop and asked the minister-favorite to offer "protection to the Church of Milan and, at the same time, myself."[17]

As the jurisdictional conflicts petered out in the early years of the seventeenth century,[18] Lerma was willing to remove what remained the greatest obstacle to a reconciliation between the Borromeos and the crown. The men he entrusted with this delicate mission were close relatives of his, the Castro brothers.[19] From his post in Rome, where he served as ambassador from 1609 onward, Francisco Ruiz de Castro (1579–1637) eagerly reached out to Federico Borromeo.[20] After a slow start, work on the thorny issue gathered speed in the mid-1610s. Starting in 1615, Castro began meeting Pope Paul V Borghese (r. 1605–1621) on a regular basis to review a draft treaty that had been drawn up by a special committee composed of five cardinals.[21] From that point, things moved along quickly. By late 1615, Castro's wife and broker with the Italian nobility, Lucrezia Legnano di Gattinara

---

[13] Gianvittorio Signorotto has been the first to highlight that Federico's relatively unpolitical stance was not a character trait, as previous historians had argued, but a clever response to the requirements of the age. Signorotto, "La scena," pp. 28, 40, 64. Also see Giannini, "Politica," p. 210.

[14] Signorotto, "La scena," pp. 34–5. [15] Ibid., p. 44. [16] Giannini, "'Con ser'."

[17] Quoted in Besozzi, "Momenti," p. 326. [18] Giannini, "Politica."

[19] Favarò, *Carriere*. On the Castro clan's ties to Lerma, see Enciso Alonso-Muñumer, *Nobleza*, pp. 14–5, 27.

[20] "Istruzione," p. 73.

[21] Giovanni Garzia Mellini to Federico III Borromeo, Rome September 6, 1614: *BAM*, mss. G 219 inf 41; Rimoldi, "L'età," p. 397.

(1590–1623), informed Borromeo that the final draft had been posted to Madrid for further amendments.[22] There, Castro's elder brother, Pedro Fernández (1576–1622), who acted as president of the Council of Italy, took care of the delicate matter, wrapping up the complex negotiations, which had involved the papacy and the Spanish crown, as well as Archbishop Borromeo.[23] In a team effort, the Castro brothers tipped Federico Borromeo into the direction into which he was already falling, putting forward a version of the peace treaty Carlo had first envisaged in the 1580s.

The deal the monarchy offered Federico Borromeo was fortuitous. Instead of taking any significant prerogatives from the archbishop, as he might have feared at first, the *concordia* redefined the broader framework within which Borromeo would henceforth exercise these powers. Reading through the document one is, in fact, struck by how much emphasis it places on adapting the role of the archbishop to the profoundly changed structure of a monarchy that was becoming more inclusive of elite groups in the peripheries.[24] The entire treaty throbbed with professions of the cooperation of worldly and ecclesiastical leaders for the good of Christendom, even if men of the Church were now clearly relegated to operating within the narrow confines laid down by the monarchy. The main impetus behind the document seems to have been to strengthen the role of the archbishop as an administrator of royal, as opposed to ecclesiastical, justice. In return for accepting the king of Spain as the uncontested lord of Lombardy and his subordinate role as a client of the monarch, Federico Borromeo was formally granted ample jurisdictional privileges over the clergy and the laity that had hitherto been disputed, with the important proviso that he accepted that these powers were not innate but emanated from the monarch.[25] While it hobbled the Borromeos' former power as an ecclesiastical dynasty, the *concordia* also put those rights that they had been able to preserve on a stronger footing and snuffed out the harrowing back-and-forth of the sixteenth century.

The *concordia* changed the Borromeos forever. By the late 1610s, the ecclesiastical dynasty that had ruled in opposition to Spanish governors no longer existed. The erstwhile rebels now poised as Habsburg loyalists, readily availing themselves of the opportunities that closeness to the ruling family promised. To be sure, Alessandro Manzoni's novel *The Betrothed* would continue to perpetuate the image of a Federico who stayed away from the temptations of the court. But, by the 1620s, when the novel is set, the archbishop was deeply entangled with the

---

[22] Lucrezia Legnano di Gattinara to Federico III Borromeo, Rome November 20, 1615: *BAM*, mss. G 221 inf 119.

[23] Ercole Ramusio to Federico III Borromeo, Madrid October 16, 1616: *BAM*, mss. G 223bis inf 347.

[24] On the "courtization" under Lerma, see von Thiessen, *Diplomatie*; Enciso Alonso-Muñumer, *Nobleza*; Benigno, *L'ombra*.

[25] Prosdocimi, *Il diritto*, pp. 321–2.

Spanish monarchy. As this book will reveal, that decade marked the beginning of the Borromeos' reinvention as clients of the Spanish monarchy. Making the most of the rise of the government of the minister-favorite in Madrid, the decrepit cardinal and his favorite nephew, Giulio Cesare, would transform the Borromeos into full-fledged members of an ascending "mass support base of Habsburg power" in Italy.[26] What follows is the story of the triumphs and tribulations of the morphing of former rebels into warriors and courtiers at the service of Habsburg Spain and the trouble through which they went to nevertheless present as disinterested actors, the image that would find its most eloquent expression in Manzoni's national novel.

---

[26] For the term "mass support base of Habsburg power," see Spagnoletti, *Principi*, p. 43.

PART I
BUCCANEERING

1

Olivaristas on the Make

The Borromeos and the Government of the Count-Duke of Olivares

The Borromeos' long haul toward Madrid had its origins in a banal rivalry between siblings. In 1613, Giovanni Borromeo (1584–1613), the designated heir to the family's possessions, died unexpectedly, leaving behind the estates the family had acquired over the course of the fifteenth century on Lake Maggiore, some 60 kilometers northwest of the capital Milan.[1] Next in line of succession was Giovanni's younger brother, Giulio Cesare (1593–1638), who had been preened for a career as a military entrepreneur in the service of sovereign princes. His lucky break did not last long. As he was on the cusp of being invested as the new lord of Lake Maggiore, his brother Carlo (1586–1652) knocked his plans on the head. Even though he had been groomed as a cleric and quite possibly the next archbishop of Milan, the second-born Carlo cited primogeniture to argue that he was the rightful heir to the *Stato Borromeo* on Lake Maggiore.[2] Cutting his losses, Giulio Cesare speculated on the anger that Carlo's about-face had elicited in the family patriarch, Archbishop Federico Borromeo. Contrasting his responsible bearings with Carlo's skittish attitude, he exhorted the cardinal to agree to an estates division between the two brothers.[3]

The settlement that was hashed out a year later, in 1614, bore the signs of the rapid advances that the idea of primogeniture had been making among the Milanese nobility.[4] Carlo, as the second-born brother, secured the lion's share of the *Stato Borromeo*, while Giulio Cesare, the third-born, obtained fewer and less lucrative fiefs on the lake.[5] By far the most painful loss for the proud knight was the fortress of Arona that topped a hill marking the southernmost point of Lake Maggiore: it went to Carlo. Never one to knuckle under, Giulio Cesare quickly set his eyes on the castle of Angera, which sat on an elevation across the lake from Arona. The fortress had originally been in the Borromeos' possession but had been confiscated by the Spaniards in 1577 as punishment for Archbishop Carlo's

---

[1] Annoni, "Lo Stato."
[2] Cremonini, "Storia," pp. 482–3, 485; Zunckel, "Handlungsspielräume," p. 445.
[3] Giulio Cesare to Federico III Borromeo, Bologna September 17, 1612: *BAM*, mss. G 211 inf 282.
[4] On primogeniture in Milan, see Álvarez-Ossorio Alvariño, "The King."
[5] Besozzi, "Ritratti," p. 43.

Aristocratic Power in the Spanish Monarchy: The Borromeo Brothers of Milan, 1620–1680. Samuel Weber,
Oxford University Press. © Samuel Weber 2023. DOI: 10.1093/oso/9780198872597.003.0003

26 ARISTOCRATIC POWER IN THE SPANISH MONARCHY

truculent stance against the crown.[6] Half a century on and on the heels of the signing of the *concordia jurisdictionalis*, Giulio Cesare hoped to bury the hatchet with the crown and reacquire the lost castle.

Favoring his prospects was a momentous shift in the court of Madrid. Since the dawn of the century, a succession of minister-favorites, or *validos*, had held sway in the royal palaces of Philip III and Philip IV. These Spanish grandees had taken control of the king's material and symbolic resources and begun to hawk them to fellow nobles in the Spanish empire's far-flung territories in a bid to form clienteles smitten with the composite monarchy. The Borromeos, as we have seen in the Prologue, were coveted allies in that new strategy. Given his uncle's settlement of the jurisdictional controversies, Giulio Cesare stood an excellent chance of recovering Angera castle and wringing vital protection out of the Spanish Habsburgs for the cadet branch that he was setting up with his wife, Giovanna Cesi (1598–1672), in the latter half of the 1610s. That plan worked out. By 1624, Giulio Cesare and Giovanna were not only the proud owners of the fortress, styling themselves as the Borromeos of Angera; but they had also put themselves on the map as *olivaristas*, supporters of Philip IV's minister-favorite, the Count-Duke of Olivares, who would give a vital push to the Borromeos' dynastic interests.

This chapter focuses on the ethical issues that the Borromeos' transition into the orbit of the Spanish court raised for a family that prided itself on its archbishops and the Christian paternalism they embodied. More perhaps than other *olivaristas*, the Borromeos had to deal with the inherent contradiction between their conception of the monarchy as a union committed to the preservation of the collective good, on the one hand, and their interests as an up-and-coming imperial family, on the other. As they hopscotched toward Madrid, they opted for a bespoke strategy: they adopted what sociologist Pierre Bourdieu calls the "misrecognition" of self-seeking behavior. Even though they acquired the castle of Angera by paying a handsome sum to the minister-favorite, the Borromeos ostentatiously denied the unsavory reality of rampant venality in the court of Madrid and chose to traffic in myths about the just government of the Count-Duke of Olivares. Though temporarily successful, that strategy was hardly sustainable. If deliberate denial helped the Borromeos ease into their rebranding as *olivaristas*, before long, the blatant distortions of its beneficiaries would spell the end of the new institution of the minister-favorite.

The Rise of the Minister-Favorite

At the turn of the seventeenth century, the royal court of the Spanish Habsburgs became the scene of far-reaching changes that would mark the monarchy for half

---

[6] Cremonini, "Storia," p. 484.

a century. With the ascent of Philip III, the era of monarchic self-rule came to an abrupt end. Along with the new monarch appeared a right-hand man whom contemporaries referred to as the king's favorite. His main task consisted of the administration of royal patronage, including honors, titles, licenses, offices, land, and membership of chivalric orders, to the king's loyal subjects. As a Venetian ambassador in the court of Madrid noted of Philip's first *privado*, the Duke of Lerma, the favorite's brief was reducible to "the dispensing of tokens of [the king's] grace" to voracious clients.[7] From the monarch's perspective, this bartering of landed titles was not without its advantages. Liberality was a marker of early modern kingship, and Philip III certainly was keen to fashion himself as a fountain of infinite bounty, always ready to cater to the needs of his subjects. At the same time, this self-positioning bore the inherent risk of incentivizing a demand for tokens of royal favor that could not be met.[8] As Philip's father, Philip II, had presciently remarked in the late sixteenth century: "With many asking and little to give, most people will remain discontented."[9] His son, therefore, thought it wise to outsource the administration of royal patronage to a trusted nobleman who could easily be deposed when the malcontents became too vocal.

Such protests were inevitable. Much as he liked to portray himself as the king's loyal servant, Lerma was a member of the Iberian high nobility. Having reached a pre-eminent position within the court of Madrid, he was forever at risk of being ousted by the heads of rival clans. The precariousness of his position forced him to co-opt an ever-larger circle of cronies. If his closest relatives were packed onto the royal councils, the nobles further afield were bought off with landed titles and admissions to the crown's military orders. In so doing, Lerma hatched a patronage pyramid with a coterie of self-appointed "favorites of the favorite (*privados del privado*)" whose influence extended to the more distant territories of the Spanish empire, notably Flanders and Italy.[10] The Borromeos, as we have seen in the Prologue, were only one of the crucial local allies Lerma sought to win over. Among a nobility in thrall to ideas of an imagined medieval past, fiefs, that age-old recompense for military service, were an especially coveted asset for which aristocrats were willing to pay handsome sums of much-needed cash.[11] The marketization of chivalric honor allowed them to style themselves as parts of what Angelantonio Spagnoletti has called the "mass support base of Habsburg power" outside Iberia.[12] Not everyone was happy with the arrangement, though. The intensified commercialization of royal favor also exacerbated the anger of the

---

[7] Soranzo, "Relazione," p. 138.   [8] Von Thiessen, "Herrschen," p. 184; Feros, *Kingship*, p. 55.

[9] Quoted ibid.

[10] The quote is from Antonio de Guevara, *Aviso de privados o despertador de cortesano*, quoted ibid. Also see Enciso Alonso-Muñumer, *Nobleza*, pp. 14–5, 27–9; Esteban Estríngana, "Flemish Elites."

[11] Ago, *La feudalità*, p. ix; Soria Mesa, *La nobleza*, pp. 319–20. On medieval feudalism, see White, "Service."

[12] Spagnoletti, *Principi*, p. 43.

28 ARISTOCRATIC POWER IN THE SPANISH MONARCHY

faction of the nobility whose interests Lerma failed to serve. They accused the favorite of fostering a new feudalism that divvied out parts of the royal demesne to the nobility, who could then hold the king to ransom.

By 1618, the left-behind had united behind the leader of the opposing faction, Baltasar de Zúñiga y Velasco (1561–1622), and ganged up on Lerma, who was swiftly dismissed as the king's broker-in-chief. The Zúñiga faction initiated legal proceedings against Lerma's inner circle with astonishing alacrity. While the disgraced *valido* himself escaped prosecution thanks to a last-gasp promotion to the cardinalate,[13] other figureheads of his dispensation stood trial on allegations of corruption. The charges brought against Lerma's son, the Duke of Uceda (1581–1624), for instance, read like an indictment of his father's style of government: "Falling short of the duties of his office and the trust His Majesty had placed in his person, he transformed all the power he had into advantages for himself and his relatives, advancing his claims and interests to the detriment of the public good and the proper administration of justice." While pretending to serve the king and the entirety of his subjects, the *valido* had violated the "proper administration of justice" and the preservation of the "public good."[14]

Despite the high-minded language of the accusations, the legal action against the Lerma faction should be read as a settlement of scores rather than a serious crackdown on embezzlement. To be sure, the ambitious social climber Rodrigo Calderón (1576–1621) was executed on Madrid's Plaza Mayor in 1621. But the exemplary punishment of a commoner was the exception that proved the rule: Calderón's co-defendants of noble stock were let off the hook with light sentences despite having been accused of high treason.[15] Although the indictments came in the lofty rhetoric of the defense of the commonwealth, the proceedings against the Lerma faction were show trials designed to make a point without challenging the fundamentals of Lerma's patronage.[16]

In fact, the trials were a way of advertising the Zúñiga's own credo.[17] As the language of the indictment made clear, the Zúñiga faction was careful to couch its palace revolt in the rhetoric of neostoicism, a philosophy that valorized individual responsibility toward the common good. Neostoicism's godfather, Justus Lipsius (1547–1606), posited that because humans were inherently passionate and greedy, it was a sign of superior being to strive for spiritual happiness through submission to God. As a practical system of ethics for a time of massive upheavals, neostoicism appealed to Protestants and Catholics alike, though the Spanish monarchy and its wider world proved particularly receptive to Lipsius's teachings.[18] These urged nobles not to view institutions as opportunities for self-enrichment

---

[13] Von Thiessen, "Familienbande," p. 121.
[14] Quoted in Mrozek Eliszezynski, *Bajo acusación*, p. 375.   [15] Ibid., pp. 337, 362–3, 419.
[16] On this function of corruption trials, see Waquet, *Corruption*, pp. 94–5, 191.
[17] Mrozek Eliszezynski, *Bajo acusación*, p. 326.
[18] Carrasco, "El conde duque," pp. 246, 248.

so much as instruments to further the well-being of the monarchy as a whole. In the effort to put distance between the Lerma and the Zúñiga clans, the new ideology seemed to hold all the right answers. By pressing charges against Lerma's high-profile associates, the new powerholders aimed to contrast the self-enrichment of their predecessors with their own purported understanding of public office as a vehicle for the advancement of the collective good.[19]

In 1623, Baltasar de Zúñiga passed the baton to his nephew, Gaspar de Guzmán y Pimentel, the future Count-Duke of Olivares (1587–1645). As the favorite of the new king, Philip IV, Olivares labored assiduously to keep up the façade his uncle had begun to erect. In the early years of his dispensation, he ruthlessly painted himself as a principled defender of the common good. If he was indeed, as John Elliott opined, a politician "unusually clean by seventeenth-century standards," his propagandists feted him as a "new Seneca" who had done away with the cronyism of Lerma and was striving to defend the common man.[20] One of Olivares's more vociferous advocates in Italy saw his reign as legitimate because Olivares allegedly put "the honor of his king" before his own, "giving heed, not to his own particular gain, but to the common good."[21]

His defenders pointed to Olivares's cleanup of the administration of patronage, which he had entrusted to bespoke committees, or *juntas*. The logic behind this move was that ministers were disinterested interpreters of the law who were much less amenable to outside pressures than the members of the high nobility who held sway in the formal councils of the monarchy.[22] While this sounded good in theory, the much-touted control function was undermined by the fact that the key positions on the committees were without fail entrusted to Olivares's relatives and allies. Much as he sought to lend the newfangled *juntas* that veneer of bureaucratic independence that the royal councils had so sorely lacked under Lerma, these efforts could not hide the fact that the perusing of patronage-related requests had been outsourced to unregulated special committees teeming with the count-duke's allies.[23]

The same continuities could be seen in the awarding of royal patronage. The marketization of royal favor that had taken root under Lerma seemed to continue unabated under Olivares. Forced to confront the mushrooming expenses of running a world-spanning empire, Olivares resorted to asset-stripping, selling off the jewels in Philip IV's crown to a nobility willing to convert them into symbolic predominance.[24] The changes Olivares implemented were ideological rather than

---

[19] Rivero Rodríguez, *El conde duque*, p. 67.   [20] Elliott, "Quevedo," p. 198.

[21] *Breve discurso donde se muestra que los Reyes han de tener privado* (1624), quoted in Muto, "'Mutation'," p. 174.

[22] Rivero Rodríguez, *El conde duque*, p. 82.

[23] Gil Martínez, "Las hechuras"; Amadori, "Privanza." See Parrott, *1652*, p. 26, for parallel developments in France.

[24] This was a constant in the history of early modern Spain. See Soria Mesa, *La nobleza*, pp. 213–4.

30   ARISTOCRATIC POWER IN THE SPANISH MONARCHY

practical. Neostoicism helped crowbar the mundane transaction between nobles and the king's ministers into a framework of contemporary values and assumptions about royal bounty that found its expression in a ubiquitous language of patronage.[25] What Linda Levy Peck writes of the court in early Stuart England is equally true of Olivares's approach: "Crucial to the success of court patronage was its disguise. While contemporaries were frank with one another about their desire for court office and titles, the rhetoric between patron and client drew on another language, one which stressed the free gift of royal patronage, the magnanimity of the patron, and the dependence of the client."[26] Despite their rhetoric, the handlers of royal patronage continued to be more partial to money and status than to merit when they distributed the monarch's bounties to those who felt their turn to collect the premium had come.

Court Patronage under Olivares

The yawning gap between theory and practice at the heart of the Olivares regime became clear when Giulio Cesare Borromeo sought to recover the long-lost castle of Angera. To do so, he dispatched an agent, Giovanni Battista Besozzo, to the court of Madrid. Brokers representing the interests of noble families in Madrid were an increasingly common sight in the seventeenth century.[27] As monarchical institutions became more complex to navigate and the rise of the minister-favorite made constant lobbying essential for stakeholders, clans from distant territories were coming to the same conclusion as the nobility of the British Isles studied by Levy Peck: "While the king promised that those who were away from court would still be thought of, out of sight all too often proved out of mind."[28] Yet, despite their significance in keeping alive the memory of distant clans, brokers remain an understudied group.[29] This is all the more surprising if one considers the hermeneutical value of their writings: occupying a liminal space as servants of the nobility without being members of that social group themselves,[30] brokers and agents often inadvertently divulged some of the hidden assumptions of elite power in early modern Europe, laying bare the reasoning their principals would rather have kept to themselves. Besozzo was no exception.[31] A member of Milan's highly selective College of Jurists, he was familiar with multiple courts and had a solid grasp of the legal aspects he was sent out to negotiate on behalf of his

---

[25] Levy Peck, Court Patronage, p. 14; Ago, La feudalità, p. 97.

[26] Levy Peck, Court Patronage, p. 18.

[27] Windler, "Städte"; Álvarez-Ossorio Alvariño, "La república," ch. II; Dandelet, "Between Courts."

[28] Levy Peck, Court Patronage, p. 37.

[29] See, however, Keblusek, "Introduction"; Fontaine, "Protektion."

[30] Kettering, "Brokerage," p. 70.

[31] Zunckel, "Handlungsspielräume," p. 488. On the College of Jurists in Milan, see D'Amico, Spanish Milan, p. 37.

masters. But as a non-noble, he did not mince his words when he discussed the goings-on in the court of Madrid. His correspondence, therefore, sheds a unique light on the functioning of the Spanish court under Olivares.

Upon arriving in Madrid in the late spring of 1623, Besozzo immediately approached the president of the Council of Italy, Manuel de Acevedo y Zúñiga, Count of Monterrey (1586–1653), who, Besozzo was careful to mention, was the count-duke's brother-in-law. In addition to Monterrey's secretary, Francesco Bonetto, he also sounded out another Olivares ally on the Council, the member (*reggente*) for Milan, Gerolamo Caimi, whose influence was apparently second to none. As Besozzo explained, "It is necessary to show that we are on friendly terms with Caimi, because here he is the oracle of Apollo: he takes part in all the *juntas*—not just of the Council of State, but of all other [councils] as well."[32] Such unthinking assertions of inconvenient truths reveal that behind the overhauled councils the old networks of friends scratching each other's backs were alive and well.

As he considered his next steps, Besozzo also debunked the myth that the councils under Olivares were institutions adhering to formal bureaucratic procedures. One of the *valido*'s favorite spin doctors, Francisco de Quevedo (1580–1645), may have likened royal councilors to the disciples of Christ who "had to be ready to give up on their property and their families, putting service to the sovereign before anything else and not using it to enrich themselves or to advance the careers of their friends or clients (*criados*)."[33] Besozzo, by contrast, had no time for this sort of self-hypnosis. Undercutting the pretense of his social betters, the broker's sole preoccupation was to constantly court and ingratiate himself with relevant councilors, coaxing them into advantageous decisions for his masters. Belying the flashy self-image of the council and its members, Besozzo was extremely worried that his interlocutors might renege on earlier promises at the last moment. At one point he wrote, for instance, "Bonetto, the secretary,…assures me that the deal will be concluded shortly, but I am very anxious that the demon might still do his thing."[34] Besozzo was constantly on edge, fearing that the Borromeos' "envious rivals" were seeking to sway his contacts.[35] As the agent saw it, his interlocutors were not bureaucrats implementing routine procedures, but skittish individuals liable to change their minds in favor of whatever party offered them most in exchange for a favorable verdict.

---

[32] Giovanni Battista Besozzo to Federico III Borromeo, Madrid May 26, 1623: *BAM*, mss. G 254bis inf 232.

[33] Quoted in Mrozek Eliszezynski, *Bajo acusación*, p. 251.

[34] Giovanni Battista Besozzo to Federico III Borromeo, Madrid June 3, 1623: *BAM*, mss. G 254bis inf 219.

[35] Giovanni Battista Besozzo to Federico III Borromeo, Madrid July 2, 1623: *BAM*, mss. G254bis inf 320.

32   ARISTOCRATIC POWER IN THE SPANISH MONARCHY

As he vied for attention, Besozzo grew increasingly convinced that there was only one way to extract an advantageous decision from erratic council members: in a letter to his patrons, he suggested helping the negotiations along by "regaling" the secretary of the Council of Italy. If his patrons disbursed a small sum of money, Besozzo explained, the secretary would accord this order of business preferential treatment. Not only would he speed up the procedure, but he would let Besozzo see the final draft of the privilege for the castle of Angera before it was ratified, "so that I may adjust it as I please, which is [a privilege] granted only to few."[36] What Besozzo was advocating in as many words was the payment of what Valentin Groebner has dubbed an "access fee," a small sum handed over to a subordinate official who would in exchange expedite a case.[37]

What are we to make of these gratuities? In her study on Renaissance France, Natalie Zemon Davis has argued that early modern people tended to think of gifts to officials as "perfectly acceptable, however much they were intended to bring favor upon the donor."[38] Indeed, preferment was the unstated goal of all gift-giving: offerings created a bond of reciprocity between the petitioner and the official, and, though this was rarely acknowledged, it would have been inappropriate for the official not to take the present proffered into consideration when he made a decision. Benefactions were ties that bound for a long time, and they did so even if they were tendered by a social inferior, such as the clients of a king. Indeed, as Lisa Klein has argued of Elizabeth I of England, her "subjects offered her gifts with an eye toward what they could expect in return" and they were under no illusion that a present was anything but "an attempt to purchase her favorable intervention" on their behalf.[39] By the seventeenth century, things had changed considerably, however: gifts had been replaced by money. This created new problems. Since cash was associated with bribery and venality, contemporaries had to go to considerable lengths to deny that the function of their humble offerings was to insinuate the donor into the good graces of the recipient. In fact, many now asserted that offerings to officials were not kickbacks but a sign of disinterested reverence whose sole purpose was to set the stage for, rather than influence, the final outcome of a procedure.[40]

Comforting though such fictions may have been to troubled seventeenth-century elites, disinterested contemporaries knew better, and a guileless agent like Besozzo inadvertently let it show. In one of his epistles, he pleaded with the Borromeos to allow him to give his contact a backhander, stating openly that "it is good to remember [this person], because he is a friend who might provide other

---

[36] Giovanni Battista Besozzo to Federico III Borromeo, Madrid June 30, 1623: *BAM*, mss. G 254bis inf 320.

[37] Groebner, *Liquid Assets*, p. 62.   [38] Davis, *The Gift*, p. 144.

[39] Klein, "Your Humble Handmaid," p. 460.

[40] Thiessen, "Normenkonkurrenz," p. 266; Andújar Castillo, Feros, and Ponce Leiva, "Corrupción," p. 290.

services" at some point in the future.[41] Besozzo may have been particularly crude in his phrasing, but the absence of a reprimand from his patrons yields the sense that they agreed with him that this transaction was far more than a fee that made no appreciable difference. There is every reason to believe that the Borromeos agreed with their agent when he trumpeted: "without paying money nothing will get done here."[42]

Once the money had changed hands, Besozzo found his interlocutors much more forthcoming. Dealing with opposition to the Borromeos' plans from competing Milanese clans was now easier. As Besozzo informed his masters, the Borromeos' "rivals" had trotted out "some frivolous reason of state [argument]," bandying about rumors about the family's supposed pro-French leanings and arguing that because of the high concentration of fiefs on Milan's north-western border under their control, "they could easily drag the French into Italy."[43] But, Besozzo went on, the Borromeos had nothing to fear: since he had been promised "a nice offering," the *reggente* of Milan in the Council of Italy was particularly eager to bounce to the family's defense.[44] In a letter to Olivares, Caimi had informed the minister-favorite that the gossipmongers "are ill-spirited and ought not to be listened to," emphasizing the Borromeos' boundless "affection" for the king.[45] For all the regime's propaganda about its rational-bureaucratic approach to governance, it was money that bought Giulio Cesare Borromeo "credit," the good name and reputation needed to acquire the castle of Angera.[46]

Money also helped the Borromeos secure what was ostensibly a sign of the king's appreciation for their loyalty to the monarchy—the castle itself. Possibly in an attempt to live up to the monarchy's reputation as a force committed to doling out tokens of royal grace in return for services rendered, Besozzo's negotiating partners in Madrid at first put forth the castle of Angera for free. This time it was the Borromeos who turned down the offer.[47] They preferred to treat the enfeoffment as a one-off transaction rather than a gift, knowing full well that presents enacted social hierarchies: asymmetrical gifting from social superiors to inferiors calcified a "'gentle' domination" over dependents that sustained asymmetrical

---

[41] Giovanni Battista Besozzo to Federico III Borromeo, Madrid June 30, 1623: *BAM*, mss. G 254bis inf 220.

[42] Giovanni Battista Besozzo to Federico III Borromeo, Madrid July 2, 1623: *BAM*, mss. G 254bis inf 320.

[43] Giovanni Battista Besozzo to Federico III Borromeo, Madrid September 6, 1623: *BAM*, mss. G 254bis inf 289; Giovanni Battista Besozzo to Federico III Borromeo, Madrid May 27, 1623: *BAM*, mss. G 254bis inf 210.

[44] Giovanni Battista Besozzo to Federico III Borromeo, Madrid July 2, 1623: *BAM*, mss. G 254 inf 278.

[45] Giovanni Battista Besozzo to Federico III Borromeo, Madrid May 27, 1623: *BAM*, mss. G 254bis inf 210.

[46] On the early modern notion of "credit," see Muldrew, *The Economy*; Fontaine, *The Moral Economy*.

[47] Giovanni Battista Besozzo to Federico III Borromeo, Madrid June 29, 1623: *BAM*, mss. G 254bis inf 213.

34   ARISTOCRATIC POWER IN THE SPANISH MONARCHY

power relations.[48] Accepting a gift from a monarch in financial dire straits would have condemned the Borromeos to eternal gratitude to Philip IV and Olivares, something they, like other contemporaries, wanted to avoid at all costs.[49] The sales mode seemed the preferable option to early modern people, because whereas the acceptance of a gift resulted in a duty to reciprocate the favor, a simple cash transaction came with the comforting sensation of "being quits once and for all."[50] As the king and his entourage reluctantly swallowed the Borromeos' effrontery, the crown made sure that the accompanying rhetoric remained unaffected by the commercial practices.[51] After the sum of 2,500 *scudi* had been exchanged, the crown stressed that Giulio Cesare was about to become lord of Angera in a sign of the Habsburgs' "consideration of, and affection for," the family.[52] Going along with the rhetoric of patronage aimed at covering up the reality of financial transactions, the Borromeos paid homage to the crown's deliberate use of the gift register: in a meeting, the agent reassured his interlocutors that even if it had paid for the fiefdom, the family "shall be as obliged to the king and his ministers as if it had been offered for free."[53] Less than a decade after the painful separation of goods, Giulio Cesare had himself become the lord of a castle that rivaled his brother's fortress.

In spite of the reassuring rhetoric from the crown, the Borromeos were worried about the venality they had just dabbled in. Characteristically, they sought to efface the painful memory through another transaction. As soon as the negotiations over Angera had been wrapped up, Besozzo threw in a request for the fishing privileges of Lake Maggiore. In early modern society, fish were highly prized perishables that Catholic baronial families, alive to their symbolic import as the sole protein permissible on fast days, sought to control in the name of their responsibility toward social inferiors.[54] Coughing up an additional 15,200 *scudi* (six times the value of the castle), Giulio Cesare basketed a privilege that put the Borromeos in a position to sell multiple angling licenses to local fishermen.[55] To appease the neostoics in Madrid, they immediately offered to exempt "Angera up to the middle of the lake." Citing the "poverty and barrenness of a good part of

---

[48] Werbner, "The Enigma," p. 150.

[49] See Bourdieu, *Outline*, p. 6. Natalie Zemon Davis calls this the "gratitude-and-obligation process of the gift mode." See her *The Gift*, p. 90.

[50] Ibid., p. 108.   [51] On the latter point, see Levy Peck, *Court Patronage*, pp. 18, 29.

[52] See the investiture in *Archivo General, Simancas*, Secretarías Provinciales, lib. 1350, ff. 321v–324r (f. 321v). The title was formally granted to Federico Sr., who bequeathed it to Giulio Cesare upon his death in 1632. See ibid., f. 322r, and Besozzi, "Ritratti," p. 43.

[53] Giovanni Battista Besozzo to Federico III Borromeo, Madrid June 29, 1623: *BAM*, mss. G 254bis inf 213.

[54] Luiten, "Friends."

[55] Giovanni Battista Besozzo to Federico III Borromeo, Madrid August 17, 1623: *BAM*, mss. G 254bis inf 309; Annoni, "Fisco," pp. 72, 90; Cavallera, "Angera," p. 164. The investiture is in *AGS*, SSP, lib. 1354, ff. 130r–135r. The privilege of September 21, 1623 is in *Archivio di Stato, Milan*, Atti di governo, Feudi camerali p.a., cart. 48, fasc. Pescagione nel Lago Maggiore.

that village," Besozzo reasoned that that sop to "Angera's poor" would honor the memory of the family saint, Carlo, and his devotedness to social justice.[56] More important, such a concession was bound to defuse any lingering doubts about the Borromeos' motives in Madrid. By ostentatiously forgoing what was theirs, they hoped to convince the *olivaristas* of their unstinting commitment to the collective good. The alleged beneficiaries, "Angera's poor," were less impressed with their lords' charity. In petitions to the Spanish authorities in Milan, they argued that the Borromeos' tokenism served only their public image and failed to bring substantive improvements to fishing communities on the lake. The *sindico* (mayor) of Angera made it clear that the waters that the Borromeos had so generously opened up to local anglers were devoid of fish so that "sometimes [the fishermen] happened to earn 30 or 40 *soldi* a day, and at others, whole weeks went by without them earning as much as a *soldo*."[57] What is only hinted at in their petition was made explicit in Besozzo's letters. As he admitted with characteristic carelessness, the display of paternalist largesse had been a ploy to win over the crown and to make sure that it "will be ever more favorably inclined toward the house."[58] If these charitable acts toward social inferiors failed to hoodwink their alleged beneficiaries,[59] they certainly functioned, to quote anthropologist James C. Scott, as "a kind of self-hypnosis within ruling groups to buck up their courage, to improve their cohesion, display their power, and convince themselves anew of their high moral purpose."[60]

The negotiations over fishing rights constituted perhaps the single most damning instance of Besozzo's continued disclosure of what Scott calls the "hidden transcript" of elites: "the practices and claims of their rule that cannot be openly avowed."[61] Not sophisticated enough to obfuscate in quite the same way as his social betters did, the clumsy agent inadvertently laid bare the unspoken assumptions of members of the emerging *olivarista* ruling class, ratting out the inconsistency between their rhetoric and their actions. His letters reveal that, despite the concerted propaganda effort of the new regime, not much had changed at the court of Philip IV. Belying all their public utterances to the contrary, key stakeholders of the monarchy continued to regard the royal demesne as spoils for them to plunder and squeeze. Provided they were willing to open their coffers, both to obtain a privilege and to bribe royal officials along the way, the monarchy's resources were theirs to dicker with. The court under Olivares remained

---

[56] Giovanni Battista Besozzo to Federico III Borromeo, Madrid July 18, 1623: *BAM*, mss. G 254bis inf 239; Giovanni Battista Besozzo to Federico III Borromeo, Madrid June 29, 1623: *BAM*, mss. G 254bis inf 213.

[57] Quoted in Besozzi, "Famiglie," p. 140.

[58] Giovanni Battista Besozzo to Federico III Borromeo, Madrid June 29, 1623: *BAM*, mss. G 254bis inf 213. On paternalism as a message sent to other members of the elite, see Scott, *Domination*, pp. xii, 10.

[59] On this point, see Thompson, "The Patricians," p. 67.   [60] Scott, *Domination*, p. 67.

[61] Ibid., p. xii.

36 ARISTOCRATIC POWER IN THE SPANISH MONARCHY

honeycombed with venal officials and greedy petitioners, though this only sprang to the attention of the losers of the passage of power, such as Matías de Novoa (1576–1652), who fumed at the blatant double standards of the representatives of a regime who were putting members of the old governing elite on trial for crimes they continued to commit themselves.[62] Even more damningly, the fledgling *olivarista* elite not only was aware of that inconsistency but also actively worked to cover it up by investing heavily in a rhetoric of responsible government for vulnerable subjects.

To this it could of course be retorted that Olivares's men—the councilors and petitioners like the Borromeos—were acting without the count-duke's knowledge. But that argument does not stand up to scrutiny. In the example discussed here, the shadow of Olivares hovered over the whole of the negotiations. In fact, Besozzo's interlocutors repeatedly reported back to the *valido*, fine-tuning their tactics in consultation with him. Besozzo himself entertained few doubts as to who was ultimately responsible. As he noted curtly: "Government is entirely in the hands of Olivares; the king, even though he holds audiences, does nothing."[63] Once the final details of the deal had been hammered out, Olivares himself no longer seemed to have an interest in keeping up the pretense either. In a note to Giulio Cesare's uncle, Archbishop Federico, the count-duke thanked the family "very much for the relics and the portrait of St. Carlo," which the archbishop had apparently sent him to acknowledge his role in the sale of Angera. Olivares went on to admit freely that he had "made sure to direct the transaction that [Besozzo] brought [here] on your behalf" to its desired outcome. He reassured Federico that "the good will that there is in [my] house toward everything that is of service to Your Most Illustrious Lordship" meant that "the same shall always be [true] on further occasions."[64] Olivares may have essayed to install the councils as a good-governance façade so as to pre-empt the charges of moral turpitude that he and his coterie had leveled at his predecessor, Lerma. But the commitment to the common good that was brandished in public was junked as soon as Olivares and his men started wheeling and dealing away from public scrutiny. Of this he was as aware as his clients.

The "Misrecognition" of Favoritism

By forking out money for the castle of Angera, the Borromeos had actively contributed to the undermining of the Olivares regime's public transcript—"the

---

[62] Mrozek Eliszezynski, *Bajo acusación*, p. 416.

[63] Giovanni Battista Besozzo to Federico III Borromeo, Madrid June 1, 1623: *BAM*, mss. G 254bis inf 217.

[64] Count-Duke of Olivares to Federico III Borromeo, Madrid November 19, 1623: *BAM*, mss. G 254bis inf 300.

self-portrait of dominant elites as they would have seen themselves."[65] Instead of reckoning with this blatant contradiction between words and actions, they chose to double down and continue invoking the neostoic myths that had sugarcoated the passage from Lerma to Olivares. Deeply aware of his own baggage as a client of Lerma's, Archbishop Federico readily pounced on the *olivaristas'* favored ideologemes to cover his tracks. Having been a prolific writer throughout his life, he reached his most productive phase as a self-styled intellectual in the role of author of treatises on princely courts during the early years of the Olivares regime.[66] Cognizant of the importance of texts as gifts for favors obtained,[67] Federico joined the hacks who hoped to make headway by adulating the minister-favorite in their writings. Quite possibly to thank the *valido* for his services to his nephew in the Angera transaction, Federico put out a treatise on *La gratia de' principi* (*The Grace of Princes*) in 1625.[68]

La gratia's content was programmatic. Historians who have studied the treatise have usually placed it within the tradition of Renaissance publications on the court and the perfect courtiers in the tradition of Baldassare Castiglione's *Courtier* of 1528.[69] The abstract language of the treatise may have contributed to scholars' overlooking the many allusions to the time in which it was written. Upon closer inspection, *La gratia* turns out to be Borromeo's contribution to the debate on favoritism that the fall of the Lerma regime and the rise of Olivares government had ushered in. For all the deliberate abstraction, the treatise contains a thinly veiled attack on Lerma and an extolling of his successor. It denies, through omission and insinuation, any continuities between the two regimes: while one is portrayed as a cesspit of corruption, the other is presented as the panacea for humanity's ills. Rather than another lackluster treatise on the court in the Renaissance tradition, then, *La gratia* was an abstruse, yet effective intervention in the debate on the regime of the minister-favorite that was raging in the early years of the Olivares administration.

Tucked between obscure disquisitions about princely rule was a savage condemnation of Lerma and the beneficiaries of his regime. Borromeo started out with a characterization of the clients of the dispensation, castigating them for their bottomless greed that had wrecked the monarchy: "those subjects squeeze and wring their lords too much, wanting to wrest too many benefits from their benevolence [and doing so] without betraying the slightest concern. And in this they resemble that greedy farmer who picks the crops from his field before the

---

[65] Scott, *Domination*, p. 18.
[66] On Borromeo's intellectual pursuits, see Jones, *Federico*, and Lezowski, *L'Abrégé*.
[67] On this function of self-authored books, see Davis, *The Gift*, pp. 59–61.
[68] I am quoting from the Italian version, which was published in 1632. On the cottage industry of favorable publications under Olivares, see Elliott, "Quevedo."
[69] See, however, Continisio, "*Il libro*," p. 106.

38 ARISTOCRATIC POWER IN THE SPANISH MONARCHY

harvest season arrives."[70] While avid subjects were the main drivers, the real culprits were the ministers who enabled them: Borromeo was relentless in his clobbering of "ministers...who impudently traffic and market the grace and benevolence of the princes and lords whom they serve, buying it up and reselling it as they please, with neither shame nor remorse reining them in."[71] The king they nominally served was a helpless victim, oblivious to how his ministers and their surrogates helped themselves to the monarchy's riches, for the plunderers were careful to present themselves as hard-working princely servants: "The mind of the prince is blinded and numbed by the pleasure he experiences when he sees his ministers relieve him of the burden of hard work, so that he does not see or feel the harm of their greed and thievery."[72]

If the criticism of behavior the Borromeos had engaged in themselves is remarkable enough, it is perhaps even more significant that these excesses were treated as a thing of the past with no bearing on the present. In fact, the incriminated practices were reminiscent "of a minister in a great court who was relieved, less than ten years ago, of the incredible treasure he had amassed in a very short time."[73] Anonymous though these aspersions were, the vigorous debate about Lerma's mismanagement that had helped stabilize the Olivares regime must have made it clear that Borromeo was traducing Philip III's *privado*, Lerma. By transposing corruption to the past, Borromeo erased the continuities between Lerma's government and the system that had landed the Borromeos the castle of Angera. Where intellectuals in hock to Olivares, such as Virgilio Malvezzi (1595–1654), sought to justify the undeniable,[74] Borromeo penned a damning indictment of the haggling over patronage under Lerma that failed to mention that these practices persisted under Olivares.

Borromeo did not leave it at omitting inconvenient truths; he actively invented a much more appealing version of reality. Although his portrait of the ideal court was, again, anonymous, the author suggested, through implication rather than declaration, that he was describing the court of Madrid. In Borromeo's rendition, the court was no longer the site of messy bargaining between the prince and self-aggrandizing courtiers, but it had been elevated to the status of a model for a well-ordered society in which accounts were squared through civil conversation.[75] With its ceremonies and "mutual offices, and honors, and tributes of respect," the court had established modes of engagement that "are especially useful to prevent the breakdown of friendships" between courtiers. In fact, the civilities of the court "serve as a remedy and a shield, as though we wanted to fight each other from afar, without coming to blows."[76] As such, the court comprised the seeds to overcome in time the free-for-all that had marred its earlier incarnations. The

---

[70] Borromeo, *Il libro*, p. 38.   [71] Ibid., p. 116.   [72] Ibid., p. 131.   [73] Ibid., p. 130.
[74] On Malvezzi's legitimation of Olivares, see Feros, "Images," p. 213.
[75] Continisio, "*Il libro*," pp. 106–7.   [76] Borromeo, *Il libro*, p. 191.

vivere civile had upended the vices that were threatening the social order—avarice and pride—and replaced them with the principle of Christian love between the higher and the lower orders, patrons and clients, who were now working together to forge a perfect society: "The inferior will be loved when the superior understands that he is beneficial to himself, and the benefit will be so much greater when the inferior is more able, willing, and inclined to offer the benefit that one expects of him."[77] The cooperation between all orders of society through the mediation of the royal court had set up the conditions for the drive to the common good to prevail.

Cryptic and recondite as the treatise was, contemporaries smitten with Olivares would have had no trouble identifying an idealized version of his regime in this description. Knowingly or not, Borromeo beguiled a credulous public with the count-duke's pieties about a government dedicated to the preservation of the collective good, pieties both men seemed to forget as soon as they felt unobserved. Not only was informal influence peddling rife in the court of Philip IV, but the monetized quid pro quo the *olivaristas* enabled could hardly be said to advance the well-being of all the king's subjects. In fact, all the references to a well-ordered *vivere civile* failed to gloss over the stark reality of the continued dominance of naked self-interest among the small circle of profiteers around Olivares.[78]

What are we to make of this glaring inconsistency between thought and action? In a wide-ranging essay on competing and conflicting normative demands thrust upon early modern men and women, Hillard von Thiessen specifically mentions the gap between actions and written accounts of them that is often noticeable in the seventeenth century. Living under the spell of neostoicism, von Thiessen argues, nobles often professed to pursue the ideal of the common good in writing, only to ditch this norm for the advancement of the narrow interests of kith and kin in social interactions with their peers.[79] Exactly which normative ideal was given precedence over the other depended very much on the situation at hand: just as writers were expected to comply with certain literary tropes, noblemen negotiating with each other were required to uphold the norms regulating social relations.[80] This constant switching between norms was possible, von Thiessen concludes, because contemporaries were far more "tolerant of ambiguities" than we tend to be today.[81]

A much less charitable interpretation has been offered by Jean-Claude Waquet. He argues that early modern elites were fully aware of the wrongness of their corruption and therefore quite deliberately resorted to lying about a reality with which they were unable to deal otherwise.[82] Like so many coping mechanisms,

---

[77] Continisio, "*Il libro*," pp. 111, 113–4. The quote is from Borromeo, *Il libro*, p. 16.
[78] On similar inconsistencies in contemporary England, see Levy Peck, *Court Patronage*, p. 29.
[79] Von Thiessen, "Normenkonkurrenz," p. 266.   [80] Ibid., pp. 266–7.   [81] Ibid., p. 266.
[82] Waquet, *Corruption*, pp. 106–7.

40 ARISTOCRATIC POWER IN THE SPANISH MONARCHY

arguments provided by casuistry and probabilism "made them feel that their much criticized actions were in fact honest and that they would not fall under the censure of either divine justice or human laws."[83] While this is objectively unde-niable, Waquet's assumption of intentionality and bad faith seems problematic. It is in fact more productive to presume that the mendacity was the product of what Pierre Bourdieu calls "misrecognition." Defined as "the deliberate oversight" of objective realities, misrecognition is "the collectively maintained and approved self-deception" among elites.[84] While this can occur in many social situations, misrecognition usually operates when elites feel compelled to elaborate mental frameworks that rationalize and normalize what they would otherwise esteem as shameful behavior at variance with their values.[85] The lies are therefore not sim-ply an expression of unfettered cynicism on the part of corrupt elites. Rather, they are coping mechanisms that are rarely the "result of rational calculation or even strategic intent"; they just happen to be "objectively organized in such a way that they contribute to the reproduction of the capital at hand, without having been explicitly designed and instituted with this end in mind."[86]

The treatise Federico Borromeo published in the aftermath of the acquisition of the castle of Angera provides a vivid illustration of these "strategies through which the agent seeks to put himself in the right."[87] For the beneficiaries of the venality of the Olivares system, the stubborn defense of an unachieved ideal helped make sense of the selfish bargain they had struck with the regime. As a dynasty committed to the common good, the Borromeos had no other choice than to idealize the regime when they became aware of its corruption. Rather than an active attempt to gaslight the public, then, the lies in Borromeo's treatise were a half-conscious way of whitewashing a reality that would otherwise have been unbearable, even when real events had long made that view untenable. The willful distortions in the treatise are "second-order strategies" accompanying profit-driven behavior "whose purpose is to give apparent satisfaction to the demands of the official rule, and thus to compound the satisfactions of enlightened self-interest with the advantage of ethical impeccability."[88]

If swindling was useful to the Borromeos themselves, it also upheld the system as a whole. To make sense of this apparent paradox, it is instructive to turn to the vibrant historiography on political patronage in southern Europe in the late nineteenth and early twentieth centuries. In France, for example, the Radical Party under the Third Republic responded to public criticism of the corruption that was rife within its ranks by encouraging its members to couch their request for personal favors in the language of republicanism. If this gave rise to charges of hypocrisy that ultimately undermined the Third Republic, in the short term, this

---

[83] Ibid., p. 192.   [84] Bourdieu, *Outline*, p. 6.
[85] See Fitzpatrick, *Everyday Stalinism*, pp. 104–5; Swartz, *Symbolic Power*, pp. 37–8, 81–2.
[86] Bourdieu, *The State Nobility*, p. 272.   [87] Bourdieu, *Outline*, p. 22.   [88] Ibid.

duplicity enabled party members to negotiate the gap between their professed republicanism, with its inherent commitment to equality before the law, and the reality of favoritism. As such, it propped up a system destined to collapse.[89] This edifice is best described as "hypocrisy," though not in the moralistic sense of the term deployed by the party's detractors, but, rather, in the way Nils Brunsson has employed it to make sense of the seeming paradox that "ideology and action can systematically conflict with one another" and still lend legitimacy to organizations.[90] Through the verbal commitment to a norm that is constantly violated in action, Barbara Stollberg-Rilinger has argued, hypocrites convince themselves and others of their investment in an unachievable ideal.[91]

All the obvious differences notwithstanding, a similar hypocrisy permeated the *olivaristas'* approach to the regime of the count-duke. Behind closed doors they engaged in the very horse-trading that they publicly denounced as an assault on the common good. In the process, they brought forth a disconnect between ideas and action that, ironically, helped shore up the Olivares regime. The mental misrecognition of the corruption in which they themselves participated, along with tokenistic paternalist interventions, helped reinforce their commitment to a regime that sat at odds with their own values. In the same way it allowed the self-righteous Borromeos to ease into their role as clients of the count-duke, the hypocrisy probably enabled many others among the regime's noble cronies, who were happy to turn rationalization into lived reality. The collective delusion of the emerging elite buttressed the system much longer than it would have survived if its inner contradictions had been addressed openly. What Pierre Bourdieu wrote of Kabyle society seems to be equally true of the Spanish monarchy under Olivares: "In social formations in which the expression of material interests is heavily censored and political authority relatively uninstitutionalized, political strategies for mobilization can be effective only if the values they pursue or propose are presented in the misrecognizable guise of the values in which the group recognizes itself."[92] In fact, the system began to crumble only when forces that had been excluded from the large-scale redistribution of common resources began to query the ruling class's sincerity and demanded that the powers-that-be live up to their own ideals.[93]

Conclusion

Spawned from a rivalry between two brothers, the cadet branch of the Borromeos took off for good when Giulio Cesare Borromeo acquired the long-lost castle of

---

[89] Monier, "A 'Democratic Patronage,'" pp. 106, 112. [90] Brunsson, *The Organization*, p. vii.
[91] Stollberg-Rilinger, *The Emperor's Old Clothes*, p. 244. [92] Bourdieu, *Outline*, p. 22.
[93] On this dynamic, see Grüne, "'Gabenschlucker,'" p. 232.

42   ARISTOCRATIC POWER IN THE SPANISH MONARCHY

Angera from the minister-favorite of Philip IV, the Count-Duke of Olivares. In so doing, Giulio Cesare and his young family entrammeled themselves in the elite networks of the Spanish monarchy that the rise of the minister-favorite had begun to weave across Italy. First instituted under the Duke of Lerma, these networks had come under criticism for the corruption and self-enrichment they had fostered. Lerma's successor, Olivares, had therefore taken great care to present his continuation of Lerma's policy as a way of preserving what he, as a devotee of neostoicism, called the collective good of all the king's subjects. Even though the power-sharing arrangements with provincial nobilities continued unabated, Olivares's propagandists averred that the count-duke had ferreted out a way to wed his clients' interest in self-aggrandizement to the goal of strengthening the realm.

The Borromeos of Angera's transition into the ranks of Olivares's *protégés* complicates this optimistic picture. The surviving record shows that the court of Spain continued to be rife with the administrative malpractice of which the *olivaristas* had accused their adversaries from the Lerma faction. It also reveals that not only were the Borromeos aware of this state of affairs, but they felt uncomfortable with the goings-on in Madrid. Try as they might, they proved ultimately unable to splice together their venality and their nominal commitment to the values of the day. On the contrary, attempts to address the conflict through a treatise on the court deepened a hypocrisy that "reflected and responded to the unresolvable contradiction between two fundamental values."[94] The Borromeos' public utterances may have pulled the wool over the eyes of nobles who were equally invested in the idea of keeping the patronage market humming; they proved a much tougher sell with the subject population in their fiefdoms. As rhetoric and action drifted apart, the Borromeos' hypocrisy elicited searching questions about the elite's conception of good governance. If economic prosperity mitigated some of the resulting tensions, the Borromeos' open embrace of war as a vehicle for upward social mobility would galvanize resistance they'd find increasingly hard to restrain.

---

[94] Stollberg-Rilinger, *The Emperor's Old Clothes*, p. 244.

2

Becoming Military Leaders

The Borromeos, the Union of Arms, and the Franco-Spanish War in Italy

About midway along its western shore, Lake Maggiore widens to form the aptly named Golfo Borromeo, a bay studded by an archipelago of four islands. Of these, Isola Madre is by far the largest. In the early seventeenth century, the islet was the jewel in the crown of the budding Angera branch of the Borromeo family. Against the backdrop of the snow-capped Alps, the island's orchard, complete with Mediterranean fruits ranging from citrus to prickly pears, turned this fief into an earthly Eden.[1] So "pleasant" was the Isola with its late-Renaissance villa and luscious nature that it was a place "worthy of princes."[2] One such prince was Ferdinand of Austria (1609–1641), the younger brother of King Philip IV, whom the Borromeos hosted on the islet in 1633. After an extensive hunt in the Ticino Valley south of the lake, the cardinal-infante, as Ferdinand was known, sallied out to the island, which had been revamped for the occasion.[3] When he reached Isola Madre, he was met "with the highest princely honors (*principalissimamente*)" by Giulio Cesare and his eldest son, the then 17-year-old Giovanni (1616–1660).[4]

The cardinal-infante's visit was part of his new duties. By the 1630s, Ferdinand and the king's other brother, Carlos, had become central players in the administration of the composite Spanish monarchy.[5] Philip IV's favorite, the Count-Duke of Olivares, had long feared them because, unlike himself, they were blood relatives of the king and could stake a claim to power the *valido* did not possess. The count-duke spent the best part of the 1620s trying to find a proper role for them to fill. Offering them appointments as viceroys seemed an appropriate solution: not only would it keep them away from Madrid and the king, but it would secure the loyalty of indomitable provincial elites. Thus, Carlos was dispatched to Lisbon, while the cardinal-infante was sent to that other hotbed of resistance and rebellion, Brussels, with the express order to consolidate the ties between the local nobility and the court of Madrid. En route to Flanders, Ferdinand passed through another strategically important component of the monarchy, Milan, where he courted *olivaristas* like the up-and-coming Borromeos of Angera. What he had to

---

[1] Buratti Mazzotta, *L'Isola Madre*, p. 38. [2] Moriggia, *Historia*, p. 159.
[3] Galli, "I Borromeo," p. 218. [4] Johnsson, ed., *Storia*, p. 101.
[5] Esteban Estríngana, "Los Estados."

Aristocratic Power in the Spanish Monarchy: The Borromeo Brothers of Milan, 1620–1680. Samuel Weber,
Oxford University Press. © Samuel Weber 2023. DOI: 10.1093/oso/9780198872597.003.0004

44 ARISTOCRATIC POWER IN THE SPANISH MONARCHY

sell them was nothing less than the count-duke's Union of Arms, an ambitious plan to incorporate the territories of the Spanish monarchy through closer military cooperation.

Unlike the more established nobility, precarious families like the Borromeos of Angera latched on to these proposals.[6] To them, the Union of Arms served up an opportunity to fashion themselves as responsible landholders, willing to stick up for their vassals in the case of a military attack. As the 1630s wore on and the prospect of a war between the French and the Spanish crowns grew, the duty to protect their subjects on Milan's western border with Piedmont, an ally of France, became more pressing. What went unacknowledged in this self-positioning as responsible feudatories was the hope of upward social mobility that rode on the display of military prowess. Building on Davide Maffi's groundbreaking work on these mechanisms, this chapter details the upward trajectory within the Spanish military of one exemplary family.[7] As will become clear, the link between military defense and the promise of dynastic aggrandizement took on an uncontrollable dynamic of its own. It encouraged men like Giulio Cesare and Giovanni Borromeo to embrace a jingoism that would inflict untold harm on the subjects they claimed to protect. Once the war reached Lombardy in the late 1630s, the crisis deepened even further. As the initial skirmishes turned into an endless conflict fought by a nobility cantering after dynastic greatness, the vassals started questioning the Borromeos' commitment to their well-being.

The Union of Arms

The Borromeos' self-assertion as military leaders needs to be situated in the context of developments in the Spanish monarchy since the rise of the Count-Duke of Olivares. As he consolidated his hold on power in the 1620s, the *valido* fought an uphill battle against what he perceived as the decline of the Spanish Habsburgs' global empire. Convinced that the legacy of Philip IV's grandfather, Philip II, could be salvaged only if the monarchy underwent fundamental changes, Olivares put forward a program of radical reform.[8] Some of these policies were measures to rekindle the ailing economy of Castile, the heartland of the monarchy. The most ambitious aspect of his platform, however, was a plan to strengthen the ties between the disparate territories of the composite monarchy by creating a "stakeholder culture" among the elites of its constituent parts.[9] His stratagem was, in his own words, to "familiarize...the natives of the different kingdoms with each

---

[6] D'Amico, *Spanish Milan*, p. 64; Donati, "The Profession."   [7] Maffi, *Il baluardo*.
[8] Elliott, *The Count-Duke*, pp. 179–81.
[9] Elliott, "A Europe." The term "stakeholder culture" to describe the Spanish elite is used in Malcolm, *Royal Favouritism*, p. 110.

other so they forget the isolation in which they have hitherto lived."[10] Olivares believed that this diversification of the monarchy's power base would not only buttress the nobility's loyalty to the monarchy, but the concomitant fragmentation of authority would inevitably strengthen the king's authority and restore some of the decision-making powers the monarch had supposedly lost since Philip II.[11]

One of the first policy areas in which Olivares tried to implement his project was the military. In 1625, he unveiled a proposal called the Union of Arms. Its premise was simple enough: the nobilities of the composite monarchy should all contribute monetary and human resources to the defense of the empire. By rallying the disparate parts of the monarchy against common enemies, Olivares hoped to initiate the cooperation that would deepen the union between the kingdoms and duchies that constituted the empire.[12] The Union of Arms was, in Olivares's own words, "one way of possibly achieving that all the kingdoms of His Majesty acted as one for all and all for one."[13] Defense was to blaze the trail for the transformation of the *monarquía* into "a supra-national Monarchy, its focal point of loyalty a king who commanded the obedience of a cosmopolitan service nobility, and who governed a complex of kingdoms which recognized their obligations to each other, and shared a common set of laws and institutions."[14]

Historians have not been kind in their treatment of the Union of Arms and the nobilities it sought to ensconce in the shared defense of the empire. Ever since the publication of John Elliott's influential work, the conventional wisdom has been that if Olivares's ambitious plan was not exactly dead on arrival, it certainly foundered on the stark realities of noble and corporate particularism in the territories it was supposed to lift up.[15] Instead of uniting the monarchy, the mooted Union of Arms produced a growing polarization between a reform-minded but authoritarian minister-favorite and a nobility hostile to his agenda. In the long run, the Union of Arms, rather than bringing the monarchy together, ended in large-scale disruption and set the stage for a return to the regional prerogatives Olivares had been so impatient to overcome.[16] The *valido's* attempts to discipline the nobility and to nudge it into sharing the burden of administering an empire came to naught, as the dogged pursuit of an unpopular policy gave rise to perilous centrifugal forces in the latter half of his tenure, centrifugal forces that famously culminated in rebellions in Catalonia and Portugal in 1640, and the count-duke's demise three years later.[17]

A very different story has been told of Olivares's opposite number in France. In his work on the military reforms of Cardinal Richelieu (1585–1642), the favorite

---

[10] Quoted in Parker, *Global Crisis*, p. 255.   [11] Benigno, *L'ombra*, p. 100.
[12] Elliott, "El programa," pp. 375–6.   [13] Quoted ibid., p. 376.
[14] Elliott, *The Count-Duke*, pp. 199–200.
[15] Elliott, "El programa." A similar argument is made by Thompson, "Aspectos."
[16] Elliott, "El programa," p. 335.   [17] See Jago, "The 'Crisis,'" p. 82.

46 ARISTOCRATIC POWER IN THE SPANISH MONARCHY

of Louis XIII (r. 1610–1643), David Parrott has suggested that the cotemporaneous French attempt to integrate the nobility through the army was a success. The starting point of Parrott's argument is that Richelieu's army was not modernized from on high; instead, the cardinal portrayed himself as a member of a noble warrior elite within whose hierarchies he sought to advance the interests of his own dynasty alongside those of allied families.[18] Viewing the minister-favorite as an integral part of the caste he was trying to draw closer to the throne rather than as a minister above the fray has important implications for the way Parrott assesses the nobility's response to Richelieu's plans. As he goes on to argue, the nobility's reaction was not exclusively hostile, but ranged from open rejection to enthusiastic support, depending on individual "status, aspirations, and traditional rivalries" with other families. Seeing the army that was being built up as an opportunity to accrue honor and *gloire*, precarious families rallied behind Richelieu.[19] Thus, Parrott concludes, while "some families or individuals proved consistently hostile to the cardinal," other dynasties "gave him their explicit cooperation" because "their individual interests within the competitive world of the high aristocracy complemented, and coincided with," Richelieu's.[20]

There is reason to believe that similar familist considerations permeated Olivares's Union of Arms. In recent years, Manuel Rivero Rodríguez has challenged the old orthodoxy of Olivares as a modern statesman *avant la lettre* and made the argument that Olivares's project was driven not by the desire to promote state-building but, rather, by a wish to advance the interests of the Habsburgs and the noble families they held in tow, not least his own.[21] The resemblance to Richelieu is striking. Like the cardinal in France, Olivares seems to have seen himself as a member of the aristocracy that he was essaying to mold into a pan-Spanish service elite. Rather than as a prime minister who administered the monarchy from above, Olivares should be understood as the head of a dynasty tethered to a small circle of fellow nobles.[22] Meeting their expectations, Olivares, like Richelieu, deftly deployed the royal patronage to which he had gained temporary access to wheedle fellow nobles into royal service.

Olivares's preferred method was to appeal to the nobility as a warrior caste primed to succor the monarch. As he explained in his manifesto, the Great Memorial of 1624, he was convinced that if his fellow aristocrats were led "to believe and expect that their conduct will promote them, that they will obtain the first and most honorable military ranks," this would "restore the reputation of Spanish arms by land and sea" and turn Philip IV into "the most glorious

---

[18] Parrott, "Richelieu," p. 142, and Parrott, *1652*, p. 25.
[19] This point is made most powerfully by Guy Rowlands, who studied the evolution of the French army in the latter half of the seventeenth century. See his *The Dynastic State*.
[20] Parrott, "Richelieu," pp. 140, 172.   [21] Rivero Rodríguez, *El conde duque*, pp. 9–10.
[22] Von Thiessen, "Der entkleidete Favorit," p. 135.

monarch ever known in these kingdoms in any era."[23] Such plans accorded well with the perceived need to reconcile clientelism with the neostoic ideology of public service. Military cooperation allowed aristocrats to bundle dynastic ambitions with the common good: what was to entice the nobility was the old idea of lesser nobles basking in the glory of their social betters, of the great allowing them to envision themselves in a relationship of service with the king for the good of the realm.[24]

Since research into the question remains meager, the nobility's response to the count-duke's call to arms continues to be a matter of some speculation. Newer research has revealed that nobles were not as impervious to the idea as historians once used to claim. Luis Salas Almela, in a study of the dukes of Medina Sidonia, has shown that although they later rebelled against what they took for Olivares's tyrannical rule, the dynasty had initially embraced the count-duke's platform, which "fit very nicely with the concerns and priorities" of this influential Andalusian family.[25] As a matter of fact, if clans like the Medina Sidonia ultimately turned their backs on the project, this was less to do with the Union of Arms per se than with outrage at Olivares's tinkering with consecrated hierarchies and his increasingly unrestrained promotion of families of lesser status from outside Castile.[26] Unfortunately, not much is known about these *parvenus*, though it seems fair to assume that they must have welcomed the opportunity to accede to the ranks of the nobility through military cooperation. Thus, while the support of Castilian grandees may have hemorrhaged over time, Olivares's preferment of peripheral clans likely boosted the identification of lesser dynasties with the regime.[27]

This was certainly the case in Milan. It has been pointed out that the nobilities of southern Italy were chary of joining the Union of Arms.[28] Milanese families, by contrast, took up the offer to integrate into the military structures of the house of Habsburg with gusto.[29] The reason for this enthusiasm gap was the peculiar character of Milanese feudalism. Seventeenth-century nobles agreed that governing a fiefdom encompassed three obligations: in addition to administering justice (*giustizia*) and providing sufficient foodstuff (*grascia*), feudatories had a duty to

---

[23] Quoted in González de León, *The Road*, pp. 161–2. Manuel Rivero Rodríguez has recently questioned the authenticity of the Great Memorial, arguing that what historians have long treated as a secret instruction that Olivares penned sometime in the 1620s was one of the many French propaganda tracts that circulated in the 1640s to foment the insurgence in Catalonia. See Rivero Rodríguez, "El 'Gran Memorial.'"

[24] On this ideology, see Neuschel, *Word*, pp. 94–6.   [25] Salas Almela, *The Conspiracy*, p. 25.

[26] Benigno, "Il fato," p. 84.

[27] See the few hints in Jiménez Moreno, "Las Órdenes," pp. 328, 336; Del Mar Felices de la Fuente, "Hacia la nobleza," p. 24.

[28] On Sicily, see Ribot García, "La época"; Benigno, "Aristocrazia"; on Naples, see Sodano, "Le aristocrazie," pp. 154, 157, 160–1; Spagnoletti, *Principi*, pp. 183, 196.

[29] Ibid.

48 ARISTOCRATIC POWER IN THE SPANISH MONARCHY

protect their subjects from harm (*protezione*).[30] If Neapolitan and Sicilian nobles could draw legitimacy from the judicial authority they exercised in the country-side, Milanese feudatories had lost all significant jurisdictional powers to rela-tively centralized Milan-based courts of law.[31] With leading families unable to fashion themselves as administrators of justice, the armed defense of subject pop-ulations stepped in as a justification for their exalted position in a society that was slouching toward a bloody war with France that would inevitably play out on Milanese soil.

The Milanese Warrior Nobility under Olivares

In the 1630s, a war between Spain and France seemed increasingly likely. In France, Cardinal Richelieu saw an armed conflict against the kingdom's main competitor as a way to shore up his precarious position in the hierarchy of the court of Louis XIII.[32] On the other side of the Pyrenees, Olivares pushed for a war with France for very similar reasons. While strategic designs did play a role, the decisive factor in his decision was assuring his own survival as minister-favorite: as with Richelieu, Olivares's interest in a conflagration lay primarily in making himself indispensable to his king and thus consolidating his informal position as *valido*.[33] As his *valimiento* dragged on and the Union of Arms came under attack from Castilian grandees, he pushed for a military conflict that would prove the necessity of his common defense policy. What the Spanish empire needed, Olivares believed, was "a good war, or else we will slowly be losing everything."[34]

The belligerent rhetoric did not match Spain's preparedness. As during the Italian Wars of the previous century, northern Italy was going to be one of the main theaters of a renewed armed conflict between the French and the Spanish crowns. The French viewed Milan as Spain's Achilles heel, believing that an attack on Milan would inflict a fatal blow on the Spanish empire as a whole.[35] The Spaniards concurred. They too saw Milan as either the "key to Italy" or the "heart of Italy."[36] Olivares and the military establishment in Madrid were convinced that if the French captured Milan, they would be able to expand their control rapidly to the other Spanish possessions in southern Italy.[37] To strengthen their position, the Spanish upped their investment in the defense of their bastion in northern Italy. Throughout the early 1630s, they dispatched additional troops to Milan.[38]

---

[30] Spagnoletti, "Il governo," p. 61.
[31] Sella, *Crisis*, p. 172; Mozzarelli, "Strutture," pp. 438–9, 455–7.   [32] Parrott, "The Causes."
[33] Ibid., p. 89; for these dynamics at a later point in the Thirty Years' War, see Malcolm, *Royal Favouritism*, pp. 13, 181, 188.
[34] Quoted in Elliott, "El programa," p. 340.   [35] Oresko, "The House," p. 307.
[36] Fernández Albaladejo, "De 'llave'," pp. 41–2.   [37] Coloma, "Discurso," p. 5.
[38] Maffi, *Il baluardo*, p. 80; Hanlon, *Italy 1636*, p. 34.

BECOMING MILITARY LEADERS   49

Despite these efforts, the Spanish army stationed in Lombardy remained woefully underprepared for a French attack. Even the last-minute appointment of Olivares's cousin, Diego Felípez de Guzmán, Marquis of Leganés, as governor of Milan and commander-in-chief of the army in northern Italy in 1635 came too late to turn things around.

The first French attack proved an unmitigated disaster. Throughout the early 1630s, Richelieu had worked hard to form an alliance with Victor Amadeus I (r. 1630–1637), Duke of Savoy. The plan was to use his territories to the west of Milan to launch an attack on the State of Milan, which finally materialized in 1636. On June 22, the Franco-Savoyard coalition army led by Marshal Créquy had managed to cross the Ticino river, a natural *cordon sanitaire* shielding Milan's heartland from westerly attacks.[39] Upon hearing of this exploit, a panicking Leganés dove headfirst into open battle, near Tornavento, with an army against which his stood no chance. As it happened, the invading coalition fought on for an entire day and only desisted at the eleventh hour because of the sweltering heat and an infestation of insects. Leganés's ramshackle troops stood exposed as worthless in an emergency. As one contemporary diarist sardonically noted, "Mosquitoes and gadflies have accomplished more than the governor of Milan."[40]

Coming to terms with the structural weaknesses of the standing army, the military establishment fled into the arms of the local aristocracy. In the wake of the rout at Tornavento, appointments of local heads of household as *maestri di campo* (the first rung of the career ladder within the Spanish army in Lombardy) skyrocketed, with forty-four out of a total of forty-nine *maestri di campo* nominated in the following two decades hailing from the ranks of the nobility.[41] Social status often trumped other considerations, so much so that the great military specialist on Olivares's team, Carlos Coloma, allegedly complained that noblemen "wanted to begin to be Generals and soldiers on the same day."[42] The apologists of this heavily skewed nomination process maintained that nobles' sense of honor induced a distinct zeal that made them better placed to command troops than venal commoners.[43] One writer, Galeazzo Gualdo Priorato (1606–1678), made the genealogical argument explicit, advising princes to pick military leaders based on "the stock of the mercenaries, in the same way horse traders take into consideration the breed of colts."[44] Convoluted as these arguments were, they failed to conceal that it was the inadequacy of his own troops rather than the innate superiority of the local nobility that forced the Spanish king to co-opt Milan's leading families.[45]

---

[39] On the rout of Tornavento, see the microhistorical account in Hanlon, *Italy 1636*. On the Ticino as a *cordon sanitaire*, see Dalla Rosa, *Le milizie*, p. 119.

[40] Johnsson, ed., *Storia*, p. 122.   [41] Hanlon, *Italy 1636*, p. 64.

[42] Quoted in González de León, *The Road*, p. 166.   [43] Spagnoletti, "Onore," p. 214.

[44] Priorato, *Guerriero prudente e politico*, quoted in Donati, *L'idea*, p. 279.

[45] Signorotto, "Guerre," p. 371.

50 ARISTOCRATIC POWER IN THE SPANISH MONARCHY

Local grandees were happy to oblige. To Milanese feudatories with limited jurisdictional prerogatives, the benefits of a war outweighed the costs. Granted, nobles needed to make the most of the authority they enjoyed in local communities to replenish the *tercios* (early modern infantry companies of 3,000 men, comparable to modern-day regiments) with a steady supply of soldiers.[46] But in the context of the Union of Arms, nobles who shouldered this responsibility could hope for an entrée in Madrid. Thanks to their participation in the war effort on behalf of the empire, Milanese nobles would be locked into an alliance with the leading dynasties of the Spanish monarchy and boost their dynastic capital in ways they would not previously have thought possible. The semantic category used to rationalize this deal was what contemporary nobles called *reputación*, the fame and respect they commanded among their peers.[47] If they risked life and limb on the battlefields of Lombardy, Milanese families could expect to earn *reputación*. This symbolic capital they could later convert into offices and titles, including access to the chivalric orders of the crown, all of which would allow them to shine within an emerging Hispanic nobility.[48] While such careerist behavior would later be frowned upon (see chapter 4), the *olivaristas* were convinced, for the time being, that the striving for *reputación* of noble families would benefit not just the single head of household trying to climb the social ladder but the kingdom as a whole.[49]

One family hoping to partake in the race for *reputación* was the cadet branch of the Borromeos. When the French hit Lombardy in 1636, Giulio Cesare was promoted to the rank of *maestro di campo* with immediate effect. Betraying the despair at the top, the monarchy noted that his preferment was particularly advantageous "because of the many vassals that he can and does appoint when the governors order him to, sparing neither trouble nor expenses in the process."[50] (So zealous was Giulio Cesare that his repeated conscription drives wound up decimating the population in the family holdings around Lake Maggiore.[51]) In the aftermath of the rout of Tornavento, as Leganés plotted revenge and hatched plans for a sortie to Piedmont, the governor stressed the crucial importance of Giulio Cesare Borromeo. In a memorandum submitted to the Council of State in

---

[46] Ibid., p. 375; Jiménez Estrella, "'No ha interesado,'" p. 152. Also see Parrott, "Richelieu," p. 143. The number of soldiers per tercio diminished from an average of 2,000 in the early years of the war to just 500 toward its end. Maffi, *Il baluardo*, p. 82.

[47] Schumacher, "Felipe IV," p. 126.

[48] Signorotto, *Milano*, p. 127; Spagnoletti, *Principi*, p. 181; Jiménez Estrella, "'No ha interesado,'" pp. 151–2.

[49] This phenomenon was widespread. See Schumacher, "Felipe IV"; Sandberg, *Warrior Pursuits*, pp. 147–8.

[50] The quote is from the *consulta* of the Council of Italy, Madrid February 26, 1646: *AGS*, SSP, lib. 1135, ff. 1r–4r (f. 2v).

[51] For an early indication of the problem, see Rappresentanza del Conte Borromeo per ripari, e munizioni..., Arona March 22, 1617: *ASM*, Atti di governo, Militare p.a., cart. 325, fasc. Piazzaforte Arona; Maffi, *Il baluardo*, pp. 121–2.

March 1638, Leganés informed the councilors that Giulio Cesare had promised to raise sixteen *compañías* comprising thirty men each, whereas his closest competitors were anticipating less than one-third of that number.[52] The Borromeos, he concluded, deserved a key place in the planned invasion of Piedmont because of their unique ability to recruit soldiers.

By June 1638, the campaign against Piedmont was underway. The main booty on which Leganés had set his eyes was the fortified town of Vercelli, located in the Po Valley midway between Novara and Turin.[53] Not only was the town surrounded by lush countryside offering food and fodder for the troops, but the conquest of a strategically sensitive outpost also promised to deal the Franco-Savoyard military establishment a heavy blow.[54] After a six-week siege, the Milanese army finally entered the town center on July 6. The Vercellesi were informed that they would henceforth be "true and natural vassals and subjects of His Majesty," the king of Spain.[55] To drive that point home, the city was illuminated with torches for three consecutive nights. Celebrating the victory, Leganés readily acknowledged that that triumph had been a collective endeavor of Milan's *olivaristas*. As he phrased it in a letter to Philip IV, alluding to the unwritten contract at the heart of the Union of Arms, "all the *maestres de campo*, colonels, and corporals of this army have acted with the very *reputación* they have offered to the royal arms of Your Majesty." It was therefore only fair that "Your Majesty will offer them very splendid rewards."[56]

The Borromeos promptly queued up for the promised premiums. They had good reason to expect much. Giulio Cesare had not only fought particularly valiantly in the conquest of Vercelli, but he had lost his life during the siege when a cannonball hit his head on June 6.[57] Hoping that this violent death as the king's loyal servant would procure him eternal glory,[58] the Borromeos besieged Leganés to bequeath Giulio Cesare's position to his son, Giovanni. Giulio Cesare's intrepid widow, Giovanna, penned a letter to the governor in which she begged him to reward her son for her late husband's services. She first reminded the governor of the "loving desire with which my count (may he rest in peace) committed himself to the king's service ... putting it before the children and his house until he lost his

---

[52] *Consulta* of the Council of State, Madrid March 22, 1638: *AGS*, Estado collection, leg. 3346, f. 138.

[53] On the strategic significance of Vercelli, see Anselmi, *"Conservare,"* pp. 96–7. More generally on the importance of the conquest of fortified towns to seventeenth-century warfare Hanlon, *The Hero*, p. 96.

[54] Maffi, *Il baluardo*, p. 24.

[55] *ASM*, Atti di governo, Militare p.a., cart. 164, fasc. Minute di alcuni Manifesti pubblicati all'uscire delle Reali armi di Sua M.tà sopra Vercelli l'anno 1638.

[56] Leganés to Philip IV, Vercelli July 6, 1638: *AGS*, EST, leg. 3348, f. 138.

[57] Patente de Capitán, Milan [no date]: *Archivio Borromeo dell'Isola Bella*, Famiglia Borromeo collection, Giovanni V, Carriera militare, fasc. Sua Carriera Militare da....

[58] On the centrality of martyrdom for the king in the warrior nobility, see Sandberg, *Warrior Pursuits*, pp. 143, 147.

52   ARISTOCRATIC POWER IN THE SPANISH MONARCHY

life in it."[59] She then artfully argued that his martyrdom for the Spanish cause was an unmistakable indication of "how eagerly this house has served the royal crown over the last fourteen years." Knitting a narrative in which the Borromeos' history of royal service debuted when they became seigneurs of Angera, she drew the inescapable conclusion that her eldest should be allowed to "follow in his father's footsteps" and serve the Habsburgs, as she herself was committed to doing as a widow who had "taken on the burden of this house." In response, the monarchy lauded Giovanni's "qualities, authority, and devotedness" and put him in charge of his father's *tercio*.[60]

Buoyed by this promotion, Giovanni went from strength to strength. He participated in the conquest of Trino, a fortress on the northern bank of the Po river near Casale Monferrato that the dukes of Savoy had wrested from the house of Gonzaga in 1632. The Borromeos later liked to spin the yarn that Giovanni was the first man to enter the fortress at Trino.[61] This is not borne out by contemporary accounts, which credit him along with a slew of other military leaders for this exploit.[62] An adept manager of his own publicity, Giovanni nevertheless spread the news of his alleged prominence in the conquest.[63] Such fantastic accounts were possibly lent credibility by his eminent role in the subsequent run of victories that moved the borders of the Milanese State eastward to the gates of Turin and which the Spanish over-enthusiastically celebrated as the "flooding (*inundación*)" of Piedmont.[64] What is certain is that this public relations exercise worked. Giovanni's younger brother, Federico Jr. (1617–1673), wrote from the papal court in Rome to assure Giovanni that he was being complimented "left, right, and center" for his sibling's gumption.[65] Thanks to his skilled self-promotion, Giovanni was perceived as the rising star of the Spanish army in Lombardy.

Honoring his achievements, the military establishment showered Giovanni with new offices. In 1638 he was appointed governor of the newly conquered towns of Vercelli and Ivrea.[66] Four years later, the crown saw fit to increase his powers on the Borromeos' home turf. In 1642 he was nominated governor of

---

[59] This and the following quotes are from Giovanna Cesi to Leganés, Origgio October 15, 1638: *ABIB*, FB, Giovanni V, cart. Carriera militare.

[60] *ABIB*, FB, Giovanni V, cart. Carriera militare, fasc. 1638 6 Giugno creato Maestro di Campo....

[61] The first mention of this in an official document is in Giovanni's nomination to commissioner-general in 1646 (see chapter 3): *AGS*, SSP, lib. 1362, ff. 96r–100r (f. 97r), and a letter of Haro to Philip IV? January 1, 1648: *ABIB*, FB, Giovanni V, Carriera militare.

[62] See, for example, Leganés to Philip IV, Pontestura June 6, 1639: *AGS*, EST, leg. 3350, f. 120.

[63] One early source is the diary of an anonymous cleric in Busto Arsizio. See Johnsson, ed., *Storia*, p. 130.

[64] *Consulta* of the Council of Italy, Madrid February 26, 1646: *AGS*, SSP, lib. 1135, ff. 1r–4r (f. 2r); Maffi, *Il baluardo*, p. 26.

[65] Federico IV to Giovanni VII Borromeo, Rome June 4, 1639: *ABIB*, FB, Federico IV, Corrispondenza 1634–1644.

[66] Gualdo Priorato, "Giovanni," unpag.

Lake Maggiore and the Ossola, the valley linking the lake to Valais via the Simplon Pass. This office came with the task of military organizing in this strategically sensitive area: Giovanni was to act as the long arm of the Spanish governor and commander-in-chief in Milan in matters both military and civil.[67] According to a surviving letter-patent from an earlier period, military governors were in charge of "the militia in that area, giving them orders...to prepare and arm their companies," and of liaising with the representatives of village communities about "everything that is of service to His Majesty."[68] As governor of Lake Maggiore, Giovanni was also invested with the guardianship of the castle of Arona, one of the crucial garrisons along the Milanese State's western border.[69] The appointment as *castellano* of Arona was an unequivocal sign of the monarchy's trust in the Borromeos of Angera, showing how far the late Giulio Cesare and his son Giovanni had come within a few short years thanks to their involvement with the Count-Duke of Olivares and his local middlemen.[70] Giovanni was now in a position to prove his commitment to Olivares's vision of a shared defense policy in his fiefdom, putting his life on the line to keep his own vassals out of harm's way, as he had wished to do ever since he had met the cardinal-infante on Isola Madre a decade earlier.

The Borromeos and Popular Opposition to the War

No sooner had he settled into his new role than Giovanni was called upon to act as a protector to the subjects under his tutelage. Located on a hilltop across the lake from Angera, the citadel of Arona was crucial to the defense of Milan's western border.[71] Both the French and the Savoyards agreed that Arona was the ideal "gateway" to Milan.[72] As a consequence, the fortress became an immediate target of the coalition army. As early as 1636, a group of stragglers from the battle of Tornavento had hurtled northward along the Ticino and attacked the Borromeo fief.[73] With the garrison of professional soldiers stationed at Arona dispatched to the front, the Borromeos had had to hastily recruit a peasant militia of 4,000 to push the coalition army back into Piedmont.[74] The improvised fightback had been the first occasion for Giovanni Borromeo to shine as a military leader. The Spanish ambassador in Rome had extolled him for his services to the crown,[75]

---

[67] On the duties, see Anselmi, *"Conservare,"* pp. 104–6.

[68] 1625 9 Luglio. Patente del Governo del Lago Mag.e...: *ASM*, Atti di governo, Militare p.a., cart. 230, fasc. Borromeo.

[69] Relatione d'Arona [no date]: *ASM*, Atti di governo, Militare p.a., cart. 230, fasc. Borromeo. On governors and *castellani*, see Anselmi, *"Conservare,"* ch. 4.

[70] Ibid., pp. 116, 129.   [71] Maffi, *Il baluardo*, p. 78; Hanlon, *The Hero*, p. 90.

[72] See Du Plessis-Praslin, "Mémoires," p. 199.   [73] Capriata, *Dell'historia*, p. 135.

[74] Gualdo Priorato, "Giovanni," unpag.

[75] Federico IV to Giulio Cesare III Borromeo, Rome August 26, 1636: *ABIB*, FB, Federico IV, Corrispondenza 1634–1644.

54 ARISTOCRATIC POWER IN THE SPANISH MONARCHY

and a letter-patent of the monarchy lauded the scion of the house of Borromeo for "readying people for combat and governing that place with great bravery."[76] Eight years later, a regrouped Franco-Savoyard army handed Giovanni another occasion to prove his commitment, though this time on a much larger scale.[77]

In the final days of July 1644, an army of 12,000 foot and 3,000 horse under the leadership of Prince Thomas of Savoy (1596–1656) was closing in on Arona.[78] The siege began during the night of August 1, and on the following day the enemy fighters were within a musket shot of the redoubt in which Giovanni Borromeo had entrenched himself.[79] With all access roads to Arona pinched off, the main priority was to keep the coalition army away from the lake. So long as the Spanish side remained "masters of the lake," they believed, they would be able to ship supplies into Arona, which would allow Giovanni to sit out the onslaught.[80] That plan had only one problem: as in 1636, the military establishment proved unwilling or unable to assist Giovanni with regular troops. Holding out with a peasant militia, Borromeo fired off increasingly despondent messages, warning at one point: "The tower is shaking and will be gone after another ten cannon shots tomorrow."[81] The promised Spanish troops, led by Giovanni Pallavicino, never made it to Arona. In fact, if Prince Thomas gave up five days into the siege and flounced back into Piedmont, it was because of the prospect of additional peasant militiamen hastily recruited by the Borromeos' local clients and ferried across the lake from Angera, not because of the imminent arrival of regular soldiers from Milan.[82]

For the military high command, the siege of Arona was an embarrassing fiasco. Internal documents show that the Spanish authorities knew throughout the siege that Arona might well turn into another "Ostend or Verrua, if we are unable to come to its rescue."[83] Yet, despite the haunting imagery of garrisons that had resisted the onslaught of powerful occupiers before the risk of starvation made them surrender, the military establishment had proved unable to marshal the necessary wherewithal within a reasonable period of time, leaving Giovanni to his own devices. It is hardly surprising that the Spanish later sought to whitewash

---

[76] Patente de Capitán, Milan [no date]: *ABIB*, FB, Giovanni V, Carrieria militare, fasc. Sua Carrieria Militare da Capitano a Commissario Generale degli Eserciti.

[77] Leonida Besozzi has reconstructed the siege in painstaking detail, using the same set of sources, though he does not contextualize the events as I attempt to do here. See Besozzi, "Cronistoria."

[78] For the figures, see ibid., p. 278.

[79] Giovanni VII Borromeo to Valeriano Sfondrati, Arona August 1, 1644; Gerolamo Cignardi to Valeriano Sfondrati, Arona August 2, 1644: *Società Storica Lombarda, Milan*, Fondo Crivelli Serbelloni, vol. 15 (VIII).

[80] Juan Vázquez de Coronado to Valeriano Sfondrati, Mortara August 3, 1644: *SSL*, FCS, vol. 15 (VIII).

[81] Giovanni VII Borromeo to Valeriano Sfondrati, Arona [no date]: *SSL*, FCS, vol. 15 (VIII).

[82] Gualdo Priorato, *Relatione*, p. 142.

[83] Juan Vázquez de Coronado to Valeriano Sfondrati, Mortara August 3, 1644: *SSL*, FCS, vol. 15 (VIII).

their dismal record. Writing a few years after the siege, Philip IV's spin doctor, Pier Giovanni Capriata, claimed that Arona had been saved thanks to the backup sent in from the heartland of the State of Milan. Thomas of Savoy would have easily conquered Arona, he asserted, "if the *maestro di campo* Giovanni Pallavicino had not thwarted the prince plans by leaving Mortara with his tercio and marching [toward Lake Maggiore] with incredible speed."[84] Such rewriting of history made perfect sense: the monarchy, after all, had to contain what had for all intents and purposes been a military campaign outside the ranks of the official army.[85] But despite their best efforts, the inconvenient truth remained that it was Giovanni, not the official army, who had driven out the Franco-Savoyard troops.

In his own rendition of the denouement at Arona, Giovanni stressed his sense of abandonment. According to the distress signals he sent out when he was cooped up in the citadel in 1644, the militias were untrustworthy and unreliable, poorly trained and undisciplined.[86] Throughout the siege he repeatedly requested dragoons and foot soldiers from the Spanish army, warning the military high command not to waver and send in "paid people" "if you want to keep this stronghold."[87] The pleas grew increasingly desperate until Giovanni's secretary informed the military establishment that he and his master were "waiting for people" from the regular army "like the Jews for the Messiah, so as to dismiss some of these militiamen before they do so themselves."[88] The impression he left was that of a lone hero withstanding the enemy onslaught on his own, abandoned by both the Spanish military establishment and his own subjects.

In truth, the role of the militias was much more incisive than Giovanni allowed. As a military writer reported at the time, the "French" started to have second thoughts about the campaign when "militiamen from their fiefs" came to Borromeo's rescue from across the lake.[89] When it suited their purpose, the Borromeos themselves underscored the strategic significance of local militias. In the 1650s, when the monarchy attempted to introduce a new tax on fishermen, the Borromeos shamelessly argued that their subjects deserved to be exempted from such predation given that "those poor residents" had defended Milan's critical western border "so loyally and promptly" on multiple occasions, not least in the military campaign of "1644 against the French and Savoyard armies."[90] This was probably truer than the other story Giovanni Borromeo peddled. Although militias were regularly belittled by contemporary military strategists,[91] local draftees were more than willing to stand up for their local communities when

---

[84] Capriata, *Dell'historia*, p. 945.   [85] Rizzo, "I cespiti," pp. 465–6, 475.

[86] Gerolamo Cignardo to Valeriano Sfondrati, Arona August 1, 1644: *SSL*, FCS, vol. 15 (VIII).

[87] Giovanni VII Borromeo to Valeriano Sfondrati, Arona August 1, 1644: *SSL*, FCS, vol. 15 (VIII).

[88] Gerolamo Cignardo to Valeriano Sfondrati, Arona August 2, 1644: *SSL*, FCS, vol. 15 (VIII).

[89] Gualdo Priorato, *Relatione*, p. 142.

[90] Brief, ? July 26, 1653: *ASM*, Atti di governo, Acque p.a., cart. 296.

[91] Dalla Rosa, *Le milizie*, pp. 145–6, 151–3.

56   ARISTOCRATIC POWER IN THE SPANISH MONARCHY

they were under attack.[92] After all, they stood to lose most from a raid on their homes and livelihoods.

If Giovanni Borromeo nevertheless indulged in his counterfactual narrative, this owed much to his self-image. As Jonathan Dewald reminds us, the self-image of military heroes in the seventeenth century was steeped in the values of the society of orders: "Only those who had significant deeds to present had the right to speak of themselves, and only those of high social standing were likely to perform such deeds."[93] Like other warrior nobles, Giovanni viewed the commonwealth that he had defended at Arona as "a theater for individual greatness, rather than as an object to be advanced for its own sake."[94] In this solipsistic worldview, members of the militia morphed into props in a vicarious display of dynastic greatness.[95] The people who lived on Lake Maggiore and fought with Giovanni were not individuals willing to defend their livelihoods but, rather, "badges of social rank, denoting the superior status of elites against the groups below or vis-à-vis outsiders."[96] They helped Giovanni signal his *reputación* to his peers and king whose interests he was co-advancing by heaping glory on his own name.

This uneasiness about local militias pointed to the incongruity sitting at the heart of the Union of Arms. To Giovanni Borromeo, the defense of Arona was not just a military obligation in the face of a real and present danger; it was also an opportunity to accrue *reputación*. No one made this clearer than his own secretary, who wrote during the siege: "What is at play here is the reputation of a knight."[97] To use Pierre Bourdieu's useful concept, the "technical function" of warfare was indistinguishable from its "social function"—the prospected upward mobility of the members of the elite in charge of an intervention.[98] In fact, the seeming technicalities helped legitimize unacknowledged underlying social interests, producing perverse outcomes in the process. In the Borromeos' case, the amalgamation of these two interests not only pushed them into war but ensured that they would remain in it once it had begun. On the back of the cardinal-infante's visit to Isola Madre, the Borromeos' private correspondence started brimming with self-centered longings for a military conflagration. Giovanni Borromeo, like so many other scions of the Italian nobility at the time, yearned to join the Imperial troops in the Holy Roman Empire.[99] In missives to his younger brother, Federico, he hinted at that possibility, never failing to couple combat north of the Alps to the glory that could be earned on German battlefields.[100]

---

[92] See Parrott, *Richelieu's Army*, p. 551; Asch, "'Wo der soldat,'" p. 300.

[93] Dewald, "Writing," p. 24.   [94] Dewald, *Status*, p. 38.

[95] On the role of servants in the self-affirmation of Milan's leading families, see Cremonini, *Le vie*, pp. 74–5. More generally, see Daloz, *The Sociology*, ch. 6, in part. pp. 105–7.

[96] Ibid., p. 61.

[97] Gerolamo Cignardi to Valeriano Sfondrati, Arona August 3, 1644: *SSL*, FCS, vol. 15 (VIII).

[98] Bourdieu and Passeron, *Reproduction*, p. 164.   [99] Spagnoletti, *Principi*, p. 184.

[100] Federico IV to Giovanni VII Borromeo, Rome July 21, 1635: *ABIB*, FB, Federico IV, Corrispondenza 1634–1644.

BECOMING MILITARY LEADERS   57

If that dream never came true, he was all the more eager to join the army in Lombardy when the Franco-Spanish conflict broke out in 1635. In the wake of the first attack on Arona in 1636, Federico claimed to be "particularly pleased to hear that Count Giovanni has proved himself and will have been able to assuage his desire for the war in Germany with one at home."[101] While it is, of course, possible that Federico was being facetious, there was nevertheless truth in jest: like many others of their station, the Borromeos genuinely welcomed the Franco-Spanish War because of its inherent promise of upward social mobility.[102] Indeed, when battles failed to materialize with sufficient frequency, Federico expressed regret that there had not been "other military matters as one wishes."[103] The merger of the technical function of warfare with its social promises prodded the most mercurial elements within the warrior nobility to yearn for its continuation. With bloodletting being seen as an opportunity to win ever more *reputación*, war became a self-perpetuating force.[104]

What the *olivarista* warmongers failed to factor in was the consequences their preferred method of upward social mobility entailed: the wholesale destruction of vast swaths of land and endless suffering for its inhabitants. One source that allows us to get a sense of the nefarious effect of the war is a report written by an agent of the Serbelloni family, another military dynasty who held property in Taino, a village near Angera.[105] The testimonies of local residents who had survived the first Franco-Savoyard attack in 1636 give a sense of the life-threatening situation they had lived through during the raid. As one 44-year-old man recounted, "the enemy army struck when no one expected it." All of a sudden, the village was at the mercy of soldiers who ransacked every single household. Besides stealing livestock and animal fodder, they deprived the community of vital foodstuffs, including "large quantities of poultry and dairy, which were both plentiful in this village." To make matters worse, in their frenzy the soldiers destroyed everything they could not carry away. One eyewitness recalled that when he ventured outside after the raid, "I saw bedding in the countryside, with [down] feathers on the ground, torn bedsheets, broken washbowls"—all prized possessions to contemporary rural dwellers. Once the destructive fury was over, the retreating soldiers committed arson attacks on civilian homes, many of which burned to the ground. As the author of the report summarized his findings one year after the fact, the community "has been completely destroyed and sacked by

---

[101] Federico IV to Giulio Cesare III Borromeo, Rome September 23, 1636: *ABIB*, FB, Federico IV, Corrispondenza 1634–1644.

[102] On the jingoism of warrior nobles, see Sandberg, *Warrior Pursuits*, pp. 145–6.

[103] Federico IV to Giovanni VII Borromeo, Lucerne July 6, 1656: *ABIB*, FB, Federico IV, Cariche.

[104] See Parrott, "The Causes," p. 73.

[105] The following quotes are from Francesco Pigola, Relatione del Danno fatto da Francesi alla Terra di Taijno P.e d'Angera l'anno 1636, Milan June 3, 1637: *ASM*, Archivio Serbelloni, serie I, cart. 55, fasc. 85.

58 ARISTOCRATIC POWER IN THE SPANISH MONARCHY

the French army…the houses have been burned down, and what the residents owned has been destroyed."[106]

As such accounts indicate, the Borromeos' embrace of the Union of Arms called into question their self-assigned role as guardians. According to the public transcript, the family, as feudatories, had a duty to offer shelter to its vassals in the area around Lake Maggiore, a duty that included warding off attacks by enemy forces. But this defensive function of feudalism collided with the fact that, under Olivares, military entrepreneurship had become a vehicle of upward social mobility. The Borromeos' projection of being military leaders drove them toward a conflict in which they could display their credentials as heroic fighters. Seeing the opportunity to demonstrate their courage on the battlefield as a viable way forward in the climate of the 1630s, they ended up secretly rooting for an enemy attack on their landholdings.[107] Not unlike the late medieval feudal nobility studied by Gadi Algazi, the *olivaristas* seemed to invite the very violence from which they claimed to shield their subjects.[108]

Awareness of this disjunction grew only haltingly. During the first attack on Arona in 1636, one family member deplored "the damage the French have caused" in the same letter in which he congratulated Giovanni on his budding military career.[109] Engrossed in its war-induced *jouissance*, the family seemed to be largely oblivious to the wholesale destruction of large swaths of the territory around Lake Maggiore.[110] Giovanni's mother, Giovanna Cesi, was the only one in the family to acknowledge, albeit in passing, her regret for the "people you have lost," only to pivot to self-absorbed worrying about her son being supplied with sufficient "lemon juice, cookies, and preserved sour cherries."[111] The disdain the self-proclaimed heroes felt for non-nobles was such that, in open contradiction to the Borromeos' self-styling as protectors, the population's well-being became expendable if it stood in the way of self-aggrandizement.[112] But as the war roared on and the local population made its voice heard, that entitlement and insouciance proved harder to sustain. As Giovanni's distrust of the peasant militia during the second attack on Arona in 1644 showed, the Borromeos were growing aware of the drop in enthusiasm among the subject population for a war that, by that time, had been going on for almost a decade. Among a nobility that had tied itself up in knots, Giovanni was one of the first to realize that the elite's egotistical quest

---

[106] On this wanton destruction in contemporary France, see Parrott, *1652*, pp. 199–209.

[107] See Sandberg, *Warrior Pursuits*, pp. 175–7; Papagna, *Sogni*, p. 122.

[108] Algazi, *Herrengewalt*, pp. 133–4.

[109] Federico IV to Giulio Cesare III Borromeo, Rome September 23, 1636: *ABIB*, FB, Federico IV, Corrispondenza 1634–1644.

[110] See also Algazi, *Herrengewalt*, pp. 134–5.

[111] Giovanna Cesi to Giovanni VII Borromeo, Origgio July 5, 1639: *ABIB*, FB, Giovanni V, Atti diversi, cart. 881.

[112] Schumacher, "Felipe IV," p. 132.

for dynastic greatness would not be tenable unless the *olivaristas* shared the spoils of war with at least some of their subjects.

Conclusion

The Borromeos' efflorescence as a military dynasty suggests the need for a fresh appraisal of the Union of Arms. Historians have tended to study Olivares's proposal as a top-down project that foundered on the resistance of the nobility who rebutted his irresponsible stoking of the flames of conflict with France and the introduction of military cooperation. However, if we focus on the nobility itself, it becomes clear that not all nobles experienced the common defense of the realm as an imposition from above: some espoused Olivares's initial designs and twisted them to their own ends. Dictating the nobility's response was not uniform corporate interests but the dreams and aspirations of single families. Where more established dynasties might have recoiled at the idea of allowing upward social mobility to new clans, precarious dynasties willing to cash in on triumphs on the battlefield, such as the Borromeos of Angera, yoked themselves to Olivares's military adventures in the hope of improving their lot on the coattails of the rising star in the court of the Madrid. In this reading, Olivares pushed the nobility to war as much as bloodthirsty nobles hoping to ratchet up *reputación* pulled him into a conflict with the French crown.

Yet, as so often, the seeming expedient carried the seeds of its own undoing. This chapter has already gestured to the contradictions to which the reinvention of the Borromeos as military leaders gave rise: the desire to fight in the army to bring sheen to the family name led the clan to champion a destructive conflict, which in turn unleashed the ravages of seventeenth-century warfare on the populations the family had sworn to protect from harm. The nexus between the technicalities of warfare and upward social mobility proved more controversial than anticipated. Over time, the alleged beneficiaries of the Borromeos' philanthropy became more vocal in their protests at the inevitable side effects of war. Although they fought back valiantly when their towns and villages came under attack, ordinary people on Lake Maggiore must have felt that a conflict initiated by their social betters keen on acquiring *reputación* had little good in store for them. Their sentiments probably echoed those of an anonymous author of an anti-Olivares pamphlet published in 1642, who wrote of the Franco-Spanish War, "For many it means losses, but for others it is a good harvest."[113] In their petitions to the law courts in Milan, the Borromeos' subjects lifted the curtain on what went on behind the shiny façade of Giovanni Borromeo as a magnanimous protector of

---

[113] Quoted in Salas Almela, *The Conspiracy*, p. 126.

the defenseless, exposing his endeavor as a self-serving ploy in the hunt for self-betterment. If the Borromeos' dishonest handling of fishing privileges had already raised doubts about the sincerity of their motives (chapter 1), the war further undermined their paternalist credentials. Before long, the Borromeos would have to explain to themselves and others why so much charity on their part occasioned so much depredation among the people under their protection.

3

The Pitfalls of Patronage

Giovanni Borromeo as Commissioner-General of the Army in Lombardy

By the mid-1640s, Giovanni Borromeo had much to be proud of. Thanks to the valiant defense of his fiefdom, he had twice saved the State of Milan from a devastating Franco-Savoyard invasion. Despite lingering wariness at Borromeo's vigilantism, these exploits were earning him the grudging recognition of the Spanish military high command. When the commissioner-general of the army in Lombardy, Valeriano Sfondrati, passed away in 1645, Giovanni Borromeo was nominated his successor. Convinced that he was sufficiently "rich" to be "uninterested" in monetary gain, the military establishment thought he was the most suitable candidate for an office whose holder needed to be "of the best sort, especially with regard to integrity and commitment to serving Your Majesty."[1] In light of the "manifest greed of some, and the dissolute lifestyle and lowly origins of others," Giovanni Borromeo was the only military man to be trusted with the management of the significant amounts of public money that this office entailed.[2] For Borromeo, this nomination was a triumph. His careful fashioning as an *olivarista* had landed him the position of patron-in-chief in charge of troop allocation throughout the Milanese State. Thanks to his loyal service to Philip IV, the head of the cadet branch of the house of Borromeo had, within three short decades, been catapulted into the most eminent military office bestowed upon a member of the local nobility.[3]

Yet all was not well. As he eyed up the bigger stage, storm clouds were gathering. In February 1643, Giovanni's uncle Carlo (from the main branch of the family) had informed the military high command of the problems that were brewing on Lake Maggiore. In a string of petitions, he suggested that Giovanni's eagerness for military offices was little more than a "pretext" to "do whatever his passions and his interests in his nearby estates and fiefs inspire in him."[4] On the face of it, Carlo's concern about Giovanni's "high-handed behavior" toward social inferiors

---

[1] *Consulta* of the Council of Italy, Madrid February 26, 1646: *AGS*, SSP, lib. 1135, ff. 1r–4r (ff. 1r, 2r).
[2] Ibid., f. 3v.   [3] De Vit, *Il Lago Maggiore*, p. 241; Maffi, *Il baluardo*, pp. 296–7.
[4] Carlo III Borromeo to Sirvela, ? February 7, 1643: *ASM*, Atti di governo, Militare p.a., cart. 230, fasc. Borromeo.

Aristocratic Power in the Spanish Monarchy: The Borromeo Brothers of Milan, 1620–1680. Samuel Weber, Oxford University Press. © Samuel Weber 2023. DOI: 10.1093/oso/9780198872597.003.0005

62   ARISTOCRATIC POWER IN THE SPANISH MONARCHY

could be dismissed as the ramblings of a sore loser who was himself not a paragon of restraint in his dealings with the subject population on the lake.[5] What must have given the authorities pause, however, was Carlo's warnings of the social unrest that Giovanni's blatant disregard of the basic "rules of good government" might foster. "In times such as ours in which the loyalty and devotedness of the good vassals are obliging them to sacrifice their lives and talents in the service of their prince," the self-serving actions of members of the governing elite, Carlo admonished, might undermine trust and lead insurrectionists to enact their "pernicious designs" in Lombardy.[6] Such fears were not far-fetched. Over the previous three years, Catalan subjects had been in open rebellion against the inequities of the Union of Arms, as a consequence of which the Count-Duke of Olivares had been dismissed in January 1643.[7] As Giovanni Borromeo himself surmised during the siege of Arona, the ravages of seventeenth-century warfare were feeding doubts about the compatibility of elite longings for military grandeur with the preservation of the common good. As he acceded to the prestigious position of commissioner-general of the army, the charges that he was fomenting social unrest weighed down on him.

As if to prove the gainsayers wrong, Giovanni launched a flagship policy that attempted to build consensus among the king's non-noble subjects for the ongoing war effort against the French crown. According to the instruction prepared for his predecessor, Giovanni's main task as commissioner-general was to act as a coordinator and provide a transmission belt for material used in the provisioning of the Habsburg troops stationed across Lombardy. Besides collating information on the wherewithal available in the State and heading a retinue of officials, the main function of the commissioner was allocating combatants to accommodations.[8] Alive to the fact that the stationing of troops had been the motor of the uprising in Catalonia, Giovanni was determined to overhaul the quartering of soldiers, who had hitherto been allocated to private households. Upon taking office, Giovanni unearthed decades-old plans to levy a bespoke tax in order to be able to outsource the provision of housing and provender to private individuals. The case for the institution of so-called *case erme* (protected houses) hinged on the idea that the creation of distinct troop lodgings would not only take the stress of billeting off ordinary subjects and nip opposition in the bud; the unspoken part of the argument was the hope that the privatization would spawn a new crop of stakeholders among the "middling sorts" of the population: if propertied

---

[5] On Carlo's violent reputation, see Parachini and Pisoni, "La 'razza'," p. 481; Cremonini, "Storia," pp. 489–92.

[6] Carlo III Borromeo to Sirvela, ? February 7, 1643: *ASM*, Atti di governo, Militare p.a., cart. 230, fasc. Borromeo.

[7] The classic account remains Elliott, *The Revolt*. On attempted rebellions in Milan, see Signorotto, "Stabilità."

[8] Instruction to Valeriano Sfondrati, in: De Carichi dello Stato, vol. III, f. 164v: ASM, Atti di governo, Militare p.a., cart. 406.

THE PITFALLS OF PATRONAGE   63

non-nobles were called upon to provide services to the army, Giovanni speculated, they might become sufficiently invested in the war effort not to revolt against the aristocratic warlords.

Bold as it was, the plan ricocheted on Giovanni Borromeo. Constitutively reliant on the division of society into a small in-group of clients and a vast "out-group" of net contributors, this redistribution of collectively held resources emboldened opposition to the Borromeos. As the implications of the scheme became clearer, those left behind began to use the law courts in Milan to denounce the *case erme* as an intricate mechanism to funnel resources to private providers who raked in huge profits at the expense of the vast majority who ponied up for them. By mid-century, these relentless campaigns had exposed Giovanni and his clients as war profiteers whose recklessness had jeopardized what they were pretending to safeguard: the commonwealth. Sensing that his moment had finally come, Carlo, from the main branch, reheated his old accusations. Backing them up with new evidence from across Lombardy, he brought Giovanni down. This chapter, then, adds to Alessandro Buono's pioneering work on the *case erme* but does so from the perspective of the man responsible for running the scheme, revealing the social logics behind what only at the surface looked like a technical solution to a massive problem confronting seventeenth-century Milanese society.[9]

Milan under Military Occupation

When Giovanni Borromeo was nominated commissioner-general of the army in 1646, his foremost concern was to pre-empt a rerun of what had happened on the shores of Lake Maggiore five years earlier. Late in February 1640, as the troops of captain Juan de Astor trudged toward the hamlet of Brebbia, not far from the Borromeos' castle of Angera, the *sindico* (mayor) of that community, Francesco Besozzi di Cocco, ordered the church bells to be rung out to convoke the village's population.[10] Before long, men from Brebbia and the surrounding settlements had gathered to stage a guerrilla attack on the approaching Spanish company, hindering it from entering the village. When the armed troops predictably vanquished the spontaneous opposition that had gathered, Astor raided the house of the unruly *sindico* "with a goodly number of armed soldiers," who then proceeded to beat him, "with most serious insults, on the head with a pickaxe."[11] Although

---

[9] Buono, *Esercito.*
[10] Decree, Milan February 21, 1640: *ASM,* Registri delle cancellerie dello stato, serie XIV, registro 21.
[11] Statement given to the *giunta per gli eccessi delle soldatesche,* Milan March 10, 1640: *ASM,* Atti di governo, Militare p.a., cart. 2.

64 ARISTOCRATIC POWER IN THE SPANISH MONARCHY

Astor later confessed to this violent retaliation,[12] it was Besozzi di Cocco and his "crowd of people" who faced punishment for their "excesses": they stood trial on charges of *lèse-majesté* and sedition.[13]

The insubordination at Brebbia was driven by anguish at the indiscriminate billeting of troops in village communities. Since the early stages of the militarization of Lombardy in the lead-up to the Franco-Spanish War, the authorities had regularly allocated troops to private homes in communities across the Milanese State.[14] Although general guidelines on how many soldiers could be stationed in a single location existed on paper, army personnel were often left to their own devices. As a result, many took to forcing villagers at gunpoint to put them up for extended periods of time.[15] As early as 1633, a Venetian envoy to Milan reported that the Milanese were growing "impatient with the hard and tyrannical oppression of many years under the weight of warfare and the billeting of armies."[16] Sources closer to the population on the ground confirmed this. A canon from Busto Arsizio, a town near Brebbia, wrote eloquently about the burden the billeting of troops had been for ordinary people. Not only did troops occupy forty to fifty houses out of a total of 800 in that particular community, they also put a strain on the town's inhabitants with outrageous demands for foodstuffs and fodder at the trough of an economic depression.[17] Over the years, communities repeatedly complained about soldiers who helped themselves to food and drink before they looted whatever foodstuffs they were unable to consume on the spot (partly to prevent enemy troops getting their hands on these precious resources).[18] Adding insult to injury, army commanders were often complicit in these abuses, sometimes even egging on soldiers to depredate.[19] The reasons for this were structural. The plundering of civilians was a built-in mechanism of seventeenth-century warfare, the direct result of chronic delays in the payment of soldiers' wages, which made it incumbent on them to subsist at the expense of the peasantry in the areas to which they were deployed.[20] Village communities, already hard-pressed by a severe economic downturn, were bound to react to the excessive demands of the soldiery by rioting. As a tract published in Madrid the same

---

[12] Minute of the *giunta per gli eccessi delle soldatesche*, Milan March 29, 1640: *ASM*, Atti di governo, Militare p.a., cart. 2.

[13] Decree, Milan February 21, 1640: *ASM*, Registri delle cancellerie dello stato, serie XIV, registro 21. On the auditor general, see Maffi, *Il baluardo*, pp. 267–8.

[14] Ibid., p. 247. On the analogous situation in Aragon, see Sanz Camañes, "El peso," and Sanz Camañes and Solano Camón, "El impacto," pp. 77–8.

[15] Buono, *Esercito*, pp. 22–3; Maffi, *Il baluardo*, p. 248.   [16] Valier, "Relazione," p. 85.

[17] Johnsson, ed., *Storia*, pp. 13–4.

[18] Deposition to the *giunta per gli eccessi delle soldatesche*, Milan January 15, 1640, quoted in Buono, *Esercito*, p. 96. More generally, see Parrott, *1652*, pp. 208–9; Sanz Camañes and Solano Camón, "El impacto," p. 82.

[19] On France, see Parrott, *Richelieu's Army*, p. 551; Parrott, *1652*, pp. 204–9.

[20] Buono, *Esercito*, p. 25; also see San Camañes, "El peso," pp. 9–11.

year as the insurrection at Brebbia noted, "The common people will prefer rebellion in order to avoid destitution."[21]

Although riots against the Habsburg army were by that point a common occurrence across a continent ensnared in a deadly war, the insurgence in Brebbia was the first of its kind in Lombardy.[22] Up until that moment, civilians had regularly become enmeshed in petty warfare against enemy troops, but never before had they risen against soldiers of the Catholic king. For the first time, the supposed friendly fighters faced the active pushback of a population who struggled to see the difference between French and Spanish troops.[23] As some governors admitted in their correspondence with the court of Madrid, in the eyes of civilians soldiers from both sides engaged in the indiscriminate looting of communities.[24] Growing increasingly convinced that the war was a calamity that a self-aggrandizing elite had inflicted upon them, ordinary subjects made it clear that they were no longer going to put up with the negative consequences of their social superiors' quest for military grandeur.

Fueling the Milanese elite's nervousness at the riots on Lake Maggiore were parallel developments in another part of the Spanish empire. In Catalonia, the early months of 1640 had seen similar popular movements afoot against the stationing of troops. In April and May, peasants had gathered to the sound of church bells in the mountainous regions in the east of the principality around Girona to chase away troops that were lodged along the French border.[25] As the authorities' apprehension of marauding troops in Catalonia grew, the councils in Madrid urged the monarchy to assist local governments in furnishing the pillaging troops with food.[26] However, with the authorities failing to react swiftly, the peasant protests against billeting spread rapidly to the rest of the principality, sprouting into violent riots in Barcelona, which ended in the assassination of the Spanish viceroy on Corpus Christi.[27] All this did not bode well for the ruling elite of Milan. Its members were apprised of the Catalan revolt by Carlo Visconti, the emissary of the city of Milan, who, ironically, was on his way to Madrid to relitigate the billeting of troops with Philip IV when he witnessed the early days of the insurrection during a pit stop in Barcelona.[28] Singling out billeting as one of the main drivers behind the uprising, Visconti warned that Milan's elite could soon meet the same fate as Catalonia's, a tocsin to which the revolt against Spanish troops on Lake Maggiore lent additional urgency.[29] As a *consulta* of the Council of Italy drawn up after Visconti's audition at court made clear, if the "excesses" of the soldiery

---

[21] Quoted in Parker, *Global Crisis*, p. 37.

[22] On civilian riots against soldiers, see Parrott, *Richelieu's Army*, pp. 522–3.

[23] For similar problems in Aragon, see Sanz Camañes, "El peso," pp. 34–5.

[24] Maffi, *Il baluardo*, pp. 235–6; Signorotto, "Il marchese," p. 149.

[25] Elliott, *The Count-Duke*, p. 577; Sanz Camañes and Solano Camón, "El impacto," p. 67.

[26] Rivero Rodríguez, *El conde duque*, pp. 258–9.   [27] Ibid., pp. 259–60.

[28] Parker, *Global Crisis*, p. 564.   [29] Buono, "Il governo," p. 62.

were not reined in with draconian punishment, "the good order in the common-wealth (*república*) will not be preserved."[30]

Giovanni Borromeo and Troop Allocation

Upon taking office as commissioner-general, Giovanni Borromeo was eager to tackle the problem of the "excesses" of the soldiery. His nomination came not a moment too soon. In response to the Catalan crisis, the Milanese had set up a Committee against the Excesses of the Soldiery and tasked it with looking into the complaints from civilians.[31] However, in the half decade of its existence, the committee had turned out to be a toothless paper tiger. Despite its existence, skir-mishes between soldiers and civilians had not ceased. On the contrary, by 1644, they hit fever pitch. According to a report, on Lake Maggiore, troops in Spanish employ regularly "mistreated locals...and wanted to rape women."[32] To avert a new uprising of village communities upset at a local lord unable to protect them from attacks from their own side, Giovanni realized, he needed to get to grips with the quartering of troops on a structural level.[33] The new project Giovanni adumbrated sought to coordinate the sharing-out of troops centrally through the commissioner-general and to limit it to select towns.[34] In lieu of putting up troops in private dwellings, they were to be quartered in bespoke buildings, many of which had remained empty as the population of Lombardy was decimated by the plague of 1629–1631 and the subsequent war.[35] Although they had little to do with the purpose-built army barracks (*caserme* in modern Italian) of the eight-eenth century, the mooted *case erme* were to ensure that the soldiery "kept itself in a more orderly fashion and supported itself with less harm and inconvenience to the subjects."[36]

The centralization of troop allocation begot a whole new bureaucracy with hazy ties to private individuals. To fund the ambitious project, the *Magistrato Ordinario*, the judicial arm of the treasury in Milan, was tasked with raising a new tax in the long-suffering communities of Lombardy.[37] The revenues thus

[30] *Consulta* of the Council of Italy, Madrid [no date but 1640]: *AGS*, SSP, leg. 2025, 22, f. 2v.
[31] On the *giunta*, see Buono, *Esercito*, ch. 2. For a contemporary assessment, see the *consulta* of the Council of Italy, Madrid February 6, 1648: *AGS*, SSP, leg. 1808, f. 192.
[32] Antonio Briceño Ronquillo to Giovanni VII Borromeo, Milan June 24, 1644: *ASM*, Registri delle cancellerie dello stato, serie XVI, registro 23, f. 135v.
[33] For similar debates in Aragon, see Sanz Camañes, "El peso," p. 36.
[34] Ordine del Sig. Commissario generale, de 26 Aprile 1645, per far le Case Erme nel Ducato: *Biblioteca Nazionale Braidense, Milan*, Ordini, vol. 1. Although it had been announced by Giovanni Borromeo's predecessor, it was Borromeo who oversaw the rollout of the *case erme*.
[35] Maffi, *Il baluardo*, pp. 254, 256.
[36] Ordine del Sig. Commissario generale, de 26 Aprile 1645, per far le Case Erme nel Ducato: *BNB*, Ordini, vol. 1.
[37] Memoriale primo presentato à Sua Ecc., Milan May 14, 1645: *BNB*, Ordini, vol. 1.

THE PITFALLS OF PATRONAGE   67

generated would then be used to compensate contractors who rented out properties to house the troops and provided them with hay, oats, and straw for the horses, as well as firewood, food, and furnishings for the men themselves.[38] What had hitherto been organized on a case-by-case basis at a community level was to be administered through rapidly expanding state institutions, with an *impresaro* appointed by the commissioner-general in charge of the coordination of an expanding number of private contractors tasked with implementing the new policy.[39]

Its architects liked to describe the policy as a complex "machine" fueled by "cash" and administrative acumen.[40] Champions of the project praised it in glowing terms as a panacea. Community leaders from the Duchy of Milan claimed it was "undeniable" that, thanks to the *case erme*, the soldiery would behave in a more orderly fashion and that the extortions of host families would cease for good.[41] Thanks to the new policy, the *Magistrato Ordinario* insisted, the king's subjects could finally "stay comfortably in their homes and concentrate on winning their bread without being troubled by soldiers."[42] What was good for business was equally positive for the taxpayer. The centralized coordination by the commissioner-general ensured that the billeting of troops was more cost-effective.[43] To their devotees, the *case erme* were a guarantee that "everyone pays their share and the burden is distributed fairly (*con giustizia distributiva*)."[44] The *vicario di provvisione*, the functionary in charge of feeding the city of Milan, voiced the sentiments of many in the governing elite when he rhapsodized the "fatherly care" his institution and others took of communities across the State as they finally offered the public some letup.[45]

Yet such technical arguments could not easily be severed from rationales to do with social status. In an age still overshadowed by the Count-Duke of Olivares despite his ousting in 1643, state-centered solutions appealed to a nobility that

---

[38] Ordine del Sig. Commissario generale, de 26 Aprile 1645, per far le Case Erme nel Ducato: *BNB*, Ordini, vol. 1; Lettera Magistrale al Sig. Co: Georgio Rainoldi per la visita delle Cas'erme del Ducato per prevenirle per il prossimo alloggiamento, Milan September 13, 1652: *BNB*, Ordini, vol. 1.

[39] Capitoli sopra quali dalli Sindici generali del Ducato di Milano è stata deliberata à Cesare Magno l'Impresa di provedere, & mantenere le Case herme nelle Terre segnalate nel Ducato [no date]: *Archivio Storico Civico, Milan*, Materie, cart. 159. Also see Maffi, *Il baluardo*, pp. 254–5, and Sanz Camañes, "El peso," pp. 11–2.

[40] Consulta Magistrale a S.E. de 24 Febraro 1649 in cui si espone il stato delle Case Erme, e la difficoltà di sostenerle: *BNB*, Ordini, vol. 1.

[41] Beneficij raccordati da Sindici, & Inserti nel loro memorial de 10 Maggio 1645 per l'erettione delle Cas'Erme: *BNB*, Ordini, vol. 1.

[42] Consulta Magistrale à S.E. de 3 Agosto 1647 rappresentando lo stato delle Case Erme: *BNB*, Ordini, vol. 1.

[43] Beneficij raccordati da Sindici, & Inserti nel loro memorial de 10 Maggio 1645 per l'erettione delle Cas'Erme: *BNB*, Ordini, vol. 1.

[44] Consulta Magistrale à S.E. de 3 Agosto 1647 rappresentando lo stato delle Case Erme: *BNB*, Ordini, vol. 1.

[45] Risposta della Città [di Milano] della sodetta lettera Magistrale, in cui si preme nell'erettione delle case Erme, e si superano le difficoltà, Milan July 22, 1645: *BNB*, Ordini, vol. 1.

68   ARISTOCRATIC POWER IN THE SPANISH MONARCHY

was trying to tighten its hold on power through evidence of its talent to reorganize the commonwealth. Self-interest played a major role here. To Giovanni Borromeo, the *case erme* delivered a welcome opportunity for him to prove, once again, the organizational and logistical skills that had been the lifeblood of the reconstructed *olivarista* military elite to which he belonged.[46] The savvy as a guardian of the population he had demonstrated during the battle of Arona (see chapter 2) he could now display to a much larger audience, by hobbling a revolt that seemed inevitable.

Whatever technical advantages the *case erme* may have had, these soon yielded to the social uses to which they were put. As an internal memorandum of the Council of Italy had cautioned in 1640, the commissioner-general "has friends and enemies and passions like everyone else."[47] A few years on, Giovanni proved the councilors right. He handed out the patronage he had been entrusted with according to a pattern that had little to do with the bureaucratic rationalization that apologists for the scheme had promised. This became apparent when Giovanni selected the locations of future *case erme*. *Case erme* needed to be based in towns that were large enough to withstand the impact of a conspicuous number of soldiers and sufficiently connected to regional markets to provide the soldiery with adequate foodstuff.[48] Consequently, *case erme* were instituted in cities such as Abbiategrasso, Busto Arsizio, and Monza, sizeable market towns with excellent trade links.[49] The highest concentration, however, was reached around Lake Maggiore, where Arona, one of the centers of the Borromeos' fiefdom, and Pallanza, the last remaining free town on the lake, shifted the battlefield in their arms race from the control of transalpine trade to the hosting of troops.[50] Smaller clusters of *case erme* were set up in Varese, Gallarate, and Lonate Pozzolo in the immediate surroundings of the Borromeos' home turf. Much to the chagrin of the petitioners from the rest of Lombardy, Giovanni was determined to prefer the northwest of the State of Milan. While there were strategic reasons for this, Alessandro Buono is right to suggest that this decision also needs to be situated in the context of the Borromeos' strategy of affirming themselves as clients of the Spanish Habsburgs.[51]

As he implemented the *case erme* policy, Giovanni banked on the desperation of the communities in the area. The swath of land stretching from Milan to Lake Maggiore, known today as the Alto Milanese, had been wrecked by decades of war. A diarist from Busto Arsizio, a town that would soon host a *casa erma*, noted

---

[46] On this elite, see Jiménez Estrella, " 'No ha interesado'," pp. 168–9.
[47] *Consulta* of the Council of Italy, Madrid [no date but 1640]: *AGS*, SSP, leg. 2025, 22, f. 4r.
[48] Buono, *Esercito*, p. 260.   [49] Ibid., p. 258.
[50] Visita fatta dall'Ill.mo S.r Conte Giorgio Raynoldo Delegato dall'Ill.mo Magistrato Ordinario dello Stato di Milano di tutte le Case herme d'esso Ducato con l'assistenza del S.r Landio, Gio. Battista Colnago, et S.r Carlo Busso Ingegner Collegiato di Milano [no date but 1652]: *ASCM*, Materie, cart. 160.
[51] Buono, *Esercito*, p. 269.

THE PITFALLS OF PATRONAGE   69

that laboring people lived in such utter misery that they were "like worms, like children who had just been born, naked as nature had created them." They slept on the floor, using "straw as down, the air as a blanket."[52] An area that had once prided itself on its bounty could no longer feed the majority of the population: "a good share of the poor" subsisted on a diet of bran bread and turnips, which had become so sparse, riots broke out on the rare occasions when they were on sale.[53] These tribulations were the direct result of the collapse of trade in the region.[54] Unlike the agriculture-rich plains of the Po Valley, this area at the foot of a number of Alpine passes was heavily dependent on trade and commerce between Italy and Central Europe.[55] However, by the 1640s, that trade had seen an all-too-noticeable slump.[56] With most of the infrastructure lying barren, local notables were desperate for some relief. The billeting and outfitting of troops offered an alternative source of income to the social group that was particularly hard hit by the economic crisis. What Giovanni Borromeo proffered was no substitute for the trade they had lost but it was better than anything else on offer at the time.

Giovanni's attention to this clientele needs to be seen in the context of a growing awareness among the nobility in Spanish Italy of the political role of well-to-do commoners. As early as the 1610s, a memorandum on the Kingdom of Naples had acknowledged the existence of "a middling sort of people between the nobility and the plebs," such as "citizens" and "merchants."[57] In the intervening years, the "middling sorts" had reinvented themselves as the main champions of a reformist agenda to curtail the nobility's privileges and re-establish the powers of the third estate in the Kingdom's political institutions. With a nobility jealous to guard its privileges, the *ceto civile*, as it became known, ultimately saw no other choice than to form an alliance with the populace against the war profiteers, and rise in what is now known as the Masaniello rebellion of 1647–1648.[58] Giovanni Borromeo was acutely aware of these developments thanks to his younger brother who was serving as a papal governor of Benevento, an exclave of the Papal States surrounded by the Kingdom of Naples. When news of the insurrection broke, Federico warned Giovanni against lazy prejudices: the fact that the revolt in Naples was led by a "fishmonger" named Masaniello was no reason for complacency; the true masterminds behind the uprising were the "good and sensible people" of the kingdom.[59] His brother's perspicacious account of the dramatic events in Naples must have resonated with the much smaller uprising that had

---

[52] Johnsson, ed., *Storia*, p. 14.   [53] Ibid., p. 15.

[54] For a detailed account of the economic breakdown at mid-century, see Faccini, *La Lombardia*, pp. 17–39, esp. pp. 24–5.

[55] Vigo, "L'economia," p. 208.   [56] Ibid., pp. 199–210.

[57] Relacion del Arcobispo de Capua Gaetano para el Confesor del Rey N.S., quoted in Comparato, *Uffici*, p. 302.

[58] Villari, *Un sogno*.

[59] Federico IV to Giovanni VII Borromeo, Benevento July 13, 1647: *ABIB*, FB, Federico IV, 1645–1655.

70 ARISTOCRATIC POWER IN THE SPANISH MONARCHY

convulsed Lake Maggiore earlier: there, too, the masses had been tricked into a revolt against the army, that emblem of Spanish authority, by a cunning local notable, the *sindico* no less. The only way to avoid a large-scale revolt as in Naples was to harness the grievances of the "good and sensible people" against the war profiteers by offering them a share in the redistribution of collective resources that Madrid's "war government" was engineering.[60] The *case-erme* scheme seemed the perfect cure-all. It made it possible to court the social group from which ringleaders of the uprising that had taken place on the shores of Lake Maggiore in 1640 hailed: thanks to the *case erme*, these potential rebels could be turned into government contractors dependent on the warrior nobility against whom they might otherwise mutiny.

The profile of the people who came to run the *case erme* reflects these priorities. While some of the houses used as *case erme* were owned by village or town communities, most were private properties. Consider for example Arona, the town that had made Giovanni as a military man and which, at the height of the war, hosted two and a half soldiers per inhabitant.[61] According to the report of an official dispatched to monitor the situation on the ground in the fall of 1652, Giovanni Borromeo and his cousin, Renato, alone hosted about half the soldiery in their properties in the *borgo*.[62] Below them was a sprawling class of local notables who profited from the quartering of troops in equal measure, most notably old clients of the lords of Lake Maggiore. One such family was the Bernas, who were active as innkeepers and merchants in the area around the southern tip of Lake Maggiore and had acted as financial brokers for the Borromeos.[63] When the *case erme* were established, the Bernas seem to have viewed them as yet another opportunity to profit from the Borromeos' presence. One Anna Berna of Arona topped up her annual income by 200 *lire*, which she cashed for renting out property to the army.[64] Other beneficiaries included *dottori* (lawyers and notaries, as well as medical doctors) and members of the clergy.[65] A similar picture emerged in nearby Pallanza, where notables such as the Moriggia, towering figures within the town, and the local merchant community seem to have been particularly

---

[60] On this kind of thinking, see Benigno, "Il fato"; Benigno, *Specchi*; Benigno, *Favoriti*.

[61] Buono, *Esercito*, p. 263.

[62] Visita fatta dall'Ill.mo S.r Conte Giorgio Raynoldo Delegato dall'Ill.mo Magistrato Ordinario dello Stato di Milano di tutte le Case herme d'esso Ducato con l'assistenza del S.r Landio, Gio. Battista Colnago, et S.r Carlo Busso Ingegner Collegiato di Milano [no date but 1652]: *ASCM*, Materie, cart. 160.

[63] Giovanni's brother, Federico IV, was nuncio in Lucerne from 1655 through 1665 and in constant need of money that needed to be transferred from Rome and Milan to Switzerland via Lake Maggiore. See, for example, Federico V to Antonio Renato Borromeo, Rome October 29, 1661: *ABIB*, FB, Federico IV, Corrispondenza 1656–1664.

[64] Petition from Anna Berna, Arona [no date]: *ASCM*, Materie, cart. 160.

[65] Visita fatta dall'Ill.mo S.r Conte Giorgio Raynoldo Delegato dall'Ill.mo Magistrato Ordinario dello Stato di Milano di tutte le Case herme d'esso Ducato con l'assistenza del S.r Landio, Gio. Battista Colnago, et S.r Carlo Busso Ingegner Collegiato di Milano [no date but 1652]: *ASCM*, Materie, cart. 160.

THE PITFALLS OF PATRONAGE 71

prominent among the recipients of Giovanni Borromeo's patronage.[66] This pattern repeated itself in another market town not far from Lake Maggiore, Gallarate, where the Masera family, one of the two leading local clans, controlled a third of the properties used as *case erme*.[67] It was the same in all the other communities: wherever the landlords' social position can be gleaned from the documents, they were, if not members of the two leading local families, merchants, members of the clergy, or professionals.

Giovanni was an attractive patron to the middling sorts. No sooner was he nominated commissioner-general than letters of congratulation poured in from across Lombardy.[68] If some correspondents were courteous, others took fewer pains to conceal the ulterior motives behind their good wishes, putting their names forward as potential clients. Giuseppe Corio, a *maestro di campo* and future governor of Mortara,[69] for example, came straight to the point. "Having no less confidence in your kindness than in the honesty of the reward, I am now asking for the gratuity patrons are wont to give their servants."[70] If the most fearless anticipated a gratuity, the *case-erme* policy likely exceeded their expectations. The surviving account books of Cesare Magno, the man Giovanni had delegated to oversee the administration of the *case erme*, show him handling sizeable figures between 1645 and 1650. The annual patronage he could pass on to contractors and subcontractors ranged from 750.998.2 *lire* in 1648 to 1.125.361.3.1 *lire* in 1650. The same chart also turns up an impressive number of people up and down the Alto Milanese and Varesotto profiting from the policy. Throughout the five-year period covered by the surviving balance sheet, substantial sums were handed over to landlords for refurbishing, as well as renting, their houses to the army, with payments to single individuals ranging from as little as 50 *lire* to (more commonly) sums in the low three figures.[71] Not only was this good money for impoverished notables, it also was a win-win: as the "good and sensible people" of the northwest of the State of Milan scooped up the bounty, they became stakeholders in the Borromeos' vision of the monarchy.[72] Whereas discontented notables in Catalonia and Naples rose against the king of Spain, their peers in Milan were corralled into being constituents of the Catholic monarchy.

---

[66] Ibid.   [67] Buono, *Esercito*, pp. 266–7.

[68] See *ABIB*, FB, Giovanni V, Carriera militare, fasc. Conte Giovanni V del Conte Giulio Cesare III. Maestro di Campo. 1646 Consig.e Segreto, Commissario Gen.le degli Eserciti di S. M. Catt.

[69] On Corio, see Maffi, *Il baluardo*, p. 176, n. 88.

[70] Giuseppe Corio to Giovanni VII Borromeo, Mortara April 29, 1646: *ABIB*, FB, Giovanni V, Carriera militare, fasc. Conte Giovanni V del Conte Giulio Cesare III. Maestro di Campo. 1646 Consig.o Segreto, Commissario Gen.le degli Eserciti di S. M. Catt.

[71] Ristretto del debito e credito di Cesare Magno, Impres.o delle Case herme [no date but 1650]: *ASCM*, Materie, cart. 160.

[72] Buono, *Esercito*, p. 267; also see Béguin, *Les Princes*, pp. 202, 230–1.

72 ARISTOCRATIC POWER IN THE SPANISH MONARCHY

The End of Giovanni Borromeo's Billeting Scheme

Adroit as it must have seemed to Giovanni, the system he put in place stood on shakier ground than anticipated. The *case erme* soon sparked resistance. The initial catalyst of the opposition was the uncovering of instances of administrative malpractice at the hands of Giovanni's officials. The city of Milan warned from the outset that the large sums of money involved were liable to attract all sorts of "abuses" and "harm."[73] This structural problem was rendered more acute by the fact that those involved in the running of troop allocations were, in the words of Philip IV, "untrustworthy people of little means" who topped up their salaries by plundering whatever source of additional income they had access to.[74] Embezzlement was rife at all levels. The people tasked with farming the *case-erme* tax made up additional levies to line their pockets, while the less inventive tried to collect the same impost multiple times.[75] Contractors were not much better. According to internal documents, they filched the money handed out to them without providing the services they had promised. Others seem to have sold the victuals, furniture, and bedding they had been issued by the *impresaro* at a profit before the soldiers arrived.[76] By 1651, an internal document of the *Magistrato Ordinario* stated that "the alleged lack of furniture, houses, and fodder risked upsetting this machine," broaching concerns that such irregularities were not just uncomfortable for the soldiery but were undermining trust in the "public benefit" of the policy.[77]

The most glaring sign of discontent was the widespread refusal to pay the special tax that had been introduced to finance the *case erme*. There were, of course, sound economic reasons for this. Large swaths of land were so ravaged by war and economic breakdown, their inhabitants were unable to shoulder the new imposition. The authorities themselves conceded that the imploding income from agricultural produce made it well-nigh impossible to generate enough wealth that some of it could be skimmed off as taxes.[78] By 1650, tax farmers regularly reported that although they had resorted to "various tricks to collect [the tax], no remedy has worked."[79] If the parlous state of the economy was one motive for tax

---

[73] Circa l'admettersi un Controscrittore al Commiss.o delle Case Erme, Milan January 19, 1650: *ASCM*, Materie, cart. 160.

[74] Dispatch of Philip IV, Madrid August 19, 1638, quoted in Buono, *Esercito*, p. 98.

[75] Decree of the *Magistrato Ordinario*, Milan December 13, 1650: *ASCM*, Materie, cart. 160.

[76] Syndiconem Ducatus contra Franciscum Garischettum Impresarium Domorum Heremanum et contra Civitatem Mediolani [no date]: *ASCM*, Materie, cart. 160; City of Milan to the governor, Milan December 10, 1650: *ASCM*, Materie, cart. 160.

[77] Memoriale del 30 settembre 1651 di Annone Presidente delle R. D. Entrate Ordinarie: *ASCM*, Dicasteri, cart. 51, fascicolo Consiglio Generale—Ordinazioni.

[78] Ibid.

[79] Consulta a S.E. de 20 Febraro 1652, & sua rissolutione sopra il memoriale del Commissario del Ducato in cui richiese la trasmissione de Soldati in poenam riffiutata dal Magistrato: *BNB*, Ordini, vol. 1.

THE PITFALLS OF PATRONAGE 73

resistance, the latter was further fomented by the realization that, contrary to the promises of the elites, the new scheme did not free villagers of the old obligation of hosting and outfitting troops in their communities. In the designated sites of *case erme*, taxpayers were repeatedly asked to step into the breach for contractors who had failed to deliver. In 1648, for example, Giovanni Borromeo in person issued the stern order that the people of Melegnano, a town south of Milan, prepare hay and oats for the cavalry, specifying the rations he expected them to proffer to His Majesty's army.[80] In other communities, soldiers continued to help themselves to food and wine as if, under the new regime, these necessities were not provided by contractors.[81] The situation was not much better outside the official sites of *case erme*. Communities that failed to scrape together enough money for the *case-erme* tax were still compelled to lodge troops, in a breach of the stated aims of the policy. As part of the coercive powers the military establishment was endowed with to counter the problem of insolvent communities, Borromeo ordered that soldiers be dispatched to debtor villages to stay there for "as many days as it takes for them to pay off their debt."[82] By 1651, the commissioner-general regularly stationed entire companies in debtor communities.[83]

Apologists for the harsh reprisals claimed that they were a necessary part of going after recalcitrant local potentates who had always refused to host troops in their communities and were now mobilizing kin and friends to avoid defraying taxes to finance the *case erme*.[84] Internal documents, however, told a different story: the real victims of the crackdown were not local lords but their tenants.[85] Indeed, if troops were sent to debtor villages and towns, the better-off members of the community could usually avoid the punitive allocation of troops by bribing the *impresaro*.[86] (Giovanni's own correspondence files contain letters from minor nobles who implored him to spare their fiefs.[87]) Given these get-out clauses in the

---

[80] Decree, Milan September 3, 1648: *ASCM*, Materie, cart. 12; Faccini, *La Lombardia*, p. 124.

[81] Buono, *Esercito*, p. 277.

[82] *Magistrato Ordinario*, Milan January 21, 1647, in: De Carichi dello Stato di Milano, vol. III, f. 254r: *ASM*, Atti di governo, Militare parte antica, cart. 406. Also see Decreto di S.E. perché si possino mandar li Soldati ad alloggiar nelle Terre renitenti à pagar l'Imposte, per il mantenimento delle Case herme, per discontar il loro debito: *ASCM*, Materie, cart. 159. In a letter to the governor, Giovanni Borromeo "agreed" with this course of action. Letter of Giovanni VII Borromeo to the governor of Milan, Milan March 24, 1648: *ASCM*, Materie, cart. 159.

[83] Decree of the governor of Milan, Milan January 16, 1651: *BNB*, Ordini, vol. 1; Consulta a S.E. de 20 Febraro 1652, & sua rissolutione sopra il memoriale del Commissario del Ducato in cui richiese la trasmissione de Soldati in poenam riffiutata dal Magistrato: *BNB*, Ordini, vol. 1.

[84] Lettera alla Congregatione del Patrimonio de 20 Aprile 1648 in cui si significa il stato delle Case Erme, e gli rimedij, che sono di bisogno: *BNB*, Ordini, vol. 1.

[85] *Magistrato Ordinario*, Milan July 17, 1647: *BNB*, Ordini, vol. 1.

[86] Buono, *Esercito*, p. 237, n. 130. On contemporary notions of fairness in contributing to the war effort, see MacKay, *The Limits*, p. 147.

[87] Annibale Somaglia to Giovanni VII Borromeo, Piacenza April 24, 1646: *ABIB*, FB, Giovanni V, Carriera militare, fasc. Conte Giovanni V del Conte Giulio Cesare III. Maestro di Campo. 1646 Consig.o Segreto, Commissario Gen.le degli Eserciti di S. M. Catt. On communities' attempts to bribe officials, see Anselmi, *"Conservare,"* p. 190.

74   ARISTOCRATIC POWER IN THE SPANISH MONARCHY

social contract, it is hard to take seriously the pieties of the military administration under Borromeo who claimed that they were just ensuring that "everyone pays their share, regardless of how high-ranking or powerful they happen to be."[88] For many, the rapacious old billeting system continued unabated, but in addition to victualing soldiers in their own homes, communities now also had to shoulder a new imposition that officially alleviated their strains. In the eyes of a growing number of Milanese, the *case erme* were a black hole for war profiteers that left them worse off than when they were asked simply to host troops in their quarters.[89] In these circumstances, many seemed to believe that a return to the previous system of allocating troops to private dwellings was preferable to the *case erme*.[90]

These protests tell us much about popular politics in Milan. The exact composition of the anti-*case erme* movement remains a mystery; its individuals often disappear behind the deliberately blurred collective terminology employed in the petitions. Indeed, it cannot be excluded that some of the dissent was stage-managed by local notables aghast at plummeting profit margins now that they had to share their tenants' diminishing earnings with the exactors of the state.[91] However, in light of the favoritism of the military administration, which often exempted nobles, it seems far more likely that the majority of the protest came from village communities who availed themselves of the few literate members in their midst to articulate their disapproval.[92] What is certain is that the petitioners were motivated by the idea of "active obedience" to the king, a notion they had learned from elites in the debates over the legitimacy of opposition to the government of the minister-favorite.[93] Citing their status as vassals of the king, which they shared with members of the nobility, commoners appropriated the much-vaunted duty to impart advice.[94] If nobles were obligated to bring problems in his realm to the king's attention, commoners were likewise bound to inform His Majesty if and when one of his ministers failed to live up to the standards of good governance.[95] Much like the Barcelona artisans studied by Luis Corteguera, ordinary Milanese came to see justice as a right they could demand from the sovereign against the particular interests of their social betters.[96]

---

[88] Consulta a S.E. de 31 Agosto 1648 ripigliando il Stato delle Case Erme, con inserto un papele delle ragioni, che militano intorno ad esse: *BNB*, Ordini, vol. 1.

[89] On similar dynamics in France, see Parker, *Class*, p. 102.

[90] Giorgio Rec.o? to ?, ? 1652: *ASCM*, Materie, cart. 160.

[91] For such protest movements in France, see Parrott, *1652*, pp. 175, 210–1.

[92] On the role of literate members of the community in popular protest, see Coast, "Speaking."

[93] Corteguera, *For the Common Good*, p. 47.

[94] See Benigno, "Un país," p. 91; Walter, *Crowds*, pp. 20–1. On the tradition of the duty to counsel, see Windler, "*Arbitrismo*," pp. 19–41.

[95] MacKay, *The Limits*, p. 133.   [96] Corteguera, *For the Common Good*, p. 126.

THE PITFALLS OF PATRONAGE   75

In their petitions, most notably to the *Magistrato Ordinario*, protestors flayed the proponents of the *case erme* with their own knife.[97] Petitioners limberly couched their defiance in the political language of the ruling elite, harnessing the values of the elite as a benchmark with which to pass judgment on their rulers.[98] Discourses centered on governance in the name of the collective good, once flaunted by those in power, were now weaponized by the masses over whom they ruled. The favored public transcript of those who had risen under Olivares furnished protesters with new legitimation.[99] Surely, the masses argued through their mouthpieces in Milan's institutions, "Your Lordships' commitment to the public good of the city and duchy of Milan" would not allow the elite to let the *case erme* continue to exist in their current form.[100] The preservation of the "public benefit," asserted the powerless across Lombardy, required each member of society to contribute their fair share to the well-being of all, but, surely, the nobility had a special obligation to protect the defenseless.[101] Citing "distributive justice," the same buzzwords that had justified the introduction of the *case erme*, laboring people complained that the regressive taxation meant they were lumbered with the economic and human cost of a war that sat at odds with their most fundamental interests. Put simply, they reprised the feelings of an anonymous Neapolitan cleric who wrote around the same time that taxes "have been placed exclusively on the shoulders of the poor because the majority of the powerful have found a way not only to extricate themselves but to enrich themselves from the misfortunes of others."[102]

As these vocal protests made clear, the purported solution to the riots against looting soldiers was creating intractable problems of its own.[103] The *case erme* may have placated local notables who were showered with contracts, but the policy was now threatening to stoke discontent among the masses who were asked to chip in for the allocation of Habsburg troops. What had been sold as a plan to protect civilians from the ravages of marauding soldiers had degenerated into a system of redistribution of wealth and income from the bottom of society to the middling sorts without really resolving the problem of the imposition of troops on communities. Contemporaries outside the elite understood that the main issue with the policy was rooted in its structure: the *case erme* remained wedded to the logic of clientelism, and, as was the nature of early modern patronage, they

---

[97] On these dynamics, see Grüne, "'Gabenschlucker'," p. 232; MacKay, *The Limits*, p. 172.

[98] Corteguera, *For the Common Good*, p. 192.

[99] On this use of the rhetoric of the powerful, see Walter, *Crowds*, pp. 10, 20.

[100] See, for example, City of Milan to *Magistrato Ordinario*, Milan June 18, 1650: *ASCM*, Materie, cart. 160.

[101] On this point, see Corteguera, *For the Common Good*, pp. 38, 43.

[102] Quoted in Rovito, "La rivoluzione," p. 461.

[103] On the situation in France, see Parrott, *Richelieu's Army*, p. 544.

76 ARISTOCRATIC POWER IN THE SPANISH MONARCHY

were beneficial to a few and predatory on the many.[104] As patronage revealed itself to be incompatible with ideas about organizing society around the preservation of the collective good,[105] as the Borromeos claimed they were doing, villagers across Lombardy began clamoring for the promises of the restoration of distributive justice finally to be honored.[106] For an elite that hewed to the belief that revolts emanated from disgruntled nobles and the middling sorts,[107] it was a shocking discovery that they could originate with the bottom of the pile and, more importantly, be inspired by an alternative vision of the monarchy. Without ever acknowledging it openly, laboring people strongly implied that the king's resources were really the product of their toil and that the least they could expect was that royal ministers dispersed them fairly among the king's vassals.[108] Not only did they stake a claim to participation in government, but they forced open the premises of ruling-class ideology, fostering new ideas about how the Spanish monarchy ought to be run in the process.[109]

The main addressee of these grievances, the *Magistrato Ordinario,* slowly but inexorably came around to the protesters' opinion. If its members had been among the loudest champions of the *case erme,* they progressively changed their minds in the face of the growing volume of petitions that flooded their offices.[110] Having warned from the beginning that the regressive taxation imposed for the policy could "scare" the taxpayers, in the early 1650s they declared the model unsustainable.[111] Having kept a finger on the pulse of the Milanese State throughout the policy's implementation, the *Magistrato* concluded that although the *case erme* were undoubtedly beneficent, ramming through the program at this point "would entail the downfall of the duchy, instead of bringing it relief."[112] Based on intelligence from the ground, the *Magistrato* advised the termination of the scheme. Its officials argued that since those subjects who refused to pay taxes were made to host troops in their own homes and that numbers of the insolvent were shooting up, the obligation to put up troops in their homes was still a reality for many people, thus rendering the *case erme* redundant.[113] This admission was

---

[104] On the nature of early modern patronage, see Béguin, *Les Princes,* p. 391, and Karsten and von Thiessen, eds., *Nützliche Netzwerke.*

[105] On the tensions between these two ideals, see Engels, *Die Geschichte,* p. 60, and Béguin, *Les Princes,* p. 394.

[106] On this, see von Thiessen, "Der entkleidete Favorit," pp. 136, 147; Corteguera, *For the Common Good;* Walter, *Crowds,* p. 21.

[107] Villari, "La cultura," p. 20.

[108] On the ideology of popular movements in Spanish Italy, see Villari, "Discussioni," p. 46.

[109] Benigno, *Specchi,* p. 285.

[110] On the *Magistrato,* see Signorotto, *Milano,* ch. 6, esp. pp. 109–10; Buono, *Esercito,* p. 202.

[111] Risposta della Città [di Milano] della sodetta lettera Magistrale, in cui si preme nell'erettione delle case Erme, e si superano le difficoltà, Milan July 22, 1645: *BNB,* Ordini, vol. 1.

[112] Memoriale del 30 settembre 1651 di Annone Presidente delle R. D. Entrate Ordinarie: *ASCM,* Dicasteri, cart. 51, fasc. Consiglio Generale—Ordinazioni.

[113] Consulta a S.E. de 20 Febraro 1652, & sua rissolutione sopra il memoriale del Commissario del Ducato in cui richiese la trasmissione de Soldati in poenam riffiutata dal Magistrato: *BNB,* Ordini, vol. 1.

nothing short of an endorsement of the arguments of those taxpayers who had been hectoring institutions into the restoration of the *status quo ante*. In line with the countless petitions received from across Lombardy, the *Magistrato* now made the case that by returning to the old system, the troops "will encounter only a few more disadvantages than if they were to be hosted in *case erme*."[114] Sensing the potential of a revolt among the lower orders if the magistrates failed to protect them from a rapacious nobility and their middle-class clients, the *Magistrato* officials belatedly scrambled to live up to their duty as royal functionaries and shielded the peasantry.[115]

Embracing the rhetoric from below, the *Magistrato* convinced others. In 1653, Governor Luis de Benavides Carrillo, Marquis of Caracena (r. 1648–1656), for the first time, allowed communities to choose between continuing to transact the *case-erme* tax or return to the billeting of troops in private homes. The following year, the *case erme* were discontinued, and with them, Giovanni Borromeo's seemingly unstoppable rise to the commanding heights of the Spanish monarchy.[116] If he had implemented a policy that was meant to quell the rumors of the self-interestedness of his actions, he now stood exposed as a war profiteer before a Castilian elite that accepted common people's argument that the *case erme* were a boondoggle for the military establishment and its surrogates. Without phrasing it in such stark terms, the ruling elite of the monarchy conceded that, as the representative of the Duchy of Milan, Carlo Francesco Ridolfi, pithily put it in a memorandum to the king, "nobility and wealth" had turned out to be "two highly effective means to oppress the poor."[117] By taking the latter's concerns seriously, the *Magistrato* in particular had set out to restore some semblance of the balance that the war had thrown out.

Behind the posture of social responsibility lurked the vindictiveness of the main branch of the Borromeo family. The *Magistrato Ordinario* was headed by Bartolomeo Arese who, in 1652, had married his eldest daughter, Giulia, to Giovanni's rival on Lake Maggiore, his cousin, Renato (the son of Giovanni's *bête noire*, Carlo).[118] For all his self-fashioning as the "soul of the laws and the living law of civil government," Arese's disquietude about the well-being of the ruled was about as genuine as Giovanni's.[119] An unlikely candidate to channel the interests of those lower down the social ladder, Arese nevertheless showed no qualms about weaponizing popular protest against Giovanni's iron-fisted rule. To the arguments against Giovanni's tyranny toward social inferiors Carlo had first deployed ten years earlier, Arese added the mounting evidence from the

---

[114] *Magistrato Ordinario* to the City of Milan, Milan [no date but 1652]: *BNB*, Ordini, vol. 1.
[115] On this idea of public service, see Rovito, "La rivoluzione," p. 371.
[116] Buono, *Esercito*, pp. 254–5.   [117] Quoted in Signorotto, "Il marchese," p. 159.
[118] On Arese, see Signorotto, *Milano*, ch. 9.
[119] The quote is from one of Arese's sycophants, Pietro Crescenzio Romani, in his *La Monarchia di Spagna* (1650), quoted in Signorotto, *Milano*, p. 114.

78 ARISTOCRATIC POWER IN THE SPANISH MONARCHY

Magistrato to drive home the same point: as much as officials in faraway Madrid wanted to see Giovanni as a loyal servant committed to the common good, he had always used that argument as a pretext to further the narrow goals of his family and the clientele he had been able to build up thanks to the resources to which the "war government" had given him access.

With his reputation as a disinterested public servant on the line, Giovanni Borromeo fought back vigorously. As the *case erme* went out of business in the winter of 1654, he drummed up the support of his cronies. In 1655, several *sindici* from around Lombardy—the very group that had engaged in guerrilla warfare against Spanish troops fifteen years earlier—penned a letter to Philip IV in which they extolled Giovanni for how he had "managed the arduous allocation of lodgings" in Milan.[120] In their eyes, Giovanni was an exemplary noble hero who alloyed military bravery with cool-headed administrative savvy. Not only had he performed his function "with steadfast farsightedness," but his "fatherly love" had "made our pain more sufferable and less distressing." Committed to royal service like no other, Giovanni was a beacon of "incorruptible justice and merit" who had not once tired of ensuring that "our offices were rewarded to much universal benefit." All this, to their mind, went to show "the universal satisfaction" that derived from "the most exacting and unflinching diligence with which he has been serving in his post as commissioner-general." Tone-deaf from start to finish, this epistle did more harm than good. After all, the authors simply regurgitated trite talking points in a defense oddly out of kilter with the evidence that had been piling up over the preceding decade. Even less helpful was the fact that the senders formed part of that small section of Milanese society who had, by their own admission, been "compensated" by Giovanni. This point alone made it easy for others to dismiss the petition out of hand.

Realizing that he would not be able to make the charge of self-interest evaporate, Giovanni settled on a new argument. He surreptitiously altered the criteria against which his tenure as commissioner-general should be measured. As the monarchy regrouped after the string of rebellions that had rocked it since 1640, Giovanni Borromeo and his cronies could point to the fact that Milan, as one of the few territories of the monarchy, had not seen an insurrection and attribute this conspicuous absence to Giovanni's flagship policy. The case, such as it was, rested on the idea that the trickle-down effect of the *case erme*, however detrimental to the collective good, had not only coerced the king's non-noble subjects to become tributaries to the war effort but had spawned a stakeholder culture among the middling sorts, something that had failed to materialize in other parts of the monarchy. Deplorable as it may have been, the large-scale profiteering that

---

[120] This and the following quotes are from *Sindici* to Philip IV, Milan June 20, 1655: *ABIB*, FB, Giovanni V, Carriera militare.

those who had to bankroll it were now mauling had prevented Milan from ending up in the same turmoil as Catalonia.

Having discontinued the *case erme* at the behest of the *Magistrato*, Governor Caracena threw his weight behind this revisionist take on Giovanni's stint as commissioner-general. In a letter to Luis Méndez de Haro, Olivares's successor as minister-favorite, he praised the track record of the commissioner-general. According to the governor, Borromeo had held that function for the past nine years, during which he had always attended "most diligently to the wellbeing of the soldiers and the relief of the State, about which both are very satisfied."[121] In an enclosed letter to the king, Caracena went even further, emphasizing that Giovanni had excelled at "allocating the resources in such a way that the soldiers could be hosted and the locals could tolerate the pressure."[122] Indeed, it was thanks to his "integrity and attention [to detail]" that "we have been able to get by for so long."[123]

Conclusion

Caracena's argument about Giovanni's contribution to securing Milan's loyalty was of course not entirely without merit. Indeed, it adds nuance to the ongoing debate on Milan's relative stability during the crisis of the 1640s.[124] Giovanni had defied the conventional wisdom of the time and understood from early on that the revolts that were jolting the Spanish monarchy were spearheaded neither by rebellious nobles nor by the populace but by an emergent group contemporaries referred to as the *ceto civile*. Borromeo realized that he could break the insurrectionary spirit of these "middling sorts" if he succeeded in forming an alliance between the local notables in Lombardy's ravaged northwest and the warrior nobility. Once in power as commissioner-general, he proceeded to neutralize the middling sorts by outsourcing the provisioning of designated *case erme* to merchants and professionals in towns and villages of the Alto Milanese. The intense exchange of favors between Giovanni and notables in the communities on the ground helped create a climate that kept the population engaged enough not to rebel against a seemingly endless war. In so doing, Giovanni helped lend the Spanish monarchy new legitimacy and played a part, however mediocre, in restoring the power of the Catholic king during the monarchy's deepest crisis of

---

[121] Luis de Benavides Carrillo, Marquis of Caracena, to the Count of Haro, Milan June 20, 1655: *ABIB*, FB, Giovanni V, Carriera militare.

[122] Luis de Benavides Carrillo, Marquis of Caracena, to Philip IV, Milan June 20, 1655: *ABIB*, FB, Giovanni V, Carriera militare.

[123] Luis de Benavides Carrillo, Marquis of Caracena, to the Count of Haro, Milan June 20, 1655: *ABIB*, FB, Giovanni V, Carriera militare.

[124] For two opposing viewpoints, see Signorotto, "A proposito della fedeltà," and Buono, "Il governo."

80   ARISTOCRATIC POWER IN THE SPANISH MONARCHY

the century. If the Catalans had rebelled against the lodging of troops in their principality and the Neapolitans had risen against punitive war taxes, the Milanese had not mutinied despite being subjected to both.[125] Even the Council of State in Madrid was bound to acknowledge in an otherwise critical assessment of Giovanni's operation that considering "the distress, dangers, and afflictions of that State [Milan]," "the loyalty of the locals could serve as a model to any other subject [of the king of Spain]."[126]

What was equally true, however, was that this attempt to outsmart the governing elites of other territories of the Spanish monarchy was hardly compatible with ideas of governance in the name of the collective good, much less with disinterested royal service. The intervention of the powerless exposed the *case erme* as a cynical ploy to trade on the emergency of the 1640s in a bid to further the special interests of a nobleman and his clientele. As the monarchy was dealt one blow after another, a group of chancers in Milan had hijacked the *case-erme* plan to turn it into a gold mine for themselves.[127] Although few probably expected it at the time, these arguments would ultimately prevail. With Giovanni's opponents eager to bring him to book, they snatched this reasoning about distributive justice and ran with it. By trying to solve the problem of patronage with the same tools that had caused it, Giovanni had undermined his aspirations to join the pan-Hispanic elite that Olivares had tried to build. The career Giovanni continued to portray as an attempt to add luster to his dynasty would now be reframed as crude opportunism. As dynastic interests were being shorn from the public good in response to resistance from below, Giovanni, the last *olivarista* standing, was headed for the same fate as the Count-Duke two decades earlier: defeat amidst accusations of embezzlement hypocritically committed in the name of the collective good.

---

[125] Buono, *Esercito*, p. 142.

[126] *Consulta* of the Council of State, Madrid March 30, 1656: *AGS*, SSP, leg. 3373, f. 18, 2r.

[127] On this point, see Elliott, *The Count-Duke*, p. 514.

4

The Decline and Fall of an *Olivarista*

Giovanni Borromeo's Failed Quest for Admission to the Spanish Governing Elite

Sometime in the late 1640s, Giovanni Borromeo commissioned Melchiorre Gherardini (1607–1668), an up-and-coming Milanese painter, to produce a canvas for the stateroom of the castle of Angera.[1] Titled *Giovanni Borromeo Drives the Goths out of Rome* (fig. 4.1), the painting is less interesting for its artistic value than its double entendre. Though ostensibly depicting a battle scene in fifth-century Rome, the allusions to the present must have been palpable to an audience "used to reading events in terms of 'type and antitype'—in which earlier events could be seen as prefiguring occurrences in the present or future."[2] While it remains questionable whether an ancestor of Giovanni Borromeo's really participated in the pushback against the Visigoth sack of Rome in 410—the earliest record of the Borromeos dates from the fourteenth century—Giovanni Borromeo's valiant resistance against the barbarians of his day, the French, seemed beyond doubt. By the time the painting was ordered, he had fended off two French attacks on Milan. In 1636 and 1644, he had repelled French-led coalition armies when they invaded his possessions on Lake Maggiore, establishing himself as a paladin of the anti-French cause in the state that his ecclesiastical forebears, the two archbishops Carlo and Federico Sr., had sought to steel into a second Rome.

The portrait was a direct intervention in the debate over Giovanni's legacy that was raging within governing circles at the time. Giovanni himself consistently fashioned himself as a military hero of a new kind. The model of noble heroism he emulated was heavily indebted to the core assumptions that underpinned Olivares's project: that the nobility's pursuit of military glory, far from being an egotistical enterprise, fed the *reputación* of the king and was, therefore, conducive to the common good.[3] Giovanni sought to portray his acts of derring-do as part of the common defense policy of the monarchy and reap the benefits Olivares had promised to his clients. To his opponents, representations such as the painting at Angera exuded a different message: solipsism. Giovanni's adversaries increasingly

---

[1] Zuffi, "La pittura," pp. 395–6; Natale, *Le Isole Borromee*, pp. 140–1.
[2] Adamson, "Policy and Pomegranates," p. 166.
[3] See Sandberg, *Warrior Pursuits*, pp. 147–8.

Aristocratic Power in the Spanish Monarchy: The Borromeo Brothers of Milan, 1620–1680. Samuel Weber, Oxford University Press. © Samuel Weber 2023. DOI: 10.1093/oso/9780198872597.003.0006

Fig. 4.1 Melchiorre Gherardini, *Giovanni Borromeo Drives the Goths out of Rome*, c.1650, oil on canvas, Angera, Rocca di Angera, Sala dei Fasti Borromeo
(Università degli Studi dell'Insubria—International Research Center for Local Histories and Cultural Diversities, Archivio Fotografico, Fondo Vivi Papi—all rights reserved)

saw the idea of serving the dynastic interests of the house of Habsburg by adding luster to one's own *casato* as a contradiction. The defense of Lake Maggiore, in this view, looked more like a self-serving ploy than the vital contribution to the strengthening of Habsburg interests in Italy as which Borromeo billed it. By the mid-1650s, these voices became more insistent. The powers that be made it clear that the much-maligned self-interest was not limited to venality, as Borromeo had believed, but comprised the pursuit of dynastic glory, a volition that was now construed as incompatible with princely service. When Giovanni came to collect the rewards for his ministrations, it was these arguments that were deployed to eject him, at the eleventh hour, from the circle of high nobles he had worked so hard to join.

In probing the downfall of Giovanni Borromeo, this chapter traces the function of charges of corruption in seventeenth-century politics.[4] Historians of the Spanish monarchy working on the crown's American possessions have recently pointed to the surprisingly complex anti-corruption measures adopted by

---

[4] The two most significant publications are Malcolm, *Royal Favouritism*, and Valladares, ed., *El mundo*.

THE DECLINE AND FALL OF AN *OLIVARISTA*   83

successive governments from Olivares forward.[5] Driving this anti-corruption consensus was the interest of competing factions to instrumentalize charges of malfeasance against rivals in order to tweak the balance of power in their favor.[6] While this had been true of earlier transitions of power, such as the passage from Lerma to Olivares (see chapter 1), the weaponization of anti-corruption was especially stark during the final days of the rule of the last minister-favorite, Olivares's successor, Luis Méndez de Haro.[7] As the last *valido* left the stage and power began to be shared between an oligarchy of equals from Spain's high nobility, the way princely service was defined changed dramatically. The pursuit of individual *reputación* that had been the beating heart of favoritism yielded to conceptions of disinterested princely service in which dynastic concerns needed to be subordinated to the wider interests of the monarchy.[8] By weaponizing this redefinition against competitors, the reformed governing elite purged pushy *olivaristas* like Giovanni from its ranks, plunging the Borromeos of Angera into a profound crisis.[9]

Spanish Honors and Rewards

If the Angera painting was a representative rendition of the way Giovanni saw himself, the written record of the period reinforces the same message of noble heroism. When discussing his stunts on Lake Maggiore, Giovanni's younger brother, Federico, praised him for his extraordinary bravery, writing at one point: "Your tireless work shows to me that you are only satisfied with those endeavors that would be impossible to anyone else."[10] Federico repeatedly lauded his sibling as a hero willing to put his life on the line for his subjects and his king. Reviving ancient myths of Alexander the Great popular among aristocrats at the time, Federico extolled Giovanni as a new "Alessandro."[11] As in contemporary France, Alexander served as a model for nobles who put their "military genius at the service of [their] king and country" in a bid to heighten the glory of the monarch, as well as their own dynasty's.[12] To the extent that there was an inherent tension at

---

[5] González Fuertes and Negredo del Cerro, "Mecanismos," p. 449.

[6] Ponce Leiva, "Acusaciones."

[7] Andújar Castillo, Feros, and Ponce Leiva, "Corrupción," p. 296; for earlier debates, see Mrozek Eliszezynski, *Bajo acusación*.

[8] Engels, *Die Geschichte*, pp. 28, 74.

[9] On the shifting nature and the function of accusations of corruption, see Bernsee, *Moralische Erneuerung*; Bernsee, "For the Good"; Asch, Emich, and Engels, "Einleitung."

[10] Federico IV to Giovanni VII Borromeo, Benevento April 20, 1647: *ABIB*, FB, Federico IV, Corrispondenza 1645–1655.

[11] Federico IV to Giovanni VII Borromeo, Benevento March 10, 1647: *ABIB*, FB, Federico IV, Corrispondenza 1645–1655.

[12] On the French nobility, see Bannister, *Condé*, p. 83; Sandberg, *Warrior Pursuits*, p. 117.

84 ARISTOCRATIC POWER IN THE SPANISH MONARCHY

work here—the threat of noblemen elevating themselves above the king—Giovanni seems to have been oblivious to it.[13]

In fact, other sources confirm this heroic self-image. While much of the written record has gone missing, the portrait that Galeazzo Gualdo Priorato, a military chronicler writing in the second half of the seventeenth century, penned provides an excellent precis of Giovanni's understanding of his role. Writing with uncritical "devotedness" to the men who had made history in the bloody first half of the century, Gualdo Priorato was adamant that his was a panegyric on his subjects' "splendors."[14] In Gualdo Priorato's rendition, Giovanni was "one of the most generous and splendid knights of our days." He shone as a paternalistic and disinterested administrator of the king's army: "He was most patent in his military work, friendly with the soldiers, and charitable with those who deserved it." "Most disinterested in all his dealings," the sole driving force of his actions was a desire to burnish "his own reputation" and "glory," something that evidently did not strike Giovanni as a contradiction.[15] Indeed, so beholden was he to the Olivares consensus that he held on to a contrived opposition between selfish "interests," meaning monetary gain, and the pursuit of "reputation" and "glory" long after the count-duke's fall. If the former deserved condemnation, the latter was part of a collective endeavor in which the glory of the nobility added credit to the ruling dynasty.[16]

Part and parcel of the *olivarista* conception of service was the conceit that the heroic nobles who had contributed to the monarchy's defense deserved to be rewarded. Hence in 1656, Giovanni Borromeo dispatched an agent, Giorgio Sorino, to the court of Madrid to participate in the "bidding war" that had been unleashed by the warrior nobility.[17] In a *pourparler* with the Count of Haro sometime in 1657, Sorino informed the minister-favorite that Giovanni had loyally served the house of Habsburg as commissioner-general, but after eleven years in that post, "the count is now tired" and he wished to be promoted to a "higher-ranking military position."[18] Which office Giovanni wanted remained unclear. Sorino's initial brief was to push his name for the post of general of the cavalry and the generalate of armed men in the Milanese State.[19] Yet when the current holder of that office failed to be removed, Giovanni did not come up with an alternative. Instead, he charged ahead with his plan to resign without a concrete

---

[13] On this tension, see Asch, *Herbst*.

[14] Gualdo Priorato, *Vite*, p. 1. Mark Bannister and Katia Béguin have made a similar use of panegyrics to reconstruct the self-fashioning of the prince of Condé. See Bannister, *Condé*, p. 5, and Béguin, *Les Princes*, pp. 57–60.

[15] Gualdo Priorato, "Giovanni," unpag.

[16] For examples from France, see Bannister, *Condé*, p. 94; Sandberg, *Warrior Pursuits*, pp. 147–8.

[17] On Sorino, see Galli and Monferrini, *I Borromeo*, p. 126, n. 204. The term "bidding war" is David Parrott's. See his *1652*, p. 261.

[18] Memoriale [no date]: *ABIB*, FB, Giovanni V, Carriera militare.

[19] On Haro, see Malcolm, *Royal Favouritism*, pp. 3–5 and passim.

THE DECLINE AND FALL OF AN *OLIVARISTA*   85

project for his future. His younger brother egged him on, suggesting that he seek a sinecure that was "honorable, advantageous and not difficult to obtain" in return for the "service rendered."[20]

Others in Giovanni's entourage warned of the negative consequences of his entitlement. On hearing the "rumors" doing the rounds in Milan, Giovanni's cousin from the main branch, Renato, buried the hatchet and besought him to carefully "weigh your decision" to resign.[21] While he conceded that Giovanni's current appointment "is really tiresome and annoying," he also reminded him that quitting without solid guarantees was aleatory. There were, in fact, many who aspired to inherit Giovanni's position. What is more, they would probably be able to secure it "thanks to favors from influential people and money," which would tempt more than one government minister to take Giovanni at his word and dump him in "some airy and seemingly purely honorific position." Having worked for decades to reach the top of the Spanish monarchy, Renato believed, Giovanni ought to think twice before turning himself into the butt of "ridicule of those who are not favorably inclined toward us."

Renato's fear turned out to be well founded. Alonso Pérez de Vivero, Count of Fuensaldaña (r. 1656–1660), the Spanish governor who had taken over from Giovanni's protector Caracena, saw Giovanni's behavior as excessive assertiveness, an act of disobedience even. On Fuensaldaña's request, the Council of State ruled on December 5, 1658, that unless Giovanni "adjusts himself to what he has to do and shows, with submission, respect, and humility, that he wants to continue in his post," Philip IV should proceed to replace him without the premium he was hoping for.[22] With his downfall looming, a panicking Giovanni ate his own words. Where he had once cited ennui and tedium as the main reason for his plans to resign, he now claimed health issues had precipitated his decision: when he announced his plan to step down, he clarified that he had fallen from a horse four months earlier and had needed to carry "his right arm at the chest."[23] More generally, he was "full of ailments in body and spirit," which had necessitated him to seek permission from the governor to leave Milan twice to cure himself. To make matters worse, his wife had fallen ill and passed away soon thereafter without having produced any offspring. Pleading for leniency, he enjoined the monarch that he "remedy, at least in appearance," given the serious reasons that had led to Borromeo's temporary retirement. Regretting his bluffing, he emphasized that he had "done everything he could," and that it had never been his "intention to leave the king's service."

---

[20] Federico IV to Giovanni VII Borromeo, Lucerne July 25, 1656: *ABIB*, FB, Federico IV, Cariche.

[21] This and the following quotes are from Renato II to Giovanni VII Borromeo, Peschiera Borromeo October 28, 1656: *ABIB*, Giovanni V, Carriera militare.

[22] *Consulta* of the Council of State, Madrid December 5, 1658: *AGS*, EST, leg. 3374, f. 131.

[23] This and the following quotes are from 5.o memorial presentado miercoles 14 Ag.o 1658: *ABIB*, FB, Giovanni V, Carriera militare.

86   ARISTOCRATIC POWER IN THE SPANISH MONARCHY

In Fuensaldaña's view, Giovanni's actions directly contradicted that claim. His decision to quit had come in the thick of the rout in the battle of Valenza in September 1657. The citadel in southwestern Lombardy had been attacked by a coalition army of the king of France and the duke of Modena and surrendered to enemy forces after eighty-two days under siege.[24] The shellacking choked Spanish superciliousness, making it plain to many contemporaries that after two decades of war, the Spanish army in northern Italy was rapidly disintegrating.[25] Having taken over as governor in the midst of the siege, Fuensaldaña bore the brunt of the blame for this triumph of French arms. In a letter to Philip IV announcing the loss of Valenza, he bemoaned the fact that "the clients, relatives, and friends of my predecessors" were eager "to erase the blame they might have had for this incident" and to pass the buck to "me alone, as if I had not arrived here when the stronghold had already been under siege for fifty days."[26] Amidst the blame game, some, including Giovanni Borromeo, preyed on Fuensaldaña's weakness to wrangle over their writ. When two of his officers disobeyed Borromeo's orders, he appealed to the governor, and when Fuensaldaña refused to come to his rescue, Giovanni announced that he was unwilling to "leave his reputation exposed [to attacks] any longer," and retired to his suburban castle at Origgio, north of Milan.[27] To Fuensaldaña, the facts were crystal clear: his reputation was so precious to Borromeo, he was willing to forsake the monarchy in one of its darkest moments. His conduct had been, if not quite an act of rebellion, then certainly one of insubordination, which did not make him deserving of the guerdon to which Giovanni seemed to think he was entitled. Fuensaldaña was not the only one to think this way. As the author of a legal brief penned at Borromeo's behest put it euphemistically, Giovanni was increasingly being subjected to "displays of mistrust rather than respect toward [his] disinterested and zealous operation."[28] Little did the author know that the conflict would soon spiral into an active interrogation of the purported disinterestedness that had landed Giovanni the position of commissioner-general a decade earlier (see chapter 3).

The Campaign against Giovanni Borromeo

For those who cared to look closer, the standoff with Fuensaldaña followed a distinct pattern: it was only the last item in a long list of similarly unedifying episodes in which Borromeo had placed his honor above the common cause.

---

[24] Socini, *L'assedio*, p. 3.
[25] Considerat.ni sincere intorno l'Essercito di S. M.tà nello Stato di Milano (1657): *ASM*, Atti di governo, Militare p.a., cart. 2. See Maffi, *Il baluardo*, pp. 58–9.
[26] Fuensaldaña to Philip IV, Tortona December 9, 1656: *AGS*, EST, leg. 3374, 18, f. 1.
[27] Memoriale [no date]: *ABIB*, FB, Giovanni V, Carriera militare.   [28] Ibid.

THE DECLINE AND FALL OF AN *OLIVARISTA*   87

It had been just a few weeks into his appointment as commissioner-general of the army in 1646 when Giovanni initiated his first feud with Antonio Arias Sotelo (?–1649), the governor of the fortress of Alessandria.[29] Given the remoteness of the area and its sensitive location wedged between the territories of minor potentates, the *castellano* of Alessandria had traditionally been possessed of powers to allocate troops in the area.[30] When Borromeo was nominated commissioner-general, he was given notice that his powers did not extend to the area known as the Oltrepò, the Lombard territories south of the Po river around Alessandria.[31] Unwilling to put up with this age-old convention, Giovanni demanded with characteristic entitlement that "I be shown justice and given what I am owed."[32]

The clash between Borromeo and Arias Sotelo soon reached the courts of law. In a legal brief, Giovanni denied that Arias Sotelo had ever possessed the prerogatives he was laying claim to. If Arias Sotelo's predecessors had occasionally overstepped their authority, this had always been recognized as an "abuse" of powers.[33] Listing a series of precedents reaching back to the reign of Philip II, Giovanni framed his plea as the "defense and preservation of the jurisdiction of his office [as commissioner-general]" and a way to squelch "the unrest, harm, and inconvenience that have come to pass because of this innovation." The king's men in Milan, Borromeo went on, had an obligation to "preserve...the pre-eminence, usefulness, and proper functioning" of his office. To add heft to his entreaty, Borromeo roped in the support of friends in high places. The city of Milan, in a petition written at Borromeo's behest, implored Philip IV to furnish Giovanni with the same prerogatives as his predecessors: the representatives argued that it would be useful to "those vassals" and "Your Majesty" in equal measure if the administration of such a sensitive area as the Oltrepò were in the hands of a trusted member of the local nobility. Giovanni's voice was heard. A special committee of the Secret Council, a representative body of Milanese nobles set up to assist the governor in making strategic decisions, ruled in Borromeo's favor.[34]

Responding to this verdict, Arias Sotelo launched a counterattack in which he questioned Borromeo's disinterestedness. In a letter of support written on his behalf, the city of Alessandria stuck up for a local "minister" who "sees our desolation with his own eyes" and "will not allow that Your Majesty's subjects in said

---

[29] On Arias Sotelo, see the *consulta* of the Council of State, Madrid March 16, 1647: *AGS*, EST, leg. 3363, f. 172; Hanlon, *Italy 1636*, pp. 112, 138; Maffi, *Il baluardo*, p. 168, n. 58.

[30] Anselmi, *"Conservare,"* pp. 167–70.

[31] Condestable de Castilla to Giovanni VII Borromeo, Milan May 13, 1646: *ASM*, Atti di governo, Militare p.a., cart. 324, fasc. Oltrepò in genere, f. 14/2.

[32] Giovanni VII Borromeo to the Condestable de Castilla, Milan [no date]: *ASM*, Atti di governo, Militare p.a., cart. 324, fasc. Oltrepò in genere, f. 14/3.

[33] This and the following quotes are from a *consulta* of the Council of Italy, Madrid October 16, 1646: *AGS*, SSP, leg. 1807, f. 14.

[34] Secret Council to the Count of Haro, Milan December 20, 1647: *ASM*, Atti di governo, Militare p.a., cart. 324, fasc. Oltrepò in genere. The first decision was handed down as early as June 27, 1646: ibid. On the Secret Council, see Cremonini, "Il Consiglio," esp. p. 242.

88 ARISTOCRATIC POWER IN THE SPANISH MONARCHY

province will be put under more pressure than they can bear."[35] In his own brief, Arias Sotelo painted Borromeo as an out-of-touch nobleman whose sole concern was to further the interests of his clients instead of looking after the well-being of the communities in Lombardy. Voicing what is probably one of the earliest attacks of Borromeo's handling of the *case erme* (see chapter 3), Arias Sotelo pointed out the need of leaving the administration of troop stationing in the hands of a simple Spanish soldier such as himself rather than a local aristocrat. "Since the governors [of Alessandria] are always Spaniards who do not hold land or property in the province, they will lodge the troops with more equity than the commissioners-general, who are always locals and do have [land and property], as well as relatives and friends, which is why they are necessarily interested."[36]

To Arias Sotelo's mind, the handling of his dispute was a case in point. Giovanni had been saved by the very same coteries who he wanted to cajole by dumping Arias Sotelo. As he explained, the Secret Council comprised "four relatives" of Borromeo's, which had yielded inevitable results: "Although they know that justice is on my side," the councilors had closed rank and, driven by their "passion," had voted to suit the interests of one of their own.[37] Arias Sotelo portrayed the whole episode as a David-versus-Goliath story in which Borromeo could not only count on his "more refined style," but also on "many relatives, ministers, and friends who will take his side" to traduce a "soldier who has been serving Your Majesty for forty years of active war." Biased institutions preferred a power-hungry nobleman over a conscientious military specialist.

When reviewing the case, the Council of State in Madrid agreed with Arias Sotelo. The councilors concluded that Borromeo's sole fear was "that, after so many years of service, his reputation will suffer," while Arias Sotelo had comported himself responsibly, going as far as to "waive his right for the duration of the [military] campaign," so as not to "hamper the king's service."[38] Still, given the stakes, Madrid saw no other way than to cave to Borromeo and excise the powers Arias Sotelo and his predecessors had held for many decades.[39] As Arias Sotelo had predicted, social standing trumped technical considerations when the going got tough.

A similar picture emerged in Borromeo's feud with another army functionary. No sooner had his tiff with Arias Sotelo ended than Borromeo openly questioned the *maestro di campo generale*'s prerogatives to oversee the movement of officers across the State of Milan.[40] On paper, the division of labor between these two

---

[35] City of Alessandria to Philip IV, Alessandria [no date]: *AGS*, EST, leg. 3363, f. 178.

[36] Legal brief [no date]: *AGS*, EST, leg. 3363, f. 174.

[37] This and the following quote are from Antonio Arias Sotelo to Philip IV, Alessandria October 5, 1646: *AGS*, EST, leg. 3363, f. 173.

[38] *Consulta* of the Council of State, Madrid May 16, 1647: *AGS*, EST, leg. 3363, f. 172.

[39] Order of Philip IV to the governor of Milan, Madrid March 27, 1647: *AGS*, SSP, leg. 1808, f. 370.

[40] Decreto del Sig. Contestabile di Castiglia sopra la differenza vert.e tra il Castellano di Milano don Gio. Vazquez Coronado, & il Commissario Generale dello Stato Conte Giovanni Borromeo [no date]: *ASM*, Registri delle cancellerie, serie XI, pezzo 2, p. 292.

functions seemed clear enough: the *maestro di campo generale* was a military specialist who assisted the governor and commander-in-chief in moving troops on military grounds.[41] The commissioner-general, on the other hand, was not part of the military hierarchy; his was a "political" office charged with guaranteeing that troops were distributed with "equity and proportionality" between communities.[42] Borromeo niftily turned this argument on its head to widen the remit of his office. He claimed that in order to lift the burden off of some communities, the commissioner-general needed to be involved in decisions regarding troop allocation. The fact that officers regularly put more strain on the king's vassals than was allowed made it necessary to quarantine officers from soldiers and station them in different locations.[43] Juan Vázquez Coronado, the *maestro di campo generale*, would have none of it. Officers were the "most eminent members" of the military, and even the dramatic conditions in which many communities found themselves afforded Borromeo no right to station "the highest ranks (*las primeras planas*)" of the military at will.[44]

The Spanish authorities in Milan shared Vázquez Coronado's point of view. While they never mentioned it explicitly, they certainly implied that Borromeo's bold plan to administer troop movement under the guise of the current emergency was a maneuver to be more responsive to backhanders from communities who wanted to avoid hosting troops. They concluded that Borromeo used the potential for social unrest in Milan to extend the ambit of his office and to undermine the commander-in-chief by laying claim to responsibilities that were "alien to his office and beyond its limits."[45] Governor Caracena was adamant that Borromeo "cannot order anything to a village ... without arrogating" powers that transcended the narrow remit of his office.[46] In his view, Borromeo's point of honor on the issue was an act of "disobedience worthy [of being used] to teach a lesson to others in order to preserve the authority of the governor and his orders."[47]

In spite of these warnings, the Council of State in Madrid decided to wait out the crisis. While it seemed clear that Borromeo had none of the prerogatives that he had grabbed, it seemed politically expedient not to beard him. In "such turbulent times," it was "not only right but necessary to see to it that [the king's] subjects be relieved."[48] Given this, it made sense to entrust Borromeo with the prerogatives that he claimed for himself. As the Council of State phrased it, "this matter must not be judged according to the lesser rules and principles of a contentious prerogative but according to the superior reasons and maxims of justice and convenience at the heart of it, which have to be taken into account in a

---

[41] *Consulta* of the Council of State, Madrid August 27, 1648: *AGS*, EST, leg, 3366, f. 13/1v; Maffi, *Il baluardo*, pp. 159–60.

[42] *Consulta* of the Council of State, Madrid August 27, 1648: *AGS*, EST, leg, 3366, f. 13/7r.

[43] Ibid., f. 13/4r.   [44] Ibid., f. 13/6r.   [45] Ibid., f. 13/8r–v.   [46] Ibid., f. 13/3v.

[47] Ibid., f. 13.   [48] Ibid., f. 13/9v.

90 ARISTOCRATIC POWER IN THE SPANISH MONARCHY

controversy of this sort."[49] The "position and condition of the subject" meant that Borromeo's defection "would be a loss for Your Majesty's service." A lenient treatment would not only help to keep Borromeo in line, but would send an important signal to other Milanese nobles at a time when the monarchy was under attack from all sides: "Besides its ties to, and dependence on, the house of Borromeo, the [Milanese] nobility views this office as theirs and its convenience as their own, because of the hope" of many to be appointed to it one day. In light of this, Caracena was advised to act as an authority figure and try to liaise between Borromeo and the *maestro di campo generale* while being careful not to enrage the former. Painful as it was to admit, the Council of State concluded, this nondecision was the only course of action the monarchy could afford to take. In these fraught times, the only safe way was to ensure that "no party, at this point, wins, or can pity itself for losing, or stops hoping for justice." Such a blunt admission of impotence in the face of the local warrior nobility did not sit well with Caracena, who had hoped to see Borromeo punished for his delaying tactics that had imperiled military operations.[50]

Some of the repeated conflicts involving Borromeo were, of course, systemic. What looked like a military hierarchy on paper was often a muddle of competences and privileges that frequently contradicted each other and forced the governing elite to constantly strike a balance between conflicting normative frameworks.[51] This, however, is only one part of the explanation. The truth is that often neither of the parties involved had any interest in reaching a clear definition of their duties. Accounting for this was the fact that the writ of an office was sutured to the personal honor of its holder.[52] In the political culture of the seventeenth century, any attempt to whittle away at prerogatives was seen as an assault on the officeholder's honor, an attack to be fended off on pain of the complete loss of reputation.[53] In fact, one of the main problems in these conflicts was that Borromeo, a representative of the high nobility, refused to bow to lower-ranking Spanish military experts.[54] Reared in Olivares's military culture in which the social function inevitably trumped military necessity (see chapter 2), Borromeo made a virtue of what successive governors described as disobedience, the malicious use of the monarchy's desperate situation to extend his own powers and, by corollary, his own glory.

The flipside of this relentless quest for *reputación* was that Giovanni actively jeopardized Spanish military supremacy. For instance, the events that Borromeo had weaponized most to consolidate his reputation as a Habsburg surrogate—the siege of Arona in 1644 (see chapter 2)—had been marred by a conflict over precedence. The painting commissioned for the castle of Angera displayed his military

---

[49] This and the following quotes are ibid., f. 13.   [50] Ibid., f. 13/3r.
[51] Maffi, *Il baluardo*, p. 209.   [52] Ago, *Carriere*, p. 14.   [53] Ibid., p. 144.
[54] Maffi, *Il baluardo*, p. 215.

THE DECLINE AND FALL OF AN *OLIVARISTA*   91

triumph as an exploit that was his alone. But part of the reason why he was forced to fend off the Franco-Savoyard coalition army on his own was a conflict of precedence that had prevented support troops reaching Arona. The troops that trickled into Angera on the opposite shores of Lake Maggiore were commanded by Giovanni Pallavicino, a knight of Malta who held the same military rank as Borromeo. As the Franco-Savoyard army took aim at the fortress of Arona, Pallavicino's status sparked a row over precedence between two men of the same rank, which ended with Pallavicino staying put in Angera, unable to intervene in what Giovanni's obsession with precedence might well have turned into a rout for Spanish arms.[55] Retrospectively, the perilous behavior at Arona was the first in a long series of occurrences in which the social function of the military eclipsed its technical one to the detriment of an ongoing military operation.

If this contradiction had been a built-in mechanism of the Spanish army under Olivares,[56] in the late 1640s and early 1650s, many within the military hierarchy began to see the blending of social and technical functions as a drain on time and resources. When Borromeo began renegotiating his prerogatives in the Oltrepò with Arias Sotelo's successor, Pedro González del Valle, in the 1650s, the military establishment turned against him.[57] Taking heed of Caracena, the Council of State advised Borromeo to seek "moderation" and to "keep himself within the limits to which he is entitled, without asking for more than his predecessors."[58] In light of Giovanni's chronic overreach (and the crown's toleration of it), more and more within the Spanish governing elite took note. From their angle, Giovanni's career now looked like a succession of points of honor that were a dangerous distraction from a war threatening to tear the monarchy asunder. When he retired, without consideration and consultation, in 1657, many had long had enough of what even his own brother openly described as Giovanni's "obstinacy and caviling." As he remarked forbiddingly in a letter to Giovanni's wife, Giovanni was "headed for serious problems and a major breakdown [in relations] simply because he does not want to give in on any point…Let us hope that, God willing, this will not be the ruin of the house, for which Count Giovanni should have so much consideration."[59]

The Fall of Giovanni Borromeo

Exacerbating "the serious problems" his brother had anticipated was Giovanni's nerve in putting in a request for admission to the Order of the Golden Fleece at

---

[55] Besozzi, "Cronistoria," p. 289.
[56] See Maffi, *Il baluardo*, pp. 209–10, 215–6; for similar problems in Flanders, see González de León, *The Road*, pp. 207–8.
[57] *Consulta* of the Council of Italy, Madrid April 24, 1653: *AGS*, SSP, leg. 1810, f. 245.
[58] *Consulta* of the Council of Italy, Madrid November 22, 1657: *AGS*, SSP, leg. 1811, f. 202.
[59] Federico V Borromeo to Isabella Arcimboldi, Rome March 29, 1657: *ABIB*, FB, Federico IV, Corrispondenza 1656–1664.

92 ARISTOCRATIC POWER IN THE SPANISH MONARCHY

the height of the crisis. The Order of the Golden Fleece was a tight-knit and exclusive community of high nobles, founded in 1430 by Philip the Good of Burgundy.[60] In the sixteenth century, it had become a preserve of the Castilian high nobility and select sovereign princes from across Europe. By the early decades of the seventeenth century, access to the order was being widened to nobles lower down the social ladder.[61] As a result of the rise of the minister-favorite, requests from members of the peripheral nobilities in places like Italy became more frequent.[62] In the difficult decades of the Franco-Spanish War, the number of titles awarded to this group grew exponentially: research has shown that the granting of honorary rewards first doubled, then trebled during the reign of Philip IV.[63] Under the minister-favorites' watch, the conferring of symbolic signs of distinction became an integral part of the reconstructed relationship between the king and a nobility desperate to showcase its inner qualities with external markers.[64] The result was an inflation of pleas, which in turn devalued the honorifics of those who had already been endowed with them.[65]

If symbolic markers of the sort were closely associated with the government of the minister-favorite, that era was coming to an end. To be sure, Olivares's position had been taken over by the Count of Haro, but his hold on power had always been more tenuous than his predecessors'. For the first time in decades, the *valido* was no longer the focal point of a patronage network: under Haro, other grandees had been able to preserve a share of power.[66] Slowly but surely the court of Madrid was morphing into "a framework of different clientage networks led by a group of men who were united in their loyalty to the *valido*, but also by their close connections with each other."[67] Over the course of the 1650s, Haro shrank into a *primus inter pares*, with the minister-favorite being subsumed into "an oligarchy of equals" who ran the monarchy collectively.[68] The *valimiento* had relied on the fiction that the minister-favorite observed noblemen's behavior and rewarded them accordingly. Under the new dispensation, the nascent oligarchy in Madrid was eager to take on the role of supreme judge.[69] In the Spanish court, the eclipse of the last minister-favorite seems to have fostered what Jay Smith has called "the ideal of autosurveillance, a surveillance exercised over and *by* the servants of the king," who were to pass judgment on the actions of their peers and, if necessary, block their advancement.[70] Their task was to drive home the message to the provincial nobilities that "the glory of birth loses all its luster when it is not

---

[60] Spagnoletti, *Principi*, p. 52.   [61] Donati, *L'idea*, pp. 279–80.
[62] Spagnoletti, *Principi*, p. 57.   [63] Hanlon, *The Twilight*, p. 118.
[64] Spagnoletti, *Principi*, p. 70; Asch, *Nobilities*, p. 12; Dewald, *Status*, p. 14.
[65] A similar inflation plagued France. See Parrott, *1652*, pp. 261–3.
[66] Malcolm, *Royal Favouritism*, pp. 138–9.   [67] Ibid., p. 139.   [68] Ibid., p. 244.
[69] On similar developments in France, where the function was taken on by Louis XIV himself, see Smith, *The Culture*, ch. 4.
[70] Ibid., p. 268.

accompanied by loyalty and other civic virtues," as one pamphleteer phrased it at the time.[71]

The first to experience the full thrust of the new autosurveillance was the nobility of Spain's southern Italian possessions. Rattled by the popular uprising that had rocked the Kingdom of Naples, the Spanish governing elite first showered loyal clans with unusual honors before proceeding to put them in their place.[72] Among the many losers of the restoration of Spanish power in Naples, Giangirolamo Acquaviva (1600–1665), a nobleman who ruled over large swaths of land in and around Conversano and Nardò in Apulia, stood out. The clan's history with the crown had been marred by bouts of disloyalty, with the Acquaviva repeatedly threatening that they would side with the French to topple the Catholic king as ruler of southern Italy. By the 1640s, however, the counts of Conversano had come around, reinventing themselves as vehement supporters of the Habsburg cause. When Acquaviva's subjects rebelled in the Masaniello revolt and laid bare his track record of gratuitous violence against his vassals, he joined forces with other nobles in the kingdom to quash a rebellion that was calling into question his own predominance in the region. Once law and order had been restored, Acquaviva made a bid for a grandeeship and a Golden Fleece for his son, citing his services to the crown in putting down the insurgency of 1647–1648. This plea was duly rejected. The crown argued that although Acquaviva maintained that he had fought for the king, the "squinter of Apulia," as his cowed subjects called him, was really fending off an attack of his peasants against his brutal rule.[73] What he and his secretary were trying to sell as loyal royal service was, in actuality, brazen self-interest. In the crown's view, the fact that Acquaviva's petty ambitions dovetailed with the designs of the monarch was not sufficient grounds for him retrospectively to argue that he had been acting for the king alone. As Elena Papagna paraphrases the crown's reasoning, Giangirolamo may have stood up "to save the crown but, even more so, to safeguard himself from the subversive thrust of other social groups."[74]

Though the sources are fragmentary, it seems likely that Giovanni Borromeo fell victim to the same dynamics. His agent Sorino followed the example of Giangirolamo Acquaviva's representative in the Spanish court and produced a flurry of briefs in which he portrayed Giovanni's merit as part of a long family tradition of military service, with the virtue of birth reinforcing the merits of the individual.[75] Borromeo, Sorino argued, was a "knight of many qualities and so

---

[71] Crescenzio Romani, *La Monarchia*, p. 32.

[72] See Minguito Palomares, *Nápoles*, pp. 144–7, 175, 227–9, 232–3.

[73] Spagnoletti, "Giangirolamo," pp. 10–1, 14.   [74] Papagna, *Sogni*, p. 123.

[75] For Giangirolamo Acquaviva, see Spagnoletti, "Giangirolamo." Borromeo's briefs are in *ABIB*, FB, Giovanni V, Carriera militare. If these manuscripts were printed, as seems likely, I have been unable to locate them. On this conception of nobility, see Smith, *The Culture*, and Dewald, *Aristocratic Experience*, ch. 1.

94 ARISTOCRATIC POWER IN THE SPANISH MONARCHY

many merits, both inherited and of his own, from a house that is eminent and slavishly devoted to the king's service."[76] The new oligarchs in Madrid were desperate to undo this narrative. Borromeo's agent suspected at the time that an embittered Fuensaldaña was the driving force behind this rewriting of history.[77] However, internal documents show Paolo Spinola, Marquis of Los Balbases (1628–1699), to be the instigator. Los Balbases knew Borromeo well, having assisted multiple governors in their dealings with Giovanni's caviling over precedence over the past decade. When Giovanni came knocking on the door of the Council of State, Los Balbases was ready to take him down.

As the institutions in Madrid saw it, Borromeo had failed to match up to the responsibility he held as a nobleman. Not only had the *case-erme* scandal shown that the king's Milanese subjects had been ill-served by a reckless governing elite,[78] but with his repeated power grabs, Borromeo had torpedoed the war effort in a bid to extend his writ at the expense of military specialists. With the benefit of hindsight on the most dramatic years of the monarchy, it was impossible to argue in good faith that Giovanni's pursuit of individual power and grandeur had furthered the larger cause he claimed to be advancing. The image of the *olivarista* hero he was continuing to affect no longer convinced at a time when others had cut back on individual aspirations in the face of the great distress of the 1650s.[79] The acts of bravery on Lake Maggiore that he had painted by one of the emerging artists of the day now looked like a self-interested stunt to protect his landholdings and, as his uncle had insinuated earlier, fashion himself as a responsible seigneur to subjects who had long lost belief in the fiction that undergirded the Borromeos' involvement with the Spanish crown. Reflecting broader trends elsewhere, the oligarchs in Madrid equated the heroism of the warrior nobility with naked ambition and nudged it in the direction of implicit accusations of intentions to undermine the monarch's authority.[80] In this climate, the Council of State unceremoniously shelved Borromeo's application for admission to the Order of the Golden Fleece.

What played out in the court of Madrid was what Pierre Bourdieu calls a "classification struggle." As Bourdieu scholar Steven Loyal explains, this is a form of "worldmaking," "a cognitive struggle for the power to impose the legitimate vision of the social world—that is, the power to (re)make reality by establishing, preserving or altering the categories through which agents comprehend and construct the world."[81] Giovanni, like all *olivaristas*, plied his mind to believe that the elevation of the sovereign houses whom the nobility served was a result, a byproduct almost, of the self-aggrandizement of their servants. Yet, that model of elite

---

[76] Memoriale [no date]: *ABIB*, FB, Giovanni V, Carriera militare.   [77] Ibid.
[78] *Consulta* of the Council of State, Madrid March 30, 1656: *AGS*, EST, 3373, 18, f. 3v.
[79] Maffi, *Il baluardo*, p. 224.
[80] Jiménez Estrella, "La corrupción," p. 140. For France, see Bannister, *Condé*, p. 94.
[81] Loyal, *Bourdieu's Theory*, p. 84.

THE DECLINE AND FALL OF AN *OLIVARISTA* 95

integration had brought on widespread disruption, leading to multiple uprisings across the Hispanic world in the 1640s as the alienated masses took to the barricades to clamor for the restoration of the commonwealth that *olivaristas* like Giovanni had sworn to uphold. In response to this pressure from below and through a revival of old arguments,[82] more nimble elements within the ruling elite in Madrid sought to redefine good governance as the ability to put the interests of the king and the monarchy ahead of individual dynastic concerns.[83]

In the process, the striving for *reputación* became associated with "interested" actions, that is, venality. As the minister-favorite was obliterated, the high aristocrats who inherited his position worked hard to impose their definition of royal service on their competitors in the scramble for shrinking resources. Drawing on images of good kingship,[84] they took it upon themselves to weed out the corruption of the king's disloyal servants. The *olivarista* conception of royal service—the idea that the pursuit of family interests would somehow reflect on the house of Habsburg—was negated as private interests were being more neatly sundered from public ambitions.[85] They redefined "self-interest" (*interés* in Spanish, *interesse* in Italian): what had hitherto been circumscribed as monetary gain was expanded to include the search for glory for one's house. Based on this semantic shift, they crushed Giovanni's dream of joining their ranks.[86]

The changes to the way in which the imperial elite thought about princely service were momentous, though historians do well to question the sincerity of this new commitment. According to Gianvittorio Signorotto, the novel rhetoric was less indicative of profound changes in attitude than of a shifting balance of power within the elite.[87] The governor who ended Giovanni's career, Fuensaldaña, was probably as self-interested as his predecessors. The *Congregazione dello Stato*, who had earlier agitated against Giovanni Borromeo's administration of the *case erme*, complained that Fuensaldaña was not "the great man as whom Don Luis de Haro depicted him": he had turned out to be much more interested in the "advantages" of life than in really advancing a reform agenda.[88] Indeed, what goaded the new oligarchy in Madrid to adopt the particular line of argument against Giovanni was opportunism. In this sense, G. W. Bernard's reminder rings true here: "courtiers and ministers who accused others of corruption were not engaged in a moral crusade intended to purify public life, but rather were out to seize a moral advantage and to embarrass their rivals."[89]

---

[82] Jiménez Estrella, "'No ha interesado,'" pp. 166–7.

[83] On this shift, see Malcolm, *Royal Favouritism*, p. 182.   [84] Corteguera, "King."

[85] For similar developments in France, see Rowlands, *The Dynastic State*, p. 341.

[86] To date there is no detailed study of the term's changing meaning. For a limited contextualization of its uses in the Catholic Mediterranean, see Emich, Reinhard, von Thiessen, and Wieland, "Stand," pp. 236–7; von Thiessen, "Der entkleidete Favorit," p. 131; Kettering, *Patrons*, p. 31.

[87] Signorotto, *Milano*, p. 71.

[88] Congregazione dello Stato, Milan September 26, 1656, quoted in Signorotto, *Milano*, pp. 59–60.

[89] Bernard, "'A Water-Spout,'" p. 135. Also see Engels, "Corruption," p. 173, and Ponce Leiva, "Acusaciones."

96   ARISTOCRATIC POWER IN THE SPANISH MONARCHY

As Robert Bernsee has shown in his study of late-eighteenth-century Germany, charges of corruption proved particularly effective to invalidate an old order (and implicitly lend legitimacy to a new one).[90] As a recomposed nobility captured the monarchy, its members used their weight to legitimize their own self-interested categories of public service and to reject alternative claims to predominance.[91] When the *olivarista* service nobility showed up to collect its dues, the novel oligarchy had recourse to an alternative conception of princely service to discredit as corrupt what had once been a perfectly acceptable way of engaging with the monarchy—indeed, one that had been encouraged by the center.[92] In a bid to license the nascent oligarchic form of government, the in-group weaponized the notion of disinterested service and retrospectively applied it as a benchmark to exclude competitors from the court. It was a classic case of new powers shifting and readjusting the prevailing value system.[93] As the truly powerful in the field, they were "in a position to make it function to their advantage" by tailoring "the immanent rules of the game" to their needs.[94] As a disgruntled nobleman from the Kingdom of Naples remarked at the time, the political leaders of the post-*valido* age had effectively "destroyed the engine of our hopes...and fabricated the exaltation of their glories on the ruins of our credit and merit with His Majesty," leaving "not one part of our loyalty free from their slander."[95]

Like this Neapolitan, Giovanni Borromeo appears to have been left behind by one of the most significant "transformations in the structure of the field of power" of his time.[96] He seems to have been taken down, if not by the commoners whom he had exploited to make his way to the top, then at least by the arguments they had brought forth. His subjects on Lake Maggiore had been the first to question Giovanni's motives, suggesting that what was peddled as a mission to protect the monarchy and its subjects might, in reality, be a solipsistic quest for dynastic aggrandizement. Partly in reaction to their petitioning, the 1650s witnessed the rise of nobles invested in an ethic of royal service with which Giovanni's record of accomplishment was bound to clash. Despite his best efforts, the sort of capital he was able to invest could no longer be parlayed into symbolic power.[97] In the ongoing "struggles over the imposition of a new definition of legitimacy," Giovanni's understanding of public service had failed to prevail.[98] The preservation of the collective good as he and his erstwhile protector had defined it jarred with new ideas foisted upon a debilitated aristocracy from below.

---

[90] Bernsee, *Moralische Erneuerung*, p. 29.
[91] This is a classic classification struggle. See Swartz, *Symbolic Power*, p. 36.
[92] Jiménez Estrella, "'No ha interesado,'" pp. 151–2, 168.   [93] Swartz, *Symbolic Power*, p. 35.
[94] The quote is from Bourdieu and Wacquant, *An Invitation*, p. 99.
[95] Quoted in Rovito, "La rivoluzione," p. 456.
[96] The quote is from Bourdieu, *The State Nobility*, p. 336.   [97] Eribon, *Returning*, pp. 175–80.
[98] The quote is from Bourdieu, *The State Nobility*, p. 338.

THE DECLINE AND FALL OF AN *OLIVARISTA*   97

As far as Borromeo himself was concerned, the monarchy had failed to keep its end of the deal he had entered with Olivares three decades earlier. By accusing him of egotism, the new aristocracy in Madrid rescinded the unwritten contract on which Giovanni had become entangled with the Spanish monarchy. Having banked on a military career to be lavished with the highest honors the king of Spain could vouchsafe, Giovanni ended up going home empty-handed. A combination of greed and unfavorable circumstances had prevented him entering the closed ranks of the pan-Spanish governing elites taking shape in the second half of Philip IV's reign. In their private letters, the Borromeos openly described the unexpected turn of their fortunes as evidence of the crown's "ingratitude" for years of loyal service on the terms laid down by none other than Olivares.[99]

Conclusion

Worn down by the inglorious end of his career, Giovanni retreated to religious life. As a founding member and patron of the Accademia dei Faticosi, which was housed inside the Theatine monastery of Sant'Antonio Abate in Milan, he dedicated himself to intellectual pursuits. His younger brother Federico had long feared that "handling arms and the sword too much" would deprive him of the "custom of handling the pen."[100] Now that his time as a "soldier" had expired, he could finally unleash his inner "refined courtier," for which his education under the guidance of Archbishop Federico Sr. had groomed him.[101] Giovanni followed his brother's advice. In the late 1650s, he produced a number of erudite treatises in which he put his sophisticated intellect on show.[102] As his brother wrote in 1659 in an attempt to lift Giovanni's mood: "Your hunting, breeding horses, and playing *pallone* give the lie to those who said that you are unable to adapt to a new climate, and thus I pray the Lord to save you for the more fortunate and prosperous times that will come in the end."[103] Alas, these "more fortunate and prosperous times" never materialized. Giovanni died unexpectedly the following year, aged 45 and childless, with the whiff of disloyalty to the king of Spain still hovering over him.[104]

---

[99] Federico IV to Giovanni VII Borromeo, Lucerne April 24, 1659: *ABIB*, FB, Federico IV, Corrispondenza 1656–1664.

[100] Federico IV to Giovanni VII Borromeo, Rome February 6, 1638: *ABIB*, FB, Federico IV, Corrispondenza 1634–1644. On aristocratic education, see Gaston, "All the King's Men."

[101] Federico IV to Giovanni VII Borromeo, Rome March 24, 1635: *ABIB*, FB, Federico IV, Corrispondenza 1634–1644. On Giovanni's education, see Lezowski, *L'Abrégé*, pp. 310–1.

[102] Carpani, *Drammaturgia*, pp. 9–11; Cremonini, *Le vie*, pp. 64–5. On the uneasy alliance of culture and war, see Sodano, *Da baroni*, pp. 35–6, 40–1, 238–40.

[103] Federico IV to Giovanni VII Borromeo, Lucerne April 24, 1659: *ABIB*, FB, Federico IV, Corrispondenza 1656–1664.

[104] Bosca, *De origine*, p. 159.

98   ARISTOCRATIC POWER IN THE SPANISH MONARCHY

The torch passed to Giovanni's younger brother, Federico Jr. As a member of the clergy, he was in a much better position to push the family agenda forward in an age when his more ethical standards were required to make headway. What Loïc Wacquant calls the "social division of the labor of domination" swung into action as "ecclesiastical authority was deployed to justify and thereby solidify the rule of the new warrior class" that had sowed bitter division.[105] This old trick, dating back to the Middle Ages, worked a treat. In a stunning reversal of fortunes, Federico would use the 1660s to carry his brother's Hispanophile legacy forward and ensure that the Borromeo family finally got a seat at the negotiating table in Madrid.

Federico's was no small feat for a family that had been brought to its knees by opposition to its self-aggrandizement. The Borromeos had come to venerate military entrepreneurship as a roadmap to success in the age of the minister-favorite. To rationalize this interested behavior, they claimed that they were pursuing military careers to protect the poor and needy in their fiefs. Yet, as time wore on and dynastic interests pulled them toward a catastrophic war against the French crown, that position became steadily more untenable: the blatant contradictions that had marred the Borromeos' project of social affirmation from the outset were rendered unmissable by the family's jingoistic pursuit of a bloody conflict. Much as Giovanni tried to capitalize on the battles he was fighting in the family's fiefdom on Lake Maggiore, his efforts were brought to naught by the people in whose name he was supposedly acting. As the Borromeos unleashed the sanguinary horrors of the Franco-Spanish conflict on ordinary people, they spurred village communities into unprecedented activism for what these ordinary Milanese, borrowing the language of their social betters, referred to as the common good.

If such demands originated at the bottom of the pile, they soon traveled up the social ladder, and it was at that point that they wrongfooted the Borromeos. Desperate to save its pre-eminent position in society in the face of protest from below, the hegemonic faction of the nobility redefined self-interested behavior as the pursuit of glory for one's own dynasty, which had been at the heart of Olivares's conception of service. Impelled by popular agitation, these aristocrats divorced the pursuit of individual *reputación* from ideas of the common good and took down the most vocal champions of what now stood exposed as an oxymoron. As a new conception of princely service gained traction, there emerged a reformed courtier nobility that saw its purpose in administering good governance to the king's subjects rather than in feathering its own nest. While it was too late for Giovanni to turn the ship around, his brother, Federico, would deploy his credentials as a man of the Church to do just that. By positioning himself as a disinterested servant of the house of Habsburg and a champion of good governance, he would single-handedly save the Borromeos of Angera from what, for a short moment in the late 1650s, looked like certain oblivion.

---

[105] Wacquant, "Foreword," p. x.

PART II
BLEARING

5

"A Faithful Vassal of His Majesty"

Federico Borromeo as Papal Nuncio and the Ideology of Disinterested Service

The first occasion for Federico Borromeo Jr. to prove the house's continued loyalty to the Habsburgs after Giovanni's demise did not go well. In the fall of 1665, Federico had finished a 10-year stint as papal envoy to the Swiss Confederacy and was on his way to Rome, where a new appointment in the papal court awaited him. As he passed through the State of Milan, he stopped over in the family's holdings at Origgio and sent a messenger to the Spanish governor in the capital. In his letter he requested to meet Luis Ponce de León (r. 1662–1668), not "in public, as is usual," but rather "incognito and without the ceremonies that would be customary" on such occasions.[1] Referencing a specifically early modern ceremonial practice, the nuncio asked the governor that both men strip themselves temporarily of their identities in order to steer clear of conflicting claims to rank that would otherwise arise.[2]

Such a plea was the stock-in-trade of any diplomat in the early modern period. But in Federico's case, it stirred controversy because, in addition to being a representative of the papacy, Borromeo was also a subject of the king of Spain. His entreaty could therefore be construed as an audacious move on the part of a Milanese feudatory keen on interacting on a par with the Catholic king's alter ego in Milan. This is exactly how Ponce de León chose to read Borromeo's petition. Even though Borromeo cited important precedents of governors who had met him while resting in their bed (a token of respect in seventeenth-century society[3]), Don Luis had no time for what he perceived as a brazen request for special treatment and an attack on his credentials as a representative of the king.[4] If Borromeo refused to meet his overlord like any other "subject and vassal,"[5] Ponce de León reasoned, this was because of the "grudge of that house, which dates back to the time when Count Juan served as commissioner-general" and "quit for some

---

[1] Pedro de Aragón to the Council of State, Rome September 29, 1665: *AGS*, EST, leg. 3038.
[2] For a history of incognito encounters, see Barth, *Inkognito*.   [3] Karsten, *Künstler*, p. 219.
[4] On the self-image of Spanish viceroys in Italy, see Guarino, *Representing*, p. 18; on ceremonial conflicts with ambassadors, see ibid., pp. 31–2.
[5] Zapata to Ponce de León, Milan September 24, 1665: *AGS*, EST, leg. 3038.

Aristocratic Power in the Spanish Monarchy: The Borromeo Brothers of Milan, 1620–1680. Samuel Weber,
Oxford University Press. © Samuel Weber 2023. DOI: 10.1093/oso/9780198872597.003.0007

102   ARISTOCRATIC POWER IN THE SPANISH MONARCHY

quarrel" with Governor Fuensaldaña.[6] The family prelate's stubborn insistence on specious prerogatives was a petty vendetta for Giovanni's comeuppance.

For Federico Borromeo, these accusations were a direct attack on the image of himself as a disinterested servant of the papacy and the Spanish king that he had constructed over the course of his 10-year stint in Switzerland. There, the second-born Borromeo had used his ecclesiastical offices, and the status they conferred upon him, to advance the interests of the clan whose reins he had taken over after Giovanni's passing. One of his trump cards was the idea of disinterestedness that contemporaries generally ascribed to members of the clergy.[7] Federico himself liked to claim that "as a priest" he did everything "without interest."[8] His training as a future cardinal had endowed him with a conception of public office that was more in line with the new understanding of princely service in vogue among the new oligarchy in post-*valido* Madrid. As a celibate cleric, his conception of office had always been more clearly disjointed from dynastic concerns than Giovanni's. This made him the ideal candidate to advance the interests of the house of Borromeo in the austere climate of the 1660s. As in the Sacchetti family studied by Irene Fosi, Federico the family cleric became "the positive, safe, and prestigious representation that the house had to offer" to the outside world in an age when the privileged felt an urge to legitimize their existence in novel ways.[9]

The second element conspiring toward his success was the momentous changes his protector, Pope Alexander VII Chigi (r. 1655–1667), had initiated in the papal court. After serving Innocent X Pamphili (r. 1645–1655) in the capacity of secretary of state amidst the collapse of papal nepotism, Chigi overhauled the papacy's diplomatic service to respond to the pontiffs' dramatic loss of standing in Europe's society of princes. Doing away with the outward signs of nepotism, Chigi's moral cleanup buoyed up a new generation of cardinal hopefuls, often associated with the so-called *Squadrone Volante* faction in the college of cardinals, who made the most of their training as conscientious papal administrators. Federico Borromeo was one of the rising stars of this reinvigorated diplomatic apparatus. Having been insufficiently implicated with the nepotism of the first half of the seventeenth century, he grabbed the mantle of disinterested service and convincingly presented himself as a dispassionate papal servant committed to strong ties with the Spanish crown. Although the years spent in Switzerland furnished ample evidence of his Hispanophile inclinations, Governor Ponce de León forced Federico to position himself even more clearly lest he compromise his project of rebuilding the burned bridge to the court of Madrid.

---

[6] Ponce de León to Philip IV, Milan September 27, 1665: *AGS*, EST, leg. 3038.

[7] Signorotto, "La 'verità'," p. 204.

[8] Federico IV to Giovanni VII Borromeo, Rome August 6, 1639: *ABIB*, FB, Federico IV, Corrispondenza 1634–1644.

[9] Fosi, *All'ombra*, p. 192.

The Education of Federico Borromeo

One day in 1625, Federico Borromeo Jr., then aged 8, put quill to paper and announced a fateful decision to Federico Sr., his great-uncle, the cardinal-archbishop of Milan. In the epistle, he voiced his wish "that you let me keep this priest's vestment because (to tell you the truth) I feel a strong desire to."[10] For the addressee of this letter, this was a major triumph. Aristocratic families in Catholic Europe usually partook in a specific "social division of labor" by grooming first-borns as heads of household and cadets as clerics.[11] The Borromeos had in the past struggled with the ready acceptance of that division of roles between brothers.[12] As noted in chapter 1, Federico Jr.'s father and uncle had failed to reach an agreement on who pursued which career, and this quarrel had culminated in a division of estates on Lake Maggiore and deprived that generation of a family cardinal. One generation on, however, the second-born son seemed to accept the destiny the order of birth had assigned him. Where his father's generation had actively rebelled against their fate, Federico reassured his great-uncle that he wanted nothing more than "to be able to serve you perfectly, and to meet the expectation you have placed in me."[13]

One of the key factors in yielding the desired outcome was the boarding school, the Congregazione dei Santissimi Chiodi in Siena, to which Federico Jr. had been dispatched at the tender age of 6.[14] The school was to inculcate in him a habitus that made him internalize the norms and practices of aristocratic culture. The objective of such an education, writes Karin MacHardy, was to teach young boys to "perceive opportunities for, and collaborate in, the requirements of social and dynastic reproduction."[15] What they were meant to acquire was, in the words of Pierre Bourdieu, "necessity internalized and converted into a disposition that generates meaningful practices" and, by corollary, the preservation of inherited social position.[16] In Federico's case, this sheltered upbringing far away from the temptations that lurked outside the world of organized religion seems to have been sufficient to bring about what Renata Ago calls the "internalization of family interests" and to foster his voluntary acceptance of the role the order of birth had wrought for him.[17]

The early separation from the family setting and the transfer to a religious institution had yet another function: it served as a character-building exercise, setting the future cleric up to withstand the indignities of the competitive court in

---

[10] Federico IV to Federico III Borromeo, [Siena] December 13, 1625: *BAM*, mss. G 254 inf 370.
[11] On the "social division of labor," see Wacquant, "Reading," p. 156.
[12] On the roles of brothers, see Álvarez-Ossorio Alvariño, "The King"; Ago, "Ecclesiastical Careers."
[13] Federico IV to Federico III Borromeo, [Siena] December 13, 1625: *BAM*, mss. G 254 inf 370.
[14] Galli, "Federico IV Borromeo: Scelte," pp. 297–8.   [15] MacHardy, *War*, p. 166.
[16] Bourdieu, *Distinction*, p. 170.   [17] Ago, "Giovani nobili," p. 406.

104 ARISTOCRATIC POWER IN THE SPANISH MONARCHY

Rome where Federico was likely to pursue his career.[18] By the early seventeenth century, the papal court was pullulating with aspiring cardinals: it has been estimated that at any given time 150 young men were gunning for a red hat.[19] With everyone scheming to gain advantage in a system based on favorability rather than predictability, men like Federico needed, as he himself put it, to be steeled "to feel the blow any day."[20] An important part of their education was therefore geared toward acquiring the social capital necessary to advance in the papal court.[21] Boys like Federico learned how to cultivate ties to friends in high places and, more importantly still, how to machinate against potential rivals.[22] The entitlement necessary to do the latter without too many scruples was taught them early on through the cruel treatment they were encouraged to mete out to social inferiors. Judging by the surviving evidence, this pedagogy begot startling results: when Federico's coachman was injured by a horse and died of internal bleeding a few hours later, the aspiring clergyman's main preoccupation was not the tragic death of a servant but the fact that he would henceforth have "to use a groom as a coachman."[23] Rehearsed in interactions with flunkies, solipsism of the sort was to be of service in the scrum for limited resources in the court of Rome.

If a lack of empathy was undoubtedly useful, the right sort of cultural capital was equally important. From a purely practical standpoint, the education of future cardinals was in many ways defective. As Renata Ago concluded in her study of the career paths of future prelates, the most remarkable aspect of their training was the paucity of specialization in the fields they would end up working in.[24] This was because rather than the acquisition of a set of narrowly defined skills, the main thrust of such schooling was a specific elite culture that enabled the sons of noble families to signal their belonging to an exclusive club.[25] Based on bluff and bluster, their education placed more weight on languages than theology. Latin in particular served as a marker of distinction, with a curriculum based on classical languages rather than Italian widening the gulf between the elite and the masses.[26] Even the degree *in utroque iure* (in both canon and civil law) most future cardinals attained at the end of their formal schooling was not just useful but, first and foremost, propitious to honing "the young nobleman's natural

---

[18] Fosi, *All'ombra*, p. 252; Papagna, *Sogni*, p. 132; Ago, *Carriere*, p. 46; Dewald, *The European Nobility*, p. 173.

[19] Weber, *Familienkanonikate*, pp. 171–2.

[20] Federico IV to Giovanni VII Borromeo, Malta January 7, 1654: *ABIB*, FB, Federico IV, Corrispondenza 1645–1655.

[21] Galli, "Federico IV Borromeo: Scelte," pp. 296–7.

[22] On this point, see Duindam, *Myths*, p. 32.

[23] Federico IV to Giovanni VII Borromeo, Rome July 21, 1635: *ABIB*, FB, Federico IV, Corrispondenza 1634–1644.

[24] Ago, *Carriere*, p. 43.   [25] MacHardy, *War*, p. 174.   [26] Roggero, *Le vie*, pp. 18, 46–8.

capacity for prudence, valor, grace and refined taste, all of which entitled them to serve the ruler."[27]

Pompous though they may have been, these credentials set clerics apart from their non-celibate brothers. As Ago has argued, ecclesiastics were perhaps the first among the nobility to embrace academic learning and a notion of meritocracy.[28] Federico, for one, was adamant that it was "through my studies and knowledge of things that I truly acquire the virtues" inherited from his aristocratic progenitors.[29] Defined almost exclusively by their professional status as trained jurists, cadets in ecclesiastical office could not rely on bequeathed material wealth to stay afloat. To survive, they were forced to rely on educational credentials, which, unlike other forms of capital, required hard work and unremitting discipline in the early years of their lives. Inured to deferred gratification, celibate clerics were widely seen as standing above the narrow interests that guided the actions of heads of household with their duty to bequeath as much economic and social capital as possible to their progeny.[30] Thanks to the qualities contemporaries ascribed to ecclesiastics, Federico would be ideally placed to reinvent himself as a disinterested papal servant in the early 1650s and shepherd the Borromeos out of the crisis that marred their relationship with the crown.

The Crisis of Nepotism in the Papal Court

Federico's fortunes rose as those of nepotism fell. Nepotism, as an institutionalized system of patronage, was Rome's equivalent to Spain's *valimiento* discussed in part 1: its main function was to further the integration of local elites by showering them with the papacy's material and symbolic resources.[31] The papacy's status as an elective monarchy meant that the role of minister-favorite was assigned to a close relative of the reigning pontiff, usually his nephew (*nepos* in Latin). That peculiarity aside, the cardinal-nephew in Rome, like the minister-favorite in Madrid, sought to advance the interests of his own family, as well as those of the clientele he assembled in the provinces. Such were the similarities between the two systems that Spaniards regularly described the cardinal-nephew as "his uncle's minister-favorite (*el valido de su tío*)."[32] With the average pontificate in the early modern period lasting only a few years, papal nephews had a relatively small window of opportunity during which to establish their families at the top of the Roman hierarchy and amass as much wealth as possible before the torch was

---

[27] MacHardy, *War*, p. 172.   [28] Ago, *Carriere*, p. 70; Ago, "La costruzione."
[29] Federico IV to Federico III Borromeo, [Siena] December 13, 1625: *BAM*, mss. G 254 inf 370.
[30] Ago, "Giovani nobili," p. 413.
[31] On the similarities, see Emich, *Bürokratie*, ch. I.1. and VI.3.
[32] See Visceglia, "Factions," p. 114. On the analogies between nepotism and other systems of patronage, see Menniti Ippolito, *Il tramonto*, pp. 9–10, 17.

106 ARISTOCRATIC POWER IN THE SPANISH MONARCHY

passed on to a rival clan.[33] That frantic self-enrichment, which peaked in the early decades of the seventeenth century, made nepotism especially vulnerable to criticism when a new era dawned in the 1640s.

The brewing legitimacy crisis of the institution was deepened by Pope Innocent X Pamphili's choice of favorite. In the absence of a qualified male relative, Innocent appointed his sister-in-law, Olimpia Maidalchini (1591–1657), as the gatekeeper between the pontiff and the nobility.[34] The woman in the Apostolic Palace soon faced a barrage of criticism. According to her detractors, Donna Olimpia was bad government personified. They lamented her disturbing tendency to flout "all the good rules of true politics, trampling the innocent and elevating the guilty."[35] In their eyes, her tenure witnessed a worrying preferment for relatives and old friends of the family.[36] Compounding her favoritism was Olimpia's unrestrained venality. Under her aegis, cardinals' hats were sold to the highest bidder and bishoprics exchanged hands not on the basis of a candidate's "merits and virtues but, rather, the quantity of money" he was willing to fork out.[37] Her greed was the stuff of legends. She was insatiable, her critics groaned, "like the bottom of the sea, which the more wealth it receives, the more voracious it becomes."[38] Such was her avidity that she imperiled the salvation of ordinary Christians, such as when she left entire bishoprics vacant for as long as five years so as to be able to stuff their revenues into her own pockets during the interim period.[39]

What kindled this debate was Olimpia's gender. As Marina D'Amelia has pointed out, Olimpia's handling of her role did not differ from that of her predecessors: she administered papal patronage, divvying it out to friends, withholding it from foes, all while looking after her own, converting the resources under her temporary control into opportunities to enrich the Pamphili family.[40] The real problem, in the eyes of her male critics, was that the rise of Olimpia turned the disconcerting prospect of a woman lording it over the pope into reality. Contemporaries trafficked in shocking images of a henpecked pontiff, with one of them fretting, "In the papal command of Innocent X, the moon was seen almost earlier than the sun."[41] Though conspicuous in the screeds against Olimpia, gender really served the purpose of expressing a deep-seated malaise at social processes on which gender had no objective bearing.[42] In developments mirroring those in the France of the Fronde, the "woman on top" metaphor encapsulated

---

[33] Reinhard, "Papal Power," pp. 329, 337, 339–41.

[34] D'Amelia, "Nepotismo," p. 387; Teodori, *I parenti*, p. ix.

[35] La caduta di Donna Olimpia: *Biblioteca Apostolica Vaticana, Vatican City*, Vat. Lat. 9729, ff. 263r–288v (f. 264v).

[36] Ibid.   [37] Ibid., f. 283r.   [38] Ibid., f. 266v.

[39] Quoted in D'Amelia, "La nuova Agrippina," p. 55.   [40] D'Amelia, "Nepotismo," pp. 364–5.

[41] La caduta: *BAV*, Vat. Lat. 9729, f. 263r.   [42] On this point, see Davis, "Women," p. 127.

and symbolized a rotten system that had been depleted by decades of relentless nepotism.[43]

By the late 1640s, the nefarious effects of the system were palpable everywhere. In the Papal States, the Pamphili's milking of ordinary people stoked food riots,[44] and Olimpia stood accused of "building her splendors on the destruction of her subjects."[45] Oblivious to any notion of the collective good, the critics lamented, the pope's sister-in-law had recklessly governed the commonwealth "to the detriment and destruction of the population, looking only after her own interests."[46] The situation was even gloomier on the European stage. There, nepotism was undermining the pontiff's authority among the princes whose representatives were gathering in Westphalia for the peace talks that would end the Thirty Years' War. If the papacy had long been losing influence as a peace broker, the negotiations at Münster sealed the end of papal peacemaking.[47] Protestant princes, pamphleteer Gregorio Leti (1630–1701) noted, were by now more shocked at the grifting "relatives of the popes" than the "popes themselves."[48] More worryingly still, even Catholic kings were beginning to distance themselves from a pontiff who comported himself "more like a private lord than a universal prince."[49]

By the early 1650s, the situation was dire enough for Innocent to dismiss Olimpia and hand much of her erstwhile writ over to his new secretary of state. The man he appointed to the secretariat in 1652, Fabio Chigi, was everything Olimpia was not.[50] Where her track record had been one of cronyism and greed, his was that of an austere professional. At the time of his appointment, he was a seasoned diplomat who had moved up the career ladder from the Tuscan patriciate and won his spurs as a mediator at the Westphalian peace talks. He also had no prior association with the Pamphili: they had inherited him from the previous pontiff and left him to fend for himself as nuncio in faraway Cologne. (In fact, Innocent had never met Chigi in person before his promotion to the secretariat of state.[51]) In a change from Olimpia's dissipation, his lifestyle was notoriously frugal.[52] Leti, no friend of the papacy, described him as "so devoted to evangelical life" that he seasoned his meals with ashes and slept on a bed of straw "like the world's most despicable Capuchin," while he "loathed wealth, glory, and pomp."[53] In short, Chigi was the sober professional the pope needed to rehabilitate an institution that had become associated with the selfish plundering of papal relatives and their clients.[54]

---

[43] D'Amelia, "La nuova Agrippina," pp. 45–7. [44] Bercé, *La sommossa.*
[45] La caduta: *BAV*, Vat. Lat. 9729, f. 278v. [46] Ibid., f. 274v. [47] Schneider, "Types."
[48] Leti, *Il nipotismo*, p. 16. [49] Quoted in D'Amelia, "La nuova Agrippina," p. 52.
[50] On Chigi, see Fosi, "Fabio Chigi."
[51] On the circumstances of his appointment, see Emich, *Bürokratie*, p. 419, and Menniti Ippolito, *Il tramonto*, pp. 50–1.
[52] Teodori, *I parenti*, p. 46. [53] Leti, *Il nipotismo*, p. 166. [54] Rodén, *Church*, pp. 13–4.

108   ARISTOCRATIC POWER IN THE SPANISH MONARCHY

Thanks to this posture, Chigi went from strength to strength. He quickly imposed his austerity on a court hankering for change. Living up to his reputation as a consummate official, he remodeled the secretariat of state, greatly enhancing its role in the process.[55] Until a few years prior, secretaries of state had been scribes of minor noble or patrician extraction under the thumb of the papal nephew. While Innocent's predecessor, Urban VIII Barberini (r. 1623–1644), had begun to staff the position with legally trained prelates,[56] it was only with the ascent of Chigi that secretaries of state became themselves seasoned diplomats.[57] In Chigi's plans, the secretariat of state stood at the top of a reinvigorated diplomatic network that showcased the papacy's new commitment to good governance to Catholic rulers. Reflecting Innocent's meritocratic turn, Chigi was appointed cardinal in recognition for his services to the papacy. From there, everything pointed upward. Grateful for his restoring "the reputation of the Apostolic See and ending the chatter" on the papacy's corruption, fellow members of the college of cardinals elevated him to the Apostolic See when Innocent passed away in 1655.[58] Taking the name of Alexander VII, Chigi, in his new role, continued the moral cleanup and professionalization of the papacy, working closely with the faction in the college of cardinals who had elected him, the *Squadrone Volante*.

The members of the *Squadrone Volante* were, accidentally and inadvertently, a major driver behind the professionalization of the curia. Not unlike Chigi, many of the faction's original adherents had impressive records of accomplishment in the administration of the Church and constituted an antidote to the cronies who had run the curia before Chigi's time.[59] They embodied the metamorphosis of the cardinal from Renaissance prince to loyal servant who scaled the heights of the papacy thanks to merit and talent rather than kith and kin.[60] Following Chigi's lead, members of the *Squadrone* embraced his program of clean hands. Opportunistic though this change of heart might have been,[61] their commitment to disinterested service in the name of good governance nevertheless wrought important changes in the papal court. While their espousal of professionalism was often only skin-deep, it boxed them into the pursuit of reforms, including predictable career progressions, that undermined nepotism in the long run.[62] As they consolidated their pre-eminence in the 1650s and 1660s, their ideology percolated to the new charges. With the papal missions, or nunciatures, rapidly growing in importance as a new recruiting ground for future cardinals,[63] the

---

[55] See Emich, "Die Karriere."   [56] Visceglia, "'La giusta statera,'" p. 174.

[57] Emich, "Die Karriere," pp. 347–8.

[58] The words are those of the resident of the Medici family in Rome, quoted in D'Amelia, "La nuova Agrippina," p. 62.

[59] Signorotto, "The *Squadrone*," pp. 181–2.

[60] Visceglia, "'La giusta statera,'" p. 191; Fosi, *All'ombra*, p. 253.

[61] Signorotto, "The *Squadrone*," p. 187. Also see Pattenden, *Electing*, p. 53.

[62] Rodén, *Church*, pp. 24–7, 72.

[63] On Chigi's innovations in diplomacy, see ibid., pp. 195–6.

"A FAITHFUL VASSAL OF HIS MAJESTY" 109

nuncios serving under Alexander VII readily adopted the new creed, in the hope that it would further their careers under a pope who had forsworn nepotism. Like the self-styled "disinterested defenders of universal causes" studied by Pierre Bourdieu, the new crop of papal officials had developed "an interest in disinterestedness."[64]

Federico Borromeo's Career in the Court of Alexander VII

One of the fortune-seekers who hewed to the ideology of disinterested service was Federico Borromeo. Since arriving in Rome in 1635, he had failed to make significant headway. Having struggled to climb the first rungs of the Roman career ladder under Urban VIII, his career stalled under Innocent X and Donna Olimpia, who instead promoted his toughest competitor, his cousin Giberto from the main line of the Borromeo family.[65] Much of his bad luck was down to the lack of financial support from his family, which was necessary in the early steps of a curial career when the expenditures of an office regularly exceeded the salary that was paid out to officeholders.[66] The Pamphili rated his chances of sustaining the costs of a nunciature—the ticket to the cardinalate—so low, they parked him as a local administrator of Montalto, a town in the Marches, for the better part of five years. Such were his financial dire straits, he complained, that his debts "are a ladder for my rivals and a liability for myself, for in Rome it is now a maxim that I will not be able to recover."[67] As he wrote to his family, he had resigned himself to "having a cushy time watching the merry-go-round turn until the next scene change."[68]

When the scene did change with Chigi's advent, Federico turned his lackluster career into an asset. Sensing the austere turn underway, he embraced the posture of the disinterested papal servant, saddled with debt and suffering from intermittent fever attacks and hemorrhoids,[69] who deserved a promotion but had been ignored by the powers that be for shunning their corrupt ways. (In reality, his letters indicate that his refusal to resort to venality was due to entitlement rather than genuine anti-corruption. When his brothers suggested he bribe the papal family to secure a remunerative office, he responded: "It is unbecoming of a house of the quality of ours that there should be rumors that we acquired through

---

[64] Bourdieu, *The State Nobility*, p. 382. [65] Galli, "Giberto."
[66] See Ago, "Ecclesiastical Careers," p. 274.
[67] Federico IV to Giovanni VII Borromeo, Ascoli December 8, 1649: *ABIB*, FB, Federico IV, Corrispondenza 1645–1655.
[68] Federico IV to Giovanni VII Borromeo, Rome March 11, 1645: *ABIB*, FB, Federico IV, Corrispondenza 1645–1655.
[69] Federico IV to Giovanni VII Borromeo, Montalto July 21, 1650: *ABIB*, FB, Federico IV, Corrispondenza 1645–1655.

110 ARISTOCRATIC POWER IN THE SPANISH MONARCHY

money and interested interventions what we are owed anyway."[70]) Under Chigi, Federico's greatest shortcoming—his slow advancement over the previous two decades—was construed as a sign of his willingness to defer gratification and put in long years of hard graft on missions far away from Rome before earning a spot in the more prestigious nunciatures.[71]

Chigi actively assisted Borromeo in revamping his image along these lines.[72] In an audience he had with Innocent X shortly after Chigi's appointment as secretary of state, the pope spun Borromeo's tenaciousness in the face of adversity as "disinterested conduct," and argued that his "good services" in the provincial administration of the Papal States cut him out for the diplomatic service Chigi was relaunching.[73] As the pope saw it, Federico was exactly what the papacy needed after Westphalia: a "subject who, thanks to his distinguished birth and other qualities, restored the reputation" of the pope's diplomatic network. Although Chigi first appointed him to the inquisition of Malta, he promised him "a more suitable and important post" as soon as the first nunciature became vacant. The once hapless Federico left the Apostolic Palace a new man, drunk on the "thousand signs of the remarkable praises the Holy Father, not without criticizing his own [approach to] distributive justice, has bestowed on my service."

Chigi kept his word. After his appointment to Malta, Borromeo was quickly promoted to the nunciature in the Swiss Confederacy and the Grisons. In October 1654, almost twenty years after arriving in the Eternal City, Federico was ordained to the major orders and appointed patriarch of Alexandria in Egypt, a see "in the region of the infidels" (which meant that although he now enjoyed the rank of bishop, he could circumvent the Tridentine obligation to reside in his diocese while still collecting its benefices).[74] What was an enormous boost to his standing in the court in its own right also signaled the departure for his first diplomatic mission as nuncio.[75] After two long decades, he had coaxed a post out of a hesitant pope in a place where "our house" was much appreciated by dint of the Borromeos' long-standing ties with the Swiss cantons and Carlo Borromeo's role as patron saint of Catholic Switzerland.[76] It was from there that he would

[70] Federico IV to Giovanni VII Borromeo, Rome March 25, 1645: *ABIB*, FB, Federico IV, Corrispondenza 1645–1655.

[71] Federico IV to Antonio Renato Borromeo, Lucerne December 21, 1656: *ABIB*, FB, Federico IV, Corrispondenza 1656–1664.

[72] Federico IV to Giovanni VII Borromeo, Malta September 2, 1653: *ABIB*, FB, Federico IV, Corrispondenza 1645–1655; Federico IV to Giovanni VII Borromeo, Rome October 24, 1654: *ABIB*, FB, Federico IV, Corrispondenza 1645–1655.

[73] This and the following quotes are from Federico IV to Giovanni VII Borromeo, Rome August 3, 1652: *ABIB*, FB, Federico IV, Corrispondenza 1645–1655.

[74] On bishoprics *in partibus infidelium,* see Köchli, *Urban,* p. 37.

[75] Federico's nunciature has been studied in depth in Giovannini, *Federico,* but the author's account is ideologically tinged and fails to place Federico's activities in the broader context of the Borromeos' family strategy.

[76] Federico IV to Giovanni VII Borromeo, Rome August 27, 1652: *ABIB*, FB, Federico IV, Corrispondenza 1645–1655. On Carlo Borromeo's legacy in Catholic Switzerland, see Sidler, *Heiligkeit,* pp. 157–67, and Fink, *Die Luzerner Nuntiatur,* pp. 55–6.

continue to build his reputation as a disinterested servant, a reputation that would help him save his clan from the jaws of defeat when his elder brother fell foul of the Spanish monarchy.

The task awaiting Federico Borromeo in Switzerland was formidable. Although the Swiss cantons stood outside the European society of princes, the republican entity in the heart of the continent had become a major battleground since the sixteenth century.[77] Especially in the parts of the Confederacy that had remained Catholic, pensions from the two superpowers of the day, France and Spain, remained a vital source of revenue for elites hooked on foreign patronage, and as a consequence, a French and a Spanish faction were vying for hegemony in each canton.[78] In the late sixteenth century, Spain had benefited from the French Wars of Religion and deployed its diplomatic network to acquire predominance over the ruling elites of Catholic Switzerland, enticing them with annuities and educational opportunities in Milan.[79] Yet, by the time Federico Borromeo made for Switzerland, Spain's honeymoon had long been over. A reinvigorated French monarchy had wrenched back control as the main patron of the patriciates of most cantons. In Federico's own words, the resident of the Spanish crown was struggling to "counterbalance" the French crown's patronage with "pensions and payments" from Milan.[80] In internal correspondence, Philip IV was fretting about "the risk we are running of losing that nation because of the many efforts the French are making to keep them from serving me."[81]

The papacy was equally interested in curtailing France's angling in the confessionally mixed territories on Milan's doorstep.[82] Alexander VII in particular shared Spain's assessment of Catholic Switzerland as part of its sphere of informal influence, a vital *cordon sanitaire* protecting Italy from Protestant heresies about which the French, desperate for mercenaries from the densely populated Reformed cantons of Bern and Zurich, seemed increasingly nonchalant.[83] In this climate of interconfessional *rapprochement*, Federico was determined to "to ensure that no political gain is made at the expense of religion."[84] Given these anti-French reflexes, the interests of the papacy and the Spanish monarchy dovetailed to a large degree. Federico therefore resuscitated what Paolo Sarpi (1552–1623) had once polemically referred to as the *diacatholicon*—a dispositif

---

[77] Windler, "'Ohne Geld'"; Behr, *Diplomatie*, p. 143.   [78] Ibid., pp. 143–4.

[79] Bolzern, *Spanien*.

[80] Federico IV Borromeo to Giulio Rospigliosi, Lucerne July 15, 1655: *Archivio Apostolico Vaticano, Vatican City*, Segr. Stato, Svizzera, vol. 48, f. 151r.

[81] Philip IV to the viceroys of Naples and Sicily, quoted in Minguito Palomares, *Nápoles*, p. 397.

[82] Federico IV Borromeo to Giulio Rospigliosi, Lucerne November 30, 1656: *AAV*, Segr. Stato, Svizzera, vol. 50, f. 294v.

[83] Zwyssig, *Täler*, pp. 111–6.

[84] Federico IV Borromeo to Giulio Rospigliosi, Lucerne July 20, 1656: *AAV*, Segr. Stato, Svizzera, vol. 50, f. 20v.

112   ARISTOCRATIC POWER IN THE SPANISH MONARCHY

"painted with religion but gilded with Spanish *doblas*"—to crawl back control from the French crown.[85]

The representative of the Spanish king in Switzerland proved a vital part of the coalition of the cross and the sword Federico wanted to forge. From the moment he set foot on Swiss soil Federico sidled up to Francesco Casati (*c.*1610–1667), regularly sending him such exclusive gifts as silk stockings to thank him "for the many inconveniences he suffers because of me."[86] From Milan like the Borromeos, the Casatis had the Spanish mission in Switzerland on lock, with residents from that family regularly bequeathing the office to their sons or nephews for most of the seventeenth century.[87] Deeply embedded in local society with its complex republican government, the Casatis sought to preserve local elites' loyalty to Spain by offering them access to the economic and symbolic capital of the crown and, more importantly, the markets for agricultural produce in Lombardy.[88] As specialists with strong ties to local society, the Casatis were a valuable contact for Federico, who had little prior knowledge of the Swiss Confederacy when he set out to bridle French ambitions.[89]

Given the dramatic gains the French had been making in the Swiss Confederacy proper, Borromeo and Casati increasingly concentrated their activities on the Grisons, an allied territory in south-eastern Switzerland.[90] Good relations with the Grisons' leading families were vital to secure access to the Valtelline, a valley squeezed between the State of Milan and Tyrol that served as a crucial corridor between the possessions of the Spanish and the Austrian Habsburgs. During the Thirty Years' War, the valley had been a bone of contention and had been repeatedly invaded and occupied by Spanish and French troops.[91] It was only in 1637 that the Habsburgs gained the upper hand and, in return for major concessions, restored the territory to the Gray Leagues on the condition of extended informal control over the local administration in the Valtelline.[92] The Perpetual Peace with the Spanish crown, which was signed in Milan in 1639, went on to guarantee two decades of uncontested Spanish influence in the Grisons.

By the 1660s, that hegemony had received a dent. In the wake of the Peace of the Pyrenees, French diplomats were making significant forays into the Gray Leagues. In 1659, Casati reported to the Spanish governor in Milan that envoys of Louis XIV had come within a whisker of securing a major breakthrough in the diet, the assembly of the representatives of the fifty-two judicial communities that made up the Three Leagues: had it not been for a group of "subjects who are not of their sort (*soggetti non a loro modo*)," the French would have succeeded in

---

[85] Quoted in Tarpley, "Paolo Sarpi," p. 193.

[86] Federico IV to Antonio Renato Borromeo, Chur March 1, 1661: *ABIB*, FB, Federico IV, Corrispondenza 1656–1664.

[87] Behr, *Diplomatie*, ch. II.1.   [88] Ibid., pp. 211, 216–20, 250–1; Bundi, "Le relazioni," p. 195.

[89] On their local ties, see Behr, *Diplomatie*, pp. 146–8.   [90] Ibid., p. 40.

[91] See Wendland, *Passi*.   [92] Bundi, "Le relazioni," p. 131; Wendland, *Passi*, p. 336.

concluding a defense league with the Grisons.[93] Things went downhill from there. Emboldened by their exploit at the diet, members of the French faction set up a penal tribunal to court-martial their Hispanophile nemeses as violators of the common good.[94] Among the defendants was Ulysses von Salis (1594–1674), who had turned his back on France in the 1630s and amassed enormous riches as a punter of the Spanish crown.[95] In Federico's assessment, the legal action against von Salis was an attempt to "oppress the main partisans of Spain, to intimidate those less involved, and to dissuade others from joining that faction," so as to clear the ground for an alliance with France at a later date.[96] What made this particularly dispiriting to Borromeo was the inaction of the Spanish monarchy. Oblivious to "the fickleness of the Grisonians," the Spanish authorities failed to furnish their resident with "those quick remedies their minister has been asking for on repeated missions" to Milan.[97]

One way in which Federico could support Casati was by strengthening the diocese of Chur. The judicial communities that made up the Grisons were nominally democratic and, in this spirit, almost half of them had adopted the Reformed faith in the sixteenth century.[98] As a result, the bishop of Chur, who had once been a powerful feudatory, was a lone Catholic voice amidst "heretics."[99] Catholics agreed, in the words of one member of the cathedral chapter in Chur, that the bishopric "must be taken into particular consideration by its patrons, lest this safe haven become a seminary of errors and another Geneva, which given its proximity [to Italy] would be all the more harmful."[100] Owing to the close alliance between the papacy and the Catholic king, the bishops of Chur were also important allies of the Spanish crown. Thus, when the current occupant of the diocese, Johann Flugi von Aspermont (1595–1661), passed away in the thick of the tensions over French influence in the Grisons, Borromeo helped Casati make arrangements to replace him with a man beholden to Habsburg interests.

The candidate that fit the bill was Ulrich de Mont (1624–1692). Although he had been educated in the Grisons and in southern Germany, Borromeo viewed him as much more reliable than the runner-up, Christoph Mohr, an intellectual

[93] Francesco Casati to Fuensaldaña, Chur April 2, 1659: *ASM*, Atti di governo, Potenze estere post 1535, cart. 151.

[94] Maissen, "Das bündnerische Strafgericht," and Maissen, "Parteipolitische Kämpfe"; more generally, see Färber, "Le forze," p. 135.

[95] Wendland, *Passi*, p. 199.

[96] Federico IV Borromeo to Flavio Chigi, Lucerne February 5, 1660: *AAV*, Segr. Stato, Svizzera, vol. 54, f. 51r.

[97] Federico IV Borromeo to Flavio Chigi, Lucerne February 26, 1660: *AAV*, Segr. Stato, Svizzera, vol. 54, f. 91r.

[98] Head, *Jenatsch's Axe*.

[99] Federico IV to Flavio Chigi, Lucerne October 20, 1661: *AAV*, Segr. Stato, Svizzera, vol. 55, f. 272r.

[100] Christoph Mohr to Giulio Rospigliosi, Chur April 22, 1664: *AAV*, Segr. Stato, Svizzera, vol. 58, f. 99r. The diocese's proximity to Italy was a popular trope, used liberally to curry favor in Rome throughout the early modern period. See Zwyssig, *Täler*, pp. 110–6.

114 ARISTOCRATIC POWER IN THE SPANISH MONARCHY

lightweight ("imprudent and fickle") who may have been educated in Milan but had a perilous penchant for the French and the Protestants.[101] De Mont had been friendly with the Casatis since their endorsement had earned him the post of cantor of the cathedral chapter in 1657.[102] He was duly elected in 1661. By his own admission, Casati had "no other part than some effort and some small expenses" in bringing about this outcome.[103] Borromeo, by contrast, had not shied away from fiddling with the electoral procedure to elevate de Mont. These differences notwithstanding, both Milanese representatives saw de Mont's election as their joint victory. In a letter to his principal, Casati lauded himself for his unremitting defense of Habsburg interests in the Grisons.[104] Borromeo related to Rome that he had brought light to the "muddiness of a country that is constant only in its instability."[105] (Much later, when he was already cardinal secretary of state and Casati had long passed away, he would tout de Mont as "completely my own creature in that bishopric."[106])

His perceived meddling in the election was to have a long sequel for Borromeo. The man outgunned by de Mont, Christoph Mohr, wrote a cantankerous letter to the pope and the secretary of state in which he denounced Borromeo as a Spanish Trojan horse. Styling himself as "Jerome or Bernard," he described himself as "animated by the holy spirit" and took it upon himself to "call out, with Christian liberty, those actions that stood in the way of the well-being of Christianity."[107] Both the Swiss Confederacy and the Grisons, he explained, were deeply divided along factional lines. In this nunciature ("the most important of them all"), the representative of the pope performed a critical function in staving off the "heresy always intent on spreading its poison to the bowels of Italy, the only safe haven of apostolic purity."[108] Given these safety concerns, the papal envoy's main task was to "unite the French and the Spanish ambassadors behind the same goal, which is to protect Swiss Catholics against Zurich, Bern, and the Protestant cantons, which are far more powerful than the former."[109] Thus, if it was "praiseworthy" to dispatch "nuncios that are appreciated by this or that king" to the princely courts of

---

[101] Federico IV Borromeo to Giulio Rospigliosi, Lucerne November 18, 1655: *AAV*, Segr. Stato, Svizzera, vol. 48, f. 483v.

[102] Maissen, "Die Bischofswahl," pp. 216–7; Behr, *Diplomatie*, p. 165.

[103] Francesco Casati to Fuensaldaña, Chur April 27, 1659: *ASM*, Atti di governo, Potenze estere post 1535, cart. 151. Also see Zwyssig, "Katholische Reform," p. 165.

[104] Maissen, "Zur Bischofswahl," p. 388.

[105] Federico IV Borromeo to Flavio Chigi, Lucerne May 26, 1661: *AAV*, Segr. Stato, Svizzera, vol. 55, f. 161r.

[106] Federico IV Borromeo to Odoardo Cibo, Rome August 25, 1671: *AAV*, Arch. Nunz. Lucerna, b. 119, f. 434r.

[107] Discorso di Christofforo Moro circa l'independenza che dovrebbono haver dalle Corone li Nuntij, che si mandano a Svizzeri [no date but 1664]: *AAV*, Segr. Stato, Svizzera, vol. 58, f. 101r.

[108] Ibid.   [109] Ibid., f. 101v.

"A FAITHFUL VASSAL OF HIS MAJESTY" 115

Europe, it was equally imperative to send "nuncios who act as common fathers to a country divided into multiple factions" like republican Switzerland.[110]

When Mohr matched up Federico to this ideal, he could not help but find him wanting. Being a prominent subject of the king of Spain, Borromeo was unable to act as a neutral arbiter. Quite the contrary, "Everything he said was taken as a Spanish precept."[111] His biases shone through in his every interaction. Granted, Mohr hastened to add, this was no fault of Borromeo's: if even the powerful Roman curia had "in the past" (that is, under Innocent X) had trouble "resisting the despotic will of some" monarchs, it was hardly surprising that an impotent nuncio was completely "subject to his natural prince."[112] Seeing that "the preservation or downfall of his house" rested entirely in the hands of "his natural lord," it was unavoidable that his lodestar in the nunciature was his prince rather than "the duty of office."[113] Hence, while in theory the "eyes of a nuncio have...to be blindfolded during promotions [in local churches], so as not to take into consideration the faction to which the person to be promoted belongs," papal emissaries from Spanish Italy inevitably preferred their king's "partisans, even when they are unfit," whereas the truly meritorious candidates stood no chance if they belonged to the other faction.[114]

Mohr claimed to be speaking from experience. Over the years he had been a reliable interlocutor of Borromeo's predecessors in the nunciature of Lucerne. As he saw it, things began to go downhill under the second-to-last nuncio, Carlo Carafa della Spina (1653–1654), from an eminent Neapolitan family, and reached their nadir under Borromeo. Since the advent of these Hispanophile nuncios, Mohr lamented, there had been no place for him, a cleric "in a country divided into various factions" who "longs to live without factions and only be dependent on his supreme head," the pope. Indeed, the pro-Spanish nuncios had "exposed [him] to all sorts of malicious gossip," while "the public good suffers" as a result of his non-election.[115]

Federico readily capitalized on Mohr's ramblings. He dismissed Mohr's protest as the grumbling of a sore loser who had begun to pose as a man above the fray when the coveted title had not "fallen to him."[116] Federico had initially set out to draw up a brief that accused Mohr of crypto-Protestantism, making much of the "scandalous sentiments that, to the great detriment of the Holy See, sometimes fall from his lips."[117] In the end, wielding these spiritual arms turned out to be unnecessary. As it happened, Mohr poked holes in his self-fashioning as a man of

---

[110] Ibid., f. 103v.   [111] Ibid., f. 102r.   [112] Ibid., f. 101v.
[113] Ibid.   [114] Ibid.
[115] Christoph Mohr to Giulio Rospigliosi, Chur April 22, 1664: *AAV*, Segr. Stato, Svizzera, vol. 58, f. 99v.
[116] Federico IV Borromeo to Flavio Chigi, Lucerne October 20, 1661: *AAV*, Segr. Stato, Svizzera, vol. 55, f. 272v.
[117] Federico IV Borromeo to Giulio Rospigliosi, Chur June 2, 1664: *AAV*, Segr. Stato, Svizzera, vol. 58, f. 138r. The brief is ibid., ff. 149r–151r.

116   ARISTOCRATIC POWER IN THE SPANISH MONARCHY

God above factional strife when his secret correspondence with the French ambassador and members of the court of France surfaced.[118] As Mohr was unmasked as a French agent and fled to Paris, his accusations against the nuncio unintentionally boosted Borromeo's standing with a pope who was actively pursuing an alliance with Spain. The Spanish king himself must have been even more elated. While Federico's tireless work was no substitute for the influence Spain had once enjoyed in the Swiss Confederacy, Borromeo's tenure in Switzerland helped advance Spanish interests in the Grisons at a time when France was perilously close to becoming the hegemonic power in that contested buffer zone. As their archenemy, the hapless Mohr, wrote in a letter to the French ambassador to Switzerland, Borromeo and Casati had ensured "that everyone, even those who were believed to be reliable, had become Spanish [partisans]."[119] That grudging admission of a member of the French faction was the best propaganda Borromeo could hope for in his effort to portray himself as a faithful vassal of the king of Spain.

Given this record of achievement, it must have been all the more surprising that the governor of Milan accused Federico of disrespecting the Spanish ambassador. As he sought to justify his decision not to meet Borromeo incognito, Ponce de León claimed that he was not the first representative of the king to have been snubbed by Federico. By way of evidence, he adduced Borromeo's treatment of the Spanish envoy to the Swiss Confederacy and the Grisons, Francesco Casati. According to the governor, Federico had addressed the ambassador of the French king as "Excellency" while denying the same honorific to his Spanish counterpart, whom he greeted as "Most Illustrious," the form of address common for lower-ranking nobles. In the governor's eyes, Borromeo's unequal treatment of Casati was proof positive of his "grudge" against the king of Spain that he had also exhibited in his inconsiderate request for a private meeting.[120]

Ponce de León clearly sought to make political hay out of Casati's loosely defined status. Since the Swiss Confederacy and the Grisons had always been more important to Milan's elites than the Spanish monarchy as a whole, the permanent mission in Switzerland had long been entrusted to members of the Milanese patriciate who answered to the Spanish governor in Milan rather than the king in Madrid.[121] As locally embedded administrators of royal patronage, the Spanish envoys' function was in many ways more akin to the job of a contemporary secretary than of an ambassador proper, which explains why most in the Spanish monarchy treated the Casatis as residents rather than ambassadors.[122] In light of their ambiguous diplomatic status, the Casatis had made informal arrangements with the papal nuncios. Although nuncios were technically of

---

[118] Maissen, "Zur Bischofswahl," pp. 391–2.   [119] Quoted ibid., p. 391, n. 7.
[120] Pedro de Aragón to the Council of State, Rome September 29, 1665: *AGS*, EST, leg. 3038.
[121] Behr, *Diplomatie*, pp. 107–8, 127, 132–3, 200–1.   [122] See ibid., pp. 118–27.

superior rank, both parties addressed each other with the same title ("Most Illustrious").[123] What Ponce de León sought to pass off as an act of spite was bilateral protocol to facilitate cooperation in the name of the *diacatholicon*.

Indeed, if Borromeo had questioned Casati's status, it had been to enhance his rank rather than the opposite, as Ponce de León was alleging. When rumors started circulating in 1665 that Savoy's envoy to the Swiss cantons had had his rank upgraded to that of ambassador, Casati asked the Spanish monarchy to follow suit. The rationale behind this demand was to avoid mixing up the established hierarchy, in which the nuncio occupied the first rank and was followed by the Spanish resident and the emissary of Savoy. If the nuncio were ordered to treat the ambassador of Savoy "with the title of Excellency," while he continued to address the Spanish resident with the old honorific, Casati reasoned in his plea, there would be the risk of "confusion about titles," which "could perhaps jeopardize also the remainder of the protocol (*trattamento*)." In voicing these concerns about a potential downgrade, Casati explicitly exempted Borromeo from criticism. In a letter to Ponce de León, he stressed that Borromeo had been the first to raise the issue, explicitly asking his principals in Rome to liaise with the Spanish ambassador in the papal court to clarify Casati's ceremonial rank with a view to Savoy's modifications.[124]

Given his past lobbying for Casati's status upgrade, Federico responded to Ponce de León's accusations with disbelief. In a deposition to the Spanish ambassador in Rome, Federico admitted that he had never addressed Casati as Excellency, but also pointed out that "no nuncio has ever given such a title to the count" and that Casati himself "has interacted with all [nuncios] without demanding it."[125] Having established these facts, the ambassador leaped to Borromeo's defense. As Pedro Antonio de Aragón (r. 1662–1666) saw it, the "fault for which one wants to blame said monsignor nuncio" had never been committed. Borromeo was, quite to the contrary, "a loyal vassal of His Majesty." Not only was he the son of a man who had "sacrificed his own life" for the Catholic king, but his brothers had "offered loyal and much-appreciated service to His Majesty." As for Federico himself, he had strutted his devotion to the Spanish cause "on numerous occasions during the nunciature in Switzerland," deploying his considerable clout as a papal envoy to advance the interests of the crown. Based on Aragón's report, the Council of State in Madrid threw its weight behind Borromeo, giving Ponce de León a humiliating dressing-down about his botched meeting

---

[123] This and the following quote are from Francesco Casati to Pedro de Aragón, Lucerne January 1, 1665: *ASM*, Atti di governo, Potenze estere post 1535, cart. 150, fasc. Concernenti il Trattam.to tra l'Ambasciatore di S. M.tà, et quelli di altri Principi.

[124] Francesco Casati to [Ponce de León], Lucerne April 17, 1665: *ASM*, Atti di governo, Potenze estere post 1535, cart. 150, fasc. Concernenti il Trattam.to tra l'Ambasciatore di S. M.tà, et quelli di altri Principi.

[125] This and the following quotes are from a report on a deposition of Federico IV Borromeo to the Spanish ambassador, Rome [no date but fall 1665]: *AGS*, EST, leg. 3039.

118 ARISTOCRATIC POWER IN THE SPANISH MONARCHY

with the nuncio. Reminding him that Federico had "neither in his words nor in his demands lacked in modesty," the councilors concluded that "Don Luis" should not have been "as firm in his resistance" to accede to the nuncio's request for an incognito encounter.[126] As Ponce de León was forced into an embarrassing climb-down, Federico's reputation as a disinterested servant of the Catholic king received the stamp of approval from the imperial center.

Conclusion

Federico's triumph had hardly been a foregone conclusion in the early 1650s. Given that the crisis of the 1640s consumed the papacy as much as the Spanish monarchy, his career could have ended on the same note as Giovanni's: amid accusations of gouging to the detriment of the common good. Federico was lucky in that he had been aloof enough from the merry-go-round of the papal court under the Barberini and the Pamphili to be able to draw on his habitus as a cleric and reinvent himself as an exemplary papal servant when Alexander VII Chigi ushered in a new era of clean government. A dark horse with no record to speak of, Federico skillfully used the nunciature in Switzerland to position himself as a worthy representative of Chigi's vanguard of dedicated public servants. He willingly served the pope in a hostile and culturally alien territory for more than a decade (when others were parachuted into Switzerland for one to two years). In return, his service afforded him the reputation of a stern defender of the *diacatholicon* who spared no expense to advance the interests of pope and king. In so doing, he laid the foundations for a successful future career, limberly combining the deepening of Spanish power with the concerns of the Catholic Church, while passing it off as a selfless sacrifice.

With his impeccable track record as a votary of the Catholic and Spanish causes, Federico had imposed himself as the ideal candidate to promote the future of the Borromeo family in the more austere climate after the end of the *valimiento*. In fact, Federico's biography enabled him to preserve his family's position by espousing the habitus of the critics who had taken down Giovanni: as a legally trained cleric with a commitment to public service, Federico met the expectations of the new era much better than his chivalric brother who fancied himself something of a military hero. Drawing on the culture of the Chigi papacy, Federico wed the ambitions of his dynasty to those of the house of Habsburg in ways that would allow no one to accuse him of pursuing special interests in quite the way they had done with his late brother. What is more, his service far away from Lombardy had endowed him with an understanding of Spanish interests that

---

[126] *Consulta* of the Council of State, Madrid November 26, 1665: *AGS*, EST, leg. 3038.

transcended the narrow confines of home and hearth, allowing him to stake out a vision for both Spanish Italy and the king's global empire as he moved forward. If Giovanni's family-oriented conception of upward social mobility had run aground after the eclipse of the last *valido*, Federico's service ethic was bound to make a splash in the reconstructed court of Madrid.

6

Moral Panics and the Restoration of Consensus

Federico Borromeo and the Jurisdictional Controversies in Spanish Italy

As the dust settled on the row between Governor Ponce de León and Federico Borromeo, other explanations of the bizarre incident emerged. Some suggested that what concerned the governor was not Borromeo's past as nuncio in Switzerland so much as his future as the new secretary of the Congregation of Ecclesiastical Immunity, the papal body adjudicating jurisdictional disputes. The cause of the governor's suspicion was a furtive meeting between Borromeo and the archbishop of Milan, Alfonso Litta (1608–1679), that took place during Federico's stopover in Lombardy. Litta had spent the better part of Ponce de León's tenure reviving the old jurisdictional conflicts between Milan's ecclesiastical and secular authorities. Styling himself as the successor of the two famous archbishops from the house of Borromeo, Carlo and Federico Sr., Litta had fought a relentless battle against what he perceived as intrusions of secular law enforcement into his jurisdiction. Given Federico's appointment to the Congregation of Ecclesiastical Immunity, Ponce de León had every reason to fear that Litta had encountered Borromeo in order to "soak him in his bad maxims," as a chronicler sympathetic to the governor phrased it.[1] By casting aspersions on Borromeo's loyalty to the crown, the chronicler explained, Ponce de León had tried pre-emptively "to declare him untrustworthy so that, if need be, he will always be suspect and his intimations will not be given credit."[2] Others thought this approach counterproductive. Although he initially shared Ponce de León's worries about Borromeo's appointment, the Spanish ambassador in Rome castigated the governor for his rash reaction. He warned that this public shaming of Borromeo might spur him to wield his considerable powers as secretary, which would sabotage the

---

[1] Carlo Francesco Gorani, Libro di memorie, nel quale si fa annotazione delle cose più considerevoli che succedono alla giornata: *Biblioteca Nacional de España, Madrid*, ms. 2671, f. 154r. On Gorani, see Signorotto, "La politica."
[2] Ibid.

Aristocratic Power in the Spanish Monarchy: The Borromeo Brothers of Milan, 1620–1680. Samuel Weber, Oxford University Press. © Samuel Weber 2023. DOI: 10.1093/oso/9780198872597.003.0008

monarch's interests in the ongoing jurisdictional conflicts in Milan and Naples even more than was to be expected.[3]

To everyone's relief, none of these bleak prognostications of an obdurate and vindictive Borromeo came to pass. Once he reached Rome, Federico fashioned himself as a Hispanophile troubleshooter. Following a brief stint in the Congregation of Ecclesiastical Immunity, his appointment to the prestigious nunciature in the court of Madrid three years later, in 1668, steeled his commitment to putting an end to the jurisdictional controversies in Lombardy. His earlier positions as governor in towns of the Papal States had taught him that every sovereign needed to be able to rule with undivided powers in order to guarantee law and order. Based on his own experiences, Federico came to realize that the king of Spain needed to be able to exert the same authority in his domains as the pontiff did in his. Thus, when he was appointed prefect of the Congregation of Ecclesiastical Immunity in 1671 upon his return to Rome from Madrid, Borromeo became a staunch defender of royalism, working tirelessly toward the conclusion of what was, for all intents and purposes, a concordat between the papacy and the monarchy to end the jurisdictional conflicts in Lombardy.[4] In doing this, Federico Jr. picked up where Federico Sr. had left off (see Prologue): he actively shaped the transfiguration of the clergy from recalcitrant opponents of royal governance to loyal subjects of the Spanish king, committed to a strong monarchy that acted as a regulatory mechanism in a society that had lost its way.

The motives behind this espousal of good governance were as self-serving as the earlier embrace of disinterested princely service (see chapter 5). Having seen where the indiscriminate use of patronage could lead with Giovanni's *case-erme* scheme, Federico was determined to present himself as the restorer of the very commonwealth that his late brother had undermined. In a process not too dissimilar to the one described by sociologist Stuart Hall in his work on moral panics, Borromeo exploited the upheavals that the breakdown of public order had generated in Spanish Italy: by posturing as a tough-on-crime cardinal, he sought to win back a key constituency of aristocratic rule. In a crude sense, the adoption of a good-governance agenda based on law and order restored much of the credibility that the Borromeos had lost as defenders of the common good, helping them garner the support of the middling sorts. Stepping away from the pitfalls of pecuniary patronage, Borromeo transposed the lively debate on good governance to the far less slippery stage of symbolic interventions from above. In the process, he built anew the alliance between the nobility and the "good and wise people" he had first envisaged in the trough of the crisis and that he still saw as the only viable guarantor of the social hierarchies in which he was so invested.

---

[3] Pedro de Aragón to the Council of State, Rome September 29, 1665: *AGS*, EST, leg. 3038.

[4] On Borromeo's career, see *AAV*, Congr. Immunità Eccl., Libri Litterarum, vol. 11, f. 3.

Jurisdictional Conflicts in Spanish Italy

To understand the jurisdictional conflicts that had engulfed Milan, this episode from 1665 is as good an illustration as any. In March of that year, the collegiate church of San Nazaro in Milan became the scene of a spectacular raid.[5] The chief justice (*capitano di giustizia*) of the State had ordered his officers to blow open the door and search the property "with rifles at the ready."[6] The suspect they were looking for was by all accounts a dangerous individual. A member of the minor nobility, Ludovico Landriani was accused of having hired a killer to eliminate a rival. Upon learning that he was under investigation, he had made for the closest church, where he hoped he would be immune from arrest. As the thirty officers in the chief justice's tow cornered Landriani inside San Nazaro, he allegedly shouted that he was "in a sacred place," invoking the ecclesiastical asylum that Pope Gregory XIV Sfondrati (r. 1590–1591) had granted to all alleged criminals who took refuge in places of worship.[7] The officers were unfazed by these appeals to the Holy Father. They responded that they were under orders to "catch him, even if he were on the altar."[8] When they eventually did manage to place him under arrest, Landriani was seated in a carriage with the chief justice and escorted to the Sforza castle, the seat of the Spanish government.

Such battles over the physical appropriation of ecclesiastical spaces were widespread in the 1660s.[9] Cases of presumed criminals hiding in churches had proliferated since the end of the war between the French and the Spanish crowns. In the opinion of many, ecclesiastical asylum had become a means for felons to delay and, in some instances, completely escape prosecution for the heinous crimes they had committed.[10] The attendant moral panic was boosted by the dubious role played by some of members of the clergy. Alfonso Litta in particular had become a household name across Lombardy for his diehard opposition to secular authorities' arresting felons in places of worship. In the estimation of the Spanish authorities, Litta's rabid defense of ecclesiastical asylum meant that he willy-nilly threw his weight behind men with a long criminal record. The most flagrant example they could muster was the case of Pompeo Visconti, a career criminal who had fled to the rectory of Saronno, a town north of Milan, to dodge a death sentence for premeditated murder. Even though that verdict had been handed down many years earlier, the Council of State lamented, Visconti had gotten away scot-free because "the ecclesiastics have always interpreted immunity in his

---

[5] Gorani, Libro: *BNE*, ms. 2671, f. 135r.
[6] Report [no date]: *AAV*, Arch. Nunz. Madrid, vol. 7, f. 59v.
[7] Latini, *Il privilegio*, p. 1; Signorotto, *Milano*, p. 234. More generally, see Jemolo, *Stato*, ch. 7.
[8] Report [no date]: *AAV*, Arch. Nunz. Madrid, vol. 7, f. 59v.
[9] Carrió-Invernizzi, "Usos," p. 382.
[10] See Mrozek Eliszezynski, *Ascanio*, p. 212, for similar arguments from Naples.

MORAL PANICS AND THE RESTORATION OF CONSENSUS   123

favor."[11] As a result of their petty vindictiveness against the crown's privileges, major crimes went unpunished, which provided a "bad example to others" when only "fear of punishment" would deter villains from committing similar deeds. The de facto impunity Litta promoted was "harmful to public calm" and "detrimental to the vassals."

The trope of priests conspiring with malefactors to subvert public order was widely accepted within Spanish governing circles at the time. In Naples, many of the controversies between secular and religious authorities swirled around what contemporaries referred to as "feral clerics (*chierici selvaggi*)," members of the clergy who aided and abetted "bandits" and sometimes even engaged in illicit acts themselves.[12] As in Milan, the alleged conspiracy of priests fanned the flames of a crackdown on ecclesiastical privileges in general and ecclesiastical asylum in particular.[13] In a sign of the importance Spain now attributed to ecclesiastical immunity, all the viceroys appointed to the Kingdom of Naples in this period had a solid background in the workings of the Roman curia, where the monarchy had long been lobbying for the disciplining of the clergy.[14]

Meanwhile, the clerics on the receiving end of the crusade understood the clampdown as a continuation of the war that had recently ended. Ever the polemicist, Litta quipped: "Now that the war against the French is over, another one against the archbishop has begun."[15] Governor Ponce de León had been "enjoying himself" in his disdain for "Rome" and the Catholic Church, indulging his anger "at anyone who holds jurisdictional powers at his expense."[16] So resentful was he of the archbishop's jurisdiction, Litta averred, that he was pursuing sinister plans to "tyrannically subject" the archbishopric "to his chimeras" and "turn it into a tributary, all in the belief that this would earn the king another Flanders."[17] Indeed, the "stench of atheism" Ponce de León emitted was proof of a planned transition to a state church that Litta was willing to parry with all his might.[18]

In the face of the "most patent violation of ecclesiastical immunity" that the "king's ministers" had inflicted on him,[19] Litta turned to the Congregation of Ecclesiastical Immunity in the papal court. Unlike most other administrative

[11] This and the following quotes are from a *consulta* of the Council of State, Madrid July 16, 1669: *AGS*, EST, leg. 3043.

[12] Mrozek Eliszezynski, *Ascanio*, pp. 97–100. For a general account of "feral clerics," see Mancino and Romeo, *Clero*.

[13] Mrozek Eliszezynski, *Ascanio*, p. 182; Carrió-Invernizzi, "Usos," p. 381.

[14] Álvarez-Ossorio Alvariño, "El duque," p. 177.

[15] Alfonso Litta to Vitaliano Visconti, Milan March 29, 1667: *AAV*, Arch. Nunz. Madrid, vol. 4, f. 305r.

[16] Ibid., ff. 303r–v.

[17] Alfonso Litta to Vitaliano Visconti, Milan January 24, 1668: *AAV*, Arch. Nunz. Madrid, vol. 4, ff. 339r–v.

[18] Rodén, *Church*, p. 205.

[19] Alfonso Litta to Carlo Bonelli, Milan November 15, 1663: *Archivio Storico Diocesano, Milan*, Carteggio ufficiale, cart. 86.

124   ARISTOCRATIC POWER IN THE SPANISH MONARCHY

bodies in the Curia, which dated from the late sixteenth century, this congregation had been set up relatively late, in 1626. Although more research needs to be done on the Congregation's early years and the exact circumstances of its establishment, all available evidence suggests that it was an attempt to deal with the rise of "reason of state" arguments among Italy's secular princes and the latter's wish to exert more direct control over local ecclesiastical institutions.[20] As archbishops and bishops outside the Papal States faced the difficult task of upholding ecclesiastical privileges, the Congregation was meant to provide them moral and legal succor.[21] If that kind of support had been forthcoming under its founder, Urban VIII, the Congregation had slackened considerably under his successors. Litta experienced this firsthand when he brought his case against Governor Ponce de León. In an emotional letter to the nuncio in Madrid, he complained that the cardinals on the Congregation of Ecclesiastical Immunity had "wanted to tire me out like a [hunting] dog" to collate the necessary paperwork on the current crisis only to then ignore his complaints: "The dossier was given a round of applause and never opened again."[22]

Much to Litta's chagrin, the Congregation seemed particularly reluctant to cater to the interests of bishops who fought against violations of ecclesiastical asylum. As early as 1657, the Congregation had informed Litta that although the pope wanted "ecclesiastical immunity to be inviolably preserved and observed," he would not accept "that churches and other immune places serve as sanctuaries for criminals and thugs who very often take advantage of this privilege to flee there and sometimes even to come out again to commit new crimes."[23] This cautious response to Litta was in line with broader trends. Research on the Kingdom of Naples has revealed that while the Church instructed ecclesiastics to mount a principled defense of economic privileges, it grew increasingly wary to bat for clerics who upheld ecclesiastical immunity as a cover for illicit activities.[24] Archbishops and bishops who shielded ecclesiastical immunity were given the cold shoulder. By the 1660s, the Congregation seemed to operate a policy of ignoring the petitions of valiant defenders of ecclesiastical asylum in Spanish Italy. As Litta concluded, "The jurisdictional matters of this Church [of Milan] are really fated when those in Rome either do not want to settle them, become annoyed, or think they can pretend to be working when, in reality, they are doing nothing."[25]

---

[20] D'Avenia, La Chiesa, p. 10; Signorotto, Milano, p. 236.

[21] Latini, Il privilegio, pp. 159–61. On the functioning of the Congregation, see Menniti Ippolito, 1664, and Scalisi, Il controllo.

[22] Alfonso Litta to Federico IV Borromeo, Ponte di Magenta June 12, 1669: AAV, Arch. Nunz. Madrid, vol. 4, ff. 388r–v.

[23] Bernardino Rocci to Alfonso Litta, Rome July 10, 1657: ASDM, Carteggio ufficiale, cart. 83.

[24] De Marco, "L'immunità," p. 148.

[25] Alfonso Litta to Federico IV Borromeo, Ponte di Magenta June 12, 1669: AAV, Arch. Nunz. Madrid, vol. 4, f. 388r.

MORAL PANICS AND THE RESTORATION OF CONSENSUS   125

Things became even worse when a special committee was set up in 1666 to address the growing problem of ecclesiastical asylum in Milan and Naples.[26] The ad hoc body blatantly adopted the perspective of Litta's opponents. According to the founding document, its mission was to respond to "princes' continued grievances that churches or immune places effectively serve as safe havens for the wicked."[27] The committee unquestioningly accepted the claim of secular rulers that consecrated spaces offered felons "an escape from the exemplary punishment they would have incurred if the Church had not perverted the course of justice."[28] If this open disavowal of its own bishops was not enough, the committee singled out the secular clergy, reprimanding its members for causing "manifest harm to good governance."[29] To Litta's disappointment, the committee was to toe the Spanish line.

The Spanish authorities were pleased with the special body. Instead of listening to the bishops, the committee hired one representative for Milan and one for Naples to work with the commission. In their joint statement to the committee, Danese Casati from Milan and Antonio di Gaeta from Naples did not hold back. As they saw it, immunity for delinquents constituted a "blatant abuse of the very house of God, when wrongdoers, after having sought shelter there, keep themselves busy with dishonest trade until deep into the night, continue to deal with bandits, barter, and blackmail." As such, ecclesiastical immunity was "in open contempt" of royal justice.[30] The two representatives blamed the current morass on the bull of Gregory XIV, which was being invoked by both criminals and clerics to hamper the proper administration of justice. Given the bull's nefarious effects, the two envoys demanded that it be trimmed down drastically: it was urgent to define the crimes that fell under the remit of the monarchy's prosecution, interpret the very notion of "consecrated places" more restrictively, and to remand all suspected lawbreakers in secular custody "until their case has been reviewed."[31] The Council of State in Madrid, in its discussion of the new commission in Rome, made it even clearer what the Spanish side wanted: "a fixed rule, to the satisfaction of princes," on how "to avoid controversy and to punish criminals."[32]

The special committee of the Congregation of Ecclesiastical Immunity seemed to oblige. By the early 1670s, it had drawn up a catalog of the crimes that would henceforth be exempt from immunity to apprehension in churches and other ecclesiastical buildings. In a bonfire of privileges, highway robbers and vagabonds, murderers and their instigators, arsonists, parricides, those accused of

---

[26] See Dell'Oro, *Il regio economato*, pp. 157–74.

[27] Congregatione Particolare sopra le doglianze de' Prencipi secolari circa l'osservanza della Bolla di Gregorio XIV: *AAV*, Congr. Immunità Eccl., Varia 34, f. 6r.

[28] Ibid., f. 6v.   [29] Ibid., f. 7r.   [30] Ibid., ff. 7r–v.   [31] Ibid., f. 39r.

[32] *Consulta* of the Council of State, Madrid August 17, 1669: *AGS*, EST, leg. 3043.

126   ARISTOCRATIC POWER IN THE SPANISH MONARCHY

lèse-majesté, including conspirators against the king, and counterfeiters could now be arrested in a consecrated place, for which a narrower definition was unveiled.[33] Most importantly, secular tribunals were put in charge of determining whether an alleged criminal was exonerated.[34] Early in 1672, the committee posted its "final resolution" to the nuncio in the court of Madrid.[35] In putting forth what was essentially the revocation of the bull of Gregory XIV, the Church seemed tacitly to lay waste to centuries of legal precedent and accept the end of its erstwhile privileges.

This overhaul of the extant legal order had far-reaching implications for the relationship between the papacy and the king of Spain. While the Church had always argued that the *libertas ecclesiae* had been granted by God, the Spanish monarchs asserted that privileges such as sanctuaries had been proffered by worldly leaders who were within their rights to rescind them when they were deemed detrimental to the commonwealth.[36] Antonio di Gaeta, the envoy for Naples, put the reasoning succinctly in a legal brief: "The Church is in the commonwealth, not the commonwealth in the Church."[37] Although he did not state it explicitly, di Gaeta clearly questioned the primacy of the papacy over territorial princes, nudging the Habsburg monarchy toward the Gallican positions popular in the France of Louis XIV. Where the pope had traditionally portrayed himself as the arbiter of secular princes and their realms, the Catholic king and his men were imposing themselves as the sole authority over all the monarchy's subjects, including members of the clergy, over whom they watched as supreme protectors of religion and the God-given order.[38] What the representatives from Spanish Italy had accomplished was nothing short of the legally binding subordination of the papacy to the king of Spain, which extended to the monarchy's Italian territories what had been common practice in the Iberian kingdoms and Sicily.[39]

Federico Borromeo and the Congregation of Ecclesiastical Immunity

To understand Rome's apparent surrender to the king of Spain, we need to focus on the man who was in charge of the Congregation of Ecclesiastical Immunity at the time: its secretary and later prefect, Federico Borromeo. The irony of a

---

[33] Congregatione Particolare: *AAV*, Congr. Immunità Eccl., Varia 34, ff. 127r–129r.
[34] Respuesta al informe que hicieron al Marqués de Velada y Astorga, los dos Ministros de Nápoles y Milán, en orden a su comisión, Rome May 9, 1671: *AGS*, SSP, leg. 2041, doc. 83.
[35] Congregatione Particolare: *AAV*, Congr. Immunità Eccl., Varia 34, f. 141v.
[36] Latini, *Il privilegio*, pp. 18, 34; Lauro, *Il giurisdizionalismo*, p. 31.
[37] Quoted in Latini, *Il privilegio*, p. 146; Lauro, *Il giurisdizionalismo*, p. 42.
[38] Jemolo, *Stato*, p. 92.
[39] D'Avenia, *La Chiesa*, pp. 9, 16. On some of the consequences in Milan, see Álvarez-Ossorio Alvariño, "El duque," pp. 184–9.

MORAL PANICS AND THE RESTORATION OF CONSENSUS   127

Borromeo at the helm of the battle against ecclesiastical asylum was, of course, acute. In his writings, Litta pointed out tirelessly that his robust defense of ecclesiastical immunity was a return to the hallowed "principles of Saint Carlo and Cardinal Federico Borromeo."[40] He certainly had a point. As we have seen in the Prologue, both Carlo and Federico Sr. had fought lengthy battles over the jurisdictional privileges of their episcopal see, driven by the conviction that secular authorities should at all times be subservient to ecclesiastical power.[41] Yet, if these invocations of his forebears were meant as an overture, Federico Borromeo remained unimpressed. In a complete embrace of the Spanish position, Borromeo described the man who saw himself as the successor of his famous progenitors as "extremely impatient with anyone who exercises higher jurisdiction wherever he has his hand in."[42] Like the Spanish governors of Milan, Borromeo saw Litta's defense of ecclesiastical asylum, not as a principled vindication of ecclesiastical prerogatives, but as a self-interested battle that undermined public order. Unlike Federico's ancestors that Litta was wont to cite, Borromeo seemed to believe in a state church rather than a legal patchwork that afforded the papacy partial control over the judiciary in Spanish Italy.

That repudiation of his ancestors had several reasons. To start with, Litta's telling of the Borromeo lore lacked something essential: that the Borromeos had long distanced themselves from that oppositional part of the family legacy. As we have seen in the Prologue, when Archbishop Federico had realized at the turn of the seventeenth century that the continual bickering with the Spanish authorities excluded his clan from the all-important patronage resources of the Habsburg court, he had jettisoned the confrontational approach to the Spanish governors in Milan and reinvented himself as a loyal servant of the kings of Spain. This about-face had enabled the ascendancy of the Borromeos of Angera as clients of Philip IV, of whom Federico was now the main representative. Despite the painful setback in the 1650s, the Borromeos' ties to the monarchy were too close for them to revert to the old ways of all-out opposition through ecclesiastical institutions, as Litta had probably hoped. In fact, an unofficial hagiography of Federico Sr., which Federico Jr. had published amid the controversy surrounding Giovanni, retrospectively reinterpreted the episcopate of his great-uncle as an ultimately successful attempt to end the jurisdictional conflicts. In the manner in which the Borromeos now represented their past, Federico Sr. provided a blueprint for Federico Jr.'s unapologetic championing of a close cooperation between the Church and the monarchy, not for Litta's anachronistic caviling.[43]

---

[40] Alfonso Litta to Vitaliano Visconti, Milan July 2, 1665: *AAV*, Arch. Nunz. Madrid, vol. 7, f. 54r.
[41] Annoni, "Giurisdizionalismo," pp. 141, 151–2; Prosdocimi, *Il diritto*, p. 15.
[42] Federico IV to Giovanni VII Borromeo, Bellinzona March 25, 1655: *ABIB*, FB, Federico IV, Corrispondenza 1645–1655.
[43] Rivola, *Vita*, pp. 210, 212, 216–7, 219–20, 224.

128   ARISTOCRATIC POWER IN THE SPANISH MONARCHY

The wider circumstances were equally unfavorable to a return to the jurisdictional strife of Carlo and Federico Sr. Decades of war and emergency governance had supercharged the Spanish monarchy's clout in the Italian peninsula, while the papacy's powers had been trimmed back to a purely symbolic dimension after the peace of Westphalia. Like other members of the Congregation of Ecclesiastical Immunity, Federico had come to the painful realization that the Apostolic See's illusions of omnipotence were no longer sustainable.[44] In a radically changed world, even men of the Church such as himself needed to accept the Spanish monarchy as an overarching power structure in the territories under its direct control. Secular clerics consequently had to reinvent themselves as public servants in the service of the Catholic king.

As important as geopolitics was Federico's understanding of the proper functioning of justice. As a governor in towns across the Papal States from the 1640s through the early 1650s, he had accumulated direct experience in the administration of justice, disciplining the lower orders to preserve established hierarchies, if necessary through torture.[45] According to an instruction that was handed out to departing governors, their main task was to "defend the population from extortion, offer them peace, abundance, and good governance," in short, to "make them content and devout to the prince," even if that meant cracking down on entrenched local interests.[46] Unfortunately no documentation survives of Federico's early appointments as governor in towns in Umbria and the Marches, though his private correspondence seems to indicate that he took particular pleasure in prosecuting delinquents.[47] From Benevento, an exclave of the Papal States in the Kingdom of Naples, where he served in the late 1640s, he wrote that his brief included "keeping in check all sorts of bandits, of whom there are many who come in from the Kingdom [of Naples]."[48] To preserve God's good order, papal governors believed, it was necessary to thwart the elements within society that stood ready to unsettle it.[49]

The promotion to the governorship of Rome in 1666 seems to have heightened Borromeo's awareness of the corrosive effects of criminality on the makeup of society.[50] As Irene Fosi's research into the *governatorato* in the late sixteenth

[44] Signorotto, *Milano*, p. 264.

[45] On papal governors, see Fosi, *Papal Justice*, pp. 177–8, 192–3.

[46] Istruttione d'un Signore, ò d'un Prelato, che vada in Governo nel Stato Ecclesiastico: *BAV*, Ott. Lat. 2698, f. 43v.

[47] I have been unable to locate Borromeo's official missives from this period. However, his private correspondence contains some letters to the secretary of the Sacra Consulta (the appeals court for governors) in which he detailed the crimes he prosecuted as governor of Montalto in the early 1650s. See *ABIB*, FB, Federico IV, Corrispondenza 1645–1655.

[48] Federico IV to Giovanni VII Borromeo, Rome December 30, 1645: *ABIB*, FB, Federico IV, Corrispondenza 1645–1655.

[49] Fosi, *Papal Justice*, p. 2.

[50] Some criminal sentences handed down by Federico IV Borromeo are in *Archivio di Stato, Rome*, Tribunale criminale del governatore di Roma, Registri di sentenze, vol. 14.

century has shown, one of the main concerns of this tribunal was the fight against "bandits."[51] By the time Federico held the office, the *governatorato* increasingly acted as a court committed to eradicating crime across the Papal States and building that "moral and social order" that Fosi describes as the essence of the administration of justice in the Papal States.[52] Judging by the edicts of his predecessors and his successors (his own do not survive, though the ones that do all have the same wording), the perversion of the course of justice was a cause of distress to Rome's governors at the time. The documents contain repeated injunctions not to "exempt others from the court or justice or prevent it in the free exercise of its office," singling out influential individuals who had in the past "beaten, scared, assailed, or threatened" judicial officers.[53] Desperate times called for effective justice, and law courts could no longer turn a blind eye to the powerful who subverted the social order by conspiring with criminal elements, not even if they were men of the Church.

These ideas did not arise in a vacuum. Popes, in their role as heads of state, were much more intransigent than secular princes in jurisdictional matters, having long delegated much of the spiritual jurisdiction to secular administrators.[54] Precisely because the men staffing the governorships up and down the Papal States were members of the clergy, they could undermine the authority of the episcopate in ways that would have been unfathomable to officials of other Catholic states.[55] In a development that first peaked under Sixtus V (r. 1585–1590), the Counter-Reformation papacy had begun paring back ecclesiastical privileges in the Papal States to an extent that pontiffs, in their capacity as spiritual leaders, would not brook from other princes.[56] After the Congregation of Ecclesiastical Immunity was instituted in the 1620s, the body consistently applied a different yardstick to cases from the Papal States in comparison with petitions from the Kingdom of Naples.[57] Specifically, the papacy showed few qualms about swiftly dislodging suspected lawbreakers from places of worship and handing them over to the secular authorities, something papal officials were far less tolerant of when it happened in Naples.[58] Federico Borromeo himself, in his capacity as governor of Montalto, had wrangled with the bishop of Ripatransone over the incarceration of a murderer in a monastery.[59] During these years, he had probably matured the conviction that a strong prince was necessary to guarantee order in the Papal States. From there, it must have been a short leap to the

---

[51] Fosi, *La società*, pp. 12–3, 15–6.   [52] Fosi, *Papal Justice*, p. 111.

[53] Bando generale concernente il Governo di Roma…, Rome July 28, 1670: *AAV*, Misc. Arm. IV–V, vol. 47, f. 175r. The same wording can be found in the earlier Bando generale concernente il Governo di Roma…, Rome February 1, 1658: *AAV*, Misc. Arm. IV–V, vol. 47, f. 162v.

[54] Prodi, *Il sovrano pontefice*, p. 253.   [55] Ibid., pp. 289, 293.   [56] Ibid., pp. 231–2.

[57] Ibid., pp. 233–4.

[58] Congregatione Particolare: *AAV*, Congr. Immunità Eccl., Varia 34, ff. 7v–8r.

[59] Federico IV to Giberto III Borromeo, Montalto April 11, 1652: *ABIB*, FB, Federico IV, Corrispondenza 1645–1655.

130   ARISTOCRATIC POWER IN THE SPANISH MONARCHY

realization that the Spanish king needed the same extensive powers in his realms that the pope had in his state.

While the surviving correspondence is surprisingly silent on this point, these experiences seem to have suffused his approach to the jurisdictional controversy in Spanish Italy. From the early days of his work in the Congregation of Ecclesiastical Immunity, he used the extraordinary informal power that secretaries of Roman congregations enjoyed to establish a special committee.[60] As his successor in the post, Giacomo Altoviti (1604–1693), explained, this stratagem helped circumvent discussions in the Congregation at large, which would have been "costlier, longer, more negligent, and more exposed to breaches of confidentiality."[61] A smaller subcommittee was also easier to pack with favorably inclined cardinals. The names of the men in the red hats that Borromeo had appointed speak for themselves: Giulio Spinola of Genoa, Luigi Alessandro Omodei of Milan, and Ottavio Acquaviva d'Acquaviva from Naples all hailed from families with close and long-standing ties to the Spanish crown.[62] All of them had been equally affected by the uprisings of the 1640s and, as a consequence, had come to appreciate that they needed the monarchy more than the monarchy needed them.[63] They understood that "a monarchy that seemed highly successful and seemed to display a capacity for expansion was a better guarantee of their own existence" than the rugged individualism too many of them had previously clung to.[64] Princely service, standing shoulder to shoulder with the king and assisting him in enforcing good government, was the only way to avoid being swept away by the forces that the nobility had unleashed with its self-interested actions. With the cardinals on the committee as deeply wedded to the Catholic king as the Borromeos, Federico could be sure that they would be sympathetic to his idea of handing over some of the Church's traditional powers to a monarch who was in far better shape to enforce law and order than the papacy. Like the French nobility, they saw much that was of value in a "monarch who demanded their obedience but also gave them stability, order, and material rewards."[65]

Borromeo himself was a paragon of the "duty to obey" that members of the nobility were keen to display in the latter half of the seventeenth century.[66] He was the driving force behind the new settlement. His stint as nuncio in the court of Madrid between 1668 and 1670 further deepened that commitment. In the instruction he left his successor when he departed Madrid, he characterized the bull of Gregory XIV as the "cause of endless and serious controversies over

---

[60] On the informal power of secretaries, see Windler, *Missionare*, pp. 52–4.

[61] Giacomo Altoviti, Discorso ò Riflessioni sopra la multiplicità de Card.li nelle Congreg.ni, e se si dividessero in più, come tornerebbe ciò meglio: *BAV*, Vat. Lat., 11733, ff. 225–226 (f. 225).

[62] Congregatione Particolare: *AAV*, Congr. Immunità Eccl., Varia 34, ff. 5r, 9r.

[63] Sodano, *Da baroni*, pp. 72–7, 85.

[64] On this change of heart, see Muto, "Noble Presence," p. 292.

[65] Dee, *Expansion*, p. 8. Also see Parker, *Class*, p. 108, and Beik, *Absolutism*, ch. 13.

[66] On the "duty to obey," see Cosandey and Descimon, *L'Absolutisme*, p. 231.

the various interpretations, extent, and restrictions that one wants to give it."[67] After being promoted prefect of the Congregation of Ecclesiastical Immunity in 1671, he used the power vacuum the pontificate of the notoriously frail Clement X Altieri (r. 1670–1676) had effected to hash out a settlement that was favorable to the Spanish crown.[68] When he presented the special committee's final report to the Spanish authorities, an internal memo of the Council of State in Madrid acknowledged that Borromeo had done more than anyone else to "facilitate much of what the other cardinals resisted."[69] Although he did not go as far as secular critics of ecclesiastical jurisdictions (some of whom were beginning to argue that monarchs had the right to interfere with religious precepts that undermined their absolute power), the fight against religious asylum became one of the areas in which Federico was willing to boost the power of the monarch at the expense of the papacy.[70] Convinced that Rome was in no moral position to oppose Spanish demands, he furthered, in the words of Nicolás de Antonio, the secretary of the Spanish ambassador to Rome, "an arrangement (*temperamento*) that turns discord into concord...by laying down firm rules on how to proceed," in an attempt finally "to heal this wound instead of closing it in such a manner that it will burst open again and cause even greater illness and danger" to the body politic.[71]

The Settlement of the Jurisdictional Conflicts

The crackdown on ecclesiastical privileges Federico Borromeo engineered needs to be placed in the context of the Spanish monarchy's clampdown on the Italian nobility's arbitrary powers.[72] In Naples, the men who made a name for themselves as scourges of noble impunity were the two viceroys from the house of Cardona, Pascual and Pedro Antonio de Aragón (r. 1664–1666 and 1666–1671, respectively). As the closest surviving descendants of the house of Aragon, Pedro in particular fashioned himself as the heir to Alfonso the Magnanimous (1396–1458), Naples's famed Renaissance ruler. Aragón's panegyrists depicted him as a purveyor of good government who acted in accordance with the Virgilian maxim *parcere subiectis et debellare superbos* (to be merciful to the subjected and to vanquish the supercilious).[73] In policy terms, this invented tradition translated to a platform whose main planks included the scaling back of ecclesiastical and feudal

---

[67] Memoria delle Scritture, che si lasciano à Mons.re Ill.mo Nuntio Borromeo, e ristretto dello stato dei negotij. Al Margine del med.o ristretto resta notato il termine in che si lasciano li med.i negotij à p.o di Luglio 1670: *AAV*, Arch. Nunz. Madrid, vol. 16, f. 10r.

[68] On Clement X as a ruler, see Hohwieler, *Die Altieri*, pp. 196–8.

[69] *Consulta* of the Council of State, Madrid February 16, 1672: *AGS*, EST, leg. 3046.

[70] Jemolo, *Stato*, ch. 3; Latini, *Il privilegio*, p. 385.

[71] Nicola D'Antonio [*sic*], Riflessioni sopra l'immunità ecclesiastica e bulla gregoriana (1670), quoted in De Marco, "L'immunità," p. 125, n. 7.

[72] Minguito Palomares, *Nápoles*, pp. 201–2.   [73] Carrió-Invernizzi, *El gobierno*, pp. 249–50.

132   ARISTOCRATIC POWER IN THE SPANISH MONARCHY

privileges and immunities.[74] Although more research needs to be done on the governors of Milan in the same period, contemporaries entertained few doubts that the Spanish governing elites in Lombardy were conducting a similar campaign against the nobility. Its signature intervention targeted ecclesiastical privileges. As Litta worded it, Governor Ponce de León was chasing after "royal privileges that have been lost, mortified, wiped out in the course of fifty years of war, and hence need to be restored in times of peace," by accusing the "priests" of "usurping" them.[75] In Litta's estimation, the clergy were scapegoats whose prosecution served to legitimize what was yet to come: "a new war against the country, complete with the removal of privileges and the rescinding of many laws, so that the nobility, which has prospered in peace time, does not grow insolent."[76]

The purpose of so much repression was to rope in the middling sorts for a project of a reconstructed, rules-bound monarchy. In Naples, the Aragón brothers and their successors paid particular attention to the needs and aspirations of "the so-called 'civic class' (*ceto civile*), a socially heterogeneous urban intelligentsia comprising magistrates, lawyers, jurisprudents, physicians, government officials, university professors and several aristocrats," who had been leading the reformist movements of the 1640s.[77] A similar policy shift was discernible in the Milan of Ponce de León, whose promotion of middle-class economic and political interests earned him the applause of Carlo Francesco Gorani, a chronicler particularly in sync with these milieus.[78] Though his consciousness is harder to document than the governor's, Federico Borromeo must have been animated by a similar will to defang the *ceto civile* when he sided with Ponce de León. As noted in chapter 3, Federico had been among the first to understand that the nobility of Spanish Italy could not continue to govern without winning over "the good and wise people" just below the aristocracy. If he took sides against Litta and other bishops, it is safe to assume that he did so to impress the middling sorts, on whose goodwill the future of the nobility depended.

Borromeo's approach is best explained as a calibrated riposte to a "moral panic." This term was popularized by sociologist Stuart Hall, who borrowed it from anthropologists to describe reactions to social ills that are disproportionate to the threat that the problems actually pose.[79] In his own work on the perception of street crime in 1970s Britain, Hall argued that moral panics involved the fabrication of scapegoats onto which deep-rooted social ills are displaced.[80] The task of the student of societies is to interrogate the underlying causes of the malaise

---

[74] Fernández-Santos Ortiz-Iribas, "The Politics," p. 199.

[75] Alfonso Litta to Vitaliano Visconti, Milan March 29, 1667: *AAV*, Arch. Nunz. Madrid, vol. 4, f. 305r.

[76] Quoted in Grassi and Grohmann, "La Segreteria," p. 270.

[77] Fernández-Santos Ortiz-Iribas, "The Politics," p. 199.

[78] Gorani, Libro: *BNE*, ms. 2671, ff. 22v, 45r. Also see D'Amico, *Spanish Milan*, p. 60; Tonelli, *Investire*, pp. 100–1, 103.

[79] Hall, *Policing*, p. vii.   [80] Procter, *Stuart Hall*, pp. 76, 80.

that is being projected onto potent symbols and to ask whose interests such projections serve.[81] With a nod to Antonio Gramsci, Hall argues that moral panics surface when the common sense of a society has been busted by countercultural movements and rulers have to revert to coercion so as not to lose their grip on power.[82] While they cannot be induced from above, moral panics can be helped along and nudged into being by building on a perceived breakdown of societal norms. They are a way of misrecognizing the roots of social unease that comes with the added benefit that an intractable problem appears to be solvable through a pointed intervention from on high. Outrage at certain felonies at the expense of others helps to construct "complex ideologies of crime" that "provide the basis, in certain moments, for cross-class alliances in support of authority."[83] By going after select forms of social deviance, Hall finds, the powers that be can recuperate exhausted consensus without deploying indiscriminate violence.[84]

The situation in Milan in the 1660s fits almost perfectly Gramsci's definition of a "crisis of authority." The latter "occurs either because the ruling class has failed in some major political undertaking for which it has requested, or forcibly extracted, the consent of the broad masses (war, for example), or because huge masses...have passed suddenly from a state of political passivity to a certain activity, and put forward demands" for radical change.[85] In Lombardy the values gluing society together had turned brittle. The common-good arguments on which the Borromeos had built their power had been exposed as a myth as movements from below vociferously contested the Borromeos' administration of the *case erme* and appealed to the king to force the nobility finally to make good on its promises to deliver good governance. The demise of the Borromeos' divide-and-conquer policy at the hands of subaltern actors had left behind a discontented *ceto civile* struggling with an economic base felled by decades of war and the trickling out of alternative sources of income from war profiteering.[86] As the success of Ponce de León's government indicated, there was hunger for a disciplining of nobles who had built their fortunes on the backs of the "good and wise people" of the *ceto civile*.

In this climate, Borromeo usurped the controversies surrounding religious asylum as an "articulator of the crisis."[87] By helping promote a moral panic that relied heavily on age-old fantasies about feral priests, Borromeo caricatured parts of the clergy as colluding with felons, out to destabilize the good order. Making the most of the public outrage thus generated, he then employed it as an "ideological conductor" to reboot the debate on patronage.[88] As one of his inspirations, Nicolás de Antonio, phrased it, the prominence of priests conspiring with

---

[81] Hall, *Policing*, p. 29. [82] Ibid., p. 216; Procter, *Stuart Hall*, p. 87.
[83] Hall, *Policing*, p. 177. [84] Procter, *Stuart Hall*, pp. 87–8.
[85] Gramsci, *Selections*, p. 210. [86] See Canosa, *Milano*, ch. 16.
[87] Hall, *Policing*, p. viii. [88] Ibid.

134   ARISTOCRATIC POWER IN THE SPANISH MONARCHY

criminals recast the breakdown of the social order as the symptoms of times "in which it seems there has been a competition between the rule-breaking" of the populace and "the convenience or connivance" of parts of the clergy.[89] In addressing the collapse of consent, Borromeo accepted the lowest common denominator of what had once been a sweeping reformist program: the fight against criminal priests.[90] In so doing, he narrowed the quest for change down to curbing a particular form of patronage and favoritism: the granting of religious asylum by members of the clergy. By taking a stance against men of the Church, people from the very same group to which he belonged, he could style himself as the champion of law and order, which was in turn the precondition for the realization of the common good. As he assumed leadership of the calls for good governance, he reshaped it, sluicing it toward authoritarianism.

Such a redefinition of the crisis from above had the potential to efface fault lines stemming from the social upheavals of the 1650s and arrest a revolt against the unreformed rule of a self-seeking elite. What Federico generated through his decisive action in the moral panic of criminal priests was trust in the nobility as guarantors of good government. Enlisting paternalist arguments regarding the nobility's duty of care, he reinvented himself as a champion of law and order. Federico's was an attempt to forge anew the old alliance between the established nobility and merchants Giovanni had built through pecuniary patronage (see chapter 3). With that mode of coalition building discredited thanks to interventions from below, Federico nurtured a sense of grievances in a bid to rally the *ceto civile* behind him on the symbolic issue of the prevention of crime, which lent itself much better to the idea of disinterested public service than the squandering of the king's resources. By taking it out on fellow nobles who personified bad government, Borromeo contributed to the creation of a strong monarchy that protected the material interests of the *ceto civile,* as well as his own. As a Spanish political writer would proclaim in the 1680s: "A prince has to ensure that the maxims of his government are such that they earn him the applause of his subjects."[91] By turning on Litta, Federico Borromeo made sure that private and public aspirations came to overlap to such an extent that the self-interested nature of his quest for stability would remain forever undetected. The group that stood to lose most from social change had reshaped the meaning of that term and placed itself at the helm of the effort to deliver it.

The ploy seemed to work. In southern Italy, the jurisdictional ructions solicited enormous interest among the educated public, leading to a proliferation of newspapers and the formation of an early incarnation of a public sphere. One of the most stentorian pundits of the time, Innocenzo Fuidoro (1618–1692), commented that the people of Naples had seen "great things because of the civil

---

[89] Congregazione Particolare: *AAV*, Congr. Immunità Eccl., Varia 34, f. 34r.
[90] On crime in the reformist program in Naples, see Galasso, *Napoli*, p. 70.
[91] Juan Alfonso de Lancina, *Comentarios políticos* (1687), quoted in Maravall, *La cultura*, p. 204.

MORAL PANICS AND THE RESTORATION OF CONSENSUS 135

war in the kingdom and the wars that were fought for many years between the two crowns and other Italian princes." Over all these years, their curiosity had been duly serviced by "impassioned newsmakers and newspaper men." As they eased into the postwar settlement, however, many would not let go of their "wicked curiosity" and were eager to "have news about what was happening in the jurisdictional conflicts between royalists and ecclesiastics."[92] As the authorities proceeded to arrest criminals in churches, Fuidoro cheered them on, supplying detailed accounts of the effort to suppress what he viewed as dens of crime to an avid reading public among the *ceto civile*.[93] Much less is known about such a public sphere in Milan, though there are signs that it was as vibrant as in Naples. Carlo Francesco Gorani, a representative of the *ceto civile* if ever there was one, lauded Governor Ponce de León as a scourge of vested ecclesiastical privileges, foreshadowing the enormous support Borromeo would earn once he became the most important champion of that same agenda in the papal court.[94] Across Spanish Italy, then, the campaign against priests in cahoots with common criminals cemented the monarchy's popular appeal as a provider of good and fair administration. The persecution of priests became the symbolic scraps that were thrown to those who had criticized the Borromeos' and others' privileged relations to the Spanish crown and the implications these had for the collective good.

This arrangement changed the relationship between the nobility and the king in important ways. A comparison with contemporary France is instructive here. As Patrick Collinson has argued in his study of seventeenth-century Brittany, the experience of prolonged social unrest could foster a consciousness among both the nobility and sections of the merchant milieu of a shared interest in the preservation of the status quo. In their common quest for a social order that both legitimized extant inequalities and promised stability, both the nobility and the merchant class embraced "the king's absolute ability to make law because they believed it guaranteed order, that is, both property and inequality."[95] Over in Spanish Italy, Federico Borromeo was in search of a similar cross-class alliance in favor of a strong monarchy that guaranteed stability for all the king's subjects thanks to the indefatigable and socially responsible nobles in his service. If this reinvention forced the Borromeo family to subordinate itself to the king of Spain and abandon any hint of pursuing private interests, this was a small price to pay: at a time when so much was on the line, the new dispensation allowed the Borromeos to live up to the self-ascribed task of preserving the common good in the only way conceivable in a changed world. By rattling on about the menace emanating from rampant crime, they made themselves irreplaceable defenders of the good order in the provinces—as indispensable to the commoners below them as to the king above them.

---

[92] Quoted in Galasso, *Napoli*, p. 70. [93] Mrozek Eliszezynski, *Ascanio*, p. 257.
[94] Gorani, Libro: *BNE*, ms. 2671, f. 246r. [95] Collins, *Classes*, p. 15.

Conclusion

If news of Federico Borromeo's promotion to the Congregation of Ecclesiastical Immunity had sent shock waves through the Spanish ruling class, Borromeo himself never had doubts about his fealty. In the face of what he perceived as rampant anarchy, he positioned himself against the archbishop of Milan and came out in support of Spanish governors and viceroys across Italy. In his various functions as a member of the Congregation of Ecclesiastical Immunity, he was determined to stamp out the lawlessness in Milan and Naples. Informed by a less parochial outlook than most, he tilted the balance of power between Rome and Madrid in favor of the latter by pushing for what was to all intents and purposes the abolition of ecclesiastical asylum. That radical course of action was dictated by his own past. Drawing on his experience as a seasoned administrator of justice in the Papal States and diplomat in Switzerland, he realized that only an alliance between the Spanish crown and the Catholic Church could end the impunity that the strenuous defense of ecclesiastical immunity of some members of the clergy had unleashed. In a move that was not without irony for a member of the Borromeo clan, he went furthest in supporting innovations in government that ultimately strengthened the Spanish crown in its efforts to win back lost ground among the "good and wise people" and build a cross-class alliance between the nobility and the *ceto civile*.

If the costs were great, so were the potential rewards of this stratagem. Turning the jurisdictional controversies in Spanish Italy into his hobbyhorse was a chance for him to redeem himself and his dynasty. At the cost of disowning a venerable family tradition of principled defense of ecclesiastical immunity, he was able to launder his clan's reputation. Through his decisive action in the Congregation of Ecclesiastical Immunity, he could highlight his commitment to disinterested service and good government that his late brother's actions had called into question (see chapter 4). By becoming an unexpected Roman asset to the good government programs that were being rolled out across Spanish Italy, he made amends for a discredited system of governance. If the common good ideology that misrecognized his brother's interested actions had been exposed for the fiction it was, the *mise en scène* as a conscientious administrator of the commonwealth held the promise of the restoration of consent for the continued rule of the old guard. The symbolic appropriation and subsequent distortion of common-good ideas were useful not only to the Borromeos but to the Spanish governing elite as a whole. Recognizing Borromeo's undeniable talent in managing the Italian scene while dissimulating it for the pope, the leading lights in Madrid would soon discover that he was equally indispensable to the governance of the monarchy's heartland.

7

Dissimulation and Subterfuge

Federico Borromeo as Nuncio in Spain and Papal Secretary of State

In the early 1670s, Federico Borromeo was at the pinnacle of power. After a belated appointment to the prestigious nunciature of Madrid in 1668, Pope Clement X Altieri (r. 1670–1676) nominated him secretary of state in 1670. Another few months later, the same pontiff elevated him to the cardinalate. As he settled into Rome's court society upon his return from Madrid, Borromeo's lavish lifestyle showcased his devotedness to Spain's global empire. His menagerie of exotic animals included racehorses from Iberia, parrots from Latin America, and a clowder of big cats evoking Spain's links to Asia. The apartment he inhabited in the Quirinal Palace was crammed with objects ranging from two flasks made from "Indian" gourd, presumably from the Americas, to ivory lamps and gilded statues of black boys (*moretti*) from Africa.[1] As his trinkets suggested, Borromeo may have left Madrid, but he remained as committed as ever to the Spanish empire. In his new role as cardinal, he would continue to devote his energies to the future of the *monarquía*.

He certainly had his work cut out for himself. By the time he made it to Madrid in 1668, King Philip IV had been dead for three years, and within the oligarchy that had replaced the government of the minister-favorite, struggle over the influence on the queen-regent was rife. By 1669 the crisis had reached boiling point: Juan José of Austria, the illegitimate son of Philip IV, had placed himself at the helm of the most influential faction and was leading a coup against the queen's Jesuit confessor, Johann Eberhard Nithard (1607–1681). Federico felt that his moment had come. Posing as the monarchy's faithful subject he had always wanted to be, he sided with Juan José and employed his diplomatic channels to Rome to neutralize Nithard. The crucial part he played in the crisis raised his stock in Madrid: unlike his brother, who had been winnowed from the pool of Madrid insiders, Federico was now openly courted by the dominant faction. If this accrued his authority, it also increased his responsibility: as a client of Juan José, he was called upon to block Nithard's return to power by all means necessary.

---

[1] Galli and Monferrini, *I Borromeo*, p. 33.

Aristocratic Power in the Spanish Monarchy: The Borromeo Brothers of Milan, 1620–1680. Samuel Weber, Oxford University Press. © Samuel Weber 2023. DOI: 10.1093/oso/9780198872597.003.0009

138   ARISTOCRATIC POWER IN THE SPANISH MONARCHY

The task of catering to the needs of Spain's governing elite became more arduous after his promotion to the papal secretariat of state in Rome. As the architect of the pope's good governance façade, he had to perform his duties fairly, treating all Catholics with equanimity. In order to continue serving the Spanish governing elite with whom he was now inextricably bound up, Borromeo resorted to a secret epistolary network that served as a parallel channel to the official correspondence between the secretariat of state and the nunciature in the court of Madrid. This was a sign of the times. Haunted by the specter of rivals turning the tables on them, as had happened to Giovanni Borromeo, elites became ever more conscious of the need to separate public policy from personal strategy. As this chapter argues, this hugger-mugger birthed the "baroque state"—a structure that used an outward good-governance façade to relegate narrow dynastic and factional priorities to the backstage. For Federico Borromeo, this dispositif proved crucial in his bid to frustrate the ambitions of Nithard and thus promote his inexorable rise to the top.

By 1672, Borromeo was on the brink of a breakthrough. Where his brother had been unable to bridge the gap between dynastic interests and the common good, Federico made sure that these two priorities came to dovetail. Working his secret channels to uphold the fiction of good government before anyone else, he protected the dynastic and factional interests of his own and allied families from the sort of public scrutiny that had failed his elder brother two decades earlier. Acting out the adopted role of princely servant, he hoped that, by doing the hegemonic faction's dirty work, he would erase the accusations of interested comportment and eventually come to be seen as a valuable member of the Spanish governing elite. For a short period, it all seemed to go well, but when Nithard was elevated to the cardinalate despite Borromeo's stonewalling, Juan José threatened to turn on the secretary of state. His menaces drove home what Federico had conveniently forgotten: with all his power and influence hinging on his offices in the papal court, he could never be more than an honorary member of an elite whose members would evict him in no time when he ceased to be useful.

The Court of Madrid after Philip IV

When Philip IV passed away in 1665, he left the Spanish empire in the hands of his second wife and cousin, Mariana of Austria (1634–1696), who was to shepherd it through a regency until the heir apparent, Carlos II (1661–1700), turned 14. The queen-regent found herself almost immediately embroiled in the factional strife of the oligarchy that had emerged victorious from the romp following Haro's occlusion. After the passing of the last minister-favorite, some of the major representatives of Spain's nobility had regrouped in a so-called *junta de gobierno*, which

DISSIMULATION AND SUBTERFUGE   139

assumed collectively the tasks that had once been the *valido*'s.[2] Its members included such illustrious names as Pascual de Aragón (1626–1677), the elder brother of Pedro, who had served the monarch as ambassador in Rome and viceroy in Naples.[3] Another member was Gaspar de Bracamonte y Guzmán, Count of Peñaranda (*c*.1595–1676), who had served in Naples and Vienna and now presided over the Council of State. The latter soon emerged as an alternative pole of power, thanks not least to the influence of such personalities as Luis Guillén Moncada (1614–1672), a Sicilian aristocrat. In the face of the ongoing free-for-all at court, the Venetian ambassador to Madrid warned of the dire consequences of the "pestiferous seed of private affections that has taken hold of and has sunk roots into the bowls of the government."[4]

This tiny elite was keen to maintain the precarious equilibrium that had prevailed after Haro's passing. What perturbed its members was the prospect that one of their own should rise above them and install himself as a new minister-favorite.[5] The man they said they feared most was the queen's Jesuit confessor, Johann Eberhard Nithard, who was appointed to the junta in 1666 in a bid to make it more responsive to the regent's wishes.[6] To what extent the scenario of Nithard becoming a new *valido* was realistic is debatable. Unlike the minister-favorites of the first half of the seventeenth century, Nithard was not recognized as a member of the Castilian nobility, a quality that had been essential to the affirmation of Lerma, Olivares, and Haro.[7] Worse, the prominent grandees, who would have had to unite behind him, despised the confessor. Before long, they actively conspired to dislodge him. Adducing the commonwealth ideology so cherished by Spanish grandees in the scramble for resources, they besmirched him as a serial violator of the collective good. In 1668, the Council of State at the behest of Moncada ruled that Nithard had imperiled the good government of the monarchy and should, therefore, be asked to leave the court. The junta quickly followed suit.[8]

The commotion within the oligarchy whetted the appetite of Juan José of Austria, the stepbrother of the underage king. Born in 1629 as the son of Philip IV and a popular actress, Carlos II's half-brother nursed more than a few grievances against the regency. Although he had made a name for himself in various military hotspots during the crisis of the 1640s and 1650s,[9] his father had overlooked him in his last will, locking him out of the government of the monarchy after his

---

[2] Oliván Santaliestra, "Mariana," pp. 61–3; Mitchell, *Queen*, p. 67; on the origins of this development, see Martínez Hernández, "La cámara."

[3] Zorzi, "Relazione," pp. 340–2.   [4] Bellegno, "Relazione," p. 364.

[5] Novo Zaballos, "De confesor," pp. 781, 790.   [6] Mitchell, *Queen*, p. 71.

[7] Carrasco, "Los grandes," pp. 96–7. These arguments had earlier been deployed against Mazarin in France, see Benigno, *Specchi*, p. 142.

[8] Oliván Santaliestra, "Mariana," p. 215.   [9] Kamen, *Spain*, pp. 329–30.

140 ARISTOCRATIC POWER IN THE SPANISH MONARCHY

passing.[10] As the Nithard crisis plunged toward its nadir, Juan José fashioned himself as the heir of the dead king whose legacy as a strenuous advocate of the commonwealth needed to be defended from an illegitimate usurper. Late in 1668, he won over parts of the king's army in Catalonia and threatened to march on Madrid to enforce the Council of State and the *junta's* ruling that Nithard leave the capital. The gamble was to bring the nobility that opposed Nithard as a potential new minister-favorite to accept Juan José as a new *valido*.

Throughout this operation, Juan José was careful to appeal to the oligarchy he needed to win over for his ambitious project. Preening himself as a member of the royal family who stood above the fray of factional infighting, he argued that he, as a member of the ruling dynasty, had no "sons to provide for, no relatives to prefer, households to set up, and no one to emulate."[11] Speaking to grandees' devotedness to the "republic," he fashioned himself as the embodiment of the commonwealth, emphasizing how this idea was synonymous with the royal family.[12] These arguments seemed to persuade a governing elite under duress. As the Venetian ambassador summed up their reasoning, Juan José's blood relation with the heir-apparent allowed him credibly to act as a "shield against the blows of the Jesuit" who was inflicting "a thousand injustices on Spain's most illustrious and clean blood."[13] As Juan José and the Hispanic nobility embarked on a joint propaganda campaign, they were careful to portray their machinations, not as factional strife, but as an act to restore a commonwealth under attack from a power-hungry Jesuit and his irresponsible hogging of the underage king's patronage.[14]

What was new about this campaign was its appeal to a nascent public sphere that engaged with news from the court in unprecedent ways.[15] Inspired by Juan José, municipalities across Spain participated in a letter campaign against Nithard. At the beginning of January 1669, an epistle was found nailed to the door of the cathedral sacristy in the city of Granada. Its anonymous authors vowed to support the "just claims" of Juan José, whom they described as "moved at seeing the oppression of these poor subjects" of the monarchy.[16] Such engagement should not be misread as the beginning of more popular participation. Juan José was keen to keep the reins firmly in his hands. As Federico Borromeo, the new nuncio in the court of Madrid phrased it, Juan José portrayed himself as the "restorer of the crown"[17] in the hope that the "populace are waiting to be freed, through him,

---

[10] Ruiz Rodríguez, *Don Juan José*, pp. 243–6. [11] Quoted in Contreras, *Carlos II*, p. 97.

[12] See Burke, *The Fabrication*, pp. 9–10, for an analogous operation in France. On the common good, see Engels, "Corruption," p. 175; Bernsee, "For the Good," pp. 259, 263.

[13] Bellegno, "Relazione," p. 362.

[14] Hermant, *Guerres*, pp. 3, 18, 47; Reinhardt, *Voices*, p. 341; Oliván Santaliestra, "Mariana," p. 227.

[15] Hermant, *Guerres*, p. 23. [16] Quoted in Kamen, *Spain*, p. 334.

[17] Federico IV Borromeo to Decio Azzolini, Madrid March 30, 1669: *AAV*, Segr. Stato, Spagna, vol. 138, f. 258r.

from such an administrator of bad governance."[18] The view of society predominant among Juan José's noble followers was that humanity was divided into a small elite and the masses over whom it ruled. It was the task of the former to deliver the collective good for the latter, while also ensuring that that pursuit did not run counter to the elite's own interests.[19] Although Juan José's campaign assigned them the role of a critical public, whose interest in the monarchy was actively elicited, the people were understood to be spectators with no agency of their own: they were, in the words of Héloïse Hermant, "a shadow theater at the service of the powerful."[20] Although ordinary people were now watching them with a keen interest, decision-making remained the remit of members of a small elite of political experts who made sure to keep the masses from voicing their aspirations outside carefully policed boundaries.[21] Unsurprisingly, given his support base, Juan José and his followers dreamed of an aristocracy, a nobility born to rule in the interest of all, assisting the king in the delicate task of delivering justice. As the bastard himself put it, he wanted "the good of the poor and the firm preservation of this monarchy, which is the most stable pillar of its [Catholic] faith."[22]

Having fashioned himself as a strong man throughout 1668, Juan José was under pressure to act. As Nithard holed himself up in the queen's palace and the latter hesitated to let him go, Juan José understood that he needed to put his money where his mouth was. Starting from Barcelona, an escort of cavalrymen from the royal army accompanied Juan José in a march on Madrid until they reached Torrejón de Ardoz, outside the capital, in early January 1669. Along the way, Borromeo reported, the bastard had been "complimented and accompanied with extraordinary demonstrations of cordiality and deference by the nobility and the populace."[23] Heartened by these signs of support, on February 24, 1669, Juan José issued an ultimatum, warning that if the confessor did not leave the palace "through the door," he would make sure that he did so "through the window."[24]

Federico Borromeo and the Nithard Crisis

In the bid to oust Nithard, the support of Federico Borromeo was decisive. Federico had arrived in Spain as the papal nuncio of Clement IX Rospigliosi (r. 1668–1670) just as the Nithard crisis was heating up. In the letter of accreditation,

---

[18] Federico IV Borromeo to Decio Azzolini, Madrid March 6, 1669: *AAV*, Segr. Stato, Spagna, vol. 138, f. 165v.

[19] On these tensions, see Villari, "La cultura politica," pp. 5–31.

[20] Hermant, *Guerres*, p. 423.   [21] Ibid., p. 422.

[22] Quoted in Álvarez-Ossorio Alvariño, "La república," p. 311.

[23] Federico IV Borromeo to Decio Azzolini, Madrid February 9, 1669: *AAV*, Segr. Stato, Spagna, vol. 138, f. 94r.

[24] Federico IV Borromeo to Decio Azzolini, Madrid March 6, 1669: *AAV*, Segr. Stato, Spagna, vol. 138, f. 165r; Novo Zaballos, "De confesor," p. 765.

142 ARISTOCRATIC POWER IN THE SPANISH MONARCHY

the papal secretary of state, Decio Azzolini (1623–1689), informed the queen regent that the dispatch of a person of Borromeo's caliber was "a clear demonstration of His Holiness's respect and affection" for the crown, for Borromeo did not just boast the "splendor of birth" but could look back on a "long record of proven merit," which would be most beneficial to the monarchy.[25] The Council of State duly rejoiced at the news, lauding Federico for "being Milanese, as well as [for] his talent."[26] Borromeo made the most of the warm welcome the Council of State extended to him. He immediately accosted the rising star in the Council, the Sicilian Moncada, with whom he shared an interest in placing his house from a peripheral territory at the center of the monarchy.[27] Since Moncada was "the one who openly sides with Don Juan," Borromeo soon turned equally partisan.[28] By hitching his fate to Juan José and his faction, Federico speculated, the dream of a Borromeo in a leading position in Madrid might finally come true.

For his plan to succeed, dissimulation was *de rigueur*. As the crisis deepened, Borromeo began stirring behind the scenes. His first move was to persuade Juan José to pen a letter to the pontiff. In the epistle, the bastard argued that the "constant calamities" the confessor had visited upon Spain made it incumbent on him to "head to the court, with the help and support of the foremost nobility of these kingdoms." He also stated that he was doing so "with the presumed benediction of Your Holiness."[29] Having been put on the spot by Juan José, a fretting pontiff instructed Borromeo to "make every effort to restore calm" in Spain.[30] With this permission from on high, Borromeo was able to tender his services as a neutral mediator. Pandering to the queen's piety, the nuncio took pains to stress that he wanted to act as an intermediary, not because he was an interested party, but because his "sole aim" was to "serve the crown and Her Majesty" as a loyal vassal.[31] Playing along with Borromeo's game, Moncada and others in the Council of State leaned on the queen to accept the nuncio's generous offer to "do whatever seems most convenient for the calm of those kingdoms."[32] The plan worked out. Shortly thereafter, Borromeo was nominated the official negotiator between the queen-regent and Juan José.[33]

---

[25] Decio Azzolini to Vitaliano Visconti, Rome January 10, 1668: *AAV*, Arch. Nunz. Madrid, vol. 16, f. 375r.

[26] *Consulta* of the Council of State, Madrid February 21, 1668: *AGS*, EST, leg. 3041, f. 81.

[27] On the Moncada family, see Scalisi, ed., *La Sicilia*.

[28] Federico IV Borromeo to Decio Azzolini, Madrid February 9, 1669: *AAV*, Segr. Stato, Spagna, vol. 136, f. 352f.

[29] Quoted in Ruiz Rodríguez, *Don Juan José*, p. 289.

[30] Decio Azzolini to Federico IV Borromeo, Rome December 30, 1668: *AAV*, Segr. Stato, Spagna, vol. 136, f. 81v.

[31] Ibid. On Mariana's religious education, see Oliván Santaliestra, "Mariana," pp. 31–2.

[32] Secretary of the Council of State to Queen Mariana, Madrid February 5, 1669: *AGS*, EST, leg. 3043.

[33] Federico IV Borromeo to Decio Azzolini, Madrid February 9, 1669: *AAV*, Segr. Stato, Spagna, vol. 136, f. 352v.

DISSIMULATION AND SUBTERFUGE   143

Still cloaking his real motives beneath a discourse of royal service, Borromeo went to work as a neutral conciliator.[34] As he shuttled between Torrejón and Madrid, he came up with a Machiavellian ruse. His first concern was to win the trust of the queen and then convince her that for Nithard to stay further in the court was unviable.[35] To draw her in, he suggested a solution that would allow the queen and Nithard to save face: if the confessor resigned from his post on the junta and decamped to Rome as the queen's extraordinary ambassador, Borromeo vowed, Nithard would be made cardinal of the Roman Catholic Church at the next possible opportunity. That offer proved too hard to resist. Before the month of February was up, Nithard was en route to the Eternal City.[36]

This penchant for internal fixes was a constant in Federico Borromeo's career. As nuncio in Switzerland, he had used a similar strategy of feigned neutrality to stifle factional conflicts. Early on in his stay in Switzerland, the elites of the Catholic cantons in central Switzerland had mobilized popular resentment against a well-respected nobleman close to the house of Habsburg, Sebastian Peregrin Zwyer von Evibach (1597–1661).[37] As events unfolded, Borromeo learned quickly that papal officials were in a unique position to preserve order when local elites opportunistically roused the rabble against a rival. Realizing that the local patriciates were going to go through with their subversive actions "without consideration for the dangers that are hanging over the commonwealth," he activated his own secret diplomacy to move Zwyer out of the firing line. Exploiting his ties to the Roman curia, he rushed to offer him a position in the court of Vienna.[38] The successful averting of danger was an instructive lesson. The Zwyer affair taught Borromeo that, in order to achieve their goals, papal diplomats sometimes needed to "operate in hiding"[39] and, as his closest confidant, the Spanish resident in Switzerland, had put it, "throw the stone and then hide your hand."[40]

The same modus operandi he now applied to Spain. Capitalizing on the prestige he enjoyed as a member of the clergy and a papal envoy, he managed to pose simultaneously as a neutral arbiter to the outside world and as an ally to his cronies. With the exception of Nithard himself,[41] Borromeo fooled almost everyone. Queen Mariana thanked the pope for sending her "a nuncio she could trust" in

[34] Federico IV Borromeo to Decio Azzolini, Madrid March 6, 1669: AAV, Segr. Stato, Spagna, vol. 138, f. 165r.
[35] Federico IV Borromeo to Decio Azzolini, Madrid February 9, 1669: AAV, Segr. Stato, Spagna, vol. 136, f. 352r.
[36] Novo Zaballos, "De confesor," p. 794.   [37] Weber, "Ein Verteidiger."
[38] Federico IV Borromeo to Giulio Rospigliosi, Lucerne December 9, 1658: AAV, Segr. Stato, Svizzera, vol. 52, f. 393v.
[39] Federico IV Borromeo to Giulio Rospigliosi, Lucerne July 13, 1656: AAV, Segr. Stato, Svizzera, vol. 50, f. 12r.
[40] Maissen, "Zur Bischofswahl," p. 390.   [41] Pilo, ed., Juan Everardo Nithard, p. 242.

144 ARISTOCRATIC POWER IN THE SPANISH MONARCHY

"such grim times."[42] Borromeo's principal, secretary of state Azzolini, feted the nuncio for re-establishing order in the Spanish court.[43] Both seemed to believe that Borromeo was a neutral outsider who had saved the Spanish monarchy from civil war. Only in his correspondence with Juan José did Borromeo show his true colors, patting himself on the back for having "done my part" "according to the trust with which Your Highness has honored me."[44]

This dual strategy of outward neutrality and private partisanship was a double-edged sword. Borromeo was now a full-fledged member of the in-crowd with all the rights and duties associated with that status. Archbishop Litta of Milan, who at this point was still trying to convince Borromeo to abet him in the jurisdictional controversies in Lombardy (see chapter 6), heaped effusive praise on the nuncio for his role in concluding "the thorny negotiation between the queen and Don Juan." To Litta, it was clear that Federico had rendered the monarchy an enormous service: "the calm of that court and monarchy has to be fully attributed to the authority, caution, and wisdom of Your Most Illustrious Lordship." As he saw it, his accomplishment enhanced Borromeo's leverage as he set out to claim the "advantages" that the "generous gratitude of those majesties" would furnish "your house."[45] At the same time, the collusion with Juan José and his votaries turned these fruits of victory sour. This coterie now saw him as one of its clients whom they could blackmail into delivering more services. As his stint as a nuncio came to an end in 1670, the Council of State upped the pressure. In a *consulta* discussing Borromeo's imminent departure to Rome, the Council suggested to the queen that, given Borromeo's "affection and good deportment," it would be "very convenient" to offer him a gift to hammer home "how appreciated his comportment in this kingdom has been by Your Majesty," and, more importantly, to make clear what she "expects from this inclination for the major interests of this crown."[46] The task that his cronies of the governing elite set him through the supple use of the gift register was unenviable: he was to make sure that the papacy reneged on Borromeo's earlier public promise to elevate Nithard to the cardinalate.

Federico's promotion to the secretariat of state in Rome in 1670 turned fulfilling this promise into an impossible feat. If he had been able to pull the wool over the pope's eyes in faraway Madrid, this became well-nigh impossible in his new role, where he was under the direct supervision of Clement X Altieri and

---

[42] Federico IV Borromeo to Decio Azzolini, Madrid March 9, 1669: *AAV*, Segr. Stato, Spagna, vol. 138, f. 210v.

[43] Decio Azzolini to Federico IV Borromeo, Rome July 20, 1669: *AAV*, Segr. Stato, Spagna, vol. 351, f. 316v.

[44] Federico IV Borromeo to Juan José, Madrid March 25, 1669: *ABIB*, FB, Federico IV, Cariche: Nunzio a Madrid. On "Your Highness" as a partisan title for the bastard, see Kamen, "Spain's First Caudillo," p. 585.

[45] Alfonso Litta to Federico IV Borromeo, Milan June 24, 1669: *AAV*, Arch. Nunz. Madrid, vol. 4, f. 390r.

[46] *Consulta* of the Council of State, Madrid June 27, 1670: *AGS*, EST, leg. 3044.

his nephew, Paluzzo Paluzzi Altieri degli Albertoni (1623–1698). According to the special envoy of the house of Savoy, Giovanni Battista Luserna Bigliore (*c*.1625–1677), both men had little time for the shenanigans of their "predecessors who have thought more of enriching their relatives than of the piety and zeal of the subjects of the Church."[47] (Later investigations under Innocent XII would reveal that the cardinal-nephew had helped himself to a little over a million *scudi*, thereby coming second to only the notoriously voracious Pamphili.[48]) Borromeo's chances to influence Nithard's future took a further hit when it turned out that Paluzzi Altieri would take on a more active role than previous papal nephews, who had usually delegated the diplomatic correspondence to the secretaries of state. Paluzzi Altieri, by contrast, took exclusive charge of the correspondence with the nuncios.[49] With Borromeo's hands tied, Nithard's candidacy for the red hat was safe. Although they put up some resistance at first, the Altieri ultimately agreed that Queen Mariana, like every other Catholic sovereign, had the right to present Nithard as her candidate of choice.[50] In January 1672, Nithard copped the title of archbishop of Edessa, an archdiocese *in partibus infidelium* that did not require him to reside there.[51] The red hat followed a few months later, allowing Nithard to enter the college of cardinals, much to the disappointment of Borromeo and his cronies in Madrid.[52]

At first glance, the Nithard episode confirms the conventional wisdom about Borromeo's tenure in the secretariat of state. Based on an analysis of the correspondence of the secretariat of state, Gregor Lutz and Antonio Menniti Ippolito have both concluded that Borromeo was a lame duck who, unlike his predecessors, was almost immediately sidelined by an ambitious papal nephew.[53] There are two problems with this reading, though. First, it is directly contradicted by contemporary observers of the court of Rome. After Federico's return from Madrid, the pope was said to have exclaimed: "We can heave a sigh of relief now that we have a Borromeo running the Vatican."[54] The envoy of Savoy reported that the pope had "thrown his free will" "into [Borromeo's] arms." According to Giovanni Battista Luserna Bigliore, Borromeo was instrumental in drafting letters in matters "that are most pressing to the pope."[55] An anonymous who's who of the court confirms that Borromeo acted as a trusted "confidant" and adviser to the

---

[47] Giovanni Battista Luserna Bigliore, Relatione della Corte di Roma fatta dal Sig.r Marchese Bigliore di Lucerna stato Amb.re Straordinario d'obbedienza à Papa Clemente X.o per l'Altezza Reale di Savoia: *BAV*, Vat. Lat. 12530, f. 91v.

[48] Hohwieler, *Die Altieri*, p. 194.   [49] Ibid., p. 236.

[50] Paluzzo Paluzzi Altieri to Galeazzo Marescotti, Rome April 23, 1672: *AAV*, Segr. Stato, Spagna, vol. 139, f. 43v.

[51] Novo Zaballos, "De confesor," p. 814.

[52] See the *consulta* of the Council of State, Madrid August 3, 1669: *AGS*, EST, leg. 3113.

[53] Lutz, "Federico Borromeo"; Menniti Ippolito, *Il tramonto*, p. 53.

[54] Quoted in Galli, "Federico IV Borromeo (1617–1673)," p. 377.

[55] Luserna Bigliore, Relatione: *BAV*, Vat. Lat. 12530, f. 103v.

146 ARISTOCRATIC POWER IN THE SPANISH MONARCHY

pope and his nephew.[56] Contrary to what later historians have claimed, contemporaries concurred with the Venetian ambassador when he wrote of Borromeo: "The pope loves him and believes him."[57]

The second problem with the ready dismissal of Borromeo's role on the basis of the official correspondence is methodological in nature. As Birgit Emich has shown in her work on the secretariat of state under Paul V Borghese (r. 1605–1621), the letters secretaries of state exchanged through informal channels are as important when determining their influence as the correspondence they wrote in a formal capacity.[58] If we broaden our focus to include Borromeo's private epistolary network, he seems even less ineffective than he has been made out to be. Borromeo may have been absent from the records of the secretariat of state, but a cache of letters culled from the National Library at Madrid, as well as his correspondence in the family archive, show him to have been an assiduous correspondent. In his missives to family members, Federico frequently complained that he had been writing "from the Hail Mary until ten o'clock at night" to keep in touch with various members of the Spanish nobility.[59]

The surviving letters are only superficially inconsequential. Many correspondents let Borromeo know of weddings in their family, while others wrote to offer their condolences when his mother, Giovanna Cesi, died in 1672.[60] Still other letter-writers took the opportunity of the high holidays to congratulate Borromeo on his career achievements and woo him as a potential patron, especially after his elevation to the cardinalate.[61] One well-wisher tendered Borromeo his best wishes for Christmas and felicitated him on "the purple, which crowns your great merits and the service rendered to the Holy See."[62] Some correspondents were more straightforward: letters requesting a specific favor from Borromeo abound. Far from being mere courtesies, these letters laid bare Borromeo's influence as a barterer of ecclesiastical resources, both material and not. One typical petitioner explicitly thanked him for "speaking to His Holiness and Cardinal Altieri regarding my petition."[63] Borromeo's private letters therefore had an eminently political dimension. Not unlike the epistolary networks of noblewomen studied by James Daybell, Borromeo's privy correspondence was paramount in a political system based on "the primacy of interpersonal relationships and informal channels of power."[64]

---

[56] Compendioso Ragguaglio delle Fattioni. Nascita, età, costume, et inclinationi di tutti i Cardinali viventi nel Pontificato di Clemente Decimo: *BAV*, Barb. Lat. 4704, f. 33r.

[57] Grimani, "Relazione," p. 359.   [58] Emich, "Die Karriere," pp. 343–4, 350.

[59] Federico IV to Antonio Renato Borromeo, Rome January 24, 1671: *ABIB*, FB, Federico IV, Corrispondenza 1671–1680.

[60] Duke of San Germán to Federico IV Borromeo, Cagliari March 16, 1672: *BNE*, ms. 12877, f. 230r.

[61] See for example Francisco de Jerez to Federico IV Borromeo, Naples December 19, 1671: *BNE*, ms. 12877, ff. 106r–v. On this function of letters, see Biagioli, *Galileo*, p. 26.

[62] ? Jacinto to Federico IV Borromeo, Madrid December 3, 1670: *BNE*, ms. 12877, f. 350r.

[63] Prince of ? to Federico IV Borromeo, Milan, July 27, 1672: *BNE*, ms. 12877, f. 234r.

[64] Daybell, *Women*, p. 28.

The political nature of the correspondence becomes even clearer if we focus on the letters that directly speak to issues of high politics. Nestled between the hundreds of missives from minor nobles asking for small favors, there are the epistles from the who's who of the Spanish nobility. By far the most demanding petitioner was Juan José of Austria. As early as 1670, soon after Borromeo's return to Rome, the bastard addressed him as one of his clients: "With everything that pertains to my interests and has to go through the hands of Your Most Illustrious Lordship, I am confident that I will always experience the affection Your Most Illustrious Lordship owes me."[65] Through these blandishments, Borromeo was made to understand in no uncertain terms that he was indebted to Juan José. Once the asymmetrical relationship between the two had been firmly established, Juan José proceeded to beseech Borromeo to block Nithard's nomination. If Nithard was created cardinal, Juan José admonished, he would return to Spain to wreak more havoc. Appealing to Borromeo's own stake in the monarchy and the bastard's faction, he warned that Nithard would "finish building the throne he has planned to build out of our downfall and ruin."[66] It was therefore of the utmost importance that Borromeo did everything in his might "to prevent with your authority that return [to Spain]." Juan José's epistles were relentless. When he felt Borromeo's resolve lessen, his letters became shriller. By the spring of 1672, he put Nithard's elevation down to simony and warned of the dire consequences of the world's seeing Nithard made "prince and pillar of the Catholic Church, and (which is even harder to countenance) this thanks to the Spanish crown."[67]

While Borromeo apparently never tried to sway the pope, as Juan José suggested, he did seek to undermine the nomination. In the fall of 1671, the nuncio in the court of Madrid reported irregularities in Nithard's nomination to the cardinalate. As Galeazzo Marescotti (1627–1726) had discovered by chance, the Council of State was advising the queen to "recommend" rather than "nominate" Nithard for the biretta. This was more than nitpicking over semantics: nominations from Catholic monarchs were binding, whereas popes needed to respond to recommendations only as a "special and extraordinary act of grace," which made it unlikely the papacy would accede to such requests.[68] The mix-up of the two modalities seems to have been deliberate. As Marescotti reported, when one member of the junta opposed the recommendation of Nithard, the Count of Peñaranda clarified that the committee was not drawing up "a nomination but a

---

[65] Juan José to Federico IV Borromeo, Zaragoza December 6, 1670: *BNE*, ms. 12877, f. 2r.
[66] This and the following quote are from Juan José to Federico IV Borromeo, Zaragoza April 24, 1672: *ABIB*, FB, Federico IV, Corrispondenza 1671–1680.
[67] Juan José to Federico IV Borromeo, Zaragoza May 21, 1672: *ABIB*, FB, Federico IV, Corrispondenza 1671–1680.
[68] Paluzzo Paluzzi Altieri to Galeazzo Marescotti, Rome August 29, 1671: *AAV*, Segr. Stato, Spagna, vol. 139, f. 19r.

148 ARISTOCRATIC POWER IN THE SPANISH MONARCHY

letter of recommendation, which would have no effect."[69] Upon getting wind of this, the nuncio had no doubts that the grandees who "do not wish the promotion of Father Eberhard" were actively trying to "make the queen believe that they wanted it and were seeking it," all while torpedoing it with pettifoggery.[70] Reading the news from Madrid, the cardinal-nephew Paluzzi Altieri was equally baffled to learn that members of the Spanish high nobility should "want to deceive the queen with a ruckus and make her believe that they want something they do not actually want."[71]

It is to be doubted that such an intricate strategy originated in Madrid. The subtle difference between nominations and recommendations was such an obscure concept that even the cardinal-nephew and the nuncio needed to exchange multiple letters to clarify the papacy's position on the matter.[72] Given the unfamiliarity of the legal implications even among top diplomats in Rome, it seems highly unlikely that the Spanish grandees came up with such sophistry on their own. In fact, it is much more probable that the legal argument was fed to them by the cardinal-nephew's right-hand man, Federico Borromeo, who must have advised Paluzzi Altieri during his exchanges with Marescotti.

While there is no smoking gun, evidence abounds that the secretary of state used his privy correspondence to instruct his cronies in how to wreck Nithard's elevation. Borromeo's most likely contact was Moncada. Moncada had done his utmost from the start of the Altieri pontificate to influence decision-making processes in the secretariat of state, even writing an incriminating letter to the new cardinal-nephew in which he encouraged Paluzzi Altieri to keep himself abreast of "everything that has happened in the public affairs of this government and the effort that [Federico Borromeo] has made at the behest of the gloriously remembered Clement IX and the Apostolic See for the preservation of public calm, as well as that of Don Juan and myself."[73] Behind the scenes, Moncada continued to coordinate with Borromeo. The surviving correspondence is fragmentary, but it does contain a number of missives in which Moncada and Borromeo exchanged news about Nithard.[74] In one letter of 1670, for instance, Moncada and Borromeo

---

[69] Galeazzo Marescotti to Paluzzo Paluzzi Altieri, Madrid September 23, 1671: *AAV*, Segr. Stato, Spagna, vol. 139, ff. 264v–265r.

[70] Galeazzo Marescotti to Paluzzo Paluzzi Altieri, Madrid October 13, 1671: *AAV*, Segr. Stato, Spagna, vol. 139, f. 275r.

[71] Paluzzo Paluzzi Altieri to Galeazzo Marescotti, Rome February 24, 1672: *AAV*, Segr. Stato, Spagna, vol. 139, f. 40r.

[72] Paluzzo Paluzzi Altieri to Galeazzo Marescotti, Rome August 29, 1671: *AAV*, Segr. Stato, Spagna, vol. 139, f. 19r; Paluzzo Paluzzi Altieri to Galeazzo Marescotti, Rome September 12, 1671: *AAV*, Segr. Stato, Spagna, vol. 139, f. 20v; Galeazzo Marescotti to Paluzzo Paluzzi Altieri, Madrid October 21, 1671: *AAV*, Segr. Stato, Spagna, vol. 139, f. 280v.

[73] Luis Guillén Moncada to Paluzzo Paluzzi Altieri, Madrid July 9, 1670: *AAV*, Segr. Stato, Cardinali, vol. 34, f. 17r.

[74] The Archivio Moncada in the Archivio di Stato of Palermo does not hold letters from 1671 and 1672.

DISSIMULATION AND SUBTERFUGE   149

were plotting to park Nithard in Sicily, by offering him the archdiocese of Agrigento, an offer that Nithard promptly turned down.[75] In a subsequent epistle, Borromeo declared boldly: "Father Eberhard won't be going to Girgento because the queen does not want to force him and he won't be persuaded to go there."[76] But if Nithard hoped his stubbornness would raise his chances to obtain the red hat, Borromeo scoffed, he could not be more wrong: "He hopes that the queen will continue in her resolve to have him nominated cardinal, and hence he will be neither cardinal nor bishop."[77] Given the conspiratorial tone of this correspondence, it seems plausible that Borromeo later instructed Moncada on how to parry Nithard's preferment. Alas, the letters from the decisive months in early 1672 are missing from the file.[78] What is certain, though, is that Borromeo succeeded in delaying Nithard's nomination, news of which likely reached Madrid only after Moncada's passing in early May 1672. Though ultimately defeated, Borromeo had managed to do his patron's bidding for the better part of two years. First impressions can indeed sometimes be misleading.

The Making of the Baroque State

Borromeo's parallel correspondence was a direct outgrowth of the double-dealing in Madrid. In an age when the governing elites had to pay tribute to the notion of the common good, dissimulation, the ability to keep "secrets by rendering them unreadable or invisible to others,"[79] became an indispensable technique of governance. Politics, according to a pamphlet written at the height of the Nithard crisis of 1668–1669, was the ability to "distract others in order to slip through oneself."[80] Its practitioners, the author went on, "use Christianity as a hook in order to angle for whatever the mad greed of ambition demands."[81] Overcoming the negative connotation attached to the term "politics," which was synonymous with rank partisanship, these master dissimulators referred to themselves as "political courtiers (*cortesanos políticos*)." Federico Borromeo was one of them. He basked in descriptions of himself as a "great *politique*...completely cut off from all interests."[82] In his own writings he fancied himself a princely servant who found ways to abet his patrons in their covert misdeeds while outwardly

---

[75] Paluzzo Paluzzi Altieri to Galeazzo Marescotti, Rome September 13, 1670: *AAV*, Segr. Stato, Spagna, vol. 353, ff. 21v–22r; Novo Zaballos, "De confesor," p. 794.

[76] Quoted in Scalisi, "In omnibus," p. 562.   [77] Quoted ibid.

[78] I thank Lina Scalisi for confirming this to me.

[79] For this definition of "dissimulation," see Snyder, *Dissimulation*, p. 6.

[80] Quoted in Carrasco, "Los grandes," p. 88. On the connotation of the term "politics," see Stollberg-Rilinger, "The Baroque State," p. 828.

[81] Quoted in Carrasco, "Los grandes," p. 88.

[82] Luserna Bigliore, Relatione: *BAV*, Vat. Lat. 12530, ff. 103r–v.

150   ARISTOCRATIC POWER IN THE SPANISH MONARCHY

paying lip service to the idea that "one cannot [do] what one must not [do]."[83] With this skill set he fit in perfectly with the crowd in the Rome of the Altieri, about whom the Venetian ambassador averred: "The lodestar of that court is private interest; it does not devote itself to the public good save through specious appearance."[84]

Such a conception of politics had repercussions on the fledgling institutions of the state. If the pressure from below had stung elites into formalizing certain procedures, this very formalization created a new need for informal spheres to evade the constraints of formality und undermine the declared purpose of bureaucracies.[85] As public institutions became nominally committed to the collective good, the particular interests of officeholders needed to be advanced outside the formal channels of government.[86] The transition from a regime sworn to secrecy to a limited form of publicity that the Nithard crisis had spawned augured the necessity of informal government channels hidden from public scrutiny where the *arcana imperii* could be stowed away.[87] As Birgit Emich has shown, the elites of the Papal States were particularly adept at operating two parallel channels to meet the contradictory requirements of rational-bureaucratic governance and patronage.[88] The small group of beneficiaries of clientelism accepted to move their dealings to an emergent informal sphere as they came to see the strictures of formal proceedings as a shield from the rancor of the vast majority of left-behinds.[89]

The necessity to harmonize cronyism with good government thus engendered what Barbara Stollberg-Rilinger calls the "baroque state": an artifact steeped in the conviction that "there could be no front stage without a backstage, no formality without informal back doors."[90] In his work on the French monarchy, Peter Campbell has gone so far as to trace a direct link between the failure of rulers to live up to their own standards and the "flamboyant display" of power that is often associated with the age. In his reading, the hamminess of it all was a "*trompe l'oeil*" that, intentionally or not, distracted from the fact that the early modern "state was a socio-political entity, whose structures were interwoven with society, which it tried to rise above but with which it inevitably had to compromise."[91] In other words, the new public script, to adopt James C. Scott's apt phrase, gave birth to a hidden transcript. Although Scott's concept has mostly been applied to the study of the hidden resistance of subordinate actors, Scott himself stressed that

---

[83] Federico IV to Antonio Renato Borromeo, Rome November 14, 1671: *ABIB*, FB, Federico IV, Corrispondenza 1671–1680.

[84] Mocenigo, "Relazione," p. 376. This ambiguity was widespread at the time. See von Thiessen, *Das Zeitalter*, p. 300.

[85] Emich, "Vincoli," p. 129; Emich, "'Der Hof'," pp. 78–80; Wassilowsky, "Vorsehung," p. 72.

[86] See Béguin, *Les Princes*, p. 328.

[87] Hermant, *Guerres*, p. 15. On contemporary preoccupations with secrecy, see Burke, *The Fabrication*, p. 8.

[88] Emich, "'Der Hof'," p. 77.   [89] Ibid., p. 78.

[90] Stollberg-Rilinger, "The Baroque State," p. 828.   [91] Campbell, *Power*, p. 4.

dominant groups also resort to stealth in order to preserve their domination. As he notes: "Dominant groups often have much to conceal, and typically they also have the wherewithal to conceal what they wish."[92] Baroque institutions were as impressive an example as any of such a project: they concealed the political actions that directly contravened the stated goals of good governance.

Such an endeavor depended on subterfuge, and Borromeo was good at keeping a low profile and working behind the scenes. Antonio Grimani, the Venetian ambassador in the papal court, noted that Borromeo actively sought to give the impression that he was unimportant by toying with the faux modesty popular among Roman officeholders steeped in the novel culture of dissimulation: "Toward Cardinal Altieri, he practices all sorts of respect, and dispels doubts that he wants to acquire more power."[93] Rather than as a player in the front row, Borromeo saw himself as a "political courtier" who did the dirty work of friends in high places, hoping that his concealing of their covetousness would earn him recognition as one of the in-crowd.[94]

Deceit helped Borromeo in more than one way. It distracted from the shadow diplomacy he conducted offstage. In line with the modus operandi he had been perfecting ever since he had served as nuncio to the Swiss Confederacy, he actively strove to remain undetected, certain that this would allow him to achieve much more than when he worked in broad daylight. As he himself wrote of his informal epistolary network: "These are goods that one should not exhibit in the market square, and most often it is better to possess them than to show them off."[95] It was capital that was much more effective when it remained hidden, not least because his involvement in Spanish high politics had the potential to beget conflicts of interest with the papal family.[96] Donning the mantle of the lowly scribe helped him distract from the fact that he was doing Juan José's bidding. In fact, as he had done in Spain, he continued to dupe most. Upon Nithard's elevation, the confessor's allies thanked Borromeo for his efforts, oblivious to his role in stalling the conferral of the red hat.[97] Borromeo's duplicity helped his side without uniting its adversaries against him.

His obscurantism also saved him from the wrath of his patron and his cronies in Spain when he failed to deliver on his promises. As he explained to his brother, many of his cronies "regret to realize that the authority I have is not as unlimited

---

[92] Scott, *Domination*, p. 12.

[93] Grimani, "Relazione," p. 359. On the faux modesty of the Roman elite, see Karsten, *Künstler*, pp. 9–10.

[94] In this he resembled his predecessor, Secretary of State Decio Azzolini. See Hohwieler, *Die Altieri*, pp. 62–4.

[95] Federico IV to Antonio Renato Borromeo, Rome September 17, 1672: *ABIB*, FB, Federico IV, Corrispondenza 1645–1655, fasc. 1652.

[96] Also see D'Avenia, "Lealtà."

[97] Count of Villaumbrosa to Federico IV Borromeo, Madrid June 7, 1672: *BNE*, ms. 12877, f. 574r; Pedro Fernández to Federico IV Borromeo, Madrid June 12, 1672: *BNE*, ms. 12877, f. 580r.

152   ARISTOCRATIC POWER IN THE SPANISH MONARCHY

as they believe would be useful to the public." Many were only just beginning to understand that "my rank is to serve, not to command."[98] This argument was particularly useful in his dealings with the bastard. Thus, when Nithard's promotion to the cardinalate finally occurred, Borromeo managed to convince Juan José that he had been unable to do anything to stop the pope. Juan José swallowed this explanation. In a letter to Borromeo, he inveighed against "the common father who represents God but claims that he cannot prevent, even with prudent delays, that a man of Eberhard's qualities, full of ambition, tyranny, and ungodliness…be made, in next to no time, prince of the Catholic Church."[99] Borromeo was spared Juan José's fury.

Federico's blame-shifting fit a broader pattern. According to Gregorio Leti, Borromeo had a habit of promising the impossible to his patrons and clients only to then send their ire the cardinal-nephew's way: "Borromeo regularly blamed the cardinal-nephew for all the difficulties that representatives encountered at the Apostolic Palace as they pursued the interests of their patrons."[100] When he failed to deliver, he could simply claim that he "was only a minister dependent on the nephew, without whom he could not do anything."[101] His role in the background allowed him to shrug off responsibility while continuing to claim that he was an influential actor.

This self-fashioning was not without its disadvantages. In fact, some began to believe the tale Federico told about himself. In the fall of 1672, he needed to clarify in a letter to his brother that the "chatter…that might be invented and spread" in Milan about his diminishing influence was "all fairy tales."[102] Indeed, "I can be satisfied about the fact that there has never been a secretary of state who has received more trust from the pope and the leading voices in this court than I have."[103] The deliberate self-dwarfing was becoming dangerous, although, as his privy correspondence reveals, the Juan José faction in Madrid likely continued to see him as one of its pillars in Rome.

Conclusion

Federico's triumph as secretary of state was a rare second shot at self-affirmation after Giovanni's bid for power had foundered on his unveiled self-interest.

---

[98] Federico IV to Antonio Renato Borromeo, Rome September 17, 1672: *ABIB*, FB, Federico IV, Corrispondenza 1645–1655, fasc. 1652.

[99] Juan José to Federico IV Borromeo, Zaragoza June 4, 1672: *ABIB*, FB, Federico IV, Corrispondenza 1671–1680.

[100] Leti, *Il livello*, pp. 106–7.   [101] Ibid., p. 110.

[102] Federico IV to Antonio Renato Borromeo, Rome September 3, 1672: *ABIB*, FB, Federico IV, Corrispondenza 1671–1680.

[103] Federico IV to Antonio Renato Borromeo, Rome September 17, 1672: *ABIB*, FB, Federico IV, Corrispondenza 1645–1655, fasc. 1652.

Following a decade of stumbling to get back on their feet, Federico's ecclesiastical role afforded the Borromeos a possibility of finally becoming involved in the power struggles in the court of Madrid. The family cardinal was careful not to repeat the mistakes that had spelled the premature end of Giovanni's advancement. He laid the groundwork by acquiring impeccable credentials as a disinterested servant committed to good government: instead of pursuing narrow dynastic interests of his own, he made sure that these came to dovetail with those of the ruling elite he wanted to join. Reinventing himself as a *cortesano político*, he helped modulate monarchical government, giving rise to what has been called the baroque state, with its elaborate front stage of institutions committed to the collective good that shielded elites from the backstage on which they continued to advance their factional interests. By doing the bidding of the dominant faction as an innocuous-looking man of the Church, Federico hoped, he would ultimately succeed in advancing his family's interests in a more austere age.

In pursuing the ecclesiastical route to power in Madrid, Federico Borromeo was a trailblazer. In the decades following the end of the Franco-Spanish War, more and more families across Spanish Italy were discovering that a curial career was the safest way to secure advantages in Spain.[104] As early as the 1660s, a Milanese chronicler had noted that a family cleric's "good favors in Rome" could help deepen a clan's relationship with the Spanish crown.[105] In the absence of major military conflicts and the attendant commissions to recruit armies, high-profile roles in papal diplomacy—most notably the nunciature in the court of Madrid—became highly sought-after spots because of their inherent promise to build rapport with the Spanish governing elite.[106] The most adroit officeholders, like Federico Borromeo, even succeeded in joining the club as honorary members.[107] Thanks to the curial offices he held, Federico was catapulted into a position that his brother had failed to squeak into fifteen years earlier. Picking up the pieces, Federico brilliantly converted the symbolic power acquired thanks to his crucial work in the settlement of the jurisdictional conflicts in Spanish Italy and the Nithard crisis into influence in Spanish high politics. It was a hard-won victory, and a precarious one at that. Federico's membership of the clique of Spanish grandees was ephemeral and borrowed, inseparable from his position as a cardinal of the Roman Catholic Church: after his death, everything gained would be lost. In a society that prided itself on inherited privilege, this was a major blow, a blow that Federico and his brother, Antonio Renato, would try to soften for the better part of the 1670s.

---

[104] Spagnoletti, *Le dinastie*, pp. 271–94; Visceglia, "La nobiltà," p. 28. On the centrality of Rome for the reproductive strategies of Italian dynasties, see Osborne, "The House."

[105] Quoted in Signorotto, "La politica," pp. 324–5.

[106] Sodano, *Da baroni*, pp. 24, 41–2, 85–8; Papagna, *Sogni*, p. 132.

[107] Sodano, *Da baroni*, pp. 42–4.

8

Pining for Stability

Antonio Renato Borromeo and the Uses of Symbolic Power

In early 1671, Milan was in a festive mood. Antonio Renato (1632–1686), the straggler of the house of Borromeo, was celebrating his brother Federico's recent elevation to the cardinalate. Lasting three consecutive days, the festivities for this belated honor were designed to rival the celebrations that typically accompanied special events in royal families. Antonio Renato himself spent his days moving from one sumptuously decorated church to the next, shaking hands with throngs of well-wishers. When night fell, he used the cover of darkness for dramatic effect and proceeded to light torches. As their flames were reflected in the windows of central Milan, they reddened the night sky above the city and, if we are to believe an enthusiastic chronicler, could be seen from as far as 40 kilometers away.[1] These nightly spectacles set the stage for the main attraction on the final day of the festivities: the mass that was celebrated in Sant'Antonio Abate, the church of the Theatines, a Counterreformation order with close ties to the Borromeo family. During the divine office, symphonies segued into cannon shots, "so that Mars seemed religious and religion martial."[2] As the last salvo was fired, the message sent was unequivocal: in the Borromeo family, the sword had ceded to the cross, the warriors had morphed into courtiers.

As the Borromeos knew well, ceremonies and festivities marking extraordinary events were powerful instruments to establish sociopolitical realities amidst conflicting alternative narratives.[3] The jollity in honor of Federico signaled the beginning of Antonio Renato's attempt to moor the family's fortunes to the notion of princely service that the family cardinal embodied. In so doing, Antonio Renato laid the groundwork for the massive operation of preserving the prestige of a single family member for posterity. In anticipation of Federico's death and the forfeiture of the power conferred by his curial offices, the two Borromeo brothers faced the Herculean task of "transmitting to the next generation a fluid patrimony made of relations and unstable positions," of perpetuating what Giovanni Levi has called a "nonmaterial legacy"[4] and making it usable by other members of the

---

[1] Bosca, *De origine*, pp. 179–80. [2] Ibid., p. 179.
[3] González Tornel, *Roma*, pp. 17, 22; Stollberg-Rilinger, *The Emperor's Old Clothes*, pp. 2–5.
[4] Levi, *Inheriting*, p. 120.

Aristocratic Power in the Spanish Monarchy: The Borromeo Brothers of Milan, 1620–1680. Samuel Weber, Oxford University Press. © Samuel Weber 2023. DOI: 10.1093/oso/9780198872597.003.0010

clan. After Federico's passing, Antonio Renato doubled his efforts. In the latter half of the 1670s, he ordered painting after painting in which he visualized Federico's legacy in a bid to portray his own special bond to the Spanish monarchy. Drawing heavily on the artistic commissioning of papal families to which Federico must have introduced him, Antonio Renato's patronage of the arts was designed to create a fait accompli: it enabled the Borromeos to stake a claim to governance in a monarchy that was witnessing the final ascent of Federico's close ally, Juan José of Austria. By belaboring Federico's association with the bastard and his faction, Antonio Renato hoped to be able to thrust his family forward as purveyors of good governance who deserved to be members of an emerging aristocracy of courtiers with a track record of loyalty to Juan José and King Carlos II.

Detailing the Borromeos' consolidation as a leading family of princely servants, this chapter explores how patronage of the arts was put in the service of the reaffirmation of the established nobility in the latter half of the seventeenth century. For a family that had been tainted by charges of corruption, art was a way of reclaiming a pre-eminent role in public life. Predicated on taste and judgment as they were, art collections allowed the old nobility to distance itself from upstarts and war profiteers who were crowding into the field of politics after the Franco-Spanish War. Such was art's potency that it could help the Borromeos fabricate a past of loyal service with the aim of making it serviceable for the present. As they found out, art misrecognized the gap between ideal and reality far better than words did. Hence, investment in art became the perfect handmaiden of a new governing elite that relied on representations of a long-standing close relationship to the ruling family to legitimize its continued predominance.

The Borromeos as Patrons of the Arts

The festivities to felicitate Federico on his elevation to the cardinalate in 1671 took place against the backdrop of the reopening of the Ambrosiana three years earlier. The Ambrosiana had grown out of Cardinal-Archbishop Federico Sr.'s commitment to the patronage of the arts in the early decades of the seventeenth century. Named after Milan's legendary fourth-century bishop, St. Ambrose, it was an expression of Federico Sr.'s dedication to humanistic learning. Accordingly, in his portrait of the archbishop of Milan, the nineteenth-century novelist Alessandro Manzoni feted the Ambrosiana as a public institution devoted to spreading knowledge.[5] What Manzoni and others have failed to see is that the Ambrosiana was also a project of status affirmation devised to turn Milan into a center of intellectual production under the auspices of the Borromeo family.[6]

---

[5] Manzoni, *The Betrothed*, pp. 360–2.   [6] Lezowski, *L'Abrégé*, pp. 14–5.

156   ARISTOCRATIC POWER IN THE SPANISH MONARCHY

The Ambrosiana's most famous institution was a library whose collection rivaled those of sovereign princes: when it opened its doors in 1609, the *Biblioteca* possessed seven times as many printed books as the Vatican Library in Rome.[7] Besides the library, the Ambrosiana comprised other, lesser-known institutions, most notably a picture gallery and an art academy that instructed young artists in the Tridentine canons on painting.[8] After opening with pomp and pageantry in 1620, these two institutions fell into abeyance once the Franco-Spanish War got underway. It was only in 1668 that the art academy was re-established.

The reopening of the art academy signaled the Borromeos' newfound interest in artistic patronage as a strategy of social reproduction.[9] In the 1660s, Antonio Renato had taken over as curator of an institution that had been the sole preserve of the Angera branch of the Borromeo family since the 1620s. He limberly sold his work for the academy as part of a long story of the Borromeos as generous patrons of the arts.[10] In the tradition that was being invented, Federico Sr. was the starting point of a streak of fortune for Milan's painters that continued under Antonio Renato.[11] As one flatterer noted, Antonio Renato had spread the wings of his "mighty protection" over "most of the city's painters," which was why the Ambrosiana "flourishes today as much as any other [academy] in Italy."[12]

When Federico Jr. was granted the coveted red hat in December 1670, the Ambrosiana became an integral part of the public *mise en scène* that elevation warranted. The foyer hosted a painting (fig. 8.1) of Federico, which depicted the newly minted cardinal in the way he wished others to see him: as a courtier with aplomb and a conscientious official of the papacy. As he toyed with the bureaucratic panache popular in the circles of the Spanish nobility he frequented at the time, his quill pen evoked the memory of the Spanish paper kings he was serving.[13] This was a man ready to wield his bureaucratic acumen to shower the Catholic world with governance in the name of the common good. Thus the orchestrators of the fanfare, Federico and Antonio Renato, deliberately conscripted the symbolic capital Federico had acquired as a career diplomat in Spain to spin a new self-justifying yarn about themselves: their pre-eminent position among courtiers afforded them the means to solve the problems harrying Milanese society.

To add heft to Federico's achievement, Federico the cardinal-secretary of state was compared to his great-uncle, Federico the cardinal-archbishop. Federico Jr. had long learned to make the most of his eponymous great-uncle. As he self-deprecatingly put it, one had to "help oneself with the merits of others when one's

---

[7] Jones, *Federico*, p. 44.   [8] Rivola, *Vita*, p. 406.
[9] Bosca, *De origine*, p. 160. On the founding of the Ambrosiana, see Jones, *Federico*, pp. 39, 45–7.
[10] Lezowski, *L'Abrégé*, p. 293.   [11] Ibid., pp. 300–3.
[12] Santagostino, *L'immortalità*, p. 67.
[13] On this ideology in the Spanish ruling elite, see Mitchell, *Queen*, p. 56.

Fig. 8.1 Cesare Fiori (attr.), *Portrait of Federico Borromeo Jr.*, 1670, oil on canvas (172 × 115 cm.), Milan, Pinacoteca Ambrosiana

(Veneranda Biblioteca Ambrosiana/Paolo Manusardi/Mondadori Portfolio)

own are lacking."[14] In the new exhibition in the picture gallery founded by the archbishop, Federico Jr.'s portrait was hung next to a painting of his namesake. Although it remains unclear which canvas of Federico Sr. was chosen at the time, it seems likely that the family settled on a portrait that it had commissioned from an anonymous painter for an attempt to canonize Federico Sr. in the mid-1650s (fig. 8.2).[15] It depicted the cardinal-archbishop in a pose strikingly reminiscent of Federico Jr.: seated at a desk, quill in hand, gazing into the distance.[16] When hung next to each other, the two canvases highlighted the alleged similarities between the two men, commonalities that were reiterated with a Latin caption: "*Murice quae tyrio Federici vibrat imago, / Non una est: senior nam Federicus inest. / Ore quidem distat Federicus uterque: senili / Iunior ast eadem pectore corda gerit.*" ("The picture that glimmers with the purple of Federico's cardinalate/does not stand alone: for Federico the elder is in there, too./Indeed, the face may set one

---

[14] Federico IV to Giovanni VII Borromeo, Todi April 25, 1642: *ABIB*, FB, Federico IV, Cariche.
[15] On the failed canonization, see Signorotto, "A proposito dell'intentato processo."
[16] On the painting, see Lezowski, *L'Abrégé*, pp. 294–5; Jones, *Federico*, p. 1.

Fig. 8.2 Anon., *Portrait of Federico Borromeo Sr.*, c.1650, oil on canvas (127 × 96 cm.), Milan, Pinacoteca Ambrosiana

(Veneranda Biblioteca Ambrosiana/Paolo Manusardi/Mondadori Portfolio)

Federico apart from the other,/but the younger is as good-hearted as the elder.")[17] Combining visual and written text, the exhibition was a transparent attempt to historicize Federico Jr. by coupling him to his great-uncle.

Exactly what kind of tradition Federico Jr. was being placed in became apparent in four new *quadroni* of Federico Sr. that were unveiled on the same occasion.[18] The choice of motifs was telling. The archbishop was depicted in the company of saints, most notably Filippo Neri (1515–1595), with whom Federico had been friendly during his time in Rome in the 1590s, ending up deeply influenced by Neri's idea of bishops as Christian thinkers.[19] Another *quadrone* immortalized Federico Sr. during a visit to the lazaretto that had been erected on the outskirts of the city to host the victims of the bubonic plague that raged in Milan between 1629 and 1631. By focusing on the epidemic, the paintings amplified a message the Borromeos had been trying to push since they had published a *vita*

---

[17] Bosca, *De origine*, p. 183.   [18] On the *quadroni*, see Spiriti, "Identità," p. 325.
[19] On Federico Sr. and Neri, see Jones, *Federico*, p. 9; Lezowski, *L'Abrégé*, pp. 24–5.

of Federico Sr. some fifteen years earlier.[20] The intent of the ensemble in the Ambrosiana, as of the biography of 1656, was clearly to give an impression of a learned man of the Church committed to protecting the most vulnerable members of society.[21]

As such, the paintings had more to do with Federico and Antonio Renato's agenda than with the actual living person portrayed. As Andrea Spiriti has argued, the *quadroni* were the key ingredient of a novel strategy of social affirmation centered on the control of cultural production.[22] The ensemble, with its limber juxtaposition of past and present, was not a simple statement of fact but, rather, a "way of elaborating and disseminating" a specific self-image.[23] The exhibition gestured to a form of social reproduction based on the symbolic appropriation of princely service and charity, while editing out the Borromeos' complicity in a status quo that made their philanthropy necessary in the first place.[24] So powerful was the imagery deployed in the exhibition that it would shape the perception of the Borromeos for centuries to come. Federico Sr.'s visit to the lazaretto, for instance, enjoys pride of place in Manzoni's *The Betrothed*, where the archbishop is described as traveling to the city gates "to console the sick and inspire their attendants," before "rush[ing] about the city, bringing relief to the poor souls quarantined in their homes."[25]

The persuasiveness and longevity of the story told through the exhibition are testimony to Federico's abilities in the fabrication of a public image. He had begun collecting art from the moment he reached Rome in 1635.[26] The Rome of the Barberini, where he won his spurs, taught him the symbolic value of art. By the 1630s, the papacy's nature as an elective monarchy with its frequent changes of ruling clan had sparked a rivalry among papal families not seen anywhere else, a rivalry that found its expression in the performative magnificence that still dominates Rome today. Papal nephews in particular hired the most talented painters both to legitimize their family's accession to the Apostolic See and to pre-empt criticism of their rule. Over the course of the early half of the seventeenth century, successive nephews drove artists in their pay to ever greater heights, all in a bid to sublimate their nepotism into paintings that misrecognized the systematic violation of norms centered on the public good to which they subscribed.[27] Borromeo's first patrons, the Barberini, had taken this art of silencing their critics

---

[20] Rivola, *Vita*, pp. 562–97, 662–6. This text, which was commissioned as part of the campaign to have Federico canonized, was one of the main sources used by Manzoni in the nineteenth century.

[21] On this image of Federico Sr., see Jones, *Federico*, pp. 2, 19, 24.

[22] Spiriti, "Identità," p. 330.   [23] Ibid., p. 327.

[24] On this form of self-presentation, see Walter, *Crowds*, p. 19.

[25] Manzoni, *The Betrothed*, p. 535.

[26] See his will for an overview of his art collection: *ASR*, Notai del tribunale dell'Auditor Camerae, F. Serantonious, vol. 6562, f. 226r-v.

[27] On misrecognition, see Swartz, *Symbolic Power*, pp. 4–6, 37–8.

160   ARISTOCRATIC POWER IN THE SPANISH MONARCHY

through impressive pictorial feats to new levels.[28] Pietro da Cortona (1596–1669)'s fresco in the Barberini palace, the *Divine Providence*, persuaded through form and content, pushing back against those members of the papal court who questioned the merits of the Barberini, upstarts from the banking milieu, by portraying their rule as auspicious for the rest of humanity.[29] This obscurantism through art grew in salience as the papacy's fortunes waned. Federico Borromeo's second patron, Alexander VII Chigi, turned to massive commissions in an attempt to bolster the papacy's loss of international standing in the wake of Westphalia.[30] Interest in the symbolic was, therefore, part and parcel of the social reproduction of papal families: more perhaps than other contemporary elites, they were convinced that art had the potential to trounce inconvenient narratives, both in the present and the future.[31]

If that strategy proved bankable for ruling families in an elective monarchy, the same could be true for the courtier nobility whose power was equally evanescent. As someone in Federico's entourage remarked soon after his arrival in Rome in the 1630s: "Rome is a well of appearances, into which everyone has to throw their own lest they be laughed at behind their back."[32] Federico had arrived prepared: his retinue comprised Niccolò Tornioli (*c.*1598–1651), a Sienese painter.[33] Although his chronic lack of money soon forced him to part ways with Tornioli, Borromeo continued to live up to his reputation as a connoisseur of the arts. By the 1660s, when he finally saw return on his investment, he operationalized the stratagems of his Roman masters for his own family as it crept out of the crisis that Giovanni's pay-to-play had brought on the clan. In 1771, Federico leveraged his elevation to the cardinalate to make a lasting impression on the Milanese scene with an exhibition that presented the family history in a new and favorable light.

Besides planting a new image of the Borromeo, the exhibition of 1771 amplified Antonio Renato's reputation as an appreciator of the arts. As a young man, Antonio Renato had been dispatched to the island of Malta, where he was groomed as a knight of the Order of St. John. According to the letters family members exchanged at the time, he showed little inclination for a life on the battlefields and was drawn to the spirited conversations he had with the Carmelites, the mendicant order founded by sixteenth-century mystic Teresa of Ávila.[34] It also seems likely that he absorbed the impressive baroque art on the island, itself the product of an arms race between knights similar to the one that had produced the city of Rome. What is certain is that when the first comprehensive guide on

---

[28] Karsten, *Künstler*, p. 116.   [29] Scott, *Images*, pp. 193–5; Karsten, *Künstler*, pp. 117–8.
[30] Krautheimer, *The Rome of Alexander*.
[31] On this point, see Burke, *The Fabrication*, p. 153; González Tornel, *Roma*, pp. 22–3.
[32] Quoted in Galli, "Federico IV Borromeo: Scelte," p. 300.   [33] Ibid., p. 308.
[34] Federico IV to Giovanni VII Borromeo, Malta March 28, 1654: *ABIB*, FB, Federico IV, Corrispondenza 1645–1655.

the city's art was published in 1671, the author, the painter-cum-cataloger Agostino Santagostino, dedicated it to Antonio Renato, a "great knight" and "protector of the academy of painters that flourishes nowadays under the powerful auspices of Your Lordship."[35] Tellingly titled *L'immortalità e gloria del pennello* (*The Immortality and Glory of the Paintbrush*), the book made Antonio Renato's name as a man who knew how to use the paintbrush to immortalize his family's glory.

That skill set would prove crucial when Federico's ill-health got the better of him two years after the first exhibition at the Ambrosiana. A lifelong hypochondriac, the cardinal had adopted a strict diet in old age, forgoing such markers of culinary distinction as chocolate (presumably from Spain's American possessions) and his beloved Milanese salami.[36] When this failed to yield the desired outcome, he turned to regular purges until a bloodletting session on February 18, 1673, put a bathetic end to the aspirations of a man who, according to contemporary gossipmongers, stood an excellent chance of being elected the next pope.[37] As he faced the unexpected passing of the only weapon the Borromeos had left to wield, Antonio Renato set out to freeze the nonmaterial legacy of the family cardinal, magicking it into a useful past for himself and other family members. Availing himself of the skills Federico must have taught him, Antonio Renato would invest in artistic commissions in an attempt to perpetuate Federico's nonmaterial legacy as a public servant.

The Rise of Antonio Renato Borromeo

That need for self-affirmation was reinforced by worrying developments in Milan and Spain. Milan's new governor, Gaspar Téllez Girón, Duke of Osuna (r. 1670–1674), was setting out to craft a new social bloc, bringing together social *parvenus* from the financial sector and malcontents from the ranks of the established nobility. Under the guise of balancing the monarchy's budget, Osuna booted out the traditional *togati*, patricians from towns outside Milan who had acquired judicial offices through a university education. Instead, he began selling the posts in Milan's tribunals to the highest bidder, preferring those willing to pay for the privilege to qualified candidates with law degrees.[38] When he ran out of seats to barter, he hatched vanity offices that were equally auctioned off to the *nouveau riche*, many of whom had acquired their wealth through profiteering in

---

[35] Santagostino, *L'immortalità*, p. 3.

[36] Federico IV to Antonio Renato Borromeo, Rome April 11, 1671: *ABIB*, FB, Federico IV, Corrispondenza 1671–1680.

[37] On Federico's career prospects, see Compendioso Ragguaglio delle Fattioni. Nascita, età, costume, et inclinationi di tutti i Cardinali viventi nel Pontificato di Clemente Decimo: *BAV*, Barb. Lat. 4704, f. 33r.

[38] Álvarez-Ossorio Alvariño, "¿Los límites," pp. 174–5, 177.

162   ARISTOCRATIC POWER IN THE SPANISH MONARCHY

the Franco-Spanish War. On closer inspection, these supernumerary positions had little practical value other than buttressing the symbolic capital of their buyers.[39] Under Osuna's watch, then, Milan saw jostling for higher offices on an unprecedented scale, earning the State the unflattering moniker "the great marketplace of the world" to brand it as the territory of the monarchy where corruption was most rampant.[40]

Milan may have stood out as a particularly egregious example, but Osuna's policy was in line with developments in the imperial center. After Nithard's forced departure, the reins of power were taken over by the queen-regent's court familiar, Fernando de Valenzuela (1636–1692), who was mockingly described as the queen's goblin (*duende*) because he had cut his teeth as Mariana's secret informant.[41] The son of an impoverished *hidalgo* from Andalusia, Valenzuela had climbed the social ladder in the power vacuum created by Nithard's expulsion.[42] As a jumped-up commoner, he was responsible for an unprecedented sale of offices in royal courts in the monarchy's American and Italian possessions.[43] As the author of a broadsheet argued, Valenzuela's venality lent credence to his sobriquet "goblin, or demon, for putting justice, as well as all secular positions and holy dignities, on sale."[44] Milan's slurring into a "marketplace" was reflective of broader trends in the monarchy.

In Madrid, as in Milan, established nobles balked at the sudden rise of social *parvenus* to offices they deemed their own. In a bid to explain the unexplainable, a writer close to Federico and Antonio Renato Borromeo attributed Governor Osuna's venality to his cupidity.[45] According to the author of *Il governo del duca d'Osuna* (*The Government of the Duke of Osuna*), the governor's ravenousness came in more than one guise, with the private and the public inextricably bound up together. Not only was the king's alter ego a serial womanizer, the pamphleteer assured his gullible readers, but he also did not disdain the *pecado nefando*, a common reference to homosexual acts.[46] Such fantasies about alleged sexual debauchery were a recurring theme in slanderous campaigns against rulers in the early modern period.[47] Rather than as accurate reporting, such accusations should be deciphered as a symptom of profound unease at the topsy-turvy world the governor had created with his systematic devaluation of noble titles. To the established nobility, the governor's lavish lifestyle as a *picaro* afforded a credible explanation for his social engineering and subversion of supposedly time-honored

---

[39] Álvarez-Ossorio Alvariño, "La república," pp. 184, 187, 190–1; Álvarez-Ossorio Alvariño, "¿Los límites," p. 177; Storrs, *The Resilience*, p. 209.

[40] Álvarez-Ossorio Alvariño, "La república," p. 183; D'Amico, "Spanish Milan," p. 147.

[41] Kamen, "Spain's First Caudillo," p. 589; Álvarez-Ossorio Alvariño, "La república," pp. 196, 257, 273; Ruiz Rodríguez, *Don Juan José*, p. 375.

[42] Kalnein, *Die Regentschaft*, p. 322; Álvarez-Ossorio Alvariño, "El favor," pp. 406–7.

[43] Kalnein, *Die Regentschaft*, pp. 322–3, 356; Ruiz Rodríguez, *Don Juan José*, p. 402.

[44] Quoted ibid., p. 376.   [45] Álvarez-Ossorio Alvariño, "El duque," p. 169.

[46] Arconati Lamberti, *Il governo*, pp. 94, 96.   [47] See Crawford, "The Politics."

PINING FOR STABILITY 163

hierarchies: the Venetian emissary to Milan put it best when he speculated that the social strivers were made to cough up excessive sums for vanity offices to fund the governor's philandering.[48]

The true extent of Osuna's misrule became apparent in the mid-1670s when a special prosecutor was sent into the State to shed light on the governor's wheeling and dealing. The crown's prosecutor uncovered a group of *parvenus* that had coalesced around vanity offices in a network that was promptly dubbed the "family tree (*árbol del parentesco*)."[49] Pedro de Ledesma concluded that Osuna and Valenzuela had systematically elevated "the unworthy, or the less worthy," at the expense of "those who should be rewarded for their merits."[50] What was needed was a thorough purge to re-establish the old order in a classic move to hide the fact that the monarchy's elite was in constant flux.[51]

The Borromeos risked sinking along with Osuna's punters. According to the crown's prosecutor, elements of the established nobility were a central part of the "family tree": the social strivers who had paid for fantasy offices were the tree's branches, but its trunk was some of the leading families of Milan.[52] If the financiers and war profiteers had bought offices in the judiciary, the more entrenched aristocrats had helped themselves to equally made-up military positions. According to De Ledesma, Federico and Antonio Renato's younger brother, Paolo Emilio (1633–1690), had played merrily along, having himself appointed officer of a newly established company and governor-general of the militias in the State of Milan in the early 1670s.[53] Paolo Emilio had long been the black sheep of the family, with a history of rowdy behavior in duels with fellow nobles, which had earned him at least one prison sentence in the 1650s.[54] By dusting off the discredited military tradition under Osuna, Paolo Emilio, in Federico's estimation, did nothing but "discredit the house" in Madrid and jeopardize "everything I have tried to gain in the nunciature" in the Spanish court.[55] By the mid-1670s, as allegations of his collusion in the greatest corruption scandal in Milan's history broke and the resurgence of the repressed memory of Giovanni's tenure as commissioner-general was a real threat, Federico's legacy needed to be shored up as the official version of the family lore more than ever before.

It was against this backdrop that Antonio Renato set out to extricate the dynasty from the association with the *poseurs* from the merchant milieu. To this end, he refashioned the Borromeos as members of a state nobility.[56] Building on

[48] Canosa, *Milano*, p. 232.   [49] Álvarez-Ossorio Alvariño, "La república," pp. 337–8.
[50] Quoted ibid., p. 273.   [51] On this point, see Soria Mesa, *La nobleza*, p. 321.
[52] Álvarez-Ossorio Alvariño, "La república," p. 432; Álvarez-Ossorio Alvariño, "El duque," pp. 199–204.
[53] Galli and Monferrini, *I Borromeo*, p. 38; Dalla Rosa, *Le milizie*, p. 64.
[54] Benvenuti, *Il duca*, p. 261.
[55] Federico IV to Antonio Renato Borromeo, Rome July 16, 1672: *ABIB*, FB, Federico IV, Corrispondenza 1671–1680.
[56] On the term, see Bourdieu, *The State Nobility*.

164   ARISTOCRATIC POWER IN THE SPANISH MONARCHY

his earlier experience with the exhibition in the Ambrosiana, Antonio Renato invested heavily in the depiction of his clan as loyal servants of the Spanish crown. Backgrounding Paolo Emilio and the social strivers who had intermittently ruled the roost in Milan, he foregrounded Federico, making him the star of a series of paintings in which the family stood high above the *parvenus* with whom it had been associated in the wake of Osuna's fall. The depictions of the family's Spanish connection he commissioned from Filippo Abbiati (1640–1715), an epigone of Mattia Preti's and a rising star in Milan, in the late 1670s and early 1680s, were to be exhibited in the stateroom of the castle of Angera, where the Borromeos' liaisons with the house of Habsburg had begun half a century earlier (see chapter 1).[57]

Unlike in the Ambrosiana exhibition with its unequivocal juxtaposition of the past and the present, Antonio Renato Borromeo chose to work through history paintings at Angera. That genre was widely appreciated at the time for its pedagogical value, lending itself particularly well to deployment in the fanfare of self-congratulation Antonio Renato had in mind.[58] A knockoff of similar pictorial representations of family deeds such as the *fasti farnesiani* in the Farnese's villa in Caprarola outside Rome, Antonio Renato's *fasti borromei* centered on the Borromeos' dynastic glories, working predominantly through allusions to progenitors in order to establish continuities between past and present.[59] As Antonio Renato must have learned from Federico and his keen observation of the strategies of papal families, not only were historical allegories useful for making grandiose claims about the family without these resulting in accusations of delusions of grandeur and crude propaganda; but allegories were also more convincing than direct references to the present because they were a knowing wink that appealed to the viewers' learnedness. As Arne Karsten explains, unlike straightforward representations, allegories required spectators to marshal their knowledge of the family history to tease out the hidden meanings. The paintings worked psychologically: those who managed to connect the dots were so proud of themselves, they readily accepted the paintings' subliminal message.[60]

Among the allegorical paintings realized by Filippo Abbiati, two stand out in particular: the *Solemn Banquet Offered by Vitaliano I Borromeo to the King of Naples, Alfonso of Aragon, and the Duke of Milan, Filippo Maria Visconti* (fig. 8.3), and the *Solemn Entry of Isabella of Aragon, Bride of Gian Galeazzo Sforza, Taken to Milan by Giovanni Borromeo* (fig. 8.4), depicting two documented events of the early and late fifteenth century, respectively.[61] Although conceived as a continuation of the earlier pictures Giovanni had commissioned in the 1650s (see chapter 4),

---

[57] Zuffi, "La pittura," p. 392.

[58] Galli and Monferrini, *I Borromeo*, pp. 44–5.

[59] Ibid., p. 45. Antonio Renato's grandmother on his father's side was a Farnese. On the *fasti*, see Robertson, "Il Gran Cardinale," pp. 95–103, and Partridge, "Divinity."

[60] Karsten, *Künstler*, pp. 25–6, 226.

[61] Zuffi, "La pittura," pp. 393–4, 396; Natale, *Le Isole*, pp. 142–3.

Fig. 8.3 Filippo Abbiati, *Solemn Banquet Offered by Vitaliano I Borromeo to the King of Naples, Alfonso of Aragon, and the Duke of Milan, Filippo Maria Visconti*, 1683–1685, oil on canvas, Angera, Rocca di Angera, Sala dei Fasti Borromeo
(Università degli Studi dell'Insubria—International Research Center for Local Histories and Cultural Diversities, Archivio Fotografico, Fondo Vivi Papi—all rights reserved)

the paintings of the 1670s were indicative of the metamorphosis the family's conception of itself had undergone since mid-century. Not only did most of the new paintings allude to historical episodes more solidly moored in reality than the first canvas;[62] these *fasti* also spoke to the Borromeos' new self-positioning: whereas Giovanni had portrayed himself as the heir of maverick military entrepreneurs from late antiquity, the new series emphasized the clan's close ties to Milan's ruling dynasties of the Renaissance, the Visconti and the Sforza. The link between the past and the present rulers was established thanks to the two references to the Neapolitan house of Aragon: they brought back to life what contemporaries saw as the earliest encounter between Iberia and Italy, harnessing the Visconti and Sforza period for the Habsburg present.[63]

---

[62] On this trend, see Spagnoletti, *Le dinastie*, pp. 316–8.
[63] Carrió-Invernizzi, *El gobierno*, ch. 3. On the revival of the legacy of the last Aragonese king, Ferdinand the Catholic, during Charles II's reign, see Carrasco, "Los grandes," pp. 92–3.

Fig. 8.4 Filippo Abbiati, *Solemn Entry of Isabella d'Aragona, Bride of Gian Galeazzo Sforza, Taken to Milan by Giovanni Borromeo*, 1683–1685, oil on canvas, Angera, Rocca di Angera, Sala dei Fasti Borromeo

(Università degli Studi dell'Insubria—International Research Center for Local Histories and Cultural Diversities, Archivio Fotografico, Fondo Vivi Papi—all rights reserved)

The roles the Borromeos played in these reminiscences were equally telling: family members acted as brokers of peace settlements and dynastic marriages on behalf of Milan's rulers. The paintings created a line of continuity between a distant late medieval past and the recent past of the 1660s and 1670s.[64] Through their allegorical references to earlier princely servants, the *fasti* paid tribute to Federico as a nuncio in the court of Spain and secretary of state. To the initiated, the peace deal was an allusion to Federico's (negligible) role in brokering the peace of Aix-la-Chapelle between the Spanish and the French crowns, for which he had originally been dispatched to Madrid in 1668.[65] The painting may also have been a hint at his role as a peacemaker during the Nithard crisis (see chapter 7), which featured prominently in the collective memory: as late as 1793, the compiler of a collection of vignettes of cardinals would praise Borromeo for "making shine his wisdom and ability in settling and calming the strife that was clouding the monarchy and was close to erupting into open warfare."[66] The marital alliance, meanwhile, was an equally transparent reference to Borromeo's (also insignificant) part in arranging a failed marriage alliance between the brother of the King of England, James Stuart, Duke of York (1633–1701), and the Archduchess of Innsbruck, Claudia Felicitas (1653–1676), which he sought to finalize as secretary of state in 1672 through a secret correspondence with the

---

[64] On the need to create continuity, see Dewald, *Status*, p. 13.
[65] Pastor, *The History*, pp. 416–7.   [66] Cardella, *Memorie*, p. 204.

English ambassador in Madrid and Queen Mariana.[67] That both endeavors were hardly exploits was of little consequence: the allegorical depictions of them still drove home the point that the Borromeos were inveterate servants of the ruling dynasty in Milan, whether the Visconti, the Sforza, or the Habsburgs.[68]

In putting allusions to Federico at the center of their self-fashioning, the Borromeos asserted their membership of the pan-Hispanic courtier elite. Through recourse to allegory, Antonio Renato showed that his family was so knotted up with the house of Habsburg that its members brokered peace deals and arranged weddings on their behalf. Unlike the Viennese nobility studied by Andreas Pečar, which was in denial about its growing dependence on the ruling dynasty, the Borromeos made their proximity to the Habsburgs legible.[69] For professed closeness to the ruling family put distance between those who served the embodiment of the collective good and the self-serving strivers of the "family tree."

Form was perhaps even more decisive than content here: the artistic packaging reinforced the message the family wanted to convey. As the lines between the established nobility and *parvenus* blurred, the ability to convert economic into cultural capital had become indispensable to enforcing hierarchy on insolent strivers.[70] Like in Naples, where artistic commissions were peaking in the 1660s and 1670s, legitimate taste in art became a pattern of classification that signified membership of an elite within the elite.[71] For families like the Borromeos, an ostentatious sense of discernment was the easiest way to distance themselves from moneyed interests.[72] As Pierre Bourdieu explains: "To appropriate a work of art is to assert oneself as the exclusive possessor of the object and of the authentic taste for that object, which is thereby converted into the reified negation of all those who are unworthy of possessing it."[73] Inscrutable as it was to outsiders unfamiliar with the subtle finesse of its messaging, allegorical art was in and of itself evidence of the Borromeos' exalted position in Milan. Since the proper appreciation of art required long-term investment in education, paintings remained the preserve of the few who had the right pedigree to acquire and pass on a well-honed sense of distinction from generation to generation.[74] It was in their form, as well as in their content, that the *fasti* put down the Borromeos'

---

[67] Galeazzo Marescotti to Paluzzo Paluzzi Altieri, Madrid June 14, 1673: *AAV*, Segr. Stato, Spagna, vol. 143, f. 289r; Domenico Millanta to Federico IV Borromeo, Madrid September 22, 1672: *BAV*, Barb. Lat. 9867, f. 496r; de Gennaro, *La crisi*, pp. 108–12.

[68] On the need to create continuity where there was none in a highly volatile system, see Soria Mesa, *La nobleza*, pp. 17, 320–1.

[69] Pečar, "Status-Ökonomie," p. 104.

[70] On the conversion of economic into cultural capital, see ibid., p. 96.

[71] On Naples, see Carrió-Invernizzi, *El gobierno*, pp. 341–2; on Milan, see Cremonini, *Le vie*, p. 30.

[72] Bourdieu, *Distinction*, p. 6. Also see Pečar, "Status-Ökonomie," p. 96, and Cremonini, *Le vie*, p. 30.

[73] Bourdieu, *Distinction*, p. 280. [74] Ibid., p. 281.

168   ARISTOCRATIC POWER IN THE SPANISH MONARCHY

rivals who were arrogantly trying to outbid them from a position they had paid for rather than earned through graft, as truly meritorious nobles did.[75]

To the Borromeos, then, artistic patronage was laden with political meaning. As Pierre Bourdieu has long argued, symbolism is never disconnected from more tangible forms of power. In fact, symbolic expressions of predominance are constitutive of, and crucial to, the maintenance of social difference.[76] By lending elite rule an aura of inevitability, symbolism naturalizes hierarchies and helps elites to exercise what Bourdieu calls "symbolic violence": the power to impose meaning on others. For the Borromeos, art created a fait accompli: it foisted their own reading of reality on a skeptical public that was invited to become privy to the perpetuation of the clan's favored narrative. Repressing their own recent past as war profiteers, the Borromeos pinned their hopes on artistic commissions, believing that these would place them firmly in a small elite that wagered not on venality but on its close connection to the ruling dynasty. The family histories that French nobles commissioned at the time "reminded themselves and everyone else who listened that they rendered the king personal service and that the merits most essential to that service came from a culture to which only some families belonged."[77] The Borromeos' pictorial representations performed a similar function. Rather than as crass propaganda, the *fasti borromei* ought to be read as a legitimation of the Borromeos' will to power in the radically altered circumstances of the 1670s. Having been provincial upstarts themselves, the Borromeos were determined to defend the newly acquired position against the encroaching of new *parvenus*.[78]

If art created distinction, it also suggested presence when real influence was beginning to sag. The Spanish monarchy was itself a perfect example of this. As it staggered into the regency and the reign of an enfeebled and underage monarch after the death of Philip IV, the governing elite increasingly relied on pictorial strategies to alleviate the perceived absence of a strong monarch. The viceroys of Naples had been among the first to enhance the visibility of the Spanish monarch in the Italian peninsula.[79] This "government through images," as Diana Carrió-Invernizzi has called it, fed back to the imperial center when a Neapolitan painter, Luca Giordano (1634–1705), decorated the royal palace at El Escorial with a fresco that immortalized the grandeurs of the Spanish Habsburgs when they were already on the way out. Art became what Judith Wellen has dubbed a "panegyric safety net" that concealed a yawning power vacuum.[80]

The Borromeos, in the picture gallery at Angera, similarly eternalized the family's Spanish connection at a time when those ties had been weakened by the

---

[75] Smith, *The Culture*.
[76] Swartz, *Symbolic Power*, p. 4; Stollberg-Rilinger, *The Emperor's Old Clothes*, pp. 3–4.
[77] Smith, *The Culture*, p. 91.   [78] On this point, see Soria Mesa, *La nobleza*, p. 16.
[79] Carrió-Invernizzi, *El gobierno*, pp. 17, 218, 233.   [80] Wellen, *Bilder*, p. 335.

death of the family member who had done most to cultivate them. Knowing that he was probably going to die without an heir, Antonio Renato spent the tail end of his life investing heavily in image-making. As early as 1671, Giulio Cesare Beagna, the secretary of the Arona branch of the Borromeo family, had reported that Federico "will be spending big because he believes his branch will not have heirs."[81] When Federico, the presentable face of the clan, died, Antonio Renato availed himself of the same technique to preserve the nonmaterial legacy of the family cardinal. The interior of the fortress above Lake Maggiore was to represent the family's deeds for future generations to come, allowing them to reactivate a nonmaterial legacy and wallow in glories past when it suited them.

The Aristocratic Government of Juan José of Austria

The Angera cycle was commissioned just in time for the Borromeos to benefit from the changes underway in the monarchy. In the late 1670s, Juan José of Austria used the outrage at Valenzuela to attain the prestige he had been hankering after since the death of Philip IV. Following a failed coup in November 1675, Juan José finally succeeded in ejecting the *duende* in January 1677.[82] After years of nagging criticism from the bastard, Carlos II, who had recently come of age, finally offered his stepbrother a pre-eminent position in government as Spain's first "prime minister." In his new capacity, Juan José was able to dress himself up as a member of the royal family and the embodiment of the collective good, as he had done ten years earlier in the coup against Nithard (see chapter 7). If Olivares had been the "king's shadow," Juan José claimed to be the "king's image": he was not in the game for his own gain but the advancement of his stepbrother, the monarch, and his subjects.[83] He would now oversee the disinterested distribution of royal patronage that Valenzuela had failed to guarantee.[84]

The traditional nobility, who had been appalled at Valenzuela and the social *parvenus* in his entourage, promptly lined up to serve Juan José. Harnessing Juan José's cleanup against Valenzuela for their own ends, eminent nobles leveled charges of corruption at the *duende*'s clients to restore their former position of power.[85] A petition from Sicilian aristocrats bemoaned the fact that they had been "defrauded by Spain" of the "prerogatives" and "posts" in the court and the army they were owed.[86] Their campaign relied on a definition of nobility combining blue blood and meritocracy that had been gaining traction in Spanish Italy.[87] As early as 1673, Pedro de Avilés, in a treatise published in Naples, had argued

[81] Quoted in Galli and Monferrini, *I Borromeo*, p. 33.
[82] For a detailed account, see Kalnein, *Die Regentschaft*, ch. 5–6.
[83] Hermant, *Guerres*, p. 424.   [84] Kamen, *Spain*, p. 27.
[85] Ruiz Rodríguez, *Don Juan José*, pp. 454–5.   [86] Quoted in Rao, "I filosofi," p. 1525.
[87] Donati, *L'idea*, p. 278.

170   ARISTOCRATIC POWER IN THE SPANISH MONARCHY

that royal patronage should be allocated based on noble birth. As he saw it: "The highest dignities...belonging to the first hierarchy need to be awarded to nobles, even if they are not as well-suited or loved by the prince as others." If, instead, these were liberally parceled out to "humble people," the positions themselves risked being devalued by the "baseness of those who obtained them."[88] Such a cult of the blood nobility fell on receptive ears in Milan.[89] As the "family tree" was uprooted, established clans came to argue that the truly meritorious were not just those who had served the king but those who had done so out of a long family tradition—what they called "inherited merit."[90] To that segment of the nobility, Juan José was an ideal standard-bearer.[91] Such was his commitment to the traditional aristocracy that he was working overtime to reinstate many of the Sicilian nobles who faced trial on charges of treason after the War of Messina (1674–1678).[92] Recognizing in him a blood relative of the king, many aristocrats in other parts of Spanish Italy placed him at the helm of a project to reinstate those sections of the nobility that owed their exalted position, not to venality, but to long-standing princely service.

The Borromeos were no exception. Antonio Renato ingratiated himself with Juan José on two levels. In a pamphlet against Valenzuela and Osuna, an author close to Borromeo and his faction argued that the bastard personified the winning formula of "birth and merit" that made him an ideal purveyor of good governance.[93] As the stepbrother of the king who had finally come of age, he was a "prince no less brave and generous than noble" who had had the misfortune of being "deprived of a position that should have been conferred on him" a long time before.[94] If Juan José had been cheated out of his natural role by upstarts, this wrong had finally been righted: thanks to the new king, he had been put in charge of the monarchy along with the families who had always stood with him, even in the darkest moments when Federico Borromeo had done his utmost to support the bastard during the Nithard crisis.

Antonio Renato's artistic commissions similarly insisted on the link between Juan José and the Borromeo family. If the gallery at Angera was relatively abstract, though not without allusions to the Nithard incident, the paintings that Antonio Renato commissioned in 1678 for the main residence of the family in Milan's Via Rugabella could not have been more blatant about the intimate relationship between Juan José and the Borromeos. The centerpiece of the exhibition in the foyer of the family mansion were two paintings by an alumnus of the Ambrosiana

---

[88]   Pedro de Avilés, *Advertencias de un político a su Príncipe*, quoted in Carrasco, "Los grandes," p. 82.
[89]   Donati, *L'idea*, pp. 266–7, 279.
[90]   Álvarez-Ossorio Alvariño, "El favor," pp. 407, 419. Also see Mozzarelli, "Strutture," pp. 439–40, 446.
[91]   Álvarez-Ossorio Alvariño, "La república," p. 513.   [92]   Ribot García, *La Monarquía*, p. 614.
[93]   Arconati Lamberti, *Il governo*, p. 6. On Arconati's position, see Álvarez-Ossorio Alvariño, "El duque," p. 169, n. 17.
[94]   Arconati Lamberti, *Il governo*, p. 5.

academy, Ercole Procaccini the Younger (1605–1680). One of the now lost canvases depicted Philip IV of Spain alone, while the other featured an encounter between the king and his bastard son, Juan José of Austria.[95] If the paintings were a glowing tribute to the men to whom the Borromeos had hitched their fate in the past, they were also an indication of where the massive investment in artistic patronage was supposed to take them: within the circle of the "aristocratic republic" of high nobles who were finally consolidating their power as courtiers assisting Carlos II.[96] As the 1670s drew to a close, the Borromeos unequivocally portrayed themselves as an integral part of that benevolent elite that helped the royal family deliver good government.[97]

That fantasy turned out so stout because it had a disciplining effect on fellow nobles. It was ultimately inconsequential whether the Borromeos really believed in the embellished renditions of the family history they commissioned. Art purchased to glorify the high and mighty, Peter Burke has proposed, ought to be read as "re-presentations," as having the power to evoke something that remained elusive, bridging the gap between excessive expectations and a reality that many found wanting.[98] In a society that valued decorum more than authenticity and sincerity, paintings became convincing when they conformed to a certain set of expectations.[99] More importantly still, canvases functioned because they were embedded in a network of mutual dependencies. Since every family relied on similar stratagems to present itself, members of the in-crowd had an interest in claiming to believe their rivals' yarns, lest their own self-representations be questioned. This fostered a form of collective misrecognition at the pinnacle of society that proved infinitely more difficult to challenge from below than the blatant hypocrisy in which the Borromeos and others had dabbled when they started on their trajectory and the aging family cardinal crafted mendacious tracts to cover up the family's corruption (see chapter 1). Art, unlike the awkward bromides of the early decades of the century, boosted what Barbara Stollberg-Rilinger calls the "collective belief in the necessity, self-evident nature, and inviolability" of an established order.[100]

The Borromeos' repositioning as local oligarchs in the 1670s was typical for a family of their time and station. Historians have often noted the similarities between the Kingdom of Aragon and the Milanese State under Carlos II, placing heavy emphasis on the centrifugal forces at work in both territories. The proponents of *neoforalismo*, as this school of thought has been dubbed, are not entirely wrong: the late 1670s did see a strengthening of the local nobility, not least in response to the very real decline of what had once been the uncontested imperial

[95] Galli and Monferrini, *I Borromeo*, pp. 45, n. 221; 51; 83.
[96] On aristocratic concepts among Spain's high nobility, see Storrs, *The Resilience*, pp. 158–9.
[97] On this self-fashioning, see Karsten, *Künstler*, pp. 25–6.
[98] Burke, *The Fabrication*, pp. 5, 8, 11.   [99] Ibid., pp. 11–3; Reinhardt, "Kreise," p. 22.
[100] Stollberg-Rilinger, *The Emperor's Old Clothes*, p. 5.

172 ARISTOCRATIC POWER IN THE SPANISH MONARCHY

center—Castile.[101] What is less convincing about the well-worn narrative, though, is the underlying assumption that the push toward oligarchization meant a return to the times at the beginning of the seventeenth century, before successive minister-favorites made ultimately unsuccessful bids to unite the composite Spanish monarchy. Seen from the standpoint of local elites, the developments of the 1670s were not a return to a glorious past of local autonomy but a logical reinvention of the Olivares project after the original version had faltered under the unbridled greed of its stakeholders. Understanding that elite integration could not be achieved through clientelism alone, the eminent families of Aragon and Lombardy fought their way back from the abyss by other means: through artistic depictions of the good government that they were allegedly showering on the king's subjects.

Crucially, that reinvention was rationalized with a tradition of fealty to the house of Habsburg.[102] What the proponents of *neoforalismo* have mistaken for the strengthening of the local nobility was, really, a reinforcing of a reconstructed Spanish nobility who, redefining Olivares's dream of an integrated pan-Hispanic elite, saw themselves as purveyors of good government acting in the name of the royal family.[103] With the rise of this courtier elite, many others were pushed aside, in a process that had more in common with developments in Louis XIV's France than has hitherto been acknowledged. As Anglo-American revisionists have indicated, that of Louis XIV was a regime based on the "social collaboration" between the high nobility and a king whose might was symbolically constructed in a process of collective misrecognition.[104] If Louis XIV played a decisive role in capping off the transactionalism of Richelieu and Mazarin,[105] the nobility of the composite Spanish empire actively hardened the *monarquía* into an "aristocratic republic" that relied on projections of a strong monarch to pacify the twin threat of commoners and ennobled *parvenus* coming for the old aristocracy's predominance.[106] The Borromeos who muscled into Madrid's good graces through investment in symbolic power exalting the monarchy and a loyal aristocracy were only the most prominent example of a fundamental shift underway in seventeenth-century politics.

---

[101] See Storrs, *The Resilience*, pp. 11, 191–4, 229; Carrasco, "Los grandes," pp. 110–3.

[102] As demonstrated by Aragonese authors' enthusiasm for Charles II. See Storrs, *The Resilience*, p. 192.

[103] Jago, "The 'Crisis'," pp. 86–7. Also see Beik, *Absolutism*, p. 337.

[104] For a comparative view of France, see Horowski, *Die Belagerung*, pp. 39–43, 47–53. The classic formulation of "absolutism" as a form of "social collaboration" is Beik, "The Absolutism." The standard text on the "fabrication" of Louis XIV is Burke, *The Fabrication*.

[105] Parrott, *1652*, p. 279.

[106] See Storrs, in *The Resilience*, pp. 166, 190, who rejects the qualifier to argue that the monarchy was more "absolute" than historians had thitherto allowed. For a similar reading, see Thompson, "The Nobility," p. 218. The evidence presented here points in the opposite direction.

Conclusion

Federico's indefatigable work as a biddable servant of the Habsburgs had allowed the Borromeos to leave the odor of self-interest behind them. Thanks to his role as a member of the college of cardinals, he became so imbricated with the Spanish governing elite that he temporarily acted as a de facto member of the exclusive group to which his brother, the knight, had been denied access (see chapter 4). However, that membership was contingent on the curial offices he held, and the influence gained through them was bound to wither away after his death. To pre-empt this, he took a strategy out of the playbook of the papal families he had served and began to invest massively in artistic representations of himself and his record of accomplishments, hoping that these commissions would outlive him.

When he died much earlier than expected, his younger brother Antonio Renato took his lesson to heart. Throughout the 1670s, Antonio Renato established himself as a patron of the Milanese art scene and used his exalted position to keep Federico's nonmaterial legacy alive. The canvases he commissioned from leading local artists were to sway viewers through their form, as well as their content. In a climate where war profiteers and other upstarts were elbowing themselves into Spanish government, the Borromeos' distinction—their taste and discerning qualities—were to emphasize the message these commissions sent home: unlike the social strivers, the Borromeos had a long record as refined courtiers in the service of the rulers of the Milanese State. Depicting Federico's disinterested devotedness to the man who came out on top of the factional strife in Madrid, Juan José of Austria, the paintings suggested that the Borromeos belonged to the small group of families who deserved to be admitted to the aristocracy that was taking shape around the bastard in the late 1670s.

Unfortunately for him, Antonio Renato did not benefit from the symbolic turn he had given to the family's rule. When he died equally childless as Giovanni in 1686, the baton passed to Paolo Emilio, who passed away four years later, in 1690. His death spelled the end of the Angera branch of the Borromeo family. Yet all was not lost: the main branch quickly translated the Angera clan's *rapprochement* with the house of Habsburg into symbolic capital for itself. As early as 1678, Carlo IV Borromeo (1657–1734) had obtained the Order of the Golden Fleece that his cousin Giovanni from the Angera branch had been denied (see chapter 4). As his relationship with the Habsburgs deepened, the Borromeos handily converted the cadet branch's support of the Madrid side to the Viennese Habsburgs during the War of the Spanish Succession. When the Austrian Habsburgs eventually became lords of Milan, Carlo's fledgling career took off for good. In 1710, he was nominated viceroy of Austrian Naples before being appointed plenipotentiary of the imperial fiefs in Italy, serving the Emperor as a central coordinator of his important feudal possessions in the Italian peninsula.[107] What had looked like a long shot at the beginning of the *Seicento* had become an unassailable reality by century's end: after decades of unremitting struggle, the Borromeos were, at long last, respected servants of the Habsburgs whose beneficent power was no longer questioned by anyone, both in early modern court society and in later historiography.

[107] See Cremonini, *Ritratto*, pp. 177–213; Cremonini, "La mediazione," pp. 47–8.

Epilogue

The Crisis of Favoritism and the Courtization of the Nobility

In 1650, when the worst of the crisis of the Spanish monarchy seemed to be over, a treatise titled *La Monarchia di Spagna* (*The Spanish Monarchy*) rolled off the printing presses in northern Italy. Its author left no doubt that the beating heart of the empire was Milan and its valiant warrior nobility, the "true treasures of the most stable monarchies."[1] Even though Milan had been "the target of the thunderbolts of the enemies," he argued, it had "never collapsed regardless of how many terrible hits of the most forceful sort it took from those who had always been envious and fearful of the happiness of the Spanish monarchy."[2] Contemporaries would have had few problems decoding this encomium to the Milanese's fidelity as a veiled indictment of the revolting Catalans, Portuguese, Neapolitans, and Sicilians. Indeed, as the author reminded Philip IV: "Lucky is the monarch who does not lack great vassals to bolster his greatness."[3] Driving this effusive praise of the king's Milanese vassals was an ulterior motive: to those immersed in contemporary political culture, it was clear that this exaltation was a not-so-subtle request for the rewards that the warrior nobility felt it deserved for keeping the faith when its peers elsewhere had jeopardized the king's global empire.

One family who was impatient to be elevated in acknowledgment of its role in the preservation of the monarchy was the Borromeos. By the standards they were familiar with, there was much they could expect from the Habsburgs in 1650. One of the leading houses of the State of Milan, the Borromeos had adapted quickly to the new regime of the minister-favorite that had emerged in the Spanish court at the turn of the seventeenth century. From the 1620s onward, Giulio Cesare Borromeo and his eldest son, Giovanni, embraced the Count-Duke of Olivares's common defense policy, the Union of Arms, and positioned the family as military entrepreneurs, willing to fend off French attacks on what the crown's military strategists referred to as the "heart of the monarchy." When conflict descended on northern Italy in the 1630s, they fought off the negative repercussions. When acceptance of the war waned among an increasingly leery

---

[1] Crescenzio Romani, *La Monarchia*, p. 32.   [2] Ibid.   [3] Ibid., p. 33.

176 ARISTOCRATIC POWER IN THE SPANISH MONARCHY

population in the 1640s, Giovanni Borromeo devised an ingenious way of averting the popular revolts that had hampered the military effort elsewhere. Seeing that the lodging of troops and the taxes levied to fund the war had been a motor of the rebellions in Catalonia and Naples, he invested heavily in the establishment of a new system of troop accommodation and provisioning in Lombardy. By 1650, therefore, he felt well within his rights to make the social advancement that Olivares had promised his *protégés* finally come true. As a paragon of the fidelity that the author of *La Monarchia di Spagna* extolled, Borromeo had every reason to believe himself a suitable candidate for the honorifics that beckoned those who had stayed loyal.

What Giovanni Borromeo failed to register was that, despite the Milanese's fidelity, the entitlement to which *La Monarchia di Spagna* gave such eloquent expression was on the way out. The *valimiento* may have been a suitable method of elite integration in the early decades of the seventeenth century, but by the 1650s, it had become apparent that favoritism had incentivized a form of self-enrichment that was threatening the cohesion of the monarchy. If the Borromeos had claimed from the outset that their profiteering was conducive to the common good, the Franco-Spanish War had made it clear that the warrior nobility's commitment to kith and kin undermined the commonwealth rather than advancing it. The first to question the trickle-down theory cherished in elite circles had been the village communities that the Borromeos claimed to protect from the very ravages of the war they treated as a source of social upward mobility. These commoners were followed by rivals within the nobility who weaponized accusations of hypocrisy when Giovanni Borromeo came to collect his trophy in the 1650s. Punishing this exemplary *olivarista* for furthering private interests under the cloak of royal service, they dismantled the *valimiento* and, with it, the warrior nobility that had pinned its hopes on the minister-favorite.

The Borromeos only bounced back from Giovanni's rout when his younger brother, Federico, adapted to the new post-*valido* age. As an oligarchy of imperial grandees took over the reins of power from the last minister-favorite, Federico posed as a standard-bearer of disinterested royal service. As a member of the clergy and (in the final years of his life) of the college of cardinals, he was perhaps particularly well-suited to smoothen the transition from maverick noble to courtier-aristocrat. His last-ditch effort to save the family is an impressive illustration of, at once, the powers of adaptability in family strategies and the value of distinct masculinities as bargaining chips in rapidly changing circumstances.[4] Federico helped transform the monarchy into a commonwealth in which the king imposed himself as an arbiter of distributive justice and nobles helped him implement good government instead of sabotaging the commonwealth with their

---

[4] Rabinovitch, *The Perraults*, p. 5.

EPILOGUE: THE CRISIS OF FAVORITISM   177

narrow fixation on the social reproduction of their respective clans. The contraption with which they came up—dubbed the "baroque state"—relied on institutions publicly committed to the preservation of the common good, while shielding the persistent promotion of private interest with public displays of royal munificence.[5] As they abandoned their former illusions of military grandeur, the Borromeos became royal servants whose interests had come to dovetail with those of the royal family, that epitome of the commonwealth. Crawling out of a crisis largely of their own making, the Borromeos sought to tackle the contradiction at the heart of their rule through outward compliance with the ideal of the commonwealth.

So impenetrable was this misrecognition of private interest as disinterested public service that it has misled contemporaries and later historians alike. The Borromeos are commemorated today as the shining light of what in Italian popular culture is still deeply ingrained as the dark period of Spanish predominance. The most efficacious multiplier of this image has been Alessandro Manzoni's classic novel, *The Betrothed*, which depicts Federico Borromeo Sr. as a particularly virtuous caretaker of the collective good who stood out from the rest of the pack of rapacious nobles. In Manzoni's etching, "Federigo considered true charity his primary duty, and here, as in all else, his actions were consistent with these convictions. He gave generously to the poor throughout his life."[6] Manzoni's fiercest critic, the Marxist philosopher Antonio Gramsci, was only half-right when he brushed off this characterization as the mere projection of the author's own tendency to view "humble people" as "animals" who ought to be treated "with the kind of benevolence appropriate to a Catholic society for the protection of animals."[7] As this book has shown, Manzoni's artistic rendition of the personage was inflected as much by his own Catholic paternalism as by the very conscious misrecognition operated by the cardinal's great-nephews when they rebranded their dynasty as Spanish loyalists in the seventeenth century.

If the example of the Borromeos stands out as particularly notable, their metamorphosis speaks to the long-raging historiographical debate on the "courtization of the nobility." That trope is as old as Norbert Elias's sociological work on the French court of Louis XIV. In *The Court Society* of 1969, Elias famously argued that, during the reign of the Sun King, the French warrior nobility was "domesticated" by a farsighted monarch who deprived it of its former jurisdictional powers in the countryside and trapped it in the "gilded cage" of Versailles.[8] More recently, revisionist historians such as Ronald G. Asch, Jeroen Duindam, and Hamish Scott have drawn attention to the agency of the nobility in this process.[9] Ditching the narrative of the terminal crisis of the aristocracy in the seventeenth

---

[5] Campbell, *Power*, p. 4; Rowlands, *The Dynastic State*, p. 10; Stollberg-Rilinger, "The Baroque State."
[6] Manzoni, *The Betrothed*, p. 362.   [7] Gramsci, *Prison Notebooks*, p. 196.
[8] Elias, *The Court Society*, ch. 7–8. The book was written in the 1930s.
[9] Duindam, *Myths*, pp. 43–4, 79, 95; Asch, *Nobilities*; Scott, ed., *The European Nobilities*.

178   ARISTOCRATIC POWER IN THE SPANISH MONARCHY

century, these scholars have argued that the nobility was, on the contrary, resilient and willing to adapt to changing circumstances. Enthralled by the opportunities that centralized princely courts had to offer them, the warrior nobles of old are said to have morphed into courtiers who availed themselves of the material and immaterial resources of the court to increase their clout in the early modern society of orders. Far from opposing the growth of state institutions, as Elias believed, the high nobility had a vital interest in their expansion, an expansion that allowed the social group to rebadge itself in response to the multiple crises of the age.[10] By signing up for a "social collaboration" with the monarchy, the nobility managed to redefine its predominance as a new class of princely servants, at once dependent on and protected by monarchs whose power it actively helped construct.[11]

This argument has been an important corrective to accounts that attribute too much power to supposedly absolute kings, but it has perhaps overemphasized the agency of nobles. The Borromeos' gattopardism reveals that the courtization of the warrior nobility was not so much a voluntary act as it was a riposte to popular resistance to favoritism. What forced the clan to align its interests with those of the monarch was the protest of village communities who pointed out the inconsistencies between the Borromeos' pursuit of egotistical interests and their professed ideals of good government.[12] Like the British monarchs after the Civil Wars, clans in the Spanish monarchy adopted the notion of their inferiors that those who had gotten much out of the setup of the early seventeenth century ought to give back to the community lest they lose everything.[13] Courtization, then, was a response to the legitimacy crisis of favoritism that compelled the nobility to fine-tune the reproduction of social inequality. By holding the elite to ransom, ordinary people had nudged the Borromeos and their peers to dress up their rule. Nobles now had, in Pierre Bourdieu's words, to lend "universal form to the expression of their vested interest, to elaborate a theory of public service and of public order, and thus to work to autonomize the *reason of state* from dynastic reason."[14] Recapping the transformation of the nobility in the seventeenth century, the adage of anthropologist James C. Scott rings true: changes to elite rule often "originate in critiques within the hegemony."[15] Change, in other words, happens when subaltern actors appropriate the values of the ruling classes and hold their failure to live up to them against them.

These dynamics had long-term consequences. As families like the Borromeos took in the inconsistency of their rule, they abandoned the posture of maverick knights and morphed into princely servants, molding the clamoring from below

---

[10]   Beik, *Absolutism*; Parker, *Class*.

[11]   Bonahan, *Crown*; Beik, "The Absolutism"; Friedeburg and Morrill, eds., *Monarchy Transformed*; Stollberg-Rilinger, *The Emperor's Old Clothes*; Burke, *The Fabrication*.

[12]   On these dynamics, see Castiglione, *Patrons*.   [13]   Prochaska, *Royal Bounty*.

[14]   Bourdieu, "Rethinking," p. 16.   [15]   Scott, *Domination*, p. 106.

into benevolent initiatives from above. What they failed to anticipate was that, in so doing, they heightened the contradictions of their rule in ways that would ultimately prove unsustainable. By redefining the common good as identical with the well-being of the royal family and the collectivity of subjects it represented, they inadvertently contributed to the delegitimization of the "familism" to which they owed their fortunes as members of the Spanish ruling class. As they paid lip service to the commonwealth, they operated toward the supersession of the preferment of kith and kin which, as Jens Ivo Engels and Robert Bernsee have taught us, transpired sometime in the eighteenth century.[16] In trying to save their skin, they established a new hierarchy of norms, with the commonwealth trumping the narrow interests of the family. In due course, this rearrangement of priorities would open the floodgates to a redefinition of the commonwealth as a community of individuals with equal rights in the Atlantic Revolutions. In the long run, then, the espousal of social responsibility, insincere as it may have been, swept away a social order built on inherited privilege. Alas, the same cannot be said of the paternalism toward the poor the Borromeos affected so masterfully. Indeed, the recent rise of plutocrats feigning concern about the inequalities of our own times might be nothing more than the latest ruse to change everything in order to change nothing at all.[17] It is to be hoped that the long view only a careful examination of the past can bring to these debates will contribute toward unmasking and dismantling, once and for all, this particularly insidious form of misrecognition.

---

[16] Engels, "Corruption," p. 175; Bernsee, "For the Good," pp. 259, 263.
[17] Savage, *Inequality*, pp. 14–6.

Bibliography

Manuscript Sources

Archivio Apostolico Vaticano, Vatican City
  Archivio della Nunziatura di Lucerna: 118, 119, 120, 121, 122
  Archivio della Nunziatura di Madrid: 1, 2, 4, 7, 10, 12, 15, 16, 20, 22
  Congregazione dell'Immunità Ecclesiastica
    Acta: 1669, 1669bis, 1669ter
    Libri Litterarum: 6, 7, 8, 9, 10, 11, 12
    Varia: 34
  Miscellanea Armadio IV–V: 47
  Segreteria di Stato
    Cardinali: 31, 34, 35, 36, 37
    Malta: 9, 82A
    Napoli: 54, 331
    Spagna: 130, 132, 133, 136, 137, 138, 139, 140, 141, 142, 143, 350, 351, 353, 354A
    Svizzera: 48, 49, 50, 51, 52, 53, 54, 55, 56, 57, 58, 59, 238, 239, 240, 242
Archivio Borromeo dell'Isola Bella, Stresa
  Famiglia Borromeo
    Federico IV: Benefici ed Abbazie; Cariche; Cariche: Nunzio a Madrid; Corrispondenza
      1634–1644, 1645–1655, 1656–1664, 1665–1670, 1671–1680
    Giovanna Cesi: Corrispondenza II, Corrispondenza 1660–1672
    Giovanni V: Atti diversi; Carriera militare; Corrispondenza con diversi
Archivio di Stato, Milan
  Atti di governo
    Acque parte antica: 296
    Feudi camerali parte antica: 48, 49, 50, 65, 280, 428, 613, 673, 674, 675, 676, 677, 678, 679
    Militare parte antica: 2, 164, 165, 230, 324, 325, 406
    Potenze estere post 1535: 150, 151
  Registri delle cancellerie dello Stato
    Serie XI: 2
    Serie XIV: 21
    Serie XVI: 23
  Serbelloni
    Serie I: 55
Archivio di Stato, Rome
  Archivio Massimo d'Aracoeli: 245, 246, 247, 248, 249, 250, 251
  Fondo Cartari-Febei: 24
  Miscellanea Famiglie: 48
  Notai del tribunale dell'Auditor Camerae: 6562
  Tribunale criminale del governatore di Roma, Registri di sentenze: 14
Archivio Storico Civico, Milan
  Dicasteri: 51, 152
  Materie: 12, 13, 159, 160, 161, 648, 678

182   BIBLIOGRAPHY

Archivio Storico Diocesano, Milan
  Carteggio ufficiale: 83, 84, 85, 86, 87, 88, 89, 90
Archivo General, Simancas
  Consejo de Estado: 3038, 3039, 3040, 3041, 3042, 3043, 3044, 3045, 3046, 3047, 3048,
    3053, 3113, 3346, 3348, 3350, 3357, 3363, 3366, 3373, 3374, 3383, 3463
  Secretarías Provinciales: 1135, 1350, 1354, 1362, 1801, 1804, 1807, 1808, 1810, 1811,
    1815, 1816, 2025, 2041, 2042, 2044, 2056, 2072, 2106
Biblioteca Ambrosiana, Milan
  Manoscritti: G 205, 207, 210, 211, 212, 213, 215, 216, 218, 219, 220, 220bis, 221, 222,
    223, 223bis, 224, 226, 227, 228, 228bis, 229, 230, 237, 242, 254, 254bis, 254ter, 256
Biblioteca Apostolica Vaticana, Vatican City
  Archivio Chigi: 6, 7, 80, 87
  Barberini Latini: 4704, 9860, 9864, 9867
  Boncompagni: C.20
  Chigiani:
  E.I.: 16, 20, 21, 27 I.II.: 55
  Ottoboni Latini: 2698
  Vaticani Latini: 9729, 11733, 12530
Biblioteca Nacional de España, Madrid
  Manuscritos: 2671, 12877
Biblioteca Nazionale Braidense, Milan
  Ordini e consulti pel Ducato di Milano: vol. 1 (XA.XI.105), vol. 2 (XA.XI.106)
Società Storica Lombarda, Milan
  Fondo Crivelli Serbelloni: 15, 29

Printed Sources

Arconati Lamberti, Giovanni Girolamo. *Il governo del Duca d'Ossuna dello Stato di Milano*
  (Cologne: Battista della Croce, 1678).
Bascapè, Carlo. *I Sette Libri della Vita, & de' fatti di San Carlo Card. di S. Prassede Arcivesc.*
  di Milano, composti in Latino dal Reverendiss. D. Carlo Vescovo di Novara; e tradotti in
  volgare da Luca Vandoni Canonico Teologo della Collegiata di S. Gaudentio di Novara.
  Con l'aggiunta de' Miracoli principali del medesimo Santo (Bologna: Heredi di Giovanni
  Rossi, 1614).
Bellegno, Catterino. "Relazione di Spagna di Catterino Bellegno, ambasciatore nella
  minorità di Carlo II dall'anno 1667 al 1670." In *Relazioni degli stati europei lette al senato*
  dagli ambasciatori veneti nel secolo decimosettimo, serie 1, vol. 2, ed. Niccolò Barozzi and
  Guglielmo Berchet (Venice: Pietro Naratovich, 1860): pp. 357–79.
Borromeo, Federico. *Il libro intitolato La Gratia de' Principi* (Milan: Typographia Collegii
  Ambrosiani, 1632).
Bosca, Pietro Paolo. *De origine et statu Bibliothecae Ambrosianae Hemidecas* (Milan:
  Ludovico Monti, 1672).
Capriata, Pier Giovanni. *Dell'historia di Pier Giovanni Capriata, parte seconda, in sei libri*
  distinta (Geneva: Samuel Chouet, 1650).
Cardella, Lorenzo. *Memorie storiche de' cardinali della Santa Romana Chiesa. Tomo settimo*
  (Rome: Stamperia Pagliarini, 1793).
Coloma, Carlos. "Discurso en que se representa quanto conviene a la Monarchía española
  la conservación del Estado de Milán, y lo que necesita para su defensa y mayor

BIBLIOGRAPHY   183

seguridad (1626)." In *Lo Stato di Milano nel XVII secolo. Memoriali e relazioni*, ed. Massimo Carlo Giannini and Gianvittorio Signorotto (Rome: Ministero per i Beni e le Attività Culturali, 2006): pp. 3–13.

"Concordia giurisdizionale tra il foro ecclesiastico e il foro secolare di Milano." In *Potestà civile e autorità spirituale in Italia nei secoli della Riforma e Controriforma*, ed. Gaetano Catalano and Federico Martino (Milan: Giuffrè, 1987): pp. 141–6.

Crescenzio Romani, Giovanni Pietro. *La Monarchia di Spagna overo Dell'Unione delle Corone, e Regni dell'Augustissima Casa d'Austria* (Piacenza: Giovanni Antonio Ardizzone, 1650).

Du Plessis-Praslin, César. "Mémoires du maréchal Du Plessis." In *Collection des mémoires relatifs à l'histoire de France. Vol. LVII*, ed. Alexandre Petitot and Louis-Jean-Nicolas Monmerqué (Paris: Foucault, 1827): pp. 145–441.

Grimani, Antonio. "Relazione di Roma di Antonio Grimani Cavaliere Ambasciatore Ordinario a Clemente IX e Clemente X. 1671." In *Relazioni degli stati europei lette al senato dagli ambasciatori veneti nel secolo decimosettimo, serie III: Italia. Relazioni di Roma, vol. II*, ed. Niccolò Barozzi and Guglielmo Berchet (Venice: Pietro Naratovich, 1878): pp. 345–70.

Gualdo Priorato, Galeazzo. "Giovanni Borromeo." In his *Vite et azzioni di personaggi militari, e politici* (Vienna: Michele Thurnmayer, 1674): unpag.

Gualdo Priorato, Galeazzo. *Relatione della Città, e Stato di Milano* (Milan: Lodovico Monza, 1666).

Gualdo Priorato, Galeazzo. *Vite et azzioni di personaggi militari, e politici* (Vienna: Michele Thurnmayer, 1674).

"Istruzione a Francisco de Castro, conte di Castro. San Lorenzo del Escorial, 1609 aprile 27." In *Istruzioni di Filippo III ai suoi ambasciatori a Roma 1598–1621*, ed. Silvano Giordano (Rome: Ministero per i Beni e le Attività Culturali, 2006): pp. 68–93.

Johnsson, J. W. S., ed. *Storia della peste avvenuta nel borgo di Busto Arsizio 1630: Manuscrit original, appartenant autrefois à la bibliothèque Belgiojosa à Milan* (Copenhagen: Henrik Koppel, 1924).

Leti, Gregorio. *Il livello politico, ò sia La giusta bilancia, nella quale si pesano tutte le Massime di Roma, & attioni de' Cardinali Viventi. Parte terza* (Cartellana: Bendetto Marsetti, 1678).

Leti, Gregorio. *Il nipotismo di Roma* (no place: no publisher, 1667).

Mocenigo, Pietro. "Relazione di Roma, ambasciatore ordinario a Clemente X (1676)." In *Relazioni degli stati europei lette al senato dagli ambasciatori veneti nel secolo decimosettimo, serie III: Italia. Relazioni di Roma, vol. II*, ed. Niccolò Barozzi and Guglielmo Berchet (Venice: Pietro Naratovich, 1878): pp. 371–403.

Moriggia, Paolo. *Historia della nobiltà, et degne qualità del Lago Maggiore* (Milan: Hieronimo Bordone e Pietro Martire Locarni, 1603).

Pilo, Rafaella, ed. *Juan Everardo Nithard y sus causas no causas: Razones y pretextos para el fin de un valimiento* (Madrid: Silex, 2010).

Rivola, Francesco. *Vita di Federico Borromeo cardinale del titolo di Santa Maria degli Angeli, ed Arcivescovo di Milano* (Milan: Dionisio Garibaldi, 1656).

Santagostino, Agostino. *L'immortalità e gloria del pennello: Catalogo delle pitture insigni che stanno esposte al pubblico nella città di Milano*, ed. Marco Bona Castellotti (Milan: Il Polfilio, 1980 [1671]).

Socini, Antonio. *L'assedio di Valenza del Po dell'anno 1656*, 2nd reprint (Turin: Bartolomeo Zavatta, 1657).

Soranzo, Francesco. "Relazione di Spagna di Francesco Soranzo cav. Ambasciatore a Filippo II e Filippo III dall'anno 1597 al 1602." In *Relazioni degli stati europei lette al*

184 BIBLIOGRAPHY

senato dagli ambasciatori veneti nel secolo decimosettimo, serie 1, vol. 1, ed. Nicolò Barozzi and Guglielmo Berchet (Venice: Pietro Naratovich, 1856): pp. 27–214.

Valier, Bertuccio. "Relazione del signor Bertuccio Valier, ambasciatore veneto al serenissimo Cardinal Infante a Milano 1633." In *Relazioni degli ambasciatori veneti al senato. Volume II: Milano, Urbino*, ed. Arnaldo Segarizzi (Bari: Laterza, 1913): pp. 85–95.

Zorzi, Marino. "Relazione di Spagna di Marino Zorzi, ambasciatore a Filippo IV e nella minorità di Carlo II dall'anno 1660 al 1667." In *Relazioni degli stati europei lette al senato dagli ambasciatori veneti nel secolo decimosettimo, serie 1, vol. 2*, ed. Niccolò Barozzi and Guglielmo Berchet (Venice: Pietro Naratovich, 1860): pp. 327–53.

Secondary Sources

Adams, Julia. *The Familial State: Ruling Families and Merchant Capitalism in Early Modern Europe* (Ithaca, NY: Cornell University Press, 2005).

Adamson, John. "Policy and Pomegranates: Art, Iconography and Counsel in Ruben's Anglo-Spanish Diplomacy of 1629–1630." In *The Age of Rubens: Diplomacy, Dynastic Politics and the Visual Arts in Early Seventeenth-Century Europe*, ed. Luc Duerloo and R. Malcolm Smuts (Turnhout: Brepols, 2016): pp. 143–79.

Ago, Renata. *Carriere e clientele nella Roma barocca* (Rome and Bari: Laterza, 1990).

Ago, Renata. "Ecclesiastical Careers and the Destiny of Cadets." *Continuity and Change* 7, 3 (1992): pp. 271–82.

Ago, Renata. "Giochi di squadra: Uomini e donne nelle famiglie nobili del XVII secolo." In *Signori, patrizi, cavalieri nell'età moderna*, ed. Maria Antonietta Visceglia (Bari: Laterza, 1992): pp. 256–64.

Ago, Renata. *La feudalità in età moderna* (Rome and Bari: Laterza, 1994).

Ago, Renata. "Giovani nobili nell'età dell'assolutismo: Autoritarismo paterno e libertà." In *Storia dei giovani, vol. 1: Dall'antichità all'età moderna*, ed. Giovanni Levi and Jean-Claude Schmitt, 2nd ed. (Bari and Rome: Laterza, 2000): pp. 375–426.

Ago, Renata. "La costruzione dell'identità maschile: Una competizione tra uomini." In *La costruzione dell'identità maschile nell'età moderna e contemporanea*, ed. Angiolina Arru (Rome: Biblink, 2001): pp. 17–30.

Aikin, Judith. *A Ruler's Consort in Early Modern Germany: Aemilia Juliana of Schwarzburg-Rudolstadt* (Farnham: Ashgate, 2014).

Algazi, Gadi. *Herrengewalt und Gewalt der Herren: Herrschaft, Gegenseitigkeit und Sprachgebrauch* (Frankfurt am Main: Campus, 1996).

Álvarez-Ossorio Alvariño, Antonio. "La república de las parentelas: La corte de Madrid y el gobierno de Milán durante el reinado de Carlos II" (unpublished Ph.D. thesis, Universidad Autónoma de Madrid, 1993).

Álvarez-Ossorio Alvariño, Antonio. "El favor real: Liberalidad del príncipe y jerarquía de la república (1665–1700)." In *Repubblica e virtù: Pensiero politico e Monarchia Cattolica fra XVI e XVII secolo*, ed. Chiara Continisio and Cesare Mozzarelli (Rome: Bulzoni, 1995): pp. 393–437.

Álvarez-Ossorio Alvariño, Antonio. "El duque de Osuna y el Estado de Milán bajo Carlos II." In his *Milán y el legado de Felipe II: Gobernadores y corte provincial en la Lombardía de los Austrias* (Madrid: Sociedad Estatal para la Conmemoración de los Centenarios de Felipe II y Carlos V, 2001): pp. 163–254.

Álvarez-Ossorio Alvariño, Antonio. "¿Los límites del 'habitus'? Ministros reales en la Lombardía de Carlos II." *Studia Histórica: Historia Moderna* 39, 1 (2017): pp. 169–189.

BIBLIOGRAPHY   185

Álvarez-Ossorio Alvariño, Antonio. "The King and the Family: Primogeniture and the Lombard Nobility in the Spanish Monarchy." In *Monarchy Transformed: Princes and their Elites in Early Modern Western Europe*, ed. Robert von Friedeburg and John Morrill (Cambridge: Cambridge University Press, 2017): pp. 183–211.

Amadori, Arrigo. "Privanza, patronazgo y fiscalidad indiana en la corte de Madrid durante el reinado de Felipe IV." *Revista Complutense de Historia de América* 34 (2008), pp. 63–84.

Andújar Castillo, Francisco, Antonio Feros, and Pilar Ponce Leiva. "Corrupción y mecanismos de control en la Monarquía Hispánica: Una revisión crítica." *Tiempos modernos* 35, 2 (2017): pp. 284–311.

Annoni, Ada. "Giurisdizionalismo ed episcopalismo." In *Storia religiosa della Lombardia. Chiesa e società: Appunti per una storia delle diocesi lombarde*, ed. Adriano Caprioli, Antonio Rimoldi, and Luciano Vaccaro (Brescia: La Scuola, 1986): pp. 141–77.

Annoni, Ada. "Lo Stato Borromeo." In *L'Alto Milanese all'epoca di Carlo e Federico Borromeo: Società e territorio*, ed. AA. VV. (Gallarate: Società Gallaratese per gli Studi Patri, 1987): pp. 27–101.

Annoni, Ada. "Fisco, regalie e feudi tra '500 e '600." In *Rapporti tra città e campagna dal medioevo all'età moderna*, ed. Istituto lombardo. Accademia di scienze e lettere (Milan: Istituto Lombardo di Scienze e Lettere, 1988): pp. 63–102.

Anselmi, Paola. *"Conservare lo Stato": Politica di difesa e pratica di governo nella Lombardia spagnola fra XVI e XVII secolo* (Milan: Unicopli, 2008).

Asch, Ronald G. "'Wo der soldat hinkömbt, da ist alles sein': Military Violence and Atrocities in the Thirty Years War Re-Examined." *German History* 18 (2000): pp. 291–309.

Asch, Ronald G. *Nobilities in Transition: Courtiers and Rebels in Britain and Europe* (London: Hodder Arnold, 2003).

Asch, Ronald G. *Herbst des Helden: Modelle des Heroischen und heroische Lebensentwürfe in England und Frankreich von den Religionskriegen bis zum Zeitalter der Aufklärung. Ein Essay* (Würzburg: Ergon, 2016).

Asch, Ronald G. and Adolf M. Birke, eds. *Princes, Patronage, and the Nobility: The Court at the Beginning of the Modern Age c.1450–1650* (London: The German Historical Institute London, 1991).

Asch, Ronald G., Birgit Emich, and Jens Ivo Engels. "Einleitung." In *Integration, Legitimation, Korruption: Politische Patronage in Früher Neuzeit und Moderne*, ed. Ronald G. Asch, Birgit Emich, and Jens Ivo Engels (Frankfurt am Main: Peter Lang, 2011): pp. 7–30.

Astarita, Tommaso. *The Continuity of Feudal Power: The Caracciolo di Brienza in Spanish Naples* (Cambridge: Cambridge University Press, 1992).

Bannister, Mark. *Condé in Context: Ideological Change in Seventeenth-Century France* (Oxford: Legenda, 2000).

Barth, Volker. *Inkognito: Geschichte eines Zeremoniells* (Munich: Oldenbourg, 2013).

Béguin, Katia. *Les Princes de Condé: Rebelles, courtisans et mécènes dans la France du Grand Siècle* (Seyssel: Champ Vallon, 1999).

Behr, Andreas. *Diplomatie als Familiengeschäft: Die Casati als spanisch-mailändische Gesandte in Luzern und Chur (1660–1700)* (Zurich: Chronos, 2015).

Beik, William. *Absolutism and Society in Seventeenth-Century France: State Power and Provincial Aristocracy in Languedoc* (Cambridge: Cambridge University Press, 1985).

Beik, William. "The Absolutism of Louis XIV as Social Collaboration." *Past & Present* 188, 1 (2005): pp. 195–224.

Benigno, Francesco. "Aristocrazia e stato in Sicilia nell'epoca di Filippo II." In *Signori, patrizi, cavalieri in Italia centro-meridionale nell'Età moderna*, ed. Maria Antonietta Visceglia (Rome and Bari: Laterza, 1992): pp. 76–93.

186 BIBLIOGRAPHY

Benigno, Francesco. *L'ombra del re: Ministri e lotta politica nella Spagna del Seicento* (Venice: Marsilio, 1992).

Benigno, Francesco. *Specchi della rivoluzione: Conflitto e identità politica nell'Europa moderna* (Rome: Donzelli, 1999).

Benigno, Francesco. "Il fato di Buckingham: La critica del governo straordinario e di guerra come fulcro politico della crisi del Seicento." In *Il governo dell'emergenza: Poteri straordinari e di guerra in Europa tra XVI e XX secolo*, ed. Francesco Benigno and Luca Scuccimarra (Rome: Viella, 2007): pp. 75–93.

Benigno, Francesco. *Favoriti e ribelli: Stili della politica barocca* (Rome: Bulzoni, 2011).

Benigno, Francesco. "Un país lejano: Comunicación, política y revuelta en la Sicilia del siglo XVII." In *Soulèvements, révoltes, révolutions dans l'Empire des Habsbourg d'Espagne, XVIe–XVIIe siècle*, ed. Alain Hugon and Alexandra Merle (Madrid: Casa de Velázquez, 2016): pp. 87–99.

Benvenuti, Matteo. *Il duca d'Ossuna: Racconto cronistorico milanese*, 2nd ed. (Milano: Pio Istituto Tipografico, 1876).

Bercé, Yves-Marie. *La sommossa di Fermo del 1648* (Fermo: Andrea Livi, 2007).

Bergin, J. A. "The Decline and Fall of the House of Guise as an Ecclesiastical Dynasty." *The Historical Journal* 25, 4 (1982): pp. 781–803.

Bernard, G. W. "'A Water-Spout Springing from the Rock of Freedom?': Corruption in Sixteenth- and Early-Seventeenth-Century England." In *Anticorruption in History: From Antiquity to the Modern Era*, ed. Ronald Kroeze, André Vitória, and G. Geltner (Oxford: Oxford University Press, 2018): pp. 125–38.

Bernsee, Robert. *Moralische Erneuerung: Korruption und bürokratische Reformen in Bayern und Preussen, 1780–1820* (Göttingen: Vandenhoeck & Ruprecht, 2017).

Bernsee, Robert. "For the Good of the Prince: Government and Corruption in Germany During the Eighteenth Century." In *The War Within: Private Interests and the Fiscal State in Early-Modern Europe*, ed. Joël Félix and Anne Dubet (Cham: Palgrave Macmillan, 2018): pp. 257–80.

Besozzi, Leonida, "Ritratti dei Borromeo nei quadri dei Marchesi di Angera (sec. XVII)." *Libri e documenti* 17, 3 (1992): pp. 38–56.

Besozzi, Leonida. "Cronistoria d'un assedio fallito: Arona 1644." *Verbanus: Rassegna per la cultura, l'arte, la storia del lago* 17 (1996): pp. 275–306.

Besozzi, Leonida. "Momenti della vita del cardinale Federico attraverso la documentazione milanese." *Studia Borromaica* 14 (2000): pp. 301–43.

Besozzi, Luciano. "Famiglie e uomini della società locale e la presenza dei Borromeo." In *La Città di Angera, feudo dei Borromeo, sec. XV–XVIII*, ed. Marco Tamborini (Gavirate: Nicolini Editore, 1995), pp. 117–48.

Biagioli, Mario. *Galileo, Courtier: The Practice of Science in the Culture of Absolutism* (Chicago, IL: The University of Chicago Press, 1993).

Blockmans, Wim, André Holenstein, and Jon Mathieu, eds. *Empowering Interactions: Political Cultures and the Emergence of the State in Europe 1300–1900* (Farnham: Ashgate, 2009).

Bolzern, Rudolf. *Spanien, Mailand und die katholische Eidgenossenschaft: Militärische, wirtschaftliche und politische Beziehungen zur Zeit des Gesandten Alfonso Casati (1594–1621)* (Lucerne: Rex, 1996).

Bonahan, Donna. *Crown and Nobility in Early Modern France* (Houndmills: Palgrave, 2001).

Borromeo, Agostino. "Archbishop Carlo Borromeo and the Ecclesiastical Policy of Philip II in the State of Milan." In *San Carlo Borromeo: Catholic Reform and Ecclesiastical Politics in the Second Half of the Sixteenth Century*, ed. John M. Headley and John B. Tomaro (Washington, DC: Folger Books, 1988): pp. 85–111.

BIBLIOGRAPHY 187

Borromeo, Agostino. "La Chiesa milanese del Seicento e la Corte di Madrid." In *"Millain the Great": Milano nelle brume del Seicento*, ed. Aldo De Maddalena (Milan: Cassa di Risparmio delle Province Lombarde, 1989): pp. 93–108.

Bourdieu, Pierre. *Distinction: A Social Critique of the Judgement of Taste*, trans. Richard Nice (London: Routledge, 1984).

Bourdieu, Pierre. "The Forms of Capital." In *Handbook of Theory and Research for the Sociology of Education*, ed. John G. Richardson (New York: Greenwood, 1986): pp. 241–58.

Bourdieu, Pierre. "Rethinking the State: Genesis and Structure of the Bureaucratic Field." *Sociological Theory* 12, 1 (1994): pp. 1–18.

Bourdieu, Pierre. *The State Nobility: Elite Schools in the Field of Power*, trans. Lauretta C. Clough (Stanford, CA: Stanford University Press, 1996).

Bourdieu, Pierre. *Outline of a Theory of Practice*, trans. Richard Nice (Cambridge: Cambridge University Press, 2010).

Bourdieu, Pierre. *On the State: Lectures at the Collège de France 1989–1992*, ed. Patrick Champagne, Remi Lenoir, Franck Pompeau, and Marie-Christine Rivière, trans. David Fernbach (Cambridge: Polity Press, 2014).

Bourdieu, Pierre and Jean-Claude Passeron. *Reproduction in Education, Society and Culture*, trans. Richard Nice (London and Beverly Hills, CA: Sage Publications, 1977).

Bourdieu, Pierre and Loïc Wacquant. *An Invitation to Reflexive Sociology* (Chicago, IL: The University of Chicago Press, 1992).

Brambilla, Elena and Giovanni Muto, eds. *La Lombardia spagnola: Nuovi indirizzi di ricerca* (Milan: Unicopli, 1997).

Brunsson, Nils. *The Organization of Hypocrisy: Talk, Decisions, and Actions in Organizations*, 2nd ed. (Oslo: Abstrakt, 2002).

Bundi, Martin. "Le relazioni estere delle Tre Leghe." In *Storia dei Grigioni. Volume 2: L'età moderna*, ed. Fernando Iseppi (Chur: Pro Grigioni Italiano/Bellinzona: Casagrande, 2000): pp. 177–207.

Buono, Alessandro. *Esercito, istituzioni, territorio: Alloggiamenti militari e "case herme" nello Stato di Milano (secoli XVI e XVII)* (Florence: Firenze University Press, 2009).

Buono, Alessandro. "Il governo straordinario e la 'pazienza dei vassalli': Riflessioni attorno alla 'crisi politica generale' del Seicento." In *Proposte per un approccio interdisciplinare allo studio delle istituzioni*, ed. Giuseppe Ambrosino and Loris De Nardi (Verona: QuiEdit, 2015): pp. 57–75.

Buratti Mazzotta, Adele. *L'Isola Madre: Da Insuleta Sancti Victoris a Isola Renata, un millennio di storia* (Oggiono: Cattaneo, 2016).

Burke, Peter. *The Fabrication of Louis XIV* (New Haven, CT: Yale University Press, 1992).

Calabria, Antonio and John A. Marino, eds. *Good Government in Spanish Naples* (New York: Peter Lang, 1990).

Campbell, Peter R. *Power and Politics in Old Regime France 1720–1745* (London and New York: Routledge, 1996).

Canosa, Romano. *Milano nel Seicento: Grandezza e miseria nell'Italia spagnola* (Milan: Mondadori, 1993).

Carpani, Roberta. *Drammaturgia del comico: I libretti per musica di Carlo Maria Maggi nei "theatri di Lombardia"* (Milan: Vita e pensiero, 1998).

Carrasco, Adolfo. "Los grandes, el poder y la cultura política de la nobleza en el reinado de Carlos II." *Studia histórica. Historia moderna* 20 (1999): pp. 77–136.

Carrasco, Adolfo. "El conde duque de Olivares, un nuevo Séneca: Estoicismo romano y cultura política barroca." In *I rapporti tra Roma e Madrid nei secoli XVI e XVII: Arte, diplomazia, política*, ed. Alessandra Anselmi (Rome: Gangemi, 2014): pp. 245–64.

188 BIBLIOGRAPHY

Carrió-Invernizzi, Diana. *El gobierno de las imágenes: Ceremonial y mecenazgo en la Italia española de la segunda mitad del siglo XVII* (Madrid: Iberoamericana, 2008).

Carrió-Invernizzi, Diana. "Usos políticos del mecenazgo virreinal en los conventos de Nápoles en la segunda mitad del siglo XVII." In *España y Napoles: Coleccionismo y mecenazgo virreinales en el siglo XVII*, ed. José Luis Colomer (Madrid: Centro de Estudios Europa Hispánica, 2009): pp. 379–400.

Castiglione, Carlo. *Il cardinale Federico Borromeo* (Turin: Internazionale, 1931).

Castiglione, Caroline. *Patrons and Adversaries: Nobles and Villagers in Italian Politics, 1640–1760* (Oxford: Oxford University Press, 2005).

Cavallera, Marina. "Angera nella vita economica del Verbano." In *La Città di Angera, feudo dei Borromeo, sec. XV–XVIII*, ed. Marco Tamborini (Gavirate: Nicolini Editore, 1995): pp. 149–91.

Clancy, Laura. *Running the Family Firm: How the Monarchy Manages Its Image and Our Money* (Manchester: Manchester University Press, 2021).

Coast, David. "Speaking for the People in Early Modern England." *Past & Present* 244, 1 (2019): pp. 51–88.

Collins, James B. *Classes, Estates, and Order in Early Modern Britain* (Cambridge: Cambridge University Press, 1994).

Comparato, Vittor Ivo. *Uffici e società a Napoli (1600–1647): Aspetti dell'ideologia del magistrato nell'età moderna* (Florence: Olschki, 1974).

Continisio, Chiara. "*Il libro intitolato la gratia de' principi:* Virtù, politica e ragion di stato in Federico Borromeo." *Studia Borromaica* 18 (2004): pp. 97–115.

Contreras, Jaime. *Carlos II: El hechizado. Poder y melancolía en la corte del último Austria* (Madrid: Temas de Hoy, 2003).

Corteguera, Luis R. *For the Common Good: Popular Politics in Barcelona, 1580–1640* (Ithaca, NY: Cornell University Press, 2002).

Corteguera, Luis R. "King as Father in Early Modern Spain." *Memoria y Civilización* 12 (2009): pp. 49–69.

Cosandey, Fanny and Robert Descimon. *L'Absolutisme en France: Histoire et historiographie* (Paris: Éditions du Seuil, 2002).

Crawford, Katherine B. "The Politics of Promiscuity: Masculinity and Heroic Representation at the Court of Henry IV." *French Historical Studies* 26, 2 (2003): pp. 225–52.

Cremonini, Cinzia. "Storia di un'eclissi apparente: La famiglia Borromeo tra dissidi interni e ostracismo spagnolo (1600–1652)." In *Lombardia borromaica, Lombardia spagnola, 1554–1659*, ed. Paolo Pissavino and Gianvittorio Signorotto (Rome: Bulzoni, 1995): pp. 477–513.

Cremonini, Cinzia. "Il Consiglio Segreto tra interim e prassi quotidiana (1622–1706)." In *La Lombardia spagnola: Nuovi indirizzi di ricerca*, ed. Elena Brambilla and Giovanni Muto (Milan: Unicopli, 1997): pp. 225–61.

Cremonini, Cinzia. *Ritratto politico e cerimoniale con figure: Carlo Borromeo Arese e Giovanni Tapia, servitore e gentiluomo* (Rome: Bulzoni, 2008).

Cremonini, Cinzia. "La mediazione degli interessi imperiali in Italia tra Cinque e Settecento." In *I feudi imperiali in Italia tra XV e XVII secolo*, ed. Cinzia Cremonini and Riccardo Musso (Rome: Bulzoni, 2010): pp. 31–48.

Cremonini, Cinzia. *Le vie della distinzione: Società, potere e cultura a Milano tra XV e XVIII secolo* (Milan: Educatt, 2012).

Dalla Rosa, Enrico. *Le milizie del Seicento nello Stato di Milano* (Milan: Vita e pensiero, 1991).

Daloz, Jean Pascal. *The Sociology of Elite Distinction from Theoretical and Comparative Perspectives* (Basingstoke: Palgrave Macmillan, 2010).

BIBLIOGRAPHY 189

D'Amelia, Marina. "Nepotismo al femminile: Il caso di Olimpia Maidalchini Pamphilj." In *La nobiltà romana in età moderna: Profili istituzionali e pratiche sociali*, ed. Maria Antonietta Visceglia (Rome: Carocci, 2001): pp. 353–99.

D'Amelia, Marina. "La nuova Agrippina: Olimpia Maidalchini Pamphilj e la tirannia femminile nell'immaginario politico del Seicento." In *I linguaggi del potere nell'età barocca: Donne e sfera pubblica*, ed. Francesca Cantù (Rome: Viella, 2009): pp. 45–95.

D'Amico, Stefano, *Spanish Milan: A City within the Empire, 1535–1706* (Basingstoke: Palgrave Macmillan, 2012).

D'Amico, Stefano. "Spanish Milan, 1535–1706." In *A Companion to Late Medieval and Early Modern Milan: The Distinctive Features of an Italian State*, ed. Andrea Gamberini (Leiden: Brill, 2015): pp. 46–68.

Dandelet, Thomas James. *Spanish Rome 1500–1700* (New Haven, CT: Yale University Press, 2001).

Dandelet, Thomas James. "Between Courts: The Colonna Agents in Italy and Iberia, 1555–1600." In *Your Humble Servant: Agents in Early Modern Europe*, ed. Hans Cools, Marika Keblusek, and Badeloch Noldus (Hilversum: Uitgeverij Verloren, 2006): pp. 29–38.

Dandelet, Thomas James and John A. Marino, eds. *Spain in Italy: Politics, Society, and Religion 1500–1700* (Leiden: Brill, 2007).

D'Avenia, Fabrizio. *La Chiesa del re: Monarchia e Papato nella Sicilia spagnola (secc. XVI–XVII)* (Rome: Carocci, 2015).

D'Avenia, Fabrizio. "Lealtà alla prova: 'Casa', Monarchia, Chiesa. La carriera politica del cardinale Giannettino Doria (1573–1642)." *Dimensioni e problemi della ricerca storica* 2 (2015): pp. 45–72.

Davis, Natalie Zemon. "Women on Top." In her *Society and Culture in Early Modern France* (Stanford, CA: Stanford University Press, 1975): pp. 124–51.

Davis, Natalie Zemon. *The Gift in Sixteenth-Century France* (Oxford: Oxford University Press, 2000).

Daybell, James. *Women Letter-Writers in Tudor England* (Oxford: Oxford University Press, 2006).

Dee, Darryl. *Expansion and Crisis in Louis XIV's France: Franche-Comté and Absolute Monarchy, 1674–1715* (Rochester, NY: University of Rochester Press, 2009).

De Gennaro, Giuseppe. *La crisi della monarchia spagnola e la diplomazia pontificia (1665–1673)* (Turin: Giappichelli, 1994).

Del Mar Felices de la Fuente, María. "Hacia la nobleza titulada: Los 'méritos' para titular en el siglo XVII." In *Mérito, venalidad y corrupción en España y América. Siglos XVII y XVIII*, ed. Pilar Ponce Leiva and Francisco Andújar Castillo (Valencia: Albatros, 2016): pp. 19–40.

Dell'Oro, Giorgio. *Il regio economato: Il controllo statale sul clero nella Lombardia asburgica e nei domini sabaudi* (Milan: Franco Angeli, 2007).

De Marco, Vittorio. "L'immunità ecclesiastica nel Regno di Napoli durante il XVII secolo: Il caso delle diocesi di Puglia." *Ricerche di storia sociale e religiosa* 36 (1989): pp. 123–56.

De Vit, Vincenzo. *Il Lago Maggiore, Stresa e le Isole Borromee: Notizie storiche* (Prato: Alberghetti, 1875).

Dewald, Jonathan. *Aristocratic Experience and the Origins of Modern Culture: France, 1570–1715* (Berkeley, CA: University of California Press, 1993).

Dewald, Jonathan. *The European Nobility 1400–1800* (Cambridge: Cambridge University Press, 1996).

Dewald, Jonathan. *Status, Power and Identity in Early Modern France: The Rohan Family, 1550–1715* (University Park, PA: The Pennsylvania State University Press, 2015).

190   BIBLIOGRAPHY

Dewald, Jonathan. "Writing Failure: Aristocratic Self-Depiction in Seventeenth-Century France." In *Die "Kunst des Adels" in der Frühen Neuzeit*, ed. Claudius Sittig and Christian Wieland (Wiesbaden: Harrassowitz, 2018): pp. 23–35.

Donati, Claudio. *L'idea di nobiltà in Italia: Secoli XIV–XVIII* (Bari and Rome: Laterza, 1988).

Donati, Claudio. "The Profession of Arms and the Nobility in Spanish Italy: Some Considerations." In *Spain in Italy: Politics, Society, and Religion*, ed. Thomas James Dandelet and John A. Marino (Leiden and Boston, MA: Brill, 2007): pp. 299–324.

Duindam, Jeroen. *Myths of Power: Norbert Elias and the Early Modern European Court* (Amsterdam: Amsterdam University Press, 1994).

Duindam, Jeroen. *Vienna and Versailles: The Courts of Europe's Dynastic Rivals, 1550–1780* (Cambridge: Cambridge University Press, 2003).

Elias, Norbert. *The Court Society*, ed. Stephen Mennell (Dublin: University College Dublin Press, 2005).

Elliott, John H. "El programa de Olivares y los movimientos de 1640." In *La España de Felipe IV: El gobierno de la Monarquía, la crisis de 1640 y el fracaso de la hegemonía europea*, ed. Francisco Tomás y Valiente (Madrid: Espasa-Calpe, 1982): pp. 333–523.

Elliott, John H. *Richelieu and Olivares* (Cambridge: Cambridge University Press, 1984).

Elliott, John H. *The Revolt of the Catalans: A Study in the Decline of Spain (1598–1640)*, 2nd ed. (Cambridge: Cambridge University Press, 1984).

Elliott, John H. *The Count-Duke of Olivares: The Statesman in an Age of Decline* (New Haven, CT: Yale University Press, 1986).

Elliott, John H. "Power and Propaganda in the Spain of Philip IV." In his *Spain and Its World 1500–1700: Selected Essays* (New Haven, CT: Yale University Press, 1989): pp. 162–88.

Elliott, John H. "Quevedo and the Count-Duke of Olivares." In his *Spain and Its World 1500–1700: Selected Essays* (New Haven, CT: Yale University Press, 1989): pp. 189–209.

Elliott, John H. "A Europe of Composite Monarchies." *Past & Present* 137 (1992): pp. 48–71.

Elliott, John H., Rosario Villari, and António Manuel Hespanha, eds. *1640: La Monarquía Hispánica en crisis* (Barcelona: Crítica, 1992).

Emich, Birgit. *Bürokratie und Nepotismus unter Paul V. (1605–1621)* (Stuttgart: Anton Hiersemann, 2001).

Emich, Birgit. "Die Karriere des Staatssekretärs. Das Schicksal des Nepoten?" In *Offices et papauté (XIVe–XVIIe siècle): Charges, hommes, destins*, ed. Armand Jamme and Olivier Poncet (Rome: École française de Rome, 2005): pp. 341–55.

Emich, Birgit. "Vincoli informali in istituzioni formali: Le reti clientelari nell'amministrazione dello Stato e della Chiesa nella prima età moderna." *Filosofia politica* 1 (2015): pp. 125–41.

Emich, Birgit. "'Der Hof ist die Lepra des Papsttums' (Papst Franziskus): Patronage und Verwaltung an der römischen Kurie der Frühen Neuzeit." In *Soldgeschäfte, Klientelismus, Korruption in der Frühen Neuzeit: Zum Soldunternehmertum der Familie Zurlauben im schweizerischen und europäischen Kontext*, ed. Kaspar von Greyerz, André Holenstein, and Andreas Würgler (Göttingen: Vandenhoeck & Ruprecht, 2018): pp. 69–81.

Emich, Birgit, Nicole Reinhardt, Hillard von Thiessen, and Christian Wieland. "Stand und Perspektiven der Patronageforschung: Zugleich eine Antwort auf Heiko Droste." *Zeitschrift für historische Forschung* 32, 2 (2005): pp. 233–65.

Enciso Alonso-Muñumer, Isabel. *Nobleza, poder y mecenazgo en tiempos de Felipe III: Nápoles y el Conde de Lemos* (Madrid: Actas, 2007).

Engels, Jens Ivo. *Die Geschichte der Korruption: Von der Frühen Neuzeit bis ins 20. Jahrhundert* (Frankfurt am Main: S. Fischer, 2014).

BIBLIOGRAPHY 191

Engels, Jens Ivo. "Corruption and Anticorruption in the Era of Modernity and Beyond." In *Anticorruption in History: From Antiquity to the Modern Era*, ed. Ronald Kroeze, André Vitória, and G. Geltner (Oxford: Oxford University Press, 2018): pp. 167–80.

Eribon, Didier. *Returning to Reims*, trans. Michael Lucey (South Pasadena, CA: Semiotext(e), 2013).

Esteban Estríngana, Alicia. "Flemish Elites under Philip III's Patronage (1598–1621): Household, Court and Territory in the Spanish Habsburg Monarchy." In *A Constellation of Courts: The Courts and Households of Habsburg Europe 1555–1665*, ed. René Vermeir, Dries Raeymaekers, and José Eloy Hortal Muñoz (Leuven: Leuven University Press, 2014): pp. 123–66.

Esteban Estríngana, Alicia. "Los Estados de Flandes en el futuro político de los infantes: La designación del cardenal infante don Fernando para la lugartenencia real de Bruselas." In *La Corte de Felipe IV (1621–1665): Reconfiguración de la Monarquía católica*, ed. José Martínez Millán and José Eloy Muñoz (Madrid: Ediciones Polifemo, 2015): pp. 1615–78.

Faccini, Luigi. *La Lombardia fra '600 e '700: Riconversione economica e mutamenti sociali* (Milan: Franco Angeli, 1988).

Färber, Silvio. "Le forze e gli avvenimenti politici nei secoli XVII e XVIII." In *Storia dei Grigioni. Volume 2: L'età moderna*, ed. Fernando Iseppi (Chur: Pro Grigioni Italiano/Bellinzona: Casagrande, 2000): pp. 121–49.

Favarò, Valentina. *Carriere in movimento: Francisco Ruiz de Castro e la Monarchia di Filippo III* (Palermo: Associazione Mediterranea, 2013).

Fernández Albaladejo, Pablo. "De 'llave de Italia' a 'corazón de la monarquía': Milán y la monarquía católica en el reinado de Felipe III." In *Lombardia borromaica, Lombardia spagnola, 1554–1659*, ed. Paolo Pissavino and Gianvittorio Signorotto (Rome: Bulzoni, 1995): pp. 41–91.

Fernández-Santos Ortiz-Iribas, Jorge. "The Politics of Art or the Art of Politics?: The Marquis del Carpio in Rome and Naples (1677–1687)." In *The Spanish Presence in Sixteenth-Century Italy: Images of Iberia*, ed. Piers Baker-Bates and Miles Pattenden (Farnham: Ashgate, 2015): pp. 199–228.

Feros, Antonio. "Images of Evil, Images of Kings: The Contrasting Faces of the Royal Favourite and the Prime Minister in Early Modern European Political Literature, c.1580–c.1650." In *The World of the Favourite*, ed. J. H. Elliott and L. W. B. Brockliss (New Haven, CT: Yale University Press, 1999): pp. 205–22.

Feros, Antonio. *Kingship and Favoritism in the Spain of Philip III, 1598–1621* (Cambridge: Cambridge University Press, 2000).

Ferrier-Viaud, Pauline. *Épouses de ministres: Une histoire sociale du pouvoir féminin au temps de Louis XIV* (Paris: Champ Vallon, 2022).

Fink, Urban. *Die Luzerner Nuntiatur 1586–1873: Zur Behördengeschichte und Quellenkunde der päpstlichen Diplomatie in der Schweiz* (Lucerne: Rex, 1997).

Fitzpatrick, Sheila. *Everyday Stalinism: Ordinary Life in Extraordinary Times: Soviet Russia in the 1930s* (Oxford: Oxford University Press, 2000).

Fontaine, Laurence. *The Moral Economy: Poverty, Credit, and Trust in Early Modern Europe* (Cambridge: Cambridge University Press, 2014).

Fontaine, Laurence. "Protektion und Ökonomie: Der Markt für symbolischen Kredit am Hofe Ludwigs XIV." In *Protegierte und Protektoren: Asymmetrische politische Beziehungen zwischen Partnerschaft und Dominanz (16. bis frühes 20. Jahrhundert)*, ed. Tilman Haug, Nadir Weber, and Christian Windler (Cologne: Böhlau, 2016): pp. 261–78.

Fosi, Irene. *La società violenta: Il banditismo nello Stato pontificio nella seconda metà del Cinquecento* (Rome: Edizioni dell'Ateneo, 1985).

192 BIBLIOGRAPHY

Fosi, Irene. *All'ombra dei Barberini: Fedeltà e servizio nella Roma barocca* (Rome: Bulzoni, 1997).

Fosi, Irene. "Fabio Chigi und der Hof der Barberini: Beiträge zu einer vernetzten Lebensgeschichte." In *Historische Anstösse: Festschrift für Wolfgang Reinhard zum 65. Geburtstag am 10. April 2002*, ed. Peter Burschel (Berlin: Akademie Verlag, 2002): pp. 179–96.

Fosi, Irene. *Papal Justice: Subjects and Courts in the Papal States, 1500–1700*, trans. Thomas V. Cohen (Washington, DC: The Catholic University of America Press, 2011).

Friedeburg, Robert von and John Morrill, eds. *Monarchy Transformed: Princes and their Elites in Early Modern Western Europe* (Cambridge: Cambridge University Press, 2017).

Galasso, Giuseppe. *Napoli spagnola dopo Masaniello: Politica, cultura, società* (Florence: Sansoni, 1982).

Galasso, Giuseppe. *Alla periferia dell'impero: Il Regno di Napoli nel periodo spagnolo (secc. XVI–XVII)* (Turin: Einaudi, 1997).

Galli, Anna Elena. "Giberto III Borromeo: Strategie politiche e scelte figurative di un cardinale milanese nella Roma di pieno Seicento." *Archivio Storico Lombardo* 129 (2003): pp. 439–58.

Galli, Anna Elena. "Federico IV Borromeo (1617–1673) tra l'Europa e il Gran Teatro del Mondo." *Studia Borromaica* 22 (2008): pp. 365–80.

Galli, Anna Elena. "Federico IV Borromeo: Scelte artistiche tra Milano e Siena." In *Atti delle giornate di studio sul caravaggismo e il naturalismo nella Toscana del Seicento*, ed. Pierluigi Carofano (San Casciano in Val di Pesa: Libro Co. Italia, 2009): pp. 295–321.

Galli, Anna Elena. "I Borromeo d'Angera e l'Isola di San Vittore: 'Luogo delitioso e da Prencipe.' Nuovi elementi per la storia del palazzo e dei giardini dell'Isola Madre." In *Forme che volano, 1630–1738: Il barocco nelle province di Novara e del Verbano Cusio Ossola*, ed. Marina dell'Olmo and Sergio Monferrini (Novara: Mediaper Edizioni, 2014): pp. 217–23.

Galli, Anna Elena and Sergio Monferrini. *I Borromeo d'Angera: Collezionisti e mecenati nella Milano del Seicento* (Milan: Scalpendi, 2012).

Gaston, Ryan. "All the King's Men: Educational Reform and Nobility in Early Seventeenth-Century Spain." In *Contested Spaces of Nobility in Early Modern Europe*, ed. Charles Lipp and Matthew P. Romaniello (Farnham: Ashgate, 2016): pp. 167–88.

Giannini, Massimo Carlo. "Politica spagnola e giurisdizione ecclesiastica nello Stato di Milano: Il conflitto tra il cardinale Federico Borromeo e il *visitador* regio don Felipe de Haro (1606–1607)." *Studia Borromaica* 6 (1992): pp. 195–226.

Giannini, Massimo Carlo. "'Con ser Santo puso a riesgo de descomponerse mucho esta ciudad y estado': Carlo Borromeo da arcivescovo di Milano a santo della monarchia." *Chronica Nova* 43 (2017): pp. 19–52.

Gil Martínez, Francisco. "Las hechuras del Conde Duque de Olivares: La alta administración de la monarquía desde el análisis de redes." *Cuadernos de Historia moderna* 40 (2015): pp. 63–88.

Giovannini, Myriam. *Federico Borromeo: Nunzio apostolico. Con particolare riferimento alla nunziatura svizzera (attività diplomatica e contributo alla Controriforma) (1616–1673)* (Como: Marzorati, 1945).

González de León, Fernando. *The Road to Rocroi: Class, Culture and Command in the Spanish Army of Flanders, 1567–1659* (Leiden: Brill, 2009).

González Fuertes, Manuel Amador and Fernando Negredo del Cerro. "Mecanismos de control de la corrupción bajo Felipe IV: Los inventarios de ministros (1622–1655). Una primera aproximación." *Tiempos modernos* 35, 2 (2017): pp. 432–60.

González Tornel, Pablo. *Roma hispánica: Cultura festiva española en la capital del Barroco* (Madrid: Centro de Estudios Europa Hispánica, 2017).

Gramsci, Antonio. *Selections from the Prison Notebooks of Antonio Gramsci* (New York: International Publishers, 1971).

Gramsci, Antonio. *Prison Notebooks*, vol. 3, ed. and trans. Joseph A. Buttigieg (New York: Columbia University Press, 2007).

Grassi, Silvia and Alberto Grohmann. "La Segreteria di Stato di Sua Santità e la Milano nell'età del barocco." In *"Millain the Great": Milano nelle brume del Seicento*, ed. Aldo De Maddalena (Milan: Cassa di Risparmio delle Province Lombarde, 1989): pp. 267–83.

Groebner, Valentin. *Liquid Assets, Dangerous Gifts: Presents and Politics at the End of the Middle Ages*, trans. Pamela E. Selwyn (Philadelphia, PA: University of Pennsylvania Press, 2002).

Grüne, Niels. "'Gabenschlucker' und 'verfreundte rät': Zur patronagekritischen Dimension frühneuzeitlicher Korruptionskommunikation." In *Integration, Legitimation, Korruption: Politische Patronage in Früher Neuzeit und Moderne*, ed. Ronald G. Asch, Birgit Emich, and Jens Ivo Engels (Frankfurt am Main: Peter Lang, 2011): pp. 215–32.

Guarino, Gabriel. *Representing the King's Splendour: Communication and Reception of Symbolic Forms of Power in Viceregal Naples* (Manchester: Manchester University Press, 2010).

Hall, Stuart. *Policing the Crisis: Mugging, the State and Law and Order* (London and Basingstoke: Macmillan, 1982).

Hanlon, Gregory. *The Twilight of a Military Tradition: Italian Aristocrats and European Conflicts, 1560-1800* (London: UCL Press, 1998).

Hanlon, Gregory. *The Hero of Italy: Odoardo Farnese, Duke of Parma, His Soldiers, and His Subjects in the Thirty Years' War* (Oxford: Oxford University Press, 2014).

Hanlon, Gregory. *Italy 1636: Cemetery of Armies* (Oxford: Oxford University Press, 2016).

Head, Randolph C. *Jenatsch's Axe: Social Boundaries, Identity, and Myth in the Era of the Thirty Years' War* (Rochester, NY: University of Rochester Press, 2008).

Headley, John M. and John B. Tomaro, eds. *San Carlo Borromeo: Catholic Reform and Ecclesiastical Politics in the Second Half of the Sixteenth Century* (Washington, DC: Folger Books, 1988).

Herman, Arthur L. "The Language of Fidelity in Early Modern France." *The Journal of Modern History* 67 (1995): pp. 1–24.

Hermant, Héloïse. *Guerres de plumes: Publicité et cultures politiques dans l'Espagne du XVIIe siècle* (Madrid: Casa de Velázquez, 2012).

Hobsbawm, Eric J. "The General Crisis of the Seventeenth Century." *Past & Present* 16 (1954): pp. 35–53.

Hohwieler, Susanne. *Die Altieri - eine römische Familie: Status und Selbstdarstellung vom 15.-17. Jahrhundert. Eine Nepotengeschichte* (Bern: Peter Lang, 2019).

Horowski, Leonhard. *Die Belagerung des Thrones: Machtstrukturen und Karrieremechanismen am Hof von Frankreich 1661-1789* (Ostfildern: Jan Thorbecke, 2012).

Jago, Charles. "The 'Crisis of the Aristocracy' in Seventeenth-Century Castile." *Past & Present* 84 (1979): pp. 60–90.

James, Carolyn. *A Renaissance Marriage: The Political and Personal Alliance of Isabella D'Este and Francesco Gonzaga* (Oxford: Oxford University Press, 2020).

Jemolo, Arturo Carlo. *Stato e Chiesa negli scrittori politici del Seicento e del Settecento* (Milan: Fratelli Bocca, 1914).

Jiménez Estrella, Antonio. "'No ha interesado a cosa más que el servir a vuesta majestad': Las levas del duque de Pastrana durante el valimiento de Olivares: Servicio, mercedes y beneficio." In *Gobernar y reformar la Monarquía: Los agentes políticos y administrativos*

194 BIBLIOGRAPHY

en España y América. Siglos XVI–XIX, ed. Michel Bertrand, Francisco Andújar, and Thomas Glesener (Valencia: Albatros, 2017): pp. 151–69.

Jiménez Estrella, Antonio. "La corrupción en los tratados militares en época de los Habsburgo (siglos XVI y XVII)." In *Debates sobre la corrupción en el mundo ibérico: Siglos XVI–XVIII*, ed. Francisco Andújar Castillo and Pilar Ponce Leiva (Alicante: Biblioteca Virtual Miguel de Cervantes, 2018): pp. 133–59.

Jiménez Moreno, Agustín. "Las Órdenes Militares, la nobleza y la Monarquía española: Aspectos de una relación cambiante." In *Nobilitas: Estudios sobre la nobleza y lo nobiliario en la Europa moderna*, ed. Juan Hernández Franco, José A. Guillén Berrendero, and Santiago Martínez Hernández (Aranjuez: Ediciones Doce Calles, 2014): pp. 323–48.

Jones, Pamela. *Federico Borromeo and the Ambrosiana: Art Patronage and Reform in Seventeenth-Century Milan* (Cambridge: Cambridge University Press, 1993).

Kalnein, Albrecht Graf von. *Die Regentschaft in Spanien 1665–1677: Schwächung der Krongewalt und politische Alternativen* (Saarbrücken: Breitenbach, 1992).

Kamen, Henry. "Spain's First Caudillo: Don Juan José of Austria." *History Today* 26, 9 (1976): pp. 584–90.

Kamen, Henry. *Spain in the Later Seventeenth Century, 1665–1700* (London: Longman, 1980).

Karsten, Arne. *Künstler und Kardinäle: Vom Mäzenatentum römischer Kardinalnepoten im 17. Jahrhundert* (Cologne: Böhlau, 2003).

Karsten, Arne and Hillard von Thiessen, eds. *Nützliche Netzwerke und korrupte Seilschaften* (Göttingen: Vandenhoeck & Ruprecht, 2006).

Keblusek, Marika. "Introduction: Double Agents in Early Modern Europe." In *Double Agents: Cultural and Political Brokerage in Early Modern Europe*, ed. Marika Keblusek and Badeloch Vera Noldus (Leiden: Brill, 2011): pp. 1–9.

Kettering, Sharon. *Patrons, Brokers, and Clients in Seventeenth-Century France* (New York and Oxford: Oxford University Press, 1986).

Kettering, Sharon. "Brokerage at the Court of Louis XIV." *The Historical Journal* 36, 1 (1993): pp. 69–87.

Kettering, Sharon. *Patronage in Sixteenth- and Seventeenth-Century France* (Aldershot: Ashgate, 2002).

Klein, Lisa M. "Your Humble Handmaid: Elizabethan Gifts of Needlework." *Renaissance Quarterly* 50, 2 (1997): pp. 459–93.

Köchli, Ulrich. *Urban VII. und die Barberini: Nepotismus als Strukturmerkmal päpstlicher Herrschaftsorganisation in der Vormoderne* (Stuttgart: Anton Hiersemann, 2017).

Krautheimer, Richard. *The Rome of Alexander VII 1655–1667* (Princeton, NJ: Princeton University Press, 1985).

Krischer, André. "New Directions in the Study of the Holy Roman Empire: A Cultural Approach." In *The Holy Roman Empire, Reconsidered*, ed. Jason Philip Coy, Benjamin Marschke, and David Warren Sabean (New York and Oxford: Berghahn Books, 2010): pp. 265–70.

Kroeze, Ronald, André Vitoria, and G. Geltner, eds. *Anticorruption in History: From Antiquity to the Modern Era* (Oxford: Oxford University Press, 2018).

Latini, Carlotta. *Il privilegio dell'immunità: Diritto d'asilo e giurisdizione nell'ordine giuridico dell'età moderna* (Milan: Giuffrè, 2002).

Lauro, Agostino. *Il giurisdizionalismo pregiannoniano nel Regno di Napoli: Problema e bibliografia (1563–1723)* (Rome: Edizioni di Storia e Letteratura, 1974).

Levi, Giovanni. *Inheriting Power: The Career of an Exorcist*, trans. Lydia G. Cochrane (Chicago, IL, and London: The University of Chicago Press, 1988).

Levy Peck, Linda. *Court Patronage and Corruption in Early Stuart England* (Boston, MA: Unwin Hyman, 1990).

Lezowski, Marie. *L'Abrégé du monde: Une histoire sociale de la bibliothèque Ambrosienne (v. 1590–v. 1660)* (Paris: Classiques Garnier, 2015).

Loyal, Steven. *Bourdieu's Theory of the State: A Critical Introduction* (New York: Palgrave Macmillan, 2017).

Luiten, Loek. "Friends and Family, Fruit and Fish: The Gift in Quattrocento Farnese Cultural Politics." *Renaissance Studies* 33, 3 (2019): pp. 342–57.

Lutz, Georg. "Federico Borromeo." In *Dizionario Biografico Italiano*, vol. 13 (1971). Available at http://www.treccani.it/enciclopedia/federico-borromeo_res-a7b017a9-87e8-11dc-8e9d-0016357eee51_%28Dizionario-Biografico%29/. Accessed November 7, 2022.

MacHardy, Karin J. *War, Religion and Court Patronage in Habsburg Austria: The Social and Cultural Dimensions of Political Interaction, 1521–1622* (Basingstoke: Palgrave Macmillan, 2003).

MacKay, Ruth. *The Limits of Royal Authority: Resistance and Obedience in Seventeenth-Century Castile* (Cambridge: Cambridge University Press, 1999).

Maffi, Davide. *Il baluardo della corona: Guerra, esercito, finanze e società nella Lombardia seicentesca (1630–1660)* (Florence: Le Monnier, 2007).

Maffi, Davide. *La cittadella in armi: Esercito, società e finanza nella Lombardia di Carlo II 1660–1700* (Milan: Franco Angeli, 2010).

Maissen, Felici. "Die Bischofswahl Ulrichs VI. de Mont (1661)." *Bündner Monatsblatt* 6–7 (1957): pp. 208–22.

Maissen, Felici. "Zur Bischofswahl Ulrichs VI. de Mont (Nachtrag)." *Bündner Monatsblatt* 12 (1957): pp. 387–92.

Maissen, Felici. "Parteipolitische Kämpfe in den Drei Bünden 1657–59." *Bündner Monatsblatt* 7–8 (1968): pp. 189–209.

Maissen, Felici. "Das bündnerische Strafgericht von 1660." *Bündner Monatsblatt* 11–12 (1968): pp. 273–340.

Malcolm, Alistair. "Luis Ponce de León." In *Diccionario Biográfico Español*. Available at http://dbe.rah.es/biografias/21922/luis-ponce-de-leon. Accessed November 7, 2022.

Malcolm, Alistair. *Royal Favouritism and the Governing Elite of the Spanish Monarchy, 1640–1655* (Oxford: Oxford University Press, 2017).

Mancino, Michele and Giovanni Romeo. *Clero criminale: L'onore della Chiesa e i delitti degli ecclesiastici nell'Italia della Controriforma* (Rome and Bari: Laterza, 2013).

Manzoni, Alessandro. *The Betrothed: A Seventeenth-Century Milanese Story Discovered and Rewritten*, trans. Michael F. Moore (New York: The Modern Library, 2022).

Maravall, José Antonio. *La cultura del barroco: Análisis de una estructura histórica*, 6th ed. (Barcelona: Ariel, 1996).

Martin, John Jeffries. "Introduction: Manzoni and the Making of Italy." In Claudio Povolo, *The Novelist and the Archivist. Fiction and History in Alessandro Manzoni's* The Betrothed (Basingstoke: Palgrave Macmillan, 2014): pp. 1–19.

Martínez Hernández, Santiago. *Rodrigo Calderón, la sombra del valido: Privanza, favor y corrupción en la corte de Felipe III* (Madrid: Marcial Pons, 2009).

Martínez Hernández, Santiago. "La cámara del rey durante el reinado de Felipe IV: Facciones, grupos de poder y avatares del valimiento (1621–1661)." In *El mundo de un valido: Don Luis de Haro y su entorno, 1643–1661*, ed. Rafael Valladares (Madrid: Marcial Pons, 2016): pp. 49–96.

196 BIBLIOGRAPHY

Martínez Millán, José, ed. *La corte de Felipe IV (1621-1665): Reconfiguración de la Monarquía católica* (Madrid: Ediciones Polifemo, 2015).

Martínez Millán, José and Maria Antonietta Visceglia, eds. *La Monarquía de Felipe III* (Madrid: Fundación Mapfre, 2008).

Mellano, Maria F. and Franco Molinari. "La 'Vita di S. Carlo' del Bascapè: Vicende della pubblicazione." *Ricerche di storia sociale e religiosa* 21-2 (1982): pp. 125-89.

Menniti Ippolito, Antonio. *Il tramonto della Curia nepotista: Papi, nipoti e burocrazia curiale tra XVI e XVII secolo* (Rome: Viella, 1999).

Menniti Ippolito, Antonio. *1664: Un anno della Chiesa universale. Saggio sull'italianità del papato in età moderna* (Rome: Viella, 2011).

Merriman, Roger Bigelow. *Six Contemporaneous Revolutions* (New York: Oxford University Press, 1938).

Minguito Palomares, Ana. *Nápoles y el virrey conde de Oñate: La estrategia del poder y el resurgir del reino (1648-1653)* (Madrid: Silex, 2011).

Mitchell, Silvia Z. *Queen, Mother, and Stateswoman: Mariana of Austria and the Government of Spain* (University Park, PA: Pennsylvania State University Press, 2019).

Monier, Frédéric. "A 'Democratic Patronage': Social Integration and Republican Legitimacy in France (1880s-1930s)." In *Integration, Legitimation, Korruption: Politische Patronage in Früher Neuzeit und Moderne*, ed. Ronald G. Asch, Birgit Emich, and Jens Ivo Engels (Frankfurt am Main: Peter Lang, 2011): pp. 97-112.

Mozzarelli, Cesare. "Strutture sociali e formazioni statuali a Milano e Napoli tra '500 e '700." *Società e storia* 3 (1978): pp. 431-63.

Mozzarelli, Cesare. "Onore, utile, principe, stato." In *La corte e il "cortegiano": Un modello europeo*, vol. 2, ed. Adriano Prosperi (Rome: Bulzoni, 1980): pp. 241-53.

Mozzarelli, Cesare. "Il nero tunnel della tradizione." In his *Grandezza e splendori della Lombardia spagnola 1535-1701* (Milan: Skira, 2002): pp. 15-7.

Mozzarelli, Cesare. "Dall'antispagnolismo al revisionismo." In *Alle origini di una nazione: Antispagnolismo e identità italiana*, ed. Aurelio Musi (Milan: Guerini, 2003): pp. 345-68.

Mrozek Eliszezynski, Giuseppe. *Bajo acusación: El valimiento en el reinado de Felipe III. Procesos y discursos* (Madrid: Ediciones Polifemo, 2015).

Mrozek Eliszezynski, Giuseppe. *Ascanio Filomarino: Nobiltà, Chiesa e potere nell'Italia del Seicento* (Rome: Viella, 2017).

Muldrew, Craig. *The Economy of Obligation: The Culture of Credit and Social Relations in Early Modern England* (Basingstoke: Palgrave, 1998).

Musi, Aurelio. "L'Italia nel sistema imperiale spagnolo." In his *Nel sistema imperiale: L'Italia spagnola* (Naples: Edizioni Scientifiche Italiane, 1994): pp. 51-66.

Musi, Aurelio. *Il feudalesimo nell'Europa moderna* (Bologna: Mulino, 2007).

Musi, Aurelio. *L'impero dei viceré* (Bologna: Mulino, 2013).

Musi, Aurelio. "Antiespañolismo y decadencia en la cultura italiana." In *La Corte de Felipe IV (1621-1665): Reconfiguración de la Monarquía católica*, ed. José Martínez Millán and José Eloy Hortal Muñoz (Madrid: Ediciones Polifemo, 2015): pp. 57-129.

Muto, Giovanni. "Noble Presence and Stratification." In *Spain in Italy: Politics, Society and Religion, 1500-1700*, ed. Thomas Dandelet and John Marino (Leiden: Brill, 2007): pp. 251-97.

Muto, Giovanni. "'Mutation di corte, novità di ordini, nova pratica di servitori': La 'privanza' nella trattatistica politica spagnola e napoletana della prima età moderna." In *Con la ragione e col cuore: Studi dedicati a Carlo Capra*, ed. Stefano Levati and Marco Meriggi (Milan: Franco Angeli, 2008): pp. 139-82.

Natale, Mauro. *Le Isole Borromee e la Rocca d'Angera: Guida storico-artistica* (Cinisello Balsamo: Silvana, 2000).

BIBLIOGRAPHY   197

Neuschel, Kristen B. *Word of Honor: Interpreting Noble Culture in Sixteenth-Century France* (Ithaca, NY: Cornell University Press, 1989).

Noto, Maria Anna. *Élites transnazionali: Gli Acquavia di Caserta nell'Europa asburgica (secoli XVI–XVII)* (Milan: Franco Angeli, 2018).

Novo Zaballos, José Rufino. "De confesor de la reina a embajador extraordinario en Roma: La expulsión de Juan Everardo Nithard." In *Centros de poder italianos en la monarquía hispánica (siglos XV–XVIII)*, vol. 2, ed. José Martínez Millán and Manuel Rivero Rodríguez (Madrid: Polifemo, 2010): pp. 751–835.

Oliván Santaliestra, Laura. "Mariana de Austria en la encrucijada política del siglo XVII" (unpublished Ph.D. thesis, Universidad Complutense Madrid, 2006).

Oresko, Robert. "The House of Savoy in Search for a Royal Crown." In *Royal and Republican Sovereignty in Early Modern Europe: Essays in Memory of Ragnhild Hatton*, ed. Robert Oresko, G. C. Gibbs, and H. M. Scott (Cambridge: Cambridge University Press, 1997), pp. 272–350.

Osborne, Toby. *Dynasty and Diplomacy in the Court of Savoy: Political Culture and the Thirty Years' War* (Cambridge: Cambridge University Press, 2002).

Osborne, Toby. "The House of Savoy and the Theatre of the World: Performances of Sovereignty in Early Modern Rome." In *Sabaudian Studies: Political Culture, Dynasty, and Territory. 1400–1700*, ed. Matthew Vester (Kirksville, MO: Truman State University Press, 2013): pp. 167–90.

Papagna, Elena. *Sogni e bisogni di una famiglia aristocratica: I Caracciolo di Martina in età moderna* (Milan: Franco Angeli, 2002).

Parachini, Leonardo and Carlo Alessandro Pisoni. "La 'razza de' cavalli' di Feriolo." *Verbanus: Rassegna per la cultura, l'arte, la storia del lago* 24 (2003): pp. 481–510.

Parker, David. *Class and State in Ancien Régime France: The Road to Modernity?* (London and New York: Routledge, 1996).

Parker, Geoffrey. *Global Crisis: War, Climate Change, and Catastrophe in the Seventeenth Century* (New Haven, CT: Yale University Press, 2014).

Parrott, David. "The Causes of the Franco-Spanish War of 1635–59." In *The Origins of War in Early Modern Europe*, ed. Jeremy Black (Edinburgh: John Donald, 1987): pp. 72–111.

Parrott, David. "Richelieu, the *Grands*, and the French Army." In *Richelieu and His Age*, ed. Joseph Bergin and Laurence Brockliss (Oxford: Clarendon Press, 1992): pp. 135–73.

Parrott, David. *Richelieu's Army: War, Government and Society in France, 1624–1642* (Cambridge: Cambridge University Press, 2001).

Parrott, David. *1652: The Cardinal, the Prince, and the Crisis of the "Fronde"* (Oxford: Oxford University Press, 2020).

Partridge, Loren W. "Divinity and Dynasty at Caprarola: Perfect History in the Room of Farnese Deeds." *The Art Bulletin* 60, 3 (1978): pp. 494–530.

Pastor, Ludwig Freiherr von. *The History of the Popes from the Close of the Middle Ages, Vol. 31: Alexander VIII (1655–1667), Clement IX (1667–1669), Clement X (1670–1676)* (London: Kegan Paul, Trench, Trubner & Co., 1940).

Pattenden, Miles. *Electing the Pope in Early Modern Italy, 1450–1700* (Oxford: Oxford University Press, 2017).

Pečar, Andreas. "Status-Ökonomie: Notwendige Investitionen und erhoffte Renditen im höfischen Adel der Barockzeit." In *Die Ökonomie sozialer Beziehungen*, ed. Gabriele Jancke and Daniel Schläppi (Stuttgart: Franz Steiner Verlag, 2015): pp. 91–107.

Pissavino, Paolo and Gianvittorio Signorotto, eds. *Lombardia borromaica, Lombardia spagnola, 1554–1659* (Rome: Bulzoni, 1995).

Pollock, Linda. "Younger Sons in Tudor and Stuart England." *History Today* 39 (1989): pp. 23–9.

198 BIBLIOGRAPHY

Ponce Leiva, Pilar. "Acusaciones de corrupción y prácticas sociales infamantes: Quince años en la vida de Agustín Mesa y Ayala (1670–1685), contador de la Real Hacienda de Quito." *Revista Complutense de Historia de América* 43 (2017): pp. 49–74.

Prochaska, Frank. *Royal Bounty: The Making of a Welfare Monarchy* (New Haven, CT: Yale University Press, 1995).

Procter, James. *Stuart Hall* (London: Routledge, 2004).

Prodi, Paolo. "San Carlo Borromeo e le trattative tra Gregorio XIII e Filippo II sulla giurisdizione ecclesiastica." *Rivista di Storia della Chiesa in Italia* 11 (1957): pp. 195–240.

Prodi, Paolo. *Il sovrano pontefice. Un corpo e due anime: La monarchia papale nella prima età moderna*, rev. ed. (Bologna: Mulino, 2006).

Prosdocimi, Luigi. *Il diritto ecclesiastico dello Stato di Milano dall'inizio della Signoria viscontea al periodo tridentino (sec. XIII–XVI)* (Milan: L'arte, 1941).

Rabb, Theodore K. *The Struggle for Stability in Early Modern Europe* (New York: Oxford University Press, 1975).

Rabinovitch, Oded. *The Perraults: A Family of Letters in Early Modern France* (Ithaca, NY: Cornell University Press, 2018).

Rao, Anna Maria. "I filosofi e la corte a Napoli nel Settecento borbonico." In *La corte de los Borbones: Crisis del modelo cortesano*, ed. José Martínez Millán, Concepción Camarero Bullón, and Marcelo Luzzi Traficante (Madrid: Polifemo, 2013): pp. 1523–47.

Reinhard, Wolfgang. "Papa Pius: Prolegomena zu einer Sozialgeschichte des Papsttums." In *Von Konstanz nach Trient. Beiträge zur Kirchengeschichte von den Reformkonzilien bis zum Tridentinum: Festgabe für August Franzen*, ed. Remigius Bäumer (Paderborn: Schöningh, 1972): pp. 261–99.

Reinhard, Wolfgang. *Freunde und Kreaturen: "Verflechtung" als Konzept zur Erforschung historischer Führungsgruppen. Römische Oligarchie um 1600* (Munich: Verlag Ernst Vögel, 1979).

Reinhard, Wolfgang. "Papal Power and Family Strategy in the Sixteenth and Seventeenth Centuries." In *Princes, Patronage, and the Nobility: The Court at the Beginning of the Modern Age c.1450–1650*, ed. Ronald G. Asch and Adolf M. Birke (Oxford: Oxford University Press, 1991): pp. 329–56.

Reinhard, Wolfgang. "Amici e creature: Politische Mikrogeschichte der römischen Kurie im 17. Jahrhundert." *Quellen und Forschungen aus italienischen Archiven und Bibliotheken* 76 (1996): pp. 308–34.

Reinhard, Wolfgang, ed. *Power Elites and State Building* (Oxford: Oxford University Press, 1996).

Reinhardt, Nicole. *Voices of Conscience: Royal Confessors and Political Counsel in Seventeenth-Century Spain and France* (Oxford: Oxford University Press, 2016).

Reinhardt, Volker. "Kreise stören - Kreise schlagen: Perspektiven römischer Eliteforschung." In *Die Kreise der Nepoten: Neue Forschungen zu alten und neuen Eliten Roms in der frühen Neuzeit*, ed. Daniel Büchel and Volker Reinhardt (Bern: Peter Lang, 2001): pp. 11–27.

Ribot García, Luis Antonio. "La época del Conde-Duque de Olivares y el Reino de Sicilia." In *La España del Conde-Duque de Olivares*, ed. John Elliott and Ángel García Sanz (Valladolid: Publicaciones Universidad de Valladolid, 1990): pp. 663–77.

Ribot García, Luis Antonio. *La Monarquía de España y la guerra de Mesina (1674–1678)* (Madrid: Actas, 2002).

Rimoldi, Antonio. "L'età dei Borromeo (1560–1631)." In *Storia religiosa della Lombardia: Diocesi di Milano. Seconda parte*, ed. Adriano Caprioli, Antonio Rimoldi, and Luciano Vaccaro (Brescia: La Scuola, 1990): pp. 389–466.

BIBLIOGRAPHY 199

Rivero Rodríguez, Manuel. "El 'Gran Memorial' de 1624: Dudas, problemas textuales y contextuales de un documento atribuido al Conde Duque de Olivares." *Libros de la Corte* 4 (2012): pp. 48–71.

Rivero Rodríguez, Manuel. *El conde duque de Olivares: La búsqueda de la privanza perfecta* (Madrid: Polifemo, 2017).

Rizzo, Mario. "Centro spagnolo e periferia lombarda nell'impero asburgico tra Cinque e Seicento." *Rivista Storica Italiana* 104, 1 (1992): pp. 315–48.

Rizzo, Mario. "I cespiti di un maggiorente lombardo del Seicento: Ercole Teodoro Trivulzio e la milizia forese." *Archivio Storico Lombardo* 120 (1994): pp. 463–77.

Robertson, Clare. *"Il Gran Cardinale": Alessandro Farnese, Patron of the Arts* (New Haven, CT: Yale University Press, 1992).

Rodén, Marie-Louise. *Church Politics in Seventeenth-Century Rome: Cardinal Decio Azzolino, Queen Christina of Sweden, and the* Squadrone Volante (Stockholm: Almqvist & Wiksell International, 2000).

Roggero, Marina. *Le vie del libro: Letture, lingua e pubblico nell'Italia moderna* (Bologna: Mulino, 2021).

Rovito, Pier Luigi. "La rivoluzione costituzionale di Napoli (1647–48)." *Rivista Storica Italiana* 98 (1986): pp. 367–462.

Rowlands, Guy. *The Dynastic State and the Army under Louis XIV: Royal Service and Private Interest, 1661–1701* (Cambridge: Cambridge University Press, 2002).

Ruiz Rodríguez, Ignacio. *Don Juan José de Austria en la Monarquía Hispánica: Entre la política, el poder y la intriga* (Madrid: Dykinson, 2007).

Sabean, David Warren, Simon Teuscher, and Jon Mathieu, eds. *Kinship in Europe: Approaches to Long-Term Development, 1300–1900* (New York: Berghahn, 2007).

Salas Almela, Luis. *The Conspiracy of the Ninth Duke of Media Sidonia (1641): An Aristocrat in the Crisis of the Spanish Empire* (Leiden: Brill, 2013).

Sandberg, Brian. *Warrior Pursuits: Noble Culture and Civil Conflict in Early Modern France* (Baltimore, MD: The Johns Hopkins University Press, 2010).

Sanz Camañes, Porfirio. "El peso de la milicia: 'Alojamiento foral' y conflicto de jurisdicciones en la frontera catalano-aragonesa durante la guerra de Cataluña (1640–1652)." *Revista de historia moderna* 22 (2004): pp. 7–92.

Sanz Camañes, Porfirio and Enrique Solano Camón. "El impacto de la guerra de Cataluña en Aragón: La difícil convivencia entre las tropas y la población civil." *Revista de historia Jerónimo Zurita* 94 (2019): pp. 67–93.

Savage, Mike. *The Return of Inequality: Social Change and the Weight of the Past* (Cambridge, MA: Harvard University Press, 2021).

Scalisi, Lina. *Il controllo del sacro: Poteri e istituzioni concorrenti nella Palermo del Cinque e Seicento* (Rome: Viella, 2004).

Scalisi, Lina, ed. *La Sicilia dei Moncada: Le corti, l'arte e la cultura nei secoli XVI–XVII* (Catania: Domenico Sanfilippo, 2006).

Scalisi, Lina. "In omnibus ego: Luigi Guglielmo Moncada (1614–1672)." *Rivista Storica Italiana* 120 (2008): pp. 503–68.

Schneider, Christian. "Types of Peacemakers: Exploring the Authority and Self-Perception of the Early Modern Papacy." In *Cultures of Conflict Resolution in Early Modern Europe*, ed. Stephen Cummins and Laura Kounine (Farnham: Ashgate, 2016): pp. 77–104.

Schumacher, Ib Mark. "Felipe IV, su reputación y la política de la Monarquía Hispánica." *Pedralbes* 35 (2015): pp. 119–56.

Scott, H. M., ed. *The European Nobilities in the Seventeenth and Eighteenth Centuries* (London and New York: Longman, 1995).

200   BIBLIOGRAPHY

Scott, James C. *Domination and the Arts of Resistance: Hidden Transcripts* (New Haven, CT: Yale University Press, 1990).

Scott, John B. *Images of Nepotism: The Painted Ceilings of Palazzo Barberini* (Princeton, NJ: Princeton University Press, 1991).

Sella, Domenico. *Crisis and Continuity: The Economy of Spanish Lombardy in the Seventeenth Century* (Cambridge, MA: Harvard University Press, 1979).

Shepard, Alexandra. *Meanings of Manhood in Early Modern England* (Oxford: Oxford University Press, 2008).

Sidler, Daniel. *Heiligkeit aushandeln: Katholische Reform und lokale Glaubenspraxis in der Eidgenossenschaft (1560-1790)* (Frankfurt am Main: Campus, 2017).

Signorotto, Gianvittorio. "Il marchese di Caracena al governo di Milano (1648-1656)." In *L'Italia degli Austrias: Monarchia cattolica e domini italiani nei secoli XVI e XVII*, ed. Gianvittorio Signorotto (Brescia: Centro Federico Odorici, 1992): pp. 135-81.

Signorotto, Gianvittorio. "Stabilità politica e trame antispagnole nella Milano del Seicento." In *Complots et conjurations dans l'Europe moderne*, ed. Yves-Marie Bercé and Elena Fasano Guarini (Rome: École Française de Rome, 1996): pp. 721-45.

Signorotto, Gianvittorio. "Guerre spagnole, ufficiali lombardi." In *I Farnese: Corti, guerra e nobiltà in antico regime*, ed. Antonella Bilotto, Piero del Negro, and Cesare Mozzarelli (Rome: Bulzoni, 1997): pp. 367-96.

Signorotto, Gianvittorio. "La 'verità' e gli 'interessi': Religiosi milanesi nelle legazioni alla corte di Spagna (sec. XVII)." In *I religiosi a corte: Teologia, politica e diplomazia in Antico Regime*, ed. Flavio Rurale (Rome: Bulzoni, 1998): pp. 195-227.

Signorotto, Gianvittorio. *Milano spagnola: Guerra, istituzioni, uomini di governo, 1635-1660*, 2nd ed. (Milan: Sansoni, 2001).

Signorotto, Gianvittorio. "La politica vista dal segretario: Milano dopo la pace dei Pirenei nelle memorie di Carlo Francesco Gorani." In *L'informazione politica in Italia (secoli XVI-XVIII): Atti del seminario organizzato presso la Scuola Normale Superiore, Pisa, 23 e 24 giugno 1997*, ed. Elena Fasano Guarini and Mario Rosa (Pisa: Scuola Normale Superiore, 2001): pp. 303-40.

Signorotto, Gianvittorio. "The *Squadrone Volante*: 'Independent' Cardinals and European Politics in the Second Half of the Seventeenth Century." In *Court and Politics in Papal Rome, 1492-1700*, ed. Gianvittorio Signorotto and Maria Antonietta Visceglia (Cambridge: Cambridge University Press, 2002): pp. 175-211.

Signorotto, Gianvittorio. "A proposito dell'intentato processo di beatificazione del cardinal Federico. Milano e Roma agli esordi dell'età innocenziana." *Studia Borromaica* 17 (2003): pp. 311-45.

Signorotto, Gianvittorio. "Dalla decadenza alla crisi della modernità: La storiografia sulla Lombardia spagnola." In *Alle origini di una nazione: Antispagnolismo e identità italiana*, ed. Aurelio Musi (Milan: Guerini, 2003): pp. 313-43.

Signorotto, Gianvittorio. "A proposito della fedeltà di Milano alla Monarchia cattolica." In *Sardegna, Spagna e Mediterraneo: Dai Re Cattolici al Secolo d'Oro*, ed. Bruno Anatra and Giovanni Murgia (Rome: Carocci, 2004): pp. 275-90.

Signorotto, Gianvittorio. "La scena pubblica milanese al tempo del cardinal Federico e del conte di Fuentes." In *Carlo Borromeo e il cattolicesimo dell'età moderna: Nascita e fortuna di un modello di santità*, ed. Maria Luisa Frosio and Danilo Zardin (Rome: Bulzoni, 2011): pp. 25-71.

Smith, Jay M. *The Culture of Merit: Nobility, Royal Service, and the Making of Absolute Monarchy in France, 1600-1789* (Ann Arbor, MI: University of Michigan Press, 1996).

Snyder, Jon R. *Dissimulation and the Culture of Secrecy in Early Modern Europe* (Berkeley, CA: University of California Press, 2009).

Sodano, Giulio. *Da baroni del Regno a Grandi di Spagna. Gli Acquaviva d'Atri: vita aristocratica e ambizioni politiche (secoli XV–XVIII)* (Naples: Guida, 2012).

Sodano, Giulio. "Le aristocrazie napoletane." In *Il Regno di Napoli nell'età di Filippo IV (1621–1665)*, ed. Giovanni Brancaccio and Aurelio Musi (Milan: Guerini e Associati, 2014): pp. 131–76.

Soria Mesa, Enrique. *La nobleza en la España moderna: Cambio y continuidad* (Madrid: Marcial Pons, 2007).

Spagnoletti, Angelantonio. "Il governo del feudo: Aspetti della giurisdizione baronale nelle università meridionali del XVIII secolo." *Società e Storia* 55 (1992): pp. 61–79.

Spagnoletti, Angelantonio. *Principi italiani e Spagna nell'età barocca* (Milan: Mondadori, 1996).

Spagnoletti, Angelantonio. "Giangirolamo Acquaviva: Un barone meridionale tra Conversano, Napoli e Madrid." In *Giangirolamo II Acquaviva: Un barone meridionale nella crisi del Seicento (dai memoriali di Paolo Antonio di Tarsia)*, ed. Angelantonio Spagnoletti and Giuseppe Patisso (Conversano: Congedo, 1999): pp. 1–24.

Spagnoletti, Angelantonio. *Le dinastie italiane nella prima età moderna* (Bologna: Mulino, 2003).

Spagnoletti, Angelantonio. "Onore e spirito nazionale nei soldati italiani al servizio della monarchia spagnola." In *Militari e società civile nell'Europa dell'età moderna (secoli XVI–XVIII)*, ed. Claudio Donati and Bernhard R. Kroener (Bologna: Mulino, 2007): pp. 211–53.

Spiriti, Andrea. "Identità e scarto iconografico: I quadroni di Federico Borromeo fra eredità carliana e progettualità politica." *Studia Borromaica* 18 (2004): pp. 325–51.

Stollberg-Rilinger, Barbara. *The Emperor's Old Clothes: Constitutional History and the Symbolic Language of the Holy Roman Empire*, trans. Thomas Dunlap (New York and Oxford: Berghahn, 2015).

Stollberg-Rilinger, Barbara. "The Baroque State." In *The Oxford Handbook of the Baroque*, ed. John D. Lyons (Oxford: Oxford University Press, 2018): pp. 825–46.

Stollberg-Rilinger, Barbara. *The Holy Roman Empire: A Short History*, trans. Yair Mintzker (Princeton, NJ: Princeton University Press, 2018).

Storrs, Christopher. *The Resilience of the Spanish Monarchy, 1665–1700* (Oxford: Oxford University Press, 2006).

Swartz, David L. *Culture and Power: The Sociology of Pierre Bourdieu* (Chicago, IL, and London: The University of Chicago Press, 1997).

Swartz, David L. *Symbolic Power, Politics, and Intellectuals: The Political Sociology of Pierre Bourdieu* (Chicago, IL, and London: The University of Chicago Press, 2013).

Swartz, David L. "Metaprinciples for Sociological Research in a Bourdieusian Perspective." In *Bourdieu and Historical Analysis*, ed. Philip Gorski (Durham, NC: Duke University Press, 2013): pp. 19–35.

Tarpley, W. G. "Paolo Sarpi, His Networks, Venice and the Coming of the Thirty Years' War" (unpublished Ph.D. thesis, Catholic University of America, 2009).

Teodori, Marco. *I parenti del papa: Nepotismo pontificio e formazione del patrimonio Chigi nella Roma barocca* (Padua: Cedam, 2001).

Thompson, E. P. "The Patricians and the Plebs." In his *Customs in Common* (London: Merlin, 1991): pp. 16–96.

Thompson, I. A. A. "Aspectos de la organización naval y militar durante el ministerio de Olivares." In *La España del Conde-Duque de Olivares*, ed. John Elliott and Ángel García Sanz (Valladolid: Publicaciones Universidad de Valladolid, 1990): pp. 249–74.

Thompson, I. A. A. "The Nobility in Spain, 1600–1800." In *The European Nobilities in the Seventeenth and Eighteenth Centuries. Vol. 1: Western Europe*, ed. H. M. Scott (London and New York: Longman, 1995): pp. 174–236.

202 BIBLIOGRAPHY

Tonelli, Giovanna. *Investire con profitto e stile: Strategie imprenditoriali e familiari a Milano tra Sei e Settecento* (Milan: Franco Angeli, 2015).

Trevor-Roper, Hugh. "The General Crisis of the Seventeenth Century." In his *The Crisis of the Seventeenth Century: Religion, the Reformation, and Social Change* (Indianapolis, IN: Liberty Fund, 1999 [1967]): pp. 43–81.

Valladares, Rafael, ed. *El mundo de un valido: Don Luis de Haro y su entorno, 1643–1661* (Madrid: Marcial Pons, 2016).

Verga, Marcello. "La Spagna e il paradigma della decadenza italiana tra Seicento e Settecento." In *Alle origini di una nazione: Antispagnolismo e identità italiana*, ed. Aurelio Musi (Milan: Guerini, 2003): pp. 49–81.

Vigo, Giovanni. "L'economia lombarda nell'età dei Borromei: L'Alto Milanese." In *L'Alto Milanese all'epoca di Carlo e Federico Borromeo: Società e territorio*, ed. AA. VV. (Gallarate: Società Gallaratese per gli Studi Patri, 1987): pp. 199–210.

Villari, Rosario. *Elogio della dissimulazione: La lotta politica nel Seicento* (Rome and Bari: Laterza, 1987).

Villari, Rosario. "Discussioni sulla crisi del Seicento." In his *Politica barocca: Inquietudini, mutamento e prudenza* (Rome and Bari: Laterza, 2010): pp. 32–59.

Villari, Rosario. "La cultura politica italiana nell'età barocca." In his *Politica barocca: Inquietudini, mutamento e prudenza* (Rome and Bari: Laterza, 2010): pp. 5–31.

Villari, Rosario. *Un sogno di libertà: Napoli nel declino di un impero 1585–1648* (Milan: Mondadori, 2012).

Visceglia, Maria Antonietta. "'La giusta statera de' porporati': Sulla composizione e rappresentazione del Sacro Collegio nella prima metà del Seicento." *Roma moderna e contemporanea* 1 (1996): pp. 167–211.

Visceglia, Maria Antonietta. "La nobiltà napoletana nella prima età moderna: Studi recenti e prospettive di ricerca." In her *Identità sociali: La nobiltà napoletana nella prima età moderna* (Milan: Unicopli, 1998): pp. 9–58.

Visceglia, Maria Antonietta. "'Non si ha da equiparare l'utile quando vi fosse l'honore': Scelte economiche e reputazione: Intorno alla vendita dello stato feudale dei Caetani (1627)." In *La nobiltà romana in età moderna: Profili istituzionali e pratiche sociali*, ed. Maria Antonietta Visceglia (Rome: Carocci, 2001): pp. 203–23.

Visceglia, Maria Antonietta. "Factions in the Sacred College in the Sixteenth and Seventeenth Centuries." In *Court and Politics in Papal Rome 1492–1700*, ed. Gianvittorio Signorotto and Maria Antonietta Visceglia (Cambridge: Cambridge University Press, 2002): pp. 99–131.

Visceglia, Maria Antonietta. *Roma papale e Spagna: Diplomatici e religiosi tra due corti* (Rome: Bulzoni, 2010).

Visconti, Katia. *Il commercio dell'onore: Un'indagine prosopografica della feudalità nel Milanese di età moderna* (Milan: Unicopli, 2008).

Von Thiessen, Hillard. "Familienbande und Kreaturenlohn: Der (Kardinal-)Herzog von Lerma und die Kronkardinäle Philipps III. von Spanien." In *Die Jagd nach dem roten Hut: Kardinalskarrieren im barocken Rom*, ed. Arne Karsten (Göttingen: Vandenhoeck & Ruprecht, 2004): pp. 105–25.

Von Thiessen, Hillard. "Herrschen mit Verwandten und Klienten." In *Nützliche Netzwerke und korrupte Seilschaften*, ed. Arne Karsten and Hillard von Thiessen (Göttingen: Vandenhoeck & Ruprecht, 2006): pp. 181–207.

Von Thiessen, Hillard. *Diplomatie und Patronage: Die spanisch-römischen Beziehungen 1605–1621 in akteurszentrierter Perspektive* (Epfendorf: Bibliotheca Academica Verlag, 2010).

Von Thiessen, Hillard. "Der entkleidete Favorit: Legitimation von Günstlings-Herrschaft und politische Dynamik im Spanien des Conde-Duque de Olivares." In *Integration, Legitimation, Korruption: Politische Patronage in Früher Neuzeit und Moderne*, ed. Ronald G. Asch, Birgit Emich, and Jens Ivo Engels (Frankfurt am Main: Peter Lang, 2011): pp. 131–47.

Von Thiessen, Hillard. "Normenkonkurrenz: Handlungsspielräume, Rollen, normativer Wandel und normative Kontinuität vom späten Mittelalter bis zum Übergang zur Moderne." In *Normenkonkurrenz in historischer Perspektive*, ed. Arne Karsten and Hillard von Thiessen (Berlin: Duncker & Humblot, 2015): pp. 241–86.

Von Thiessen, Hillard. *Das Zeitalter der Ambiguität: Vom Umgang mit Werten und Normen in der Frühen Neuzeit* (Cologne: Böhlau, 2021).

Wacquant, Loïc J. D. "Reading Bourdieu's 'Capital'." *International Journal of Contemporary Sociology* 33, 2 (1996): pp. 151–70.

Wacquant, Loïc J. D. "Foreword." In Pierre Bourdieu, *The State Nobility: Elite Schools in the Field of Power* (Stanford, CA: Stanford University Press, 1996): pp. ix–xxii.

Walter, John. *Crowds and Popular Politics in Early Modern England* (Manchester: Manchester University Press, 2006).

Waquet, Jean-Claude. *Corruption: Ethics and Power in Florence, 1600–1700*, trans. Linda McCall (University Park, PA: Penn State Press, 1991).

Wassilowsky, Günther. "Vorsehung und Verflechtung: Theologie und Mikropolitik im Konklavezeremoniell Gregors XV. (1621/22)." In *Werte und Symbole im frühneuzeitlichen Rom*, ed. Günther Wassilowsky and Hubert Wolf (Münster: Rhema, 2005): pp. 51–82.

Weber, Christoph. *Familienkanonikate und Patronatsbistümer: Ein Beitrag zur Geschichte von Adel und Klerus im neuzeitlichen Italien* (Berlin: Duncker & Humblot, 1988).

Weber, Samuel. "Ein Verteidiger adliger 'Interessen' gegen republikanische 'Leidenschaften': Nuntius Federico Borromeo als Akteur im Zwyerhandel (1656–1659)." In *Beobachten, Vernetzen, Verhandeln: Diplomatische Akteure und politische Kulturen in der frühneuzeitlichen Eidgenossenschaft*, ed. Philippe Rogger and Nadir Weber (Basel: Schwabe, 2018): pp. 45–67.

Weber, Samuel. "Una *mater litigans* nella Roma chigiana: Giovanna Cesi in Borromeo (1598–1672) e il 'misconoscimento' del potere femminile nella corte pontificia di metà Seicento." *Dimensioni e problemi della ricerca storica* 2 (2021): pp. 217–50.

Wellen, Judith. *Bilder wider das Ende der Dynastie: Kunst als Vermittlungsform der königlichen Herrschaft Karls II. von Spanien in Escorial* (Frankfurt am Main: Vervuert, 2015).

Wendland, Andreas. *Passi alpini e salvezza delle anime: La Spagna, Milano e la lotta per la Valtellina 1620–1641*, trans. Gian Primo Falappi (Sondrio: L'officina del libro, 1999).

Werbner, Pnina. "The Enigma of Christmas: Symbolic Violence, Compliant Subjects and the Flow of English Kinship." *The Sociological Review* 44, 1 (1996): pp. 135–62.

White, Stephen D. "Service for Fiefs or Fiefs for Service: The Politics of Reciprocity." In *Negotiating the Gift: Pre-Modern Figurations of Exchange*, ed. Gadi Algazi, Valentin Groebner, and Bernhard Jussen (Göttingen: Vandenhoeck & Ruprecht, 2003): pp. 63–98.

Williams, Patrick. *The Great Favourite: The Duke of Lerma and the Government of Philip III of Spain, 1598–1621* (Manchester: Manchester University Press, 2006).

Windler, Christian. "Städte am Hof: Burgundische Deputierte und Agenten in Madrid und Versailles (16. –18. Jahrhundert)." *Zeitschrift für Historische Forschung* 30, 2 (2003): pp. 207–50.

Windler, Christian. "'Ohne Geld keine Schweizer': Pensionen und Söldnerrekrutierung auf den eidgenössischen Patronagemärkten." In *Nähe in der Ferne: Personale Verflechtung in*

204 BIBLIOGRAPHY

den Aussenbeziehungen der Frühen Neuzeit, ed. Hillard von Thiessen and Christian Windler (Berlin: Duncker & Humblot, 2005): pp. 105–33.

Windler, Christian. "*Arbitrismo*, Reform and the Government of the Minister-Favourites in the Spanish Monarchy." In *Reforming Early Modern Monarchies: The Castilian* Arbitristas *in Comparative European Perspectives*, ed. Christian Windler and Sina Rauschenbach (Wiesbaden: Harrassowitz, 2016): pp. 19–41.

Windler, Christian. "Redes de relaciones personales y corrupción: Culturas confesionales y culturas políticas." In *Gobernar y reformar la Monarquía: Los agentes políticos y administrativos en España y América. Siglos XVI–XIX*, ed. Michel Bertrand, Francisco Andújar, and Thomas Glesener (Valencia: Albatros, 2017): pp. 123–32.

Windler, Christian. *Missionare in Persien: Kulturelle Diversität und Normenkonkurrenz im globalen Katholizismus (17.–18. Jahrhundert)* (Cologne: Böhlau, 2018).

Wright, A. D. "Relations between Church and State: Catholic Developments in Spanish-Ruled Italy of the Counter-Reformation." *History of European Ideas* 9, 4 (1988): pp. 385–403.

Wunder, Heide. *He Is the Sun, She Is the Moon: Women in Early Modern Germany*, trans. Thomas Dunlap (Cambridge, MA: Harvard University Press, 1998).

Yun Casalilla, Bartolomé, ed. *Las redes del Imperio: Élites sociales en la articulación de la Monarquía Hispánica* (Madrid: Marcial Pons, 2009).

Zuffi, Stefano. "La pittura ad Angera e le committenze dei Borromeo: I fasti." In *La Città di Angera, feudo dei Borromeo, sec. XV–XVIII*, ed. Marco Tamborini (Gavirate: Nicolini Editore, 1995): pp. 391–6.

Zunckel, Julia. "Handlungsspielräume eines Mailänder Erzbischofs: Federico Borromeo und Rom." In *Römische Mikropolitik unter Papst Paul V. Borghese (1605–1621) zwischen Spanien, Neapel, Mailand und Genua*, ed. Wolfgang Reinhard (Tübingen: Max Niemeyer, 2004): pp. 427–567.

Zwyssig, Philipp. "Katholische Reform als soziale Praxis: Handlungslogiken eines Churer Bischofs im 17. Jahrhundert." *Traverse* 2 (2015): pp. 156–69.

Zwyssig, Philipp. *Täler voller Wunder: Eine katholische Verflechtungsgeschichte der Drei Bünde und des Veltlins (17. und 18. Jahrhundert)* (Affalterbach: Didymos, 2018).

Index

For the benefit of digital users, indexed terms that span two pages (e.g., 52–3) may, on occasion, appear on only one of those pages.

Abbiati, Filippo 163–5
absolutism. *See* social collaboration between king and nobility
Accademia dei Faticosi (Milan) 97
Acquaviva, Giangirolamo
    quest for grandeeship 93
Alessandria 86–8
Alexander VII Chigi, Pope. *See* Chigi, Fabio
Alexander the Great
    myth of 83–4
Alfonso the Magnanimous
    myth of 131–2, 164–5
Altoviti, Giacomo 130
ambiguity (von Thiessen)
    toward conflicting norms 39
Ambrosiana (Milan) 155–6, 161
Angera
    castle of 25–6
    cycle of paintings 81–2, 163–5, 168
    lords of 26
anti-corruption
    opportunistic 10–11, 77–8, 95, 109–10
Antonio, Nicolás de 130–1, 133–4
Aragón, Pascual de 131–2, 138–9
Aragón, Pedro Antonio de 117–18, 131–2
árbol del parentesco 163
Arese, Bartolomeo
    opposition to *case erme* 77–8
Arias Sotelo, Antonio
    clash with Giovanni Borromeo 86–8
aristocratic oligarchy
    after Haro 7, 82–3, 138–9
    under Haro 92–3, 96–7
aristocratic solipsism 56
Arona
    fortress of 25–6, 52–4
    siege of (1644) 54–5, 90–1
    town of 68
Astor, Juan de 63–4
autosurveillance of courtiers 92–3

baroque state (Stollberg-Rilinger) 11–12, 138, 150–1
Benevento 69–70, 128

Besozzi di Cocco, Francesco 63–4
Besozzo, Giovanni Battista 30–1
    bribery 32–3
billeting. *See* troop allocation
Bonetto, Francesco 31
Borromeo, Antonio Renato
    as client of Juan José 163–4, 170–1
    as patron of the arts 156, 160–1, 164, 170–1
Borromeo, Carlo III
    clash with Giovanni Borromeo 61–2, 77–8
    estates-division with Giulio Cesare 25
Borromeo, Carlo IV 173–4
Borromeo, Carlo, saint 18–19
    jurisdictional conflict 18–19
Borromeo, Federico III 20–1
    as archbishop 19–20
    as author 36–8, 40
    jurisdictional conflict 18, 20–1
    myth of 1–2, 21–2, 121, 156–9, 177
    relationship with Lerma 20
    stance on favoritism 38–9
Borromeo, Federico IV
    as cardinal 137, 156
    as client of Chigi 109–10
    as client of Juan José 143–4, 147
    as client of the Pamphili 109
    as governor in the Papal States 121, 128
    as governor of Rome 128–9
    as nuncio in Spain 141–4
    as nuncio in Switzerland 110–13
    as patron of the arts 159–60
    as prefect of the Congregation of Ecclesiastical Immunity 130–1
    as secretary of state 144–6, 151–2
    as secretary of the Congregation of Ecclesiastical Immunity 126–7, 130
    clash with Ponce de León 101–2, 116–18, 120–1
    education 103–5
    role in Nithard's cardinalate 143, 147–9
Borromeo, Federico V 91
Borromeo, Giovanni
    as client of Olivares 52–3
    as commissioner-general 61–3

206 INDEX

Borromeo, Giovanni (*cont.*)
  as governor of Lake Maggiore 52–3
  as *maestro di campo* 52
  as patron of the *ceto civile* 71, 79–80
  clash with Arias Sotelo 86–8
  clash with Fuensaldaña 86
  clash with González del Valle 91
  clash with Vázquez Coronado 88–9
  during siege of Arona (1644) 55
  promotion of 1657 84–5
  quest for Golden Fleece 91–4
Borromeo, Giulio Cesare
  as lord of Angera 26, 30–1, 33–4
  as military entrepreneur 50–1
  death on the battlefield 51–2
  estates-division with Carlo III 25
Borromeo, Paolo Emilio 163
Borromeo, Renato II 70–1, 77–8, 85
Bourdieu, Pierre 12–13, 39–41, 56–7, 94–5,
  103–4, 108–9, 167–8, 178
Brebbia, revolt of (1640) 63–4
Brunsson, Nils 40–1

Caimi, Gerolamo 31, 33
capital (Bourdieu) 12
  cultural 105
  social 103–4
  symbolic 50, 156, 173–4
  transubstantiation of 12
Caprarola 164
Capriata, Pier Giovanni
  on siege of Arona (1644) 54–5
Caracena, Luis Benavides de Canillo y Toledo,
  Marquis of
  case erme 77, 79–80
  clash with Giovanni Borromeo 89
Carafa della Spina, Carlo 115
Casati, Danese 125
Casati, Francesco 112
  diplomatic status 116–18
  relationship with Federico IV Borromeo 112,
  115–18
case erme
  as elite project 67–8
  as patronage 69–70
  corruption 72–4
  opposition to 72, 74
  policy 62–3, 66–7
  sites 68
  stakeholders 68–71, 78
  suppression 75–7
Castro, Francisco Ruiz de 20–1
Castro, Pedro Fernández de 20–1
Catalonia, revolt of (1640) 65–6

ceremonial
  conflict over rank and status 101–2, 116–17
  incognito 101–2
Cesi Borromeo, Giovanna 26, 51–2, 58–9, 146
ceto civile
  alliance with nobility 5–6, 79–80, 135–6
  as clients of Federico IV Borromeo 132–4
  as clients of Giovanni Borromeo 70–1, 79–80
  insurrectionary potential of 69–70
  law and order and 132, 134–5
Chigi, Fabio
  as patron of Federico IV Borromeo 110–11
  as patron of the arts 159–60
  reforms 107–9
Church-state relations in Spanish Italy 18,
  128, 130–1
classification struggle (Bourdieu) 94–6
Claudia Felicitas, Archduchess of
  Innsbruck 166–7
Coloma, Carlos 49
common good
  after favoritism 10–11, 94–6, 98
  as norm 10
  popular conception of 75
  semantic shift 11–12, 178–9
  under Olivares 28–9, 34–5, 40
  violation of 80
  vs. social norms 11–12, 39
concordia jurisdictionalis (treaty) 18, 21
conflicting norms 10, 39, 90
Congregation of Ecclesiastical Immunity
  (Rome) 123–4, 129–30
  Special Committee on the Bull of
  Gregory XIV 125–6, 130
corruption
  charges of 82–3, 95–6
  historiography of 10–11, 39–40, 82–3
cortesano político 148–9
Cortona, Pietro da 159–60
Council of Italy (Madrid)
  under Olivares 31–4
Council of State (Madrid)
  during regency of Mariana 138–9
courtization 21, 98, 177–9
Crescenzio Romani, Pietro Giovanni de 175
crime 125, 134–5
crisis of authority (Gramsci) 133

Di Gaeta, Antonio 125–6
diacatholicon 111–12
disinterested service
  as ideal 61, 96, 102, 118–19, 135
  as ideology 108–11
  vs. *reputación* 82–3

INDEX   207

dissimulation 142–3, 149–52
distinction (Bourdieu) 160, 167–9
distributive justice
    as ideal 67
    popular conception of 74–5
    violation of 73–4
D'Onofrio, Vincenzo. *See* Fuidoro, Innocenzo
duty to protect 47–8, 58

ecclesiastical asylum 122–3
    settlement between papacy and Spanish
        monarchy (1672) 125–6, 130–1
ecclesiastical dynasty 18–19
ecclesiastical immunity. *See* ecclesiastical asylum
Elias, Norbert 177–8

familism 9
fasti borromei. See Angera, cycle of paintings
favoritism
    appeal in Spanish Italy 5
    end of 7, 92–3
    function of 20–1, 26–8
    resistance to 178
feral priests (moral panic) 122–3, 131–5
Ferdinand of Austria, Cardinal
    relationship with Giulio Cesare Borromeo 43
Flugi von Aspermont, Johann 113
Franco-Spanish War
    aristocratic jingoism 48, 56–8
    causes 48
    impact on civilians 57–9
    Milanese nobility in 49
    peasant militia 55–6
    popular opposition to 58–60, 75
Fuensaldaña, Alonso Pérez de Vivero, Count of
    relationship with Giovanni Borromeo 85–6
Fuentes, Pedro Enríquez de Acevedo,
        Count of 20
Fuidoro, Innocenzo 134–5

gender. *See* masculinity
Gherardini, Melchiorre 81
gift
    as corruption 32
    book as 36–7
    vs. sale 33–4
Golden Fleece, Order of 91–2
González del Valle, Pedro 91
good governance
    as ideal 42
    as platform 121, 130, 133, 138
Gorani, Carlo Francesco 120–1, 132, 134–5
Gramsci, Antonio 132–3, 177
Gray Leagues. *See* Grisons

Grimani, Antonio
    on Federico IV Borromeo 145–6, 151
Grisons 112–13
    Spanish influence in 112–13, 115–16
Gualdo Priorato, Galeazzo 49, 54–6, 84

Hall, Stuart 121, 132–3
Haro, Luis Méndez de 79
    style of government 92–3
history painting
    as allegory 81, 164, 166–8
honor
    as threat to war effort 91, 94
    of officeholder 90
hypocrisy (Brunsson) 40–2

inequality 12–13, 178
    rationalization of 12–13, 39–40, 50, 98
informal government structures 150–2
Innocent X Pamphili, Pope 106–7, 110

Juan José of Austria
    as prime minister 169–70
    coup against Nithard 139–42
    coup against Valenzuela 169
    relationship with Federico IV Borromeo
        143–4, 147, 151–2
junta de gobierno (Madrid) 138–9
jurisdictional conflict
    public reception 134–5
    under Alfonso Litta 122
    under Carlo Borromeo 18–19
    under Federico III Borromeo 18, 20–1

La gratia de' principi (book) 36–7
Lake Maggiore
    fief of the Borromeo 25–6
    fishing privilege 34–5
Landriani, Ludovico 122
law and order 121, 133–4
Ledesma, Pedro de
    crackdown on *árbol del parentesco* 163
Leganés, Diego Felípez de Guzmán,
        Marquis of 48–9
    relationship with Giulio Cesare
        Borromeo 50–1
Legnano di Gattinara, Letizia 20–1
Lerma, Francisco Gómez de Sandoval, Duke of
    aristocratic opposition to 27–8
    as patron 27–8
    downfall 28
    Italian clients 20, 27–8
Leti, Gregorio 107, 152
Levi, Giovanni 154–5

208 INDEX

Litta, Alfonso 120–1
  as defender of ecclesiastical asylum 122–3
  conflict with Federico IV Borromeo 127
  interaction with Congregation of
    Ecclesiastical Immunity 123–4
Los Balbases, Paolo Spinola, Marquis of
  clash with Borromeo 93–4
Louis XIV, King of France 172, 177–8
Luserna Bigliore, Giovanni Battista 144–6

Magistrato Ordinario (Milan) 66–7
Maidalchini, Olimpia 106–7
Manzoni, Alessandro 1–2, 21–2, 155–6, 159, 177
Marescotti, Galeazzo 147–8
Mariana of Austria, Queen-Regent of Spain 138–9
Masaniello, revolt of (1647–1648) 69–70
masculinity
  chivalric 13–14, 97, 118–19, 176–7
  clerical 13–14, 98, 102–3, 105, 118–19, 176–7
middling sorts. See *ceto civile*
Milan
  loyalty to Spanish crown 6–7, 78–80
  strategic importance to Spanish crown 48–9
military entrepreneurship
  as self-affirmation 98
military heroism 81–2
minister-favorite
  function 5–6, 20, 26–8
misrecognition
  as analytical concept 12–13, 39–40
  as self-deception 34–5, 41, 171
  as strategy 136, 177
  through art 159–60
  through writing 40
Mohr, Christoph 113–14
  controversy with Borromeo 114–16
Moncada, Luis Guillén 138–9
  relationship with Federico IV Borromeo
    141–2, 148–9
Mont, Ulrich de
  election to bishop 113–14
Monterrey, Manuel de Acevedo y Zúñiga,
    Count of 31
moral panic (Hall) 121–3, 132–4

neoforalismo 171–2
neostoicism
  under Olivares 28–9, 39
Nithard, Johann Eberhard von
  aristocratic opposition to 139–41
  as confessor 139
  exile in Rome 143
  negotiations with Federico IV Borromeo 142
  promotion to cardinalate 144–5

nobility
  after favoritism 130, 133–4
  under Haro 81–2, 92–3
  under Juan José 169–72, 177–8
  under Olivares 5–6, 50, 81–2, 84–5, 94–5
nonmaterial legacy (Levi) 154–5, 161, 168–9

Olivares, Gaspar Guzmán y Pimentel,
    Count-Duke of
  anti-corruption 29
  asset-stripping 29–30
  corruption 42
  economic reforms 44–5
  Italian clients of 5–6
  misrecognition 35–6
  opposition to 59–60
  relationship with Federico III Borromeo 36
  royal councils under 31–4
  Union of Arms 45
Oltrepò 86–7
Osuna, Gaspar Téllez Girón, Duke of 161–3

Pallavicino, Giovanni 54–5, 90–1
Paluzzi Altieri degli Albertoni, Paluzzo
  as papal nephew 144–5
papal nepotism 105–6
  crisis of 106–7
parallel correspondence 146, 148–9, 151
paternalism 41, 134, 178–9
patronage
  as analytical concept 9–10
  ethics of 26
  iniquity of 63, 75–6
  marketization of 29–30, 39
  rhetoric of 29–30, 33–4
  symbolic 134
Paul V Borghese, Pope
  jurisdictional conflict in Milan 20–1
Peñaranda, Gaspar de Bracamonte y Guzmán,
    Count of 138–9
Philip II, King of Spain
  relationship with St. Carlo Borromeo
    18–20
Ponce de León, Luis Guzmán de
  clash with Federico IV Borromeo 101–2,
    116–18, 120–1
  reforms 123, 131–2, 134–5
princely service
  under Haro 80, 82–3, 95
  under Olivares 50, 95, 98
Procaccini, Ercole 170–1

reputación
  as driver of war 56–60

as social advancement 50–1, 56
as threat to military operations 90–1
Richelieu, Armand Jean du Plessis, Cardinal 45–6

Salis, Ulysses von 112–13
Santagostino, Agostino 160–1
Scott, James C. 34–5, 150–1, 178
Secret Council (Milan) 87–8
self-interest
   charge of 61–2, 78, 84, 86–8, 93–5
Sfondrati, Valeriano 61
social collaboration between king and
   nobility 130, 172, 177–8
social division of the labor of domination
   (Wacquant) 13–14, 98
social norms
   vs. common good 10–12, 39
social reproduction
   art in 156
   education in 103
   patronage in 8
social vs. technical function of office 56–7,
   59–60, 68, 88–91, 94
soldiers
   "excesses" against civilians 57–8, 64–6
   looting 57–8, 64–5
Sorino, Giorgio 84–5
Spanish Italy
   dark legend of 3–4
   historiography of elite networks in 4–5
   historiography of nobility in 8
   post-nationalist historiography of 4–5
   Risorgimento historiography of 2
Spanish monarchy
   crisis of 6, 89–90
   popular vision of 75–6
   resilience of 7–8
Squadrone Volante (faction in the college of
   cardinals) 108–9
Stollberg-Rilinger, Barbara 11–12, 42, 150–1, 171
Swiss Confederacy 111
   influence of papacy in 111–12
   Spanish influence in 111–12
symbolic politics
   historiography of 11–12
symbolic power 7–8, 12, 168

Taino, looting of (1636) 57–8
tax revolt 72–3, 75
Theatines 97, 154
Tornavento, battle of (1636) 49
Tornioli, Niccolò 160
transcript (Scott)
   hidden 35–6, 150–1
   public 36–7, 58
troop allocation
   outsourcing of 63, 66–7, 71
   social tensions from 64–5
   tax 66–7
   to insolvent communities 72–3
   to private homes 64–5, 73–4

Union of Arms
   aristocratic response to 47
   as social advancement 46, 50
   historiography of 45
   incongruities of 56–9
   Milanese nobility and 51
   policy 45
Urban VIII Barberini, Pope
   as patron of the arts 159–60
   jurisdictional conflicts 123–4

Valenza, siege of (1657) 86
Valenzuela, Fernando de 162, 169–70
Vázquez Coronado, Juan 88–9
Vercelli, siege of (1638) 51
Visconti, Pompeo 122–3
Visconti, Carlo
   eyewitness to revolt of Catalonia
   65–6
von Thiessen, Hillard 10–11, 39

Wacquant, Loïc 13–14, 98
warrior nobility
   as myth 27–8, 46–7
   taming of 177–8

York, James Stuart, Duke of 166–7

Zúñiga y Velasco, Baltasar de
   crackdown on Lerma 28
Zwyer von Evibach, Sebastian Peregrin 143